COWGIRLS

Cowgirls
WOMEN OF
THE AMERICAN WEST

Teresa Jordan

ANCHOR BOOKS
Doubleday & Company, Inc., Garden City, New York
1984

Anchor Books Edition: 1984

PHOTO CREDITS

Amon Carter Museum 29, 202, 205, 211, 213; **Marie Bell** 22, 27; **Amy Chubb** 5; **Colorado Historical Society** xii, 93, 125; **Barbara Davis** 66, 68, 69, 71; **Denver Public Library** xvi, xxi, 47, 189, 277, 283; **Douglas County Museum** xvii (lower), 75, 192; **Bob Gibbs** 1; **Alice Greenough** 196, 214, 217, 219, 220, 224, 225; **Teresa Jordan** xxiii, xxiv, xxv, xxvi, xxviii, xxx, xxxi, 2, 13, 20, 30, 38, 40, 41, 48, 59, 65, 73, 76, 86, 94, 97, 101, 103, 107, 110–111, 112, 114, 118–119, 126, 134, 138, 146, 155, 156, 159, 162–163, 166, 171, 173, 174, 176, 178, 227, 237, 238, 241, 242, 243, 244, 251, 259, 261, 269; **Lil Lambert** 195; **Lorena Mueller** xvii (upper), xviii; **Professional Rodeo Cowboys Association** 187; **Rodeo Historical Society** 188, 190, 193, 194, 200; **Fern Sawyer** 231; **Mrs. Herman Werner** vi, 153

BOOK DESIGN BY *Marilyn Schulman*

Library of Congress Cataloging in Publication Data

Jordan, Teresa.
Cowgirls.

Bibliography: p. 282
1. Cowgirls—West (U.S.) 2. West (U.S.)—
Social life and customs. I. Title.
F596.J62   978

AACR2
ISBN 0-385-14511-X
Library of Congress Catalog Card Number 80–1810

For Two Iron Mountain Women I Loved Dearly . . .

My Mother,
Jo Steele Jordan

And My Friend,
Sandy Hirsig

Grace (Mrs. Herman) Werner, 1922. Her divided skirt is made of a heavy, canvaslike material.

ACKNOWLEDGMENTS

IF I THANKED EVERYONE WHO HELPED WITH THIS BOOK, MY ACKNOWLEDG-ments would be longer than the text itself, but several people deserve special recognition. Patty Nelson gave me both the idea to try a book and the audacity to tackle it. Howard Lamar helped me structure my original idea to make it salable. Bill Ferris taught me the skills that made it possible.

Dick Etulain guided my study in the literature, ever ready with provocative insights about my findings. Jim Folsom also helped me in this area. William K. Everson directed my look at cowgirls in film. Although I later discarded this pursuit (it is a book in itself), Mr. Everson gave selflessly of his time.

T. A. Larson, Gene Gressley, and Agnes Wright Spring were among the many who helped me put cowgirls in a historical context. Peter Decker, in addition to his unflagging encouragement, led me to the homes of many cowgirls. Wally Throgmorton advised me on inheritance tax law as it relates to ranchwomen.

Dr. J. S. Palen lent me photographs from his extensive personal collection on rodeo and helped me identify and date other photographs. Larry Day advised my own photographic efforts.

I owe thanks, too, to the staffs of the Denver Public Library's Western History Department; the Colorado Historical Society; the Wyoming State Archives; the Wyoming State Library; the University of Wyoming Library; the Coe Collection of the Yale University Library; the Amon Carter Museum; the Oregon Historical Society; the Douglas County Museum (Oregon); the Cowgirl Hall of Fame; and the National Cowboy Hall of Fame. The Women's Professional Rodeo Association (WPRA) and the Professional Rodeo Cowboys Association (PRCA) answered endless queries.

Phil Keisling helped from the book's inception. He read more drafts of the manuscript than I care to admit I wrote, squeezing my project into his already sleep-starved schedule time and again. Whenever I grew discouraged, he drew from his own deep well of enthusiasm the energy I needed to go on.

Bill Crawford, editor of the PRCA's *ProRodeo Sports News,* kept me busy with assignments that provided my bread and butter through much of this endeavor. He also brought his excellent writing credentials to bear in a thoughtful reading of the manuscript. Bernice Harris, Kathy Jensen, and Peter Iverson helped in this way as well.

Jenny and Becky Kilgore, working for slave wages, transcribed over 200 hours of tape. Without their magnificent effort I would still be locked in my office with that damn transcribing machine glued to my ear.

The Rocky Mountain Women's Institute provided me with a place to work in Denver during 1978–79, the community of creative women, and a welcome stipend. My debt to them is great.

My family gave me support—both moral and material—and this project would have been impossible without them. My lifelong friends, the Farthings, offered me the little house on the prairie in Iron Mountain, from which I revised the manuscript.

My deepest thanks extend to the many women who befriended me, who let me enter their lives, and who fed and housed me when I rode the grub line in search of the elusive cowgirl. This book is truly theirs.

Contents

Madonna of the Trail statue at Lamar, Colorado. This image of the frontier woman as earth mother pervades our sense of women in the West. She took care of the house and children while father tamed the land. She is the frontier woman most familiar to us, but she had more adventurous sisters.

Introduction

Fifty miles from nowhere, southern Montana. Early April. 2:00 a.m. The alarm jangles. Cassie reaches from under the eiderdown and turns it off, then lies for a moment and listens to the wind beat against the windows. "It's come up," she thinks, "since I laid down. It must be even colder now," and she remembers the midnight reading of twenty below. She snuggles closer to her husband, Dave. "You O.K.?" he mumbles. "You want me to go this time?" "No, I'll go. One of the heifers is about to calve out. I want to see her through."

Cassie rolls out of bed and feels for the pair of Levi's she left on the chair. She pulls them over her long-johns and wiggles into a heavy wool sweater. Then she stumbles to the kitchen, pours herself some coffee from the pot she never unplugs during calving season, and finishes dressing. A down vest. Two pairs of wooly socks. A thick scarf. Insulated coveralls. She reaches for her heavy rubber boots by the door and catches sight of her reflection in a window. The fatigue around her eyes surprises her, but then she smiles. Padded with so many clothes, she looks like a chubby man. Only her wedge of brunette hair betrays her sex. She grabs her stocking cap off the wall peg and yanks it defiantly over her ears. She grabs gloves and a flashlight, pushes the door against the wind, and steps into the blackness.

The wind cuts through her with a cold that sucks her breath, stops her heart. She hunches against it and pushes toward the calving shed. Her flashlight beam bounces abruptly, jaggedly before her on the snow. She fumbles with the bar on the shed door. There is no heat in here, but at least there is no wind.

The labored panting of the two-year-old heifer sounds loud from the second stall. "How ya doin', Momma?" She flips on a dim yellow light that civilizes the shed.

When Cassie checked the heifers two hours before, she knew this one would calve soon, and she is not surprised to find the cow lying down, in hard labor. "Push, Momma, push," she croons softly. She approaches the cow slowly, easily. "You're O.K., little lady, just having a calf. This won't seem so scary after you've done it once or twice."

Cassie kneels next to the cow and softly strokes her rich, auburn coat. "Easy, Momma. You gotta push." But something is wrong. The heifer pants too quickly, frenetically. Her big dark eyes are pools of fear and pain. Suddenly, an unusually severe contraction wrenches her and she bellows—that clear, cutting bellow that sounds like a train whistle loosed at your shoulder, loud enough to raise the rafters or the dead.

"What's the matter, old gal? All that pushin's not doing much good, is it? I better take a look."

During the few moments Cassie crouches by the heifer's side, she feels the chill sink deep inside her. Now she gets up stiffly and walks to the medicine chest, each breath shooting plumes of smoke before her. She unzips her coveralls and slides out of the top half, tying the sleeves around her waist to hold up the pants. She removes her scarf, down vest, and sweater and hangs them on the wall. Only a thin layer of duofold separates her from the raw air. She can almost see her goosebumps under the cotton, and the cold snaps her nipples to a rigid attention. Cassie's right arm is bare—the sleeve has been cut out of the long-john top to make it easier to work in—and the skin glows almost iridescent in its whiteness "You sure better appreciate this," she says to the heifer. "Someday they are going to invent warm clothes you can *work* in!" She squirts disinfectant over her hand and up her arm, then scoops a handful of Vaseline out of a two-pound jar.

"Close your eyes, Momma, and think about England."

MMMMAAAAWWW—the heifer thrashes her head and bellows but makes no attempt to get up. Cassie leans into the cow, groping in the narrow channel for the calf. She finds a shape and her expert fingers try to read it. She makes out a tiny, cloven hoof. She pushes farther and feels two small hollows —the calf's nose. "At least you don't have a breech, pretty lady." But she cannot find the other hoof. "Ahh, that's the problem. You've got a front leg caught back. Easy, Momma, and I'll straighten it out."

Already Cassie's hand is aching as the tight cow-muscles fight her. Sometimes she has had to work inside a cow for more than an hour. She tries not to think about the calf three nights ago that hung up inside a cow and died. She'd had to skin it while it was still inside the cow, dismember it, remove it piece by piece. A lurid, dirty business, but she'd saved the cow. Thank God tonight is more routine. She struggles to work her hand back along the calf's body, find the misplaced leg, and straighten it.

"I know this is gonna hurt." The cow bellows again, throwing its head and casting a wad of thick, lathery drool back at Cassie. Another bellow, and the heifer struggles to get up. "Easy, easy, *easy*, Momma." Cassie strokes the cow's rump with her free hand and talks in a low, reassuring drone. The cow relaxes for a second. "There, I got it! Now, *push!*"

Cassie has hold of both the calf's front feet and pulls with each contraction. Finally, the calf begins to move. In a few moments its feet appear and then its nose; a few more and the calf rests in a steaming pool of blood and afterbirth. "You did it! Hey Momma! You got a fine baby here!"

The heifer looks back at the tiny creature curiously but makes no effort to stand. Cassie clears the phlegm and mucus out of the calf's nose and mouth with her fingers. The calf starts to breath. Cassie grabs a gunny sack and rubs the calf down. She can feel its heart beat in its tiny frame. She places it by the cow's nose. The cow moos softly at the calf, nudges it. Then the mother gets up, slowly, hind feet first, and finally stands above her baby. She noses it again. "MMaaaww." She licks it tentatively and then more strongly until she settles into the strong, rhythmic tongue-wash of maternal possession.

Cassie rocks back on her heels, her long-john top splattered with blood and her hand and arm dripping long crimson strands of mucus and afterbirth. "You done good, Momma," she coos. The calf struggles to get up, then falls back. In a few minutes he tries again and succeeds. He stands uncertainly on wobbly, waiflike legs, and takes his first precarious steps. Finding his mother's udder, he butts her with his nose and begins to suck. "You done *real* good." A placid smile plays across Cassie's tired face. She has witnessed this scene a hundred times before. She watches a long time, impervious to the cold and her own fatigue.

Cassie is a cowgirl. She is contemporary, but women like her lived and worked a hundred years ago. Her husband Dave, a cowboy, is more familiar to us. We can picture him—tall, lean, with a weathered face. We hear his spurs jingle softly as he walks through every Western we've ever read or seen. We know how strong he is, how quick with a rope or gun, and yet how gentle with women, kids, and critters. We know Dave and we love him. But Cassie. What a mystery she is. And how have we missed her all these years?

Almost every ranch community has at least one woman who actively ranches, either alone or hand-in-hand with her husband. Ranchers' daughters grow up working alongside ranchers' sons. Women ranch hands earn men's pay for men's work. Women's rodeo is a fast-growing professional sport. Along with competing in the tamer events like barrel race and goat-tying, women rope calves and ride broncs and Brahma bulls.

Cowgirls draw on a long tradition. Women came West as independent entrepreneurs, to take up land and build futures for themselves. From 1862 to 1934, under the auspices of the Homestead Act and related legislation, thousands of widows and single women proved up on homesteads. Women made up a significant proportion of those who took out claims—in some areas, close to 20 percent. One study indicates that women proved up more often than men.* Although some daughters or wives homesteaded to contribute to the family landholding, many independent women saw free land in the West as their opportunity. Some of the most hardy increased their original homesteads and built ranches.

Women also came West married to cowboys and cattlemen. If a woman's husband died or was badly injured, she had three choices: she could return to the East, move to town and wash clothes or teach school, or take over the spread. Some chose the latter. A few women worked outside with their spouses and paid more attention to the stock than the washing. Outside work allowed them to escape the domestic drudgery, loneliness and isolation of the plains. Women who did not work outside often had daughters who did. Some of these daughters rode with the roundup wagon, broke horses for pay, or hired out as cowhands.

From ranches, women joined Wild West shows and rodeos. Ladies' bronc riding was a standard rodeo event until the late 1930s, and the top women

* Sheryll Patterson-Black, "Women Homesteaders on the Great Plains Frontier," in *Western Women in History and Literature,* ed. by Sheryll and Gene Patterson-Black (Crawford, NE: Cottonwood Press, 1978), p. 16.

Jane Bernoudi (also spelled Burnoudy), the first woman trick roper, in 1909.

"Ma" Mueller on horse-drawn mower, 1916, at the homestead in South Dakota.

Four women on a homestead in Oregon, probably around 1920. Each woman has her hair pinned to the clothesline.

Mrs. Mueller, Sr., around 1916, at the homestead in South Dakota.

bronc riders became elegant celebrities, as well-known nationally as the most famous stars of the silver screen.

Cowboys were always much more numerous than cowgirls, to be sure. But cowgirls were—and still are—an important part of the West. Yet, for some reason, they are invisible.

Other western women come more easily to mind when we think of the cattle frontier. The Pioneer Woman, for instance. We have all seen those statues off the highway in Oklahoma, Kansas, or Nevada. Remember? She stands ramrod straight, her stoic face shielded from the sun for eternity beneath her calico sunbonnet-cast-in-bronze. With one hand she pushes her children protectively behind her flowing skirts; with the other she holds a gun. She is the prairie madonna, and she was a real and important part of the great frontier.

The prairie madonna made great pies, babies, and floursack curtains. After her children went to bed each night, she washed their school clothes and pressed them with heavy irons she heated on the wood stove. She rose in the middle of the night to punch down her bread. She kept immaculate house under impossible conditions—floors of raw dirt or unfinished wood; windows little more than holes in the wall blocked by shutters that swung insecurely shut on rawhide hinges. If a midwinter visitor left behind him a flock of bed-bugs, she had to drag the blankets outside and scrub them with lye soap; then struggle to hang them, sopping and leaden, on the line. After they froze, she had to drag them in the house to thaw, then hang them out again.

The prairie madonna could handle a gun or help with the stock if her husband were away when the Indians attacked or the cows broke down the fence on the back forty. But primarily she was an interior creature, delegated to the chores of house and family. Her husband, on the other hand, belonged to the great outdoors and the "real" work of cattle, horses, and land.

> It is either a very dull woman, or an unusually self-sufficient woman, who can escape being affected by the wearisome combination of high altitude, three-day sandstorms, and the lonely and tremendous reach of land and sky.
>
> Worst of all to me was the monotony of unaccustomed housework. It was often too heavy for me, and was always an uninteresting drudgery. No one can deny that the men worked hard too. But they were out of doors, usually on horseback and working with animals, and they were free to meet others interested in the same business.
>
> It was a truly surprised and unhappy rancher who said: "I can't figure out why my wife went crazy. Why, she ain't been out of the kitchen in twenty years!"
>
> He merely expressed the viewpoint of many another man. It had not occurred to him that woman is a gregarious animal—or should be.
>
> —Dorothy Ross,
> *Stranger to the Desert,* 1958.

The work, the sheer physical drudgery, made some pioneer women haggard and thin. The isolation, fear, loneliness, and wind—Oh God, the incessant wind—drove others insane. One woman picks up her rifle and shoots her children, her husband, and then herself. Another walks glassy-eyed from the house toward the prairie singing a wordless hymn in a tinny voice, mechanically undoing one piece of clothing after another until she walks naked, still trancelike, into the icy winter wind.†

We know, too, about the notorious women of the West—the bandittas, desperadas, and wild women; prostitutes, dance-hall girls, and faro dealers. Calamity Jane, for instance. She was a burly, mannish, fun-loving woman. An excellent horsewoman and a crack shot, she drove freight and rode with the cavalry. She swore and drank with abandon and turned a trick or two, but no one denied her kindness to children and cowboys on the down-and-out.

Or Belle Starr, "The Bandit Queen." She led a band of rustlers and killers centered at her home at Youngers Bend, Oklahoma. Well-bred and boarding-

† See, for instance, Elizabeth N. Shor, "Problems in the Land of Opportunity," *American West,* Vol. 13, ⚹1, January/February 1976, pp. 24–27.

Group portrait of cowgirls during the 1920s. Back row (left to right): Fox Hastings, Bea Kiernan, Rose Smith, Mabel Strickland. Front row: Ruth Roach, Florence Hughes.

school educated, she was reputed to be a fine pianist. She wore a black velvet gown and great white hat with a flowing ostrich plume when she thundered over the prairies on Venus, her spirited black mare.

Calamity Jane, Belle Starr, and other desperadas like Pearl Hart, Rosa Dunn, Della Rose, and Etta Place, were wild, outrageous women. They lived often outside the law and always outside convention. They were uninhibited and free-spirited, but there is something pathetic about them as well. When Calamity Jane was hungry and needed a drink, she would bum money to buy a washboard and basin, then make the round of the bars, collecting dirty clothes. She washed until she had earned enough for a binge, then left her washtub for a barstool. Belle Starr lived to see three of her lovers shot down; she lost her own life to a sniper's bullet.

Wild West cowgirl, around the turn of the century. Note her leather gauntlets, Angora chaps, and blacksnake. The bridle on the ground has a horsehair headstall. Her pistol is painted into the picture.

Why, when we think of women in the West, do we think of desperadas or prairie madonnas, but not cowgirls? Tom Robbins suggests one answer in his whimsical novel many know only by its title, *Even Cowgirls Get the Blues:*

I saw my first cowgirl in a Sears catalogue. I was three. Up until then I had heard only of cowboys. I said, "Mama, Daddy, that's what I want Santa Claus to bring me . . .

. . . they let you dress up like a cowgirl, and when you say, "I'm gonna be a cowgirl when I grow up," they laugh and say, "Ain't she cute." Then one day they tell you, "Look, honey, cowgirls are only play. You can't really be one. And that's when I holler, "Wait a minute! Hold on! Santa Claus and the Easter Bunny, I understand; they were nice lies and I don't blame you for them. But now you're screwing around with my personal identity, with my plans for the future. What do you mean I can't be a cowgirl?"

—Bonanza Jellybean

Real cowgirls don't identify much with Tom Robbins' nubile maids who know more about whooping cranes than cattle and would rather roll in the hay with each other than pitch it to the horses. But Robbins points out a basic truth. While the cow*boy* is our favorite American hero—the quintessential man—most of us see the cow*girl* as a child who will grow up someday and be something else. The cowboy's female counterpart—who can ride and rope and wrangle, who understands land and stock and confronts the elements on a daily basis—is somehow missing from our folklore.

"Cowgirls." I hesitate to use the word at all because it seems so frivolous. It makes us think of little girls in fringed felt skirts or big-eyed sweeties in tight jeans and high-heeled boots. But the term is a valid one that should carry more weight. "Women on ranches and in the rodeo" is, after all, a clumsy phrase. But more significantly, cow*boys* hold a place dear to our hearts. Their independence, self-assurance, and pragmatic savvy endear them to us as heroes. The women in this book share those qualities. I like to think they deserve an equal canonization.

Unlike Bonanza Jellybean, I was never told I could not grow up to be a cowgirl. I grew up on a ranch in Iron Mountain, Wyoming, fifty miles northwest of Cheyenne. As they say in that part of the country, I rode before I could walk. By the time I was seven or eight, each summer my older brother and I rode every day, either alone or together, and looked after the cattle while the men put up hay. We were not unusual. Up on the breaks, the Hirsig kids—Debbie, Sandy, and Tom—did the same. Over the hill, my Great Aunt Marie Bell worked hand-in-hand with her husband John. Toward town, Biddy Bonham and her daughter Jennie Mai rode and roped with husband Wayne and the boys. I grew up surrounded by women and girls who worked on the range, right beside their husbands and brothers.

Then, at college, I focused on History of the American West. I studied women on the overland trails, prairie mothers and desperadas, women in politics and on the mining frontier, women schoolteachers and even rural doctors, but few cowgirls. What about these women I grew up with? Did women throughout the cattle-West work outside at the same work, earning the same

Annette Pollard, bull and bronc rider and calf roper, with bull rope at Hereford, Texas, All-Girls Rodeo, 1978.

respect as men, or was Iron Mountain a unique community? Did the women I grew up with have an unusual sense of personal value and self fulfillment, or was that perception a product of my own nostalgia? Were cowgirls a recent phenomenon, or had they always existed? Out of these questions this book was born.

This, then, is a book about cowgirls. Or, rather, a book *of* cowgirls, for here is a collection of individuals rather than a systematic study and analysis of a type. The majority included here are from Colorado, Wyoming, and Montana, with a smattering from Arizona, New Mexico, Idaho, Oregon, and Texas. There are hundreds more in these and other western states.

Finding the women presented here was as much a matter of chance as design. The rodeo cowgirls were the easiest to find, for theirs is a public activity. The early cowgirls are recorded in rodeo histories, and I could contact many of those still alive through the Rodeo Historical Society, part of the National Cowboy Hall of Fame in Oklahoma City. For contemporary rodeo contestants, I had only to contact the Girls Rodeo Association (which changed its name to the Professional Women's Rodeo Association in 1981) in Spencer, Oklahoma, for names of top contestants. Then I spent much of the summer and fall of 1978 following the rodeo circuit, traveling from one women's rodeo to another.

Ranch cowgirls posed a larger problem, for their lives are more private. I knew several to start out with. I found some through newspaper and magazine

Frances Bentley on her ranch near Casper, Wyoming, 1979.

Vickie Lande, coming off a bull at the Hereford, Texas, All-Girls Rodeo, 1978.

articles; others through university historians and local historical societies. Most, however, I found through word of mouth.

Each cowgirl I met invariably told me about others, but I got many names from non-ranch sources. Over the two years I worked on this project, I described it to many people and a pattern emerged. Time and again their first response was, "Is there such a thing as cowgirls?" When I explained it further, they'd say, "Oh yeah, I know this woman you ought to see . . ." At cocktail parties, writers' conferences, and even in strangers' homes when I sold encyclopedias to help cover my travel expenses, people gave me names of cowgirls. I traveled over sixty thousand miles between 1978 and 1980, and interviewed close to a hundred women. I had many more names, in all the western states, than I could ever hope to contact.

I don't know how many cowgirls live in the West. Every ranch community I visited boasted at least one. Many had several.

A cowgirl is not just a woman who lives on a ranch or hangs around the rodeo. She is the female counterpart of the cowboy. "Cowboy" in its purest form means an itinerant hired hand who works with cattle, but our sense of the word is much broader. It presupposes a knowledge of horses and stock (yes, even sheep) and a daily confrontation with the elements. I use "cowgirl" in this way. Cowgirls are women who work outside, on ranches or in the rodeo, on a regular basis.

I do not include in this definition ranch wives who primarily take care of the house, feed the help, and drive to town for supplies, working outside only when the ranch is short-handed. These women are usually strong and independent, and many ranches could not exist without them. Still, if they do not work outside on a day-to-day basis, they are not a full-fledged counterpart to the cowboy. Although they deserve many volumes of their own, I have chosen not to include them here. Nor does my definition include the desperadas like Calamity Jane and Belle Starr. Their volumes have already been written. Finally, I do not include women who are unhappy with rural life. The country can be brutally hard, acutely isolating. Some women are very unhappy there. A man who dislikes the land leaves it. A woman often cannot because of family responsibilities, although she will try to avoid it by concentrating her efforts inside the house. If she does not embrace the land and the stock, she is not a cowgirl. Her story is important, but this is not the place for it.

Nancy Meyring, Meyring Ranch, North Park, Colorado, 1979.

Of course, contemporary women cannot tell the whole story of cowgirls. Woven through the primary interviews that follow are accounts by other women from autobiographies, reminiscences, diaries, oral-history projects, and magazine and newspaper articles. These allowed me to include women who are no longer alive, some from as far back as the 1870s, and women whom I could not visit myself. Occasionally these women are more farmers than cowgirls—that is, concerned more directly with crops than livestock. I have included them because they offer additional insight into a woman's particular relationship with the land.

I have also included excerpts from fiction, poems, and songs, when these present an accurate image of cowgirls. I have not tried to analyze in depth the portrayal of cowgirls in popular culture. For the most part, "cowgirls," if they exist at all, are only a *raison d'être* for the cowboy, a backdrop against which his bravery and competence can shine. Occasionally, realistic portrayals occur. The question, then, is: Why haven't we digested these images? Why don't we *know* that cowgirls exist? At least part of the answer will come through the words of the women themselves.

What, then, are some cowgirl characteristics? Their backgrounds vary widely. Mildred Kanipe has not seen all of her own Douglas County, Oregon— "Course, it *is* a big county." Marion Trick left the family ranch to attend Bennington College in Vermont, then went to Peru, where the Peruvian Air Corps taught her to fly. Linen Bliss and Gwynne Fordyce came from upper-class eastern families and never dreamed of a life on the range until they came West, met cowboys, and married them. But all share a deep emotional attachment to the land that translates in a rich, grass-roots eloquence. "I'm just like these old oak trees," says Mildred Kanipe. "I'm rooted in here so deep there's just no movin' me."

Most cowgirls are natural storytellers, their art honed by years of practice. Storytelling helps pass the time on long winter nights with no TV or on the ride to a distant pasture. It serves as entertainment; it also preserves the humor and value of a unique way of life.

To succeed on the land, cowgirls have overcome, or never considered, the factors that make other rural women unhappy. The land is hard on a woman. Weather lines her face and work gnarls her hands. But cowgirls are not concerned with fragile beauty. "It's hard on you, I know," says Frances Bentley, "but I'm happy working outside. And my horse don't care about the wrinkles. He knows who I am, anyway."

Nor do cowgirls share the fear that surfaces so often in prairie women's reminiscences. Sometimes this was a specific fear of something like Indians or prairie fires; more often it was a vague, inchoate fear of "out there," the unfathomable vastness and its potential threat to her husband and children. But cowgirls work "out there."

"Not many of our women neighbors got about as did my mother and her daughters," wrote Agnes Morley Cleaveland about her childhood in the 1880s. "Not many had reason to, with the menfolks to carry the responsibility of look-

Lorena "Ma" Mueller on her ranch near Custer, South Dakota.

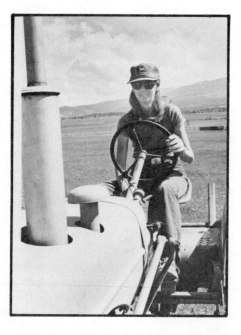

Putting up hay—Deedee Decker on the tractor, near Ridgway, Colorado, 1979.

ing after their cattle. It was this deadly staying at home month in and month out, keeping a place of refuge ready for their men when they returned from their farings-forth, that called for the greater courage, I think. Men walked in a sort of perpetual adventure, but women waited—until perhaps the lightning struck."

Cowgirls—in one way or another—simplify their domestic demands to free themselves for work outside. Some have mothers or sisters who take care of the house. Others hire a cook. Some share domestic chores with their husbands and children. A few are "superorganized," and prepare food in advance for family and crew, then freeze it. Most are content with less-than-perfect housekeeping. "This house," says Tootie Brocker, "doesn't pay for the ranch."

Cowgirls with children must cope with the responsibilities of child rearing. For some, it is the first time they have been kept from working outside, and the confinement is painful. Sometimes they take their babies on horseback or leave them in the pickup while they work cattle or fix fence. Sometimes they convince their husbands to share in the childcare and give them unencumbered time outdoors.

"I'm not a women's libber," I heard time and again when I broached the subject of the women's movement. The women's movement is primarily an urban phenomenon, and most country women see it as just one more outside interference which—like government regulation or Hollywood interpretations of the West—poorly understands their way of life and hardly relates to it. Probably because they don't feel a need for the movement in their own lives, they make little attempt to study or understand it in depth.

These women heartily embrace equal work and just inheritance taxes. But, like many people not close to the movement, they see "this women's lib stuff" as a power struggle between men and women, and find that idea alienating. Several women have absolute equality with their husbands in decision making; others let their husbands take the lead. The ones who work alone, of course, make all their own decisions. But all are intimately involved with the business and could take over the ranch tomorrow if they had to.

But liberation is not a question of who wears the pants in the family. Liberation is the ability to find fulfillment in your life, to be respected for your contribution. Cowgirls share the family business, contribute to the family income. And a man seldom takes for granted a woman who works beside him in bitter winds, bucking 80-pound bales off a hay sled.

The women in these pages feel they make a difference—to their families, the business, the stock, and the land. They work at something they love, and many will tell you they are leading exactly the life they want. That is liberation.

Of course, the West is not a feminist utopia. Some cowgirls share the frustration of women everywhere when they see their contribution, no matter how significant, devalued simply because it is the work of a woman. Others see the ranch they built with their husbands, to which they contributed their time, energy, and capital on an equal basis, always referred to as "his ranch." They

*Mary Jane Werner Sellers,
irrigating near Casper,
Wyoming, 1979.*

know that, should their husbands die before they do, the inheritance tax laws will see it as "his ranch" as well.

Some cowgirls have always worked outside. "We never thought about it," say two octagenarian sisters, Elsie Lloyd and Amy Chubb. "We just always did. Nobody ever thought anything about it." Others have had to break through local taboos against women doing "men's work." Carole Horn, who worked with her father from the beginning and had total responsibility on the ranch, married into a ranch family which thought it "very unladylike" for a woman to ride. She was a virtual prisoner in the house the first few years until her husband understood how much she needed to work outdoors and helped her buck the family inhibitions. Now she works out regularly and her in-laws accept and admire her for it.

For all its romantic appeal, life on the land is terribly, terribly hard. Accidents happen frequently. Biddy Bonham saw her father killed when his horse stepped in a gopher hole. Martha Gibbs's brother caught his foot in his rope and was dragged to death by his horse. Linen Bliss's daughter had her skull crushed by a horse and lost an eye. Almost all the women have had major accidents themselves.

And land and livestock are inviolate responsibilities. You cannot take the day off from milking the cows. You must feed in the winter; man the fire-watch in the summer. When the weather does its worst, your animals need you most. Few people are suited to country life. The women in these pages, for their individual reasons, thrive on its adversity. They meet the challenge and emerge triumphant. Perhaps a cowgirl's life is best summed up by the most female of all metaphors, birth, where out of exquisite pain is born enduring beauty.

But now, meet the women. This is a collage, a collection of individuals and materials. Take each piece separately but then step back and try to see the whole; a composite portrait of this elusive participant in the great American West, the cowgirl.

Judy Robinson, 1978 GRA (now the WPRA) All-Around Champion Cowgirl, fixing her bareback riggin' on a bronc at the Hereford All-Girls Rodeo, 1978.

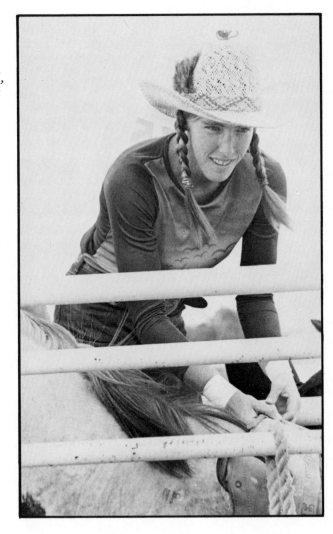

1

Cowgirls from the Cradle:

THE RANCHER'S DAUGHTER

Dorothy Gibbs,
age fourteen, 1918.

Elsie Lloyd and Amy Chubb

Near Kaycee, Wyoming

Elsie Lloyd and Amy Chubb, sisters, on their ranch near Kaycee, Wyoming, 1978.

INTERSTATE 25 NORTH FROM CASPER, WYOMING, CUTS THROUGH DESOLATE country. Miles and miles of nothing but miles and miles, the locals say. Halfway between Casper and Buffalo you pass the Sinclair oilfield at Midwest, an alkali plain cut here and there by chalk bluffs, dotted with sagebrush, and infested with giant steel mosquitoes sucking crude.

Turn west at Kaycee, though, and you head into Hole in the Wall country, once the home of Butch Cassidy and the Sundance Kid. Suddenly the dramatic "Red Wall" slashes across the plains and the monotonous gold of the late-summer prairie gives way to heather greens and blues and pinks.

Two sisters, Elsie Lloyd and Amy Chubb, live here in the Mayoworth Valley. Their simple frame houses nest inside the sunburnt arms of the red bluffs. I arrive on the tail of a cloudburst and slip-slide my way up the muddy dirt road to their home.

Elsie and Amy bought this 2,400-acre sheep ranch with their husbands, John Lloyd and True Chubb, when the men retired from Standard Oil in Midwest in 1954. It was like coming home for the sisters. They had spent their teenage and early-adult years riding the range, working the roundups, breaking horses.

In 1956, Amy and Elsie took out licenses to guide deer and antelope hunters. By their second year, they had all the business they could handle. Now their regular clients come from as far away as Iowa and Illinois. You must be a good hunter and sportsman to be invited back. If you're a son of a bitch, Chubb and Lloyd (as everyone calls the women) will tell you so. The sisters baby their Suffolk sheep but not their hunters. The hunters stay in housekeeping cabins, where they "damn well cook for themselves."

Today, at 82 and 79, the sisters are slim and sinewy. They look alike, and they'll tell you they think alike. They tame their curly white hair with hairnets and wear cotton cowboy shirts with mother-of-pearl snaps. Tooled leather belts hold up their trim Wranglers.

They do all the work on the ranch—True, Amy's husband, died in 1977; Elsie's John has been an invalid to diabetes for years.* Now they run only about eighty head of sheep, but the two have taken care of as many as twenty-five hundred.

They have deep, slow, sonorous voices. If John Wayne were a woman—or two women—he'd talk like this. And while the sisters live concretely in the present, it doesn't take too much to get them to talk about the past. Elsie takes the lead.

Elsie: We were born in England. Dad used to ride on the fox hunts, and he told us if we were going after the hounds, we'd have to learn to ride. He started us when we were about four years old, each one of us. He fixed little jumps for us and we rode bareback. When we were a little bigger, we held our reins in one hand and a pail of water in the other. If we didn't spill the water going over the jumps, we had pretty good balance.

We were crazy about horses. We rode everything with four legs and a tail.

We moved to Pennsylvania in 1906 and Dad had a milk route. He couldn't keep enough milk purchased to satisfy his customers, so we moved onto a farm and bought about thirty-five milk cows. Amy and I helped him milk.

But Dad always wanted to come farther west. One evening after supper he took a map of the population of the United States and spread it out on the table. "We want to go where there aren't too many people," he said. "That's a sparsely populated area," he was looking south, down around Nevada, "but it

* John died in 1981.

would be too hot down there." He stuck his finger on Sheridan [Wyoming] and said, "Right there is where we're going."

We came to Sheridan in 1914. Amy was fourteen and I was seventeen. Our whole family went to work. We had never worked for anybody else before, but we wanted to work until we knew where we were going to settle, and get a little money ahead. Dad worked on a ranch, Mother cooked, Amy and I did housework, and I was nursemaid for some kids. My brother went to work at Parkman, Montana.

A couple years later, Dad filed on a homestead out at the head of Hanging Woman and Buffalo creeks, twenty-one miles northeast of Fremont. He bought a couple adjoining places, so we had quite a bit of acreage there. Dad had Amy and me for his boys. My brother was not home much; he was out working and then he married.

We did everything. We helped with the farming and put up the hay. We drove four horses on a gang plow, and drove teams on the mower, the rake, the disk, the harrow, anything.

Amy: You didn't have a baler in those days. You pitched your hay with a fork. You pitched it on the wagon and then pitched it off and stacked it. We did all that. Now, at our age, it's kind of an effort to lift a fifty-pound sack of cake [cattle feed]. But when we were young, we didn't think anything about picking up a hundred-pound sack of oats.

The thing we liked to do best was ride. When we worked as domestics we had ridden here and there, helping with the cattle, because we were crazy about riding. But soon as Dad got his ranch, we really started our range riding.

It was all open range in those days. Dad and all the different neighbors turned cattle out. We rode and watched these cattle and kept them located. We kept the country pretty well covered because we had a couple unpleasant neighbors who had been picked up for rustling. We had to keep pretty close watch on our cattle and horses both.

The cattle business in those days was conducted on horseback. Any rider who knew what to do was on a parity with any other rider who knew what to do, so, as soon as we children had mastered the art of sitting on a horse with some assurance, our value to the business became out of all proportion to our age. The art of horse-sitting is acquired rapidly if one keeps at it from daylight till dark day after day, so we quickly learned to ride by the simple process of riding.

Mounted on a horse, we were useful in direct proportion to our powers of observation and our ability to interpret what we saw,

Elsie Cooksley (later Lloyd), age twenty (left), and Amy Cooksley (later Chubb), age seventeen, with a colt whose mother had died, 1917. They raised the colt. Here the sisters wear simple trousers.

faculties, of course, which are sharpened by interest. Our interest
was boundless. Cattle became the circumference of our universe,
and their behavior absorbed our entire waking hours.
—Agnes Morley Cleaveland,
No Life for a Lady.
Copyright © 1941 by Agnes Morley Cleaveland.

We always carried a branding ring on our saddle. If we found a calf that
wasn't branded, we'd rope it and build a little fire and run its momma's brand
on it.

You know how to work a branding ring? Well, you take a branding ring like
this one here [Elsie grabs an iron ring, about three inches in diameter, off the
wall.] and you get you two green sticks that won't burn. You hold the branding ring with your sticks and get the ring red-hot. Then you run the brand on
the animal, sort of draw it on.

A funny thing happened once. The Smith brothers were moving a bunch of
cows, and of course we were helping. Another neighbor of ours, Joe Buchanan,
was helping too. There was a locoed yearling heifer, and you can't drive a
locoed animal. So Al Smith said to Joe, "For ten dollars you can have this
heifer for meat." Joe said, "All right," so we dropped the yearling out and
took the cattle on.

In a day or two, Joe come over home and talked to my dad. "Cooksley," he
said, "I don't have the ten dollars I'm supposed to send Smith for that yearling. Do you want it?" Dad said, "Yeah, I'll send him ten dollars."

So we got the locoed heifer. She didn't die. She was still locoed, but the next
year she had a calf. Of course, we never did rebrand her—she had a Triple A.
I went out and put Dad's brand on the calf with the running iron. One of the
neighbors saw me, and they rode up to see what I was doing. It was somebody
that didn't like me very well, so they wrote over to Smith and told him he had
seen me run our brand on a calf that belonged to a Triangle A cow.

I rode in one evening—I was alone on the ranch—and here was the sheriff
from Buffalo, the brand inspector, and Al Smith, sitting in a car. I rode up
and said, "Hi! What in the world are you sitting out here for? Why didn't you
go in the house and make yourself some coffee?"

"Got a question to ask you first, Elsie," Al said, "before we can go in the
house. I sure hate to ask it, but I got to do it."

"Well, what do you want to know?"

"I got word that there is a Triangle A cow over here with a calf with your
brand on it."

"There is," I said. "Do you want me to show her to you?"

"Well, how come?"

"You remember that locoed heifer you sold to Joe Buchanan for ten dollars?
Well, that's her. Dad sent the money, Joe didn't."

"Oh hell!" he said. "I knew there had to be some explanation. Let's go in
and have some coffee."

When we rode, we'd leave right after breakfast and ride all day. It took us most of the day to locate all our horses and cattle; some of them would stray eight or ten miles. When the roundup wagon came through, we'd ride down while they were working the herds and make sure all our cattle were cut out and left. That's how we learned about cattle and the roundups, by doing it for ourselves and the neighbors. And then after we became acquainted with the roundup men, we started to ride circle with them and help work the herds just like the rest of the men.

We were the only girls that ever rode with the roundup. I don't know why, unless it's due to the fact that Dad sent us out to take care of our own stock and we got started doing it and nobody else did. There weren't very many girls in the country who rode to the extent we did.

The wagon we rode with was the OW roundup wagon, which belonged to Senator John B. Kendrick. He had the biggest outfit in the area, and then everybody else who ran cattle sent a rep to look after their stock.

There were two roundups each year. The first was in the spring. That was the calf roundup when we branded the calves. In the fall we had the beef roundup. We cut out the beef that was to be sold. In those days you generally sold four-year-old steers instead of calves or yearlings like you do now. We'd also brand any calves we had missed, and pick up any strays we found.

We'd eat breakfast at four and then throw the morning circle. We'd get back to camp in time for dinner at ten. Half of us would hold the herd while the other half ate. Then we'd change horses and throw a second circle [ride out and round up cattle over a circle as large as time and the number of riders would permit]. We ate supper at four and moved camp before we went to bed.

Those roundups were really something. Of course, the cattle were a lot wilder than they are now. They were never handled. They stayed on the range all winter; they weren't fed. The only time they ever saw a person was twice a year when they were gathered for roundup. They were almost like wild animals.

We shipped the cattle from Kendrick. The stockyards were built with a wing out from the corner, so you had two sides of the fence to push them in. But those steers wouldn't go in. They would get there and start to mill. And they'd just mill as hard as they could run. They weren't dehorned, and you'd have several hundred four-year-old steers running in a tight circle, with their horns clashing. The only way you could get them started in the gate was to wait until they started to slow down a little on the outside. Then you'd ride in and peel off a couple through the gate. Some more would follow and it would be just like uncoiling a spring, going around and following into that gate. It was a beautiful sight. And something that no one will ever see again.

We rode with the roundup wagon four or five years.

Amy: I remember two of the times they came and got us. One year Kendricks had an order for twelve hundred two-year-old heifers. The wagon boss came down and asked us if we would help them. We took our teepee and set that up to sleep in, and we worked right along with the cowboys, just regular roundup work.

Another time, this wagon boss—we always called him Father Tug—came around in the spring. Elsie and I were shucking grain. He said, "Cooksley, I need your girls." Dad said, "Well, you can't have them. I need them too. They are shucking grain."

"I need them worse than you do," said Father Tug. "I've got a bunch of kids out of Sheridan that don't know one end of a cow from the other, and I've got beef roundup to work. I'll make you a deal. I'll send two of those boys over here to shuck grain if you'll let me have your girls to go with the wagon."

So that pleased us! We'd lots rather ride a horse than shuck grain. And we were out all the rest of the fall.

The cowboys treated us just like we were one of them. They never swore when we were around, and there was never once in all the years we were around them that anyone ever said anything off color to either one of us. They had a lot more respect for women then than they do now. They wouldn't even tell a dirty story. They probably told plenty when we weren't around, but we didn't ever hear them. As far as working, though, they treated us like one of the boys.

The bad guys are gaining. Hurricane Nell spurs recklessly. Her stallion is game and the colt they are leading has spunk. But Cecil's mount is failing fast. The pursuing hooves of Cap'n Bob Woolf and his gang pound closer, closer, closer . . .

———

A sudden resolute light entered the desperate girl's eyes.

"Lash your animal up to my left side, here!" she suddenly cried to the young lawyer, who was pale and silent.

He obeyed, mechanically, and for a second, all three animals dashed on, abreast.

"Seize your rifle, and when I lift you, spring from your stirrups," she next commanded, bracing herself firmly in the saddle. In another instant, *she had seized him about the waist, raised him high over her head by the power of her wonderful arm, and deposited him upon the back of the wild stallion!*

A wild, unearthly yell of applause went up from the stentorian throats of the pursuers. Ruffians and cut-throats though they were, they could not but admire and cheer the accomplisher of this astounding act, and Cap'n Bob Woolf was among the loudest who shouted the "bravo!"

—From the dime novel,
  Bob Woolf, The Border Ruffian; or, The Girl Dead-Shot,
  by Edward L. Wheeler, 1878.

Amy: Well, here's an illustration. We were holding the herd one time while half the men had their dinner. We saw a lady and her daughter drive into the wagon for dinner. When the wagon came around, often the neighbors would come for a chuck wagon dinner. Our relief came out and told us we could go eat. One of the fellers that was helping hold the cattle said, "No way! I'm not going in there and eat with those women. I don't mind Amy and Elsie and the rest of the boys. But I'm not going in with those women."

I don't think the neighbors thought a thing about our riding. At least, most of them were real friendly. There were one or two of them that wondered whether or not we were cohorting with the cowboys. One of them asked me one day, and I said, "Well, if you'd like to know, why don't you go ask the cowboys." I wouldn't give her the satisfaction of answering a question like that.

Amy: She just came right out and said, "Are you girls decent?" Can you imagine!

There were a lot of dances in those days, and we had an awful lot of fun. The dances would be at different ranches or homesteads. If the people didn't have room in their house, they built a platform and laid it on the ground. Somebody would fiddle—that was all the music we had unless somebody happened to have an organ.

People would come from all around for the dances. I remember riding ten or fifteen miles in the middle of winter, subzero weather. Usually about twenty or thirty teenagers would show up, and the adults danced too. The cowboys would all go if there was any around.

People often gave dances when they knew the roundup wagon was going to be near. Of course, we'd all saddle up and go to the dance and dance all night and then come back to the wagon, change horses, and go to work.

If we went to a dance from home, we always took our dresses and shoes and stockings tied behind our saddles. We would change when we got there. But we didn't have dresses when we were out on the roundup, so we'd just dance in our britches. One or two times, the lady of the house where the dance was held furnished us dresses. But they couldn't fit us for shoes, so we wore our cowboy boots under our skirts.

If we went from home, we could stay as late as we wanted, but we had to be home in time to go to work in the morning. One time Amy and I went to a dance down on Clear Creek. On our way home we saw these two four-year-old geldings we'd been missing, running with a bunch of range horses.

We rounded the whole herd up and put them in the stockyards at Kendrick. We roped our geldings out and turned the others back where we got them.

These four-year-olds were pretty big, never been broke. We were each riding quite small horses. We each tied onto a bronc. We had a long ways to go and couldn't go very fast leading these broncs. We didn't get home until late.

My dad was kind of hot-tempered. He was always good to us, but he popped off. He heard us come riding into the yard and he opened the door and bellered, "Where in the hell . . . ohhh, where'd you get them?" Cooled him right down to see those geldings.

New version of "The Old Strawberry Roan"

Now you have all heard of that Strawberry Roan,
That famous old bronc, and the boys he has thrown.
Let me tell you a tale that will make your head swim,
How a blame country girl took that all out of him.
His fame was broadcasted until she got upset,
I know I can ride him and straight up, I'll bet.
So she bid farewell to the old folks at home,
And lit out to find that old Strawberry Roan.

Oh, that Strawberry Roan, Oh, that Strawberry Roan,
I'll find him, I'll ride him, I'll break his old heart,
I'll pound on his lattice work right from the start,
On the ribs of that Strawberry Roan.

Well she found that old horse at a big rodeo,
I'm telling you, boys, it was half of the show.
He came out of the chute a-buckin' straight up,
Making kangaroo jumps, and he wouldn't let up
Till she crawls right on him, and bit his crop ear
Right then and there they left this old sphere,
But the girl's settin' pretty and seemed right at home
As she spurred the full length of that Strawberry Roan.

Oh, that Strawberry Roan, Oh, that Strawberry Roan,
He can't jump a lick, he's puddin' to ride,
She is making lace curtains out of his old hide,
The hide of that Strawberry Roan.

Now while he's a-buckin' she jumps to the ground,
Then back in the saddle with one single bound,
She's makin' a monkey of old Roany's hide,
Says she'd like to have him for her kid sis to ride.
She 'lows that her grandma could ride him to town,
Take a settin' of eggs to the old widder Brown.
Now a man that can't ride him should never compete,
But go back to his home ranch and start herdin' sheep!

Oh, that Strawberry Roan, Oh, that Strawberry Roan,
There was never a Cowboy that couldn't be throwed,

And never a Bronc that couldn't be rode,
Including that Strawberry Roan.

Now this old outlaw is hitched to a cart
A chink huckster bought him, and he works right smart,
He peddles onions, and string beans and peas.
Old Roany's plumb gentle, and sprung at the knees.
As he patiently waits at some lady's back door,
You can see on his left hip that old forty-four.
So cowboys, beware before it's too late,
Or like Roany you'll be waitin' at some lady's gate.

Oh, that Strawberry Roan, Oh, that Strawberry Roan,
Like salty young cowboys he roamed far and wide
But now he's a-waitin' while women decide,
He's a busted old Strawberry Roan.

—possibly by **J. Western Warner**
in *Ten Thousand Goddam Cattle,* by **Katie Lee, 1976.**

Amy: In those days money was short and hard to come by, so we were always looking for something to earn a little money. We knew Senator Kendrick almost as well as we know each other. We had an awful winter one year and everyone lost a lot of cattle. Senator Kendrick saw us in town one day and said, "If you girls want to skin any of my dead cows and sell the hides, you can have the money." Well, we thought we had hit it rich. We'd skin down the legs and around the neck and make a split down the belly. Then we tied one rope to the head and one to the hide and we'd ride in opposite directions. We had our cow skinned in no time. We made quite a lot of money selling hides that year.

Another time Dad came in. "You girls are always wanting money," he said. "I was talking to Doc Gardner today and he's got ten broncs to break for ten dollars a head." We said, "When do we get them?" "Tomorrow." So we got a hundred dollars for breaking them. We thought we were on easy street!

To break them, we didn't mess around with tying their feet up or leading them or anything else. We just got on them and bucked them out. Dad would generally haze for us. [Hold the horse's head, usually from another horse, until the rider can mount.] As soon as we got the worst of the buck out of them, which was just two or three days, we took them right out on the range and put them to work. And they made a lot better stock horses that way. We taught them to work a rope and everything.

One winter I made quite a bit of money rounding up range horses. They weren't what you call wild horses today, but they were just as wild. A lot of them were never in a corral 'til they were two years old.

You see, what happened—there used to be a fellow in Montana, a horse trader, who bought and sold horses to make a living. These poor homesteaders would come out and file on a place, and this man would call on them and say, "Now the range doesn't cost you anything, and the grass is free. You don't have to feed horses in the winter. If you'll buy ten head of mares and a stud and let them raise a colt every year, in three or four years you've got a herd of horses and they haven't cost you a dime to run."

Well, the homesteaders would fall for it, and they'd buy these horses and turn them on the range. Then they had no way to catch their horses, and there were hundreds of them out there. The whole range became infested with horses and they were eating all the grass. Finally the ranchers said that the horses either had to be gathered or they were going to shoot them.

A man named Slippery Jim paid me two dollars a head to gather horses. He had a contract with an outfit up in Montana. I gathered horses all winter.

These horses were as wild as antelope. They'd see you on a ridge, and they'd go over the next one. So the way I'd get them, I'd just keep them moving and not try to run them when I first found them. I'd keep them moving for three or four hours and let them get thirsty. Then I'd let them go to water and fill up. They would get their bellies full of water, and my saddle horse could just go around them.

Amy: I didn't work with Elsie that winter but over the years I ran in several bunches with her. The easiest bunch we ever brought in was one summer when the water was low. They'd go to the reservoirs to drink. You know how long range horses' tails get. Their tails would drag in the mud and a big mud ball would form at the bottom. When they'd start to run, that would wrap around their hind legs and throw them down. So we brought that bunch in pretty easy.

You know, everybody says we've led such an interesting life. But it wasn't unusual to us. We just did it. That's what we had to do, so we did it.

Kim Taylor

Taylor Ranch, near Buffalo, Wyoming

Noon break—Kim Taylor on the NX Bar Ranch, near Sheridan, Wyoming, 1980.

I FIRST MEET KIM AT THREE-THIRTY IN THE MORNING. SHE HAS JUST CRAWLED out of the canvas teepee she shares with her brother Gordon at the Scrutchfield Corrals Camp on the NX Bar Ranch near Decker, Montana. She comes into the trailer rubbing the sleep out of her eyes and fixes coffee and pancakes while Helen Musgrave, the manager of the NX Bar, goes over breeding records with Kim's father, Wes. The Taylors have a contract to artificially inseminate two hundred of Helen's cattle.

Kim and Gordon eat; then walk to the corral to saddle up just as the sky begins to lighten. As soon as they can see the cattle in the pasture, they ride out to detect heat—watch the cattle to determine which are ready to breed; then bring them in for insemination.

Kim is the quintessential tomboy. Short blond hair, strong, thick hands, slightly stocky build. She wears a tweed, English sports cap. She moves slowly and deliberately, and speaks the same way. Her voice is surprisingly low and husky.

I'm fourteen. I want to be a veterinarian. I have ever since I can remember. I've always hung around when they went to c-section a cow instead of walking around the corner and getting sick.

I sat down and looked at veterinary school catalogues and found out what I have to take. I need science and social studies and my schedule is full of that. The only thing I haven't taken yet is a foreign language. I don't know if I can hack one.

If you are a girl, I don't think you have much of a chance to become a vet if you aren't devoted to it all your life, especially if you grew up in a city. If you were a man, maybe you could decide to become a vet on the spur of the moment. But I think a woman almost has to grow up on a ranch or around one.

I love animals more than I do people. I know that's crazy. Everybody thinks I don't have any common sense when I say that. But it's true. I couldn't live without a dog. I like dogs better than cats because dogs can go with you everywhere. You can communicate with a dog because they know their name and they'll come to you. They will do what you want, like a cow-dog will go after cows if you tell him to.

When I'm mad or something, I feel like animals are the only ones who really care. I don't want to bug somebody else with my problems. I like listening to other people's problems and trying to help them, but I couldn't really think about telling them mine. I'd rather they'd just leave me alone with my dog. A dog will lick your hand or something. They give you a lot of confidence.

I like the outside. I like how it's really open and you can be free instead of having people all around you and pushing you about. Cattle can't tell you what's up and what's down. Cattle can't really argue with you.

Some people say that vet medicine takes more strength than a woman has. But I'm stronger than most girls or women are at this stage right here, and I'm getting stronger every day, just from working around the ranch. I think I can handle most of it. Some girls get in arm wrestles with boys and get whipped. I'll beat most of the boys—you know, some of the ones who are regular-sized. Some of the bigger ones can throw my arm over like that—Whack! But I feel I can probably handle most of it. I grew up on a ranch and I went to a country school and stuff, so I grew up pretty tough.

You must know a lot of girls who are into fashion and long fingernails . . .
It's all right, you know. Only thing that really bugs me is when girls act like something really bothers them when it doesn't. You know, when they were little, they'd go up and smash a spider with their hand. Then when they get sixteen or seventeen, everybody says, "Act like a lady," and they'll scream if they

see a spider go across the floor. The same with a mouse. They change right then 'cause everybody tells them ladies aren't supposed to like that sort of thing. They scream 'cause they don't want to act like a tomboy or something. No way I could act like that! I see a mouse run across the floor, I try and catch it. [Laughs] I don't jump up on the table or something.

The only thing I dislike is snakes, because of rattlesnakes. If I see a snake, I get off my horse and kill it. Sometimes, if it's right by me when I see it, I'll kick my horse and get out of there. I'm scared to death of those things. They bite you and you're dead. There's no saving you, really. If you're out in the pasture, how are you going to keep your blood from vibrating through you when you gallop home? And you don't want to go slow 'cause it's five miles to the house.

The country has changed my whole relationship to my body—it is no longer a vehicle to get me around but has become an extension, an expression of myself. Its limits have expanded as my own have, muscles able to lift or reach, as my mind also lifts away fears, reaches out to try. But this has not been an obvious or self-conscious process; the changes have been subtle. Along the way I have at times badly misused my body or ignored its pains, following an old pattern of seeing it merely as a necessary but unimportant appendage to my "real" self. Now, body consciousness is with me all the time from aching feet to muscles stretching loose and free, naked to the sun. My body is my most precious tool.

—Jeanne Tetrault,
Country Women.
Copyright © 1976 by Jeanne Tetrault and Sherry Thomas.

Dad spends a lot more time teaching Gordon, my brother, about the ranch than he does me. It's because I'm a girl. Dad's a chauvinist, a good example of one. I don't know why he's that way. I guess he's just an old-timer and he's used to all the women staying back. Luckily, Gordon teaches me if I ask him.

Dad's attitude makes me more determined to be a hand. [Laughs] I want to go out and show him I'm going to learn how to do it whether he teaches me or not. If he doesn't teach me, somebody else will. Finally, you know, he'll teach me things.

Dad always tells me I'm not as good as I think I am, that I think I can do more than I really can. I don't know. Maybe it's true, but I'll try and do it. It's challenging, and anything that's challenging inspires me. If there's a challenge, usually I'll go after it. Sometimes I won't. But I'd rather take the challenge and see for myself. If it ends up bad, then I guess he was right and there ain't nothing I can do about it.

Besides being a vet, I'd like to have a ranch. I'm not really worried about getting a ranch as much as I am about getting to be a veterinarian. But when I want to retire, I'd like to have my ranch to back myself up, and then doctor my own cows and horses. I always figured I'd have a ranch.

I don't really know how I'd get one, with the price of land. I'm sure I'll find one somewhere. I can go into partnership with someone that might already have land, or I might inherit our land if Gordon doesn't want it. He probably will, but he might let me live on it. Or I might marry a rancher and have me a ranch, too. [Laughs] Be easy enough. I'll just step over that log when I get to it.

My impression of Montana was good, though different from anything I had ever seen [when I arrived in 1911 from Iowa to homestead with my family]. Honyokers were arriving every day. The Hocking family arrived the same month as we. They were our nearest neighbors and we became good friends at once. Edith and I spent most of the summer riding through the hills and over the prairie. How I enjoyed the little prairie dogs, who barked their welcome; the meadow larks who greeted us with their song, "I'm here and can't get away"; the white-faced cattle that ran whenever they saw us; and the gallant cowboys in their ten-gallon hats, neckerchiefs, and angora chaps. They didn't run—always had time to stop and visit.

Edith and I made one trip to Miles City [50 miles away] via horseback during that summer. It was a real lark.

. . . In June 1913 I filed on a homestead after contesting a previous filing, as it had been abandoned. It was located about one and a half miles north of the present Coalwood Store and Post Office. My father built my one-room 14′ by 16′ house mostly of native lumber, having two windows and a "boughten" door with a glass panel. When I was not teaching I spent most of my time on the homestead. I purchased a few horses and a brand and it became the 6 Triangle Quarter Circle Ranch.

Edith Hocking spent much of her time with me, so we dubbed it "Our Ranch."

—Carolyn Janssen Bird, "First Trip by Stage Coach? And Shank's Horses,"
Echoing Footsteps.

Do I think I'll get married? Oh yeah, probably. But for certain I'm not going to get married until after I go through vet school. I put my mind to that a long time ago. I know that if I get married before I finish, it's going to step in my way and I'll never get through.

I don't date very much. I don't really have any interest in it. I like to have a good time with boys and everything, but when it gets down to going out with one—they always seem to want me not to go around with any others. That gets me fed up. I'd rather have fun with everybody instead of being cut off to one certain person. I'd rather be with everybody or nobody.

I really like to sing and play my guitar. Sometimes I record it, but then I usually erase it because I think it sounds dumb. I play in the barn or anywhere —just so long as I'm not around people. That really bugs me. I think they're just going to laugh at me if I play this dumb thing around them.

I usually make up the songs I sing. I start out on a regular song and end up with my own 'cause I can never remember the real words. I like mine better, anyhow. I usually sing about animals and mountains and stuff, and they're usually sad. I guess that's just my nature.

When you're little, you know how everybody says they're going to grow up to be a nurse or a doctor or something? I said I was going to be a hermit. I'm not kidding—really. I always dreamed about being a hermit, going up into the mountains where nobody goes, and building me a cabin or living in a cave. I figured I would build things around there and maybe have a little bit of stock. I'd just work and not worry about money or anything. I'd just live off of nature. Anymore, I'm sure the BLM would start bugging me. I'm a little behind my time, thinking about being a hermit. But I'd still like to. When I get what I need out of my life being a vet, I'd like to go to the mountains and live and not bug anybody else with all my dumb problems. It's a lot easier that way.

In 1942, at the age of fifty-four, Lillian Erickson Riggs went totally blind. A bronc had thrown her twenty years before; probably the slight dislocation of her neck pinched a nerve and caused her blindness. Never again would she enjoy the sight of the cool green pastures on the Faraway Ranch she ran with her husband Ed near the Chiricahua National Monument in Arizona. Never again would she glory in the strange and awesome shapes the fantastic rock structures there assumed in the deepening magenta of an Arizona evening.

But Lillian Riggs did not give up. Even when, six years later, her husband and then her mother died, Lillian Riggs did not give up. And in 1958, when A. T. Steele wrote about the "Lady Boss of Faraway Ranch" for *The Saturday Evening Post,* Lillian Riggs was as active as ever, involved with every facet of the 7,000-acre dude and cattle ranch.

For a while Faraway Ranch was an all-woman outfit. Mrs. Riggs employed two competent cowgirls, Adeline (Del) Lemos and Donna Cramer. But according to Mr. Steele, "Faraway just wasn't big enough for three such individualists as Lillian, Del and Donna." Del and Donna moved to another ranch and Lillian hired a couple to take their place.

Seventy years old, Lillian rode over her pastures regularly, with the reins in one hand and a guide rope held by another rider in the other. Sometimes she dropped the guide rein and galloped freely over the prairies she loved. When a cow was sick, Lillian attended, listening to the cow's breathing while someone described the ailment, offering experienced advice. She supervised everything and asked questions constantly. When her tourist guests gathered at dinnertime, Lillian headed the table, spinning wonderful tales about the Chiricahua region.

Courage, that's what Lillian Riggs was made of. Courage and spunk. And that's exactly what she revealed when she talked to A. T. Steele in 1958.

––––––

When the first settlers came to this valley, the grass grew so high it brushed against a rider's stirrups. Now look at it. The old springs are going dry—and some of the wells too. Oh, we have a wet year now and then, but as long as I can remember it has been getting drier.

But it takes a lot of trouble to beat us down. Not many ranchers have quit. Once you have lived here, you don't want to live anywhere else. We've got a wonderful climate, plenty of elbowroom and beautiful surroundings. That's something. We may sell our cattle; we don't often sell our land.

When I went blind, life seemed hardly worth living. Readjustment was terribly hard. I tried learning Braille, but my fingers were not sensitive enough. I had done too much rough work in my time. I decided I must learn typing; and after a while I managed it. I used to be a fast walker. Now I had to learn to walk slowly, and I hated it. I was thankful to be able to continue my riding.

My big gray "seeing-eye" horse, Britches, knows I cannot see. He knows it, and he takes advantage of it. But he is a good horse. He stops when the going is dangerous. He never gets excited. He carries me as if I were china.

Everybody thinks I'm crazy to carry on, but if I quit, how am I going to keep busy? I'd like to travel. But I don't want to give up this old home where I've met people from all over the world and where I hope to meet many more in years to come. Nor do I want to give up my riding. When I'm in a saddle I feel I'm living again. I'm in no hurry to part company with my cattle, either. Cows are so easy to keep happy.

> —Constructed from quotes in "The Lady Boss of Faraway Ranch," by A. T. Steele,
> *The Saturday Evening Post,* March 15, 1958.

Lillian Erickson Riggs died in 1977.

Marie Bell
Iron Mountain, Wyoming

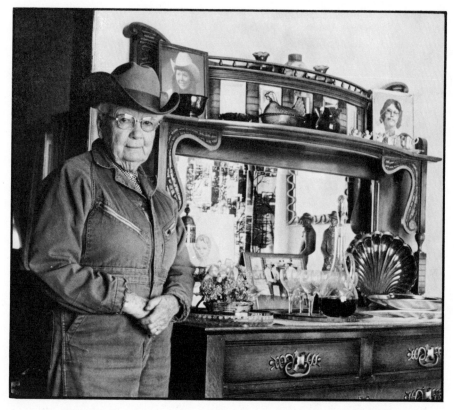

Marie Bell on her ranch at Iron Mountain, Wyoming, 1980.

I'M PROUD OF MY GREAT AUNT MARIE. SHE IS MY AUNT AND I'M PARTIAL, BUT all of Laramie County will back me up when I say she's something special. At eighty-one, she never walks, she scurries. She has pure white hair and the kind, watery blue eyes of a woman who has worked all her life out-of-doors. She wakes each morning at four-thirty, cooks breakfast for the men, rides all day through Wyoming's wicked winter or drives hay machinery in the summer heat.

Ten years ago a horse fell on Marie and broke her pelvis. Less than six weeks later she was back on a horse. Her leg has troubled her since the accident—she can't lift it high enough to reach the stirrup. She has to use a fence or a mounting block to get on. She is terribly embarrassed.

Marie was born a Jordan and raised on the ranch where I grew up. She married John Bell, a gregarious, fun-loving cowboy with an acute business sense. They started with nothing and built one of the largest ranches in south-eastern Wyoming. John loved the business end of it; Marie loved the ranching. They spent fifty happy years together.

When John died of cancer in 1972, Marie never considered leaving the ranch. "Goodness! What would I do in town? This is where I belong." She actively runs the ranch, with help from her foreman of fifty years, Floyd Hale.

It is spring and I'm going to have dinner with Marie. I've always loved the drive—from the Iron Mountain Post Office (in half a boxcar), a rugged dirt road winds seven miles around red striated bluffs and through green meadows full of fat Hereford cows. The ground owes its color to the iron, and I raise a great red cloud as I pass.

When Marie meets me at the door I can tell something is wrong. "It's my Sweetheart mare," she says. "She's sick. She's awful sick. I think she's going to die. I've been with her all day. Floyd is with her now."

Marie fixes us each a drink and we sit on the porch, watching evening settle on the valley, listening to the coyotes howl in the nearby bluffs. After a while we hear a motor. Floyd drives the loader around the corner of the shed. The lift, raised several feet above the ground, carries the body of a buckskin horse. Floyd hits a bump and the horse's head falls off the end of the lift, the long neck arching gracefully like that of a wounded swan.

"Sweetheart was such a fine horse," Marie says. "When she won the Denver Stock Show the judge told me I could take her anywhere in the country and win. And oh, how I loved her." A single tear courses down a weathered cheek. The loader makes its way down the dry, red road. Neither of us speaks for a long, long while.

Then Marie straightens herself abruptly, clears her throat, and says, "You wanted to know something about when I was a girl . . ."

Ranch life was a good deal different when I grew up. We had no conveniences—no lights or telephone, no water in the house, nothing like that. Course we never thought anything about it. It was just a way of life and I guess we all enjoyed it.

Everything was horses then. And oh, how I've always loved horses. I rode with Dad when I was about three years old—he would put me on the back of his saddle. Then when I was about four, Dad got me a horse of my own and I rode by myself. He was a black horse named Coon. He was sort of a big horse, but he was nice and gentle and I could pull myself up on him. I could either drive him or ride and I did both. Dad got me a little carriage, just a little one.

I rode everywhere. The mail came to the Underwood place, about two miles away. I would ride up there and pick up the mail. I rode up there on my fourth birthday and Mrs. Underwood said, "Oh, you've just got to come in and see me. This is your birthday." She had tiny muffins with four candles on them. I thought that was just great, 'cause we never paid any attention to birthdays. I mean, you could have a birthday and nobody would ever mention it. I sure was tickled!

Marie Jordan (later Bell) and her brother Frank at the home place on Chug Creek, Iron Mountain, Wyoming.

I rode a flat saddle for a while and I went bareback a lot of the time. I rode with Dad a lot. I remember one time he was going to ride to the Two Bar, about ten miles away, and he said I couldn't go. So I waited until he left and then I left. When I arrived at the Two Bar, he wasn't very glad to see me, I'll tell you. I guess I was about six.

Every fall we'd bring in the mare and colt bunch and brand the colts. Dad would alway take first pick. He would take eight or nine horses, whatever he thought he'd need. Then Sonny [Marie's older brother; my grandfather] got to choose, and then I did. When I was eight or nine, there was a black colt that I'd been watching for a long time and wanted so bad. Dad chose him and I said, "Would you consider letting me have him?" "No." "Why?" "Because I want him." This went on for days and days. Finally, I guess he got tired. He said, "You break him and you can have him." I named him Fashion, and he was nothing to break. He was just perfect. And that's the way I got him.

Dad, Sonny, and I each had a buckskin horse. They were half thoroughbred, and they were very fast horses. Dad's was named Tobe, Sonny had Neigh, and Turk was mine. They were half brothers, just a year apart in age. Mine turned out to be the biggest horse of the bunch—wouldn't you know it! Turk was a very showy horse. He never did buck with me, but he'd show off a bit. He'd look at people and just scare them to death.

One year—I must have been about nine—some boys came out from the Post to buy horses and Dad wanted me to wrangle. I didn't have a saddle, so Dad put his saddle on Turk and I put my feet through the stirrup leathers. One boy said, "You ain't going to send her out on that horse to bring in horses, are you?" Dad said, "I send her every day to bring horses." Oh, they couldn't get over that. They thought sure I'd get killed. But you didn't have to do a thing to Turk. He brought the horses.

Dad finally got me a saddle. Course, it was so heavy and I was so small and the horses were so big, I couldn't throw it up. Dad put up a pulley in the barn, and I could set it on a horse with that. That way I could saddle my own horse. We had a stump outside the barn that the side saddlers used to get on with. I used it too, and I could get on real easy.

We didn't raise Thoroughbreds, although sometimes we'd breed some of our mares to a neighbor's Thoroughbred stud. Lannens had a lot of Thoroughbred horses. They had awfully good horses. I'd go over to help them bring in the mares and colts. I used to love to sit on the fence and watch Mrs. Lannen cut out the horses she wanted. Mr. Lannen would say, "Tillie, you do the cutting," and she would do the whole thing. She was perfect with a blacksnake [bull-whip], just perfect. She'd cut them when she wanted just one or two at a time, and she put them just where she wanted them.

Every year the Two Bar would come through with their horse herd. I remember Dad taking me up there one time—they stopped for water at the AL. They must have had twenty-five hundred horses, all their work horses and driving horses and saddle horses. I never will forget the scene there. All those horses spread out over the meadow. Of course, they were having a little trouble with them. You always do. I can see that scene yet, just perfect. I said to Dad, "That's the nicest thing you ever did for me."

When I was real little I rode in dresses, 'cause they didn't have pants for kids or anything. Then I started wearing divided skirts. They were short—they came up just below your knees. They would flap, and oh, they just scared a horse to death. We'd tie them down with pieces of twine or rawhide. Course, the horse would get used to them pretty quick. The first time I wore Levi's my mother had a fit. I forget how old I was, but I must have been around twenty, because I'd been away to school. Mother just thought it was terrible, but they were a whole lot safer than divided skirts.

My own great concession to a new age was to abandon the sidesaddle. Why, for ten years, I continued to ride sidesaddle is a mystery to me now. I recall the steps that led to emancipation.

First, I discarded, or rather refused to adopt, the sunbonnet, conventional headgear of my female neighbors. When I went unashamedly about under a five-gallon (not ten-gallon) Stetson, many an eyebrow was raised; then followed a double-breasted blue flannel shirt, with white pearl buttons, frankly unfeminine. In time came blue denim knickers worn *under* a short blue denim skirt. Slow evolution (or was it decadence?) toward a costume suited

for immediate needs. Decadence having set in, the descent from
the existing standards of female modesty to purely human comfort
and convenience was swift. A man's saddle and a divided skirt
(awful monstrosity that was) were inevitable. This was the middle
nineties.

"I won't ride in the same cañon with you," protested [my
brother] Ray, when I first appeared thus clad.

"Put that promise in writing—you might forget it," I snapped.

And forget it he did. Vehemently he denied only a few months
later ever having said it, wherein he was not unlike many another
penitent who has rushed into delivering a premature ultimatum.

—Agnes Morley Cleaveland,
No Life for a Lady.
Copyright © 1941 by Agnes Morley Cleaveland.

Mama didn't ride. I broke a horse for her once. I got it nice and gentle, and
Dad said, "Now I think it's gentle enough so she'll like to ride." She rode one
day and she said, "Marie, I just can't do it."

Mama was a great woman, really. I never heard her complain. But she
didn't like living on the ranch. Every year she'd say, "Now this will be our last
year, won't it?" And Dad would say, "Yes." He had no more idea of moving
off of there than I had. Finally she said to him, "You're not going to move, are
you." He answered, "Yes, if you still want to, we'll go." She said, "I don't
think I want to go." That's all it took, see. If he'd said that a long time before
it would all have been over 'cause she had grown to love the ranch.

Mama raised such beautiful flowers. The sweet peas would be three and
four feet high. She was a genius with flowers. We had barrels in the yard.
Dad would get a certain kind of feed in barrels and he'd cut them in two and
make them into flower places. Our yard was full of flowers.

Mama was a great cook, and oh, she cooked for a bunch of people. We always had three or four boys at the bunkhouse, and in the summer we'd have
five or six to help put up the hay. I helped Mama because she couldn't do it
all. I worked out a lot too. I certainly liked to work out more than work in
the house. And I'm sure Mama thought I should be helping her sometimes
when I wasn't. But she never objected to me riding so much and helping my
dad.

Her mother objected. Grandma came out from the East two or three times,
and I remember she scolded Mama because I was out with the boys riding.
She thought Mama should keep me in and make me a lady. She told Dad that
she thought he was making a boy out of me; she didn't think it was very
proper. He said that I was his daughter and he would raise me the way he saw
fit. That ended that.

Prim put both hands on her hips and nodded. "Yes, the laird
himself! And your daughter just like you. What does she do for
me? Gives the work a lick and a promise and is out the door
before I can open my mouth to call her back. Then she gets on her
horse and rides all over the country like a wild Indian."

—Peggy Simson Curry,
So Far from Spring, 1956.

Course, in those days, all the girls worked outside. I guess that probably
depended on the family. Some girls worked in the house all the time. But an
awful lot of the girls I knew rode. I remember one time, Villa Moore and I
were working some cattle near the railroad. Some of Moore's cattle had gotten
in with ours, so Villa and I were roping them and dragging them out. A train
was going by right then, and suddenly we looked up and the train had stopped
and all the passengers were grouped around the windows looking at us.

Girls came through the country, riding from ranch to ranch, breaking
horses. Usually they traveled alone and they had horses with them that they
were taking home to break. Of course, in those days, everybody had fifty or
sixty saddle horses. These girls would break horses—I don't know what they
charged. Sometimes they would take a horse in trade for breaking several.
They were very nice girls. It was just a case of making some money, and that's
the only way they had.

Some of the older women worked out too. I remember there was a Mrs.
Steele. Dad went over to their place to help them brand one day. Soon after he
came home, Mrs. Steele rode up and said, "Can you come back? My husband
has completely lost his mind." She said, "I made a run for the barn because he
was carrying a gun and I was afraid he was going to kill me." So Dad went
back with her. Mr. Steele was completely out of his mind. Nobody ever knew
why. They put him in a home somewhere. Then Mrs. Steele ran that ranch for
a long, long time. She got hurt. A horse fell with her and broke her arm. In
those days they didn't set them very good, and she lost the use of that arm.
She couldn't comb her hair or anything, so she always kept her hair short, just
like a man's. She was a great ranch woman.

I took out a section homestead when I was around sixteen. It wasn't too far
from the house, up in the meadow by a tiny stream. Dad fixed up a little old
house for me and I homesteaded. I lived there three years, except for the time
I was in school. That was how long it took to prove up.

The last five years we lived [on our homestead near Broadus,
Montana], I was a widow with five children to feed and care for.
It wasn't an easy life, but we made it and didn't go hungry either.

The three oldest children attended the Bottles School through the eighth grade. The high-school problem had to be settled, so the children and I talked it over and decided to move to Lodge Grass. We sold the homestead to Lee Wilson, loaded our household possessions on a wagon, and took out across the hills towards Lodge Grass in 1929.

We took three head of horses—two to pull the wagon and one saddle horse to drive the twelve head of cattle. The children took turns riding the horse and driving the cattle. It took us a week to make the trip. Upon arriving at our destination, we started a dairy and chicken ranch. We enjoyed this and received very good returns for our efforts. A few years later I remarried.

—Alda (Wise) Maynard,
"The Charles Wise Family," *Echoing Footsteps,* 1967.

It wasn't much. I just had a bed and a little stove, and I think I had a mirror hanging in it and one little window. But I was sort of proud of it. I had a little garden up there.

Dad kept that land. He paid me so much lease on it every year and I finally said, "Well, I'm not going to use it, so why don't you just take it." He wouldn't do that, but he said, "I'll give you a thousand dollars for it." With that thousand dollars I fixed up part of our house after I was married. We couldn't have done it otherwise. We didn't have much money, I'll tell you. It was nip and tuck.

I always wanted to go to college. I had it in my mind for quite a while before I said anything to the folks. I picked out a girls' college in Baltimore. I chose that one because Dad had come from Baltimore and a lot of his family was there.

That was the first year of the war [World War I] and all the men from the ranch had gone to fight. Dad didn't want me to go to college. He said, "I need you here so badly." And I knew he did. I told him, "If I could stay this age and be here, it would be fine. But something might happen to you that I'd have to get out and do something, and I've got to have more education than I've got." I said, "I'll stay here 'til you're through haying." So I stayed and helped put up the hay, and then I went back. That made me a month late, which was a little hard, but if you want to do something bad enough, you can do it.

I'll tell you the way I paid for college. Dad said, "I don't want you to go, but as long as you're going, I'll pay your ticket back there, and I'll put a check in the bank for you for forty-five dollars. If you're sick you use it, and if you're not, you leave it there. You're to make your way after you get back there. That's up to you."

I didn't have any trouble at all. Some of those girls were quite wealthy and they were tickled to death to have me do their washing. I fixed their hair and kept the halls clean, and I didn't have any trouble making my way.

I went to Baltimore two years. It burned down eight or nine months after I left, which was sad because it was such a beautiful school. I think I got a very good education there. Better than I did at the next school I went to, which was more fun. That was Kansas University.

I made my way in Kansas too. I was in a sorority and I cooked and took care of the kitchen. We were right next to a fraternity house and they made me queen of their house 'cause when they had company I was supposed to go over and fix things for them. Oh, we had a circus there. If they had any girls come, the girls would stay at our house, and if we had boys come, the fraternity took care of them. We had a lot of fun! I graduated from Kansas, and I think I got a good education there in everything. The only thing that bothered me was they made me take foreign languages that I didn't want to take. Latin, for instance. I don't think Latin helps anybody.

Marie Bell and her husband, John, around 1924, on the Polo Ranch near Cheyenne, Wyoming. Marie always wore a divided skirt or, later, trousers when she worked outside, and a dress when she did housework— "that's just the way women did things." Today, at eighty-two, she always wears slacks. Airedale's were popular ranch dogs at that time.

I always thought so much of my father. I just worshiped him. The last time I rode with Dad I was married, and John and I had the packing plant in town. He drove some cattle over the hills to Laramie. I went halfway with him, and then I had to go back to town to work at the plant.

Mama dreamed that something would happen to Dad on that trip. She dreamed he would be terribly sick and she would have to take him to the hospital. When he got back, he had three ticks right straight across his stomach. They had all gone in. He got an awful fever, a terrible fever. Mama brought him right to town. I was at the plant when she called and said, "Come up right away 'cause your father is very sick." I did, I tell you. I just flew up there.

When I walked into the room he said, "Marie, I'm afraid this is it. I'm sick. I'm just terribly, terribly sick." Every once in a while he'd cough, but not a bad cough.

Two specialists from Denver came to look at him. They said it wasn't the ticks; they said he had a blockage in his stomach.

He kept begging me, "Marie, take me to the ranch. If I could just get to the ranch, I'd be well." Dr. Shingle came in about four o'clock and I told him that Dad wanted me to take him to the ranch. The doctor said, "Marie, he wouldn't live 'til you got him out of town. He'll be gone by eleven o'clock tonight." But Dad kept begging and begging, just as long as he could talk. It was straight up eleven that night when he died. I was holding his hand.

Just before he died, he said, "Marie, there is a horse for you out in Seven Mile Pasture. It is just for you. And I want you to have it." I looked and looked for that horse. But I never found it.

Cowgirls Carry On:

THE MOTHER-DAUGHTER TRADITION

Rodeo star Tad Lucas holding daughter Mitzi in hat. Born prematurely, Mitzi weighed only two pounds four ounces at birth and was the smallest baby up to that time to survive at the Fort Worth, Texas, hospital. She is five months old in this picture.

Jerri Wattenberg

North Park, near Walden, Colorado

JERRI WATTENBERG IS A THIRTY-EIGHT-YEAR-OLD, BIG-HEARTED KID. SHE IS A top hand, a recognized equestrian, and the first woman to sit on the North Park Stock Growers Association board of directors. But when Jerri heads out to check a herd of cattle on a warm spring day, she is likely to return with raspberry stains on her lips and fingers and a slightly guilty grin on her face.

Jerri dresses casually, in worn blue jeans and a yellow polyester top. Yet she has about her, even in her open ebullience, an almost Old World elegance. Her bewitching almond-shaped eyes, high cheekbones, and long brunette hair, which she twists into a bun on the top of her head, make Jerri a woman of unusual beauty. She has an alluring way of tipping her head just so as she speaks. The gesture is almost coquettish but completely unconscious.

Jerri is a playful person who laughs a lot. Still, she says, "I don't have much time for someone I can run the whole length of." She has a husband, Dave, and a seventeen-year-old son, Tye.

My mother is a very unusual woman. She was raised on a farm in Kansas but she did a lot of running around. She took off in a model-T once and went to California. She and her sisters worked for a man who insured the movie stars. She got to see Greta Garbo and the Marx Brothers and Jack Benny and all those stars. And she saw a lot of country. She didn't get married until she was thirty years old. That was a scandal in those days!

She and my dad went to the same high school in Kansas. They grew up together but went their separate ways. Then they got together when they were thirty. They came out West and my father worked for ranchers. Much later they bought a ranch of their own.

They got married at the end of the thirties. They didn't have anything. I suppose the wages were fifty dollars a month or something. They were so poor —well, everybody was, I don't mean to single them out. But Mother trapped muskrats.

. . . [Heather] had set traps for muskrat and mink along the small creeks that poured into the river. She pulled the traps every Sunday evening before she rode down to Plunketts' for school.

In the willows the air smelled of wet bark and damp earth. The small creeks were clear and fast, pouring like pale amber over the rocky beds. She had baited some of the traps with carrots, and others with the rank-smelling beaver-castor mixture that Jediah used. The smell of this was on the old jacket that Prim wouldn't let her wear in the kitchen. Two traps had been sprung but were empty, and she knelt to set them and placed them on the shallow ledges so the animals would tumble into the deeper water and drown, and not twist their feet. Jediah had taught her this, saying, "It's kinder, so that makes it right."

She came around a bend of a narrow creek and stopped. On the bank she saw another sprung trap, and beside it a mink, slim and dark and long, one front foot held up. At once she knew it had been caught by the toe and had worked its foot loose, but the foot still hurt from the steel bite of the trap. The mink made no effort to move. It simply stood motionless on the river bank, the foot held up, the little eyes dark and bright, its fur blue-black in the sunlight.

A mink, she thought, her heart beating hard—a wild mink. The first I've ever caught—or almost caught. She pictured taking it home, and how Kelsey would praise her, and how she would tell Jediah about it. She raised the rifle, cocked it, and sighted down the barrel. The mink looked back at her, beautiful and strangely still. Slowly she brought the barrel down, staring at the animal there before her, so close it seemed she could almost hear the quick fluttering of its heart.

The long moment drew out between them, caught in the silence of the bright, quiet day. And then the mink moved, turning and sliding over the bank in one liquid, dark motion, flowing into the water and parting it with no sound at all; the amber-colored shine separated to receive the animal. It moved across the creek and around the dripping bank and out of sight. The naked willows trembled in a small breath of wind, in a brief orange-red and golden motion, and were still. Heather's hands shook, and the water murmur rose loud in the silence.

—Peggy Simson Curry,
So Far from Spring.
Copyright © 1956 by Peggy Simson Curry.

My earliest memories are going with her to run the trap line. We'd ride out real early on cold mornings, ride up the ditch. I remember going on the same horse with her. When I was a little older, I rode my own horse. Mother would wear rubber boots and check her traps in the water. By the time I was two or three, I thought I was pretty brave with my horse. I'd ride out in the ditch where Mom couldn't get to me—the water was over the tops of her boots. She'd say, "Now Geraldine, it's time to go home." I'd ignore her. Then she'd say, "Goddam it, get that horse out of there!" [Laughs] I can remember her standing on the bank, screaming bloody murder at me. Finally I would come out and I knew every time I'd get a licking. Those are my earliest memories.

Mom always worked outside. She cooked and took care of the house too, but she didn't make a big deal out of it. She always thought the cattle and the other work was more important.

She is very good with animals. She's a very, very good equestrian, and she knows cattle. She can sense just what they are going to do next. And she loves to milk. I just hate to milk! I'd do all the other chores, and she'd milk. And she still loves to milk.

There weren't very many women who worked out in those days, and I remember some women made catty remarks about my mother. They felt sorry for her and they'd say, "Oh, poor Mrs. Bartley, she has to shovel manure," or, "Isn't it too bad she has to work and can't be playing bridge?" I don't think they ever stopped to realize that she enjoyed it. It wasn't a "have to" situation.

Come to think about it, remarks were probably made about me too, because most of my friends didn't work out. I remember once I had to take home-ec. We were supposed to be doing embroidery or something at home. The teacher came out one day to see what I was doing and make a call on the family. She wanted to know where I was and Mother said, "She's down there by the hill." The teacher asked, "What's she doing there?" "She's on the Cat [Caterpillar tractor] cleaning the ditch. You can go down and see her if you want." The home-ec teacher got in her car and drove back to town. That was the end of that. [Laughs] We had no more family calls.

One of the things I liked best about growing up on a ranch was the variety of people. We always had a lot of help around. A lot of them were drunks. Filthy drunks. They had their problems, but they all had something to offer. You know—you walk into a room where some old drunk has wet the bed and thrown up. But then you'll see him sober, and what a nice person he is! A lot of the people who worked were drunks, but they still had a sense of honor. They wouldn't steal from you or lie to you, and they were good workers when they were sober. People don't want to work on ranches today. We have a saying up here that we can't even hire a good drunk anymore.

We had a lot of hobo types come through. And you'd learn so much. You met the most fascinating people. It's amazing what's behind some of them, you know. You'd run into someone who had been a lawyer or a businessman. Or maybe nothing but a hobo. We had one little guy who worked for us every haying for years. He was nothing but a hobo. He'd get on the trains and he traveled all over the United States. And he was the most fascinating person. The things he knew, and the stories he could tell. . . .

Of course, there were the trappers, the government trappers. And then we met quite a few very wealthy, high-class people. The Pughs from Philadelphia had a ranch near us and they were great friends of my parents. So I met a wide, wide variety of people. People from one extreme to the other—from the dirtiest drunk to people like the Pughs. I've always loved livestock, but if I had to put my finger on the one single thing I like best about ranch life, I guess it would be the people I've met because of it.

I was an only child, but I was never lonely. There were so many people around. Really, I grew up with a bunch of men. But that's one thing—if I have any problems, it's relating to other women. I think like a man. I find myself not having enough patience, I guess. As far as I'm concerned, you can get in one hell of an argument—a knockdown, drag-out argument—but when you're through, you're through. That's the end of it. And I find that men generally think that way. But women—my God! "Last year you said . . ." [Laughs] To hell with last year! I just don't hold a grudge. I guess, if anything, that would be my biggest problem, relating to most women.

I am completely lost when a group of women sit down and start talking—"Well, Johnny went to the potty today." Big deal! Or, "I baked a casserole today," or, "I have a new recipe." [Laughs] It just isn't my world. And yet, I don't want to belittle them at all. I think it's great to be able to have the privilege to do what you want.

Some ranch women around here work out occasionally—like they will help on a roundup or something fun like that. But they don't work out on a regular basis. Like one of my friends says, "They're good help when the weather's nice, but when it comes time to shovel the shit, they're at women's club."

Now, there are a lot of women in the Park who I feel perfectly at ease with. We work out, we have similar interests. But there's a lot of them that I just end up thinking, "What am I doing sitting here?" And I'm sure they're just as bored with me.

I don't think I could ever be a suburban housewife. Quite frankly, I don't know what they do with their time. You can only clean so much house. You can only cook so many meals. I don't care how much start-from-scratch you do, you can only fill so many hours. I just have to be busy, or I get picky. I drive myself and everybody around me up the wall.

I went through a bad bout with hepatitis. I came down with it last year, the first of April—just when calving started, of all things. It kept me down all last summer and a good part of this winter. I've never been through anything so bad in my life! It was horrible not to be able to get out and work! I couldn't do anything! And I'm really not all that ambitious. But you have to have something to do.

An old German man worked for us for many years and I remember him saying one day, after we'd had a really long, hard day, "It's a privilege to be able to work." I thought, "Oh God." You know. [Laughs] But when I was laying in that hospital in Denver, I thought he was so right. Because it really is a privilege to be able to do what you want, to be able to get out and do it.

Staying inside all day, the smallest things suddenly mushroomed into major crises. One time, Dave was away and we had a windmill out. The repairman hadn't come from town to work on the well. I was still sick, and I went up there and found a cow down in the water. I didn't have a rope with me and while I walked back to the house to get one, she drowned. About that time Dave came home. The minute I saw him, I just stood there and bawled. It wasn't that serious a thing, but I just could not pull myself together. I must have bawled for thirty minutes before I got it all together again. But that's a classic example of sitting at home and not doing anything and then falling to pieces when some little thing happens. Can you imagine someone who lives on a ranch who could not cope with a situation like that? But after that, I could see why women who stay in the house all the time get depressed and neurotic.

I have some very positive thoughts about the women's movement. I know a lot of women panic over the Equal Rights Amendment. They think they're all going to have to go to the same bathroom or their daughters are going to have to fight. But there's a lot of good in it. The main thing I support is equal pay for equal work. And it also makes me mad that the government, or the

Internal Revenue Service, does not consider a wife. It's just like these ranch women—you work all your life, you work alongside your husband, and then when the estate is settled, you get shafted.* The ERA might change that.

As far as having trouble with men, I can't say I have had any. My theory is that if you do your job, you're not going to have problems. Oh, you have a few —there are always a few men who say, "She ought to be in bed instead of out here," no matter what you're doing. But to me, those men are funny. I find them amusing. I have a habit of digging at them, teasing them. [Laughs] I probably shouldn't do that, but it appeals to my sense of humor.

Once in a while you get a man who doesn't particularly like the idea of taking orders from a woman. But to me that's no worse than a woman who doesn't want to take orders from another woman, which you find too.

I don't think a woman should get a job if she can't handle it. There was a situation recently with a firm that hauls gravel out our way. A woman raised

---

* Inheritance tax laws are more complicated than can be explained here, but an anecdote, told me by W. L. Throgmorton, CPA, partner in McGladrey Hendrickson & Co., Cheyenne, Wyoming, will serve to illustrate the inequity Jerri mentions.

A family—let's call them the Smiths—homesteaded many years ago outside Cheyenne. They started with nothing. Actually, Mrs. Smith's family gave them a couple cows and a few pigs, but other than that, neither partner had any capital.

They worked together on the homestead until Mr. Smith was injured badly and unable to work for several years. During that time, Mrs. Smith did all the work on the homestead—planting, harvesting, taking care of what little livestock they had. As their five children grew old enough, they helped.

The homestead did well under Mrs. Smith, and by the time Mr. Smith recovered they could sell it, move onto a larger ranch, and go into the livestock business. When Mr. Smith died in 1970, they had built a sizable estate, worth roughly one million dollars.

For inheritance purposes, the entire estate was considered Mr. Smith's. Even though Mrs. Smith supplied the only capital they had in the beginning (the cows and pigs); even though her labor and management were primarily responsible for their ability to buy a larger place; and even though she continued to work after her husband recovered, she had to pay federal inheritance tax on the full estate, with the exception of the standard marital deduction. (At that time, the wife received tax free half of the estate up to a value of $100,000. In other words, she had to pay tax on $900,000.)

In 1976, partially in response to pressures brought by the women's movement, Congress acted to rectify this situation. According to part of the Tax Reform Act of 1976, a woman who worked alongside her husband and whose contribution to the estate was equal to his, in a situation similar to the Smiths', would receive tax free 2 percent of the estate for each year they were married up to a maximum of 20 years, or 40 percent over and above the current marital deduction of maximum $250,000. Hence, had the Smiths' estate been settled under this law, Mrs. Smith would have had to pay inheritance tax on only 60 percent of the estate, or $600,000 minus the marital deduction of $250,000 for a total of $350,000. (If, however, Mr. Smith died after only ten years of marriage, Mrs. Smith could have received tax free only 20 percent of the estate plus the marital deduction. In that case, she would have been taxed on $800,000 minus $250,000 or $550,000.)

Under the new law, if Mrs. Smith died first, Mr. Smith would receive 60 percent of the estate, plus the marital deduction, tax free. Thus, he would pay taxes on $400,000 minus $250,000 or $150,000. It would not be to either partner's advantage to list the estate in both names. In that case, whichever partner survived could only receive tax free 2 percent of the estate for each year of marriage up to twenty years. In other words, whoever survived would have to pay tax on a minimum of $350,000.

Cain with the company. She was going to go to court if they didn't hire her. They got spooked and hired her. She couldn't change an inside dual tire. She couldn't put the chains on. Well, she had no business driving a truck, as far as I'm concerned. That's just my little hangup. If you're capable of doing it, you should get the job, but I think it's ridiculous to scream about getting a job you can't handle.

I don't think I'm better than any man, but I do think I'm equal. In certain things. I'm well aware of the limitations of my strength. There are certainly things that Dave can do better than I can do. On the other hand, there are things that I can do better than he can.

Dave and I have a very open relationship. We give each other a lot of space. We were both only-children, and so we're both very independent. We were brought up that way. We make a lot of decisions together, but we each have a part of the ranch we more or less run ourselves. We don't tell each other everything we do. In fact, he has no idea where I am at the moment and I don't think it's bothering him in the least. Yet, we are very, very close. We have a lot of fun together.

We divide some of our responsibilities on the ranch. The horses are pretty much my responsibility. I handle the books. If there's a big purchase, we'll decide as a family. We bought a backhoe, which is eighteen thousand dollars. That was a family-type decision. But as far as the upkeep—making sure the vehicles have good tires, their oil is changed, deciding when to buy a new pickup—I basically take care of that.

Dave buys the bulls. That is something I really don't care much about. He usually makes the deals as far as when we sell our yearlings and what price we go with. He's a very good cowman and I have a lot of respect for his intuition. He does the irrigating.

As far as the help goes, we've got to have help we can both get along with. Also, Dave's mother cooks for the help, and she sees them three times a day, so she's got to get along with them too. So that is really a joint decision. We all hay together. I've run everything in the field from the swather to the baler, and now I'm back to the rakes I started out on when I was seven or eight years old. [Laughs] And that's fine with me. There's hardly anything that can happen to a rake besides a flat tire. And besides, I usually don't start raking 'til ten o'clock, and that gives me time to do other things before I start, like grab a horse and check some cattle or something.

Dave is an excellent housekeeper. That's one thing I admire so much about Eva, his mother. She always felt that men ought to be able to do something, and Dave can cook, he can iron, he can take care of himself. That's pretty unusual for men his age. And Dave's father didn't hesitate about scrubbing the floor or cleaning house. I really appreciate it. And that's one thing I'm going to give my future daughter-in-law: a husband who can take care of himself and is willing to share the load.

I'm thirty-eight and I'm not the least bit upset that I'm pushing forty. I had a great childhood, but I wouldn't want to go back to it. People say, "Oh, to be sixteen again." No way! I like my independence. I like to make plans and do what I want. If I make a mistake, I straighten it out and I like the privilege of being able to do that. My age doesn't bother me at all.

I think I get a lot of that from my mother, because she's never been one to moan, "Oh, my God, the wrinkles, I'm getting old." Dave's mother is the same way. She's seventy-four and she is very aware of what's going on in the world. She reads a lot. She's a crack bridge player. She cooks for a crew of seven every summer. She's a very energetic lady. Neither of them worry about their age or getting old. They both have the attitude that you look towards tomorrow. I guess I'm lucky. I had a mother that was that way. And then to have a mother-in-law too. I'm very, very lucky.

The years creep up no matter what you do. You don't know that yet, but in another twenty years, you'll see how fast they go. Oh, they do go fast.

I try to think young. I remind myself of this woman who was on the Johnny Carson show one night. She worked on a rig off the coast of Texas, out in the bay. I told my daughter-in-law, I said, "You see what weather does to women?" Now men can go out in the sun and the wind and they just seem to stay the same, they don't look old and wrinkled. But that woman—I bet she looked ten or fifteen years older than the men she worked with. A woman's skin doesn't take the weather.

A friend of mine was saying something about wrinkles and I said I didn't have room for any more! [Laughs] Oh dear! It's hard on you, I know, but I'm happy working outside. That's the main thing. And wrinkles are character. Some people say that. Sometimes I'd just as soon have a little glamor. I don't know what for, though, 'cause the alfalfa plants don't care. And my horse don't care. He knows who I am, anyway.

—Frances Bentley,
    deemed "the best damn irrigator in Natrona County [Wyoming]"
    by a neighbor.

Biddy Bonham

Bonham Ranch, Northwest of Cheyenne, Wyoming

Biddy Bonham, Bonham Ranch, northwest of Cheyenne, Wyoming, 1980.

SEEN FROM THE TOP OF MERRITT'S HILL, THE BONHAM RANCH SEEMS somnolent, peaceful, picturesquely still, as if caught in an old-fashioned water-colored postcard. Yet, drive down the steep hill and turn off the highway into the yard and you will be met by a whirlwind of vocal dogs and—lurking more quietly in the background—an even greater number of cats. As on many ranches, the dogs are mostly Blue Heelers, ferocious in voice but usually friendly. They have the run of the house as well as the ranch. The cats are a motley lot—Siamese, Manx, alley cat, and all possible permutations thereof. They have more or less house privileges depending on their needs, personality, and persistence. All the critters like company and greet it with enthusiasm.

Bonhams get lots of company. They live twenty-five miles northwest of Cheyenne on a ranch straddling the Horse Creek Road, a well-maintained, paved, secondary highway. They live far enough in the country to seem isolated to city folk, yet close enough to Cheyenne for easy access. When the Travel Commission entertains visiting dignitaries or journalists who want to see a genuine Wyoming ranch, Bonham's is the logical (and usual) choice. Among those they have entertained are Walter Mondale's daughter Eleanor and the staff of Japan's *Playboy* magazine.

This would not be particularly remarkable except that Bonhams are not native to the area. They bought this ranch nineteen years ago. Ranch communities tend to be close-knit, not overly enthusiastic about newcomers, and the Iron Mountain-Horse Creek-Federal area is no exception. In a community where many ranches have been in the same families for a century, "old" and "genuine" mean the same thing. Town folks subscribe to this formula as much as ranchers. That Bonhams have been chosen as the prototypical ranch family is one of the many tokens of their complete acceptance in the community.

But from the first, Biddy and Wayne and their four children (now ages nineteen to twenty-five) fit right in. They are, first and last, ranch people. They know cattle and horses, they love the land, they work hard. And they have the ready, if sometimes ironical, humor of the range.

A particularly handsome couple, Wayne and Biddy both have striking, angular faces, more carved or hewn than molded, full of quiet strength and subtle pride. Wayne, with his hawklike nose and rugged profile, could be the Marlboro Man. Biddy looks slightly Indian, with black hair now streaked with gray, and high cheekbones.

I have known Bonhams since they first moved in and they are like a second family to me. Biddy and I talk over what must be the thousandth cup of thick, black coffee I have enjoyed under their roof.

Biddy, now fifty-two, grew up near Steamboat Springs, Colorado. Her father, Marshall Peavy, was the son of an Alabama doctor and came to the area as a boy. He cowboyed throughout Colorado, Wyoming, and Utah before starting a ranch near Steamboat Springs. Biddy's mother, Mavis, was a schoolteacher from Denver when she met Marshall. The Peavys raised top-notch Quarter Horses and their name is fundamental in the American Quarter Horse Association. They sold the Steamboat ranch in 1944, when Biddy was sixteen, and bought another in northeast Colorado. Marshall was killed soon after. Mavis, Biddy, and Biddy's older sister, Mary, carried on.

Before Daddy got killed, we really didn't think about Mother very much. You know, daughters are very father-oriented. Daddy was very much a Southerner, and he had his idea of the role a woman should play—or rather, his wife should play. Mother was always supposed to be a lady. She was allowed to ride and she was allowed to buy horses, but she didn't work outside doing the everyday nitty-gritty.

I think I always respected Mother's horse judgment. I remember when she bought Beulah. Beulah was the mother of Gold Heels, which Daddy kept for stud. Gold Heels was the first champion Quarter Horse at the Denver Stock Show, so I think that gave us respect for Mother. But since she didn't work outside, she sort of got left out of our memories. She was definitely the underdog, if you stop and think about it.

[My older sister] Mary and I went with Daddy right from the start. Why he was so liberal as to let us ride, I don't know. There were definitely some things ladies didn't see. If we were moving cattle and a bull mounted a cow, Daddy made sure that we turned our heads. He always checked to make sure we were

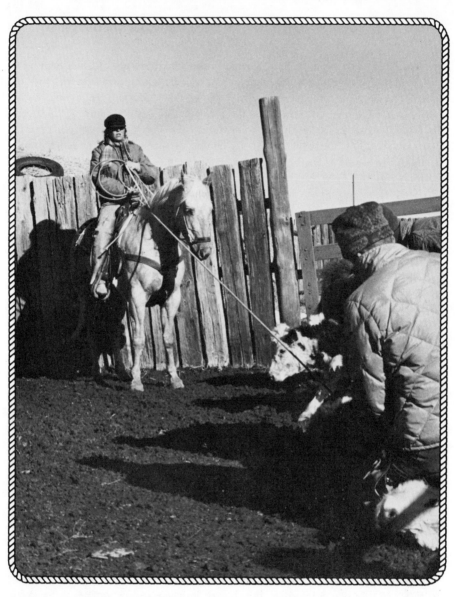

Jennie Mai Bonham, holding rope on a steer being castrated, Iron Mountain, Wyoming, 1980.

looking the other way. I still turn my head. It's funny the things you don't outgrow.

Daddy was such a hero to me. He was the greatest, outside of Paul Bunyan. Now, he told great Paul Bunyan stories. When we were little and we had been riding a long way and we'd see a pile of rocks, he'd tell a story about how Paul Bunyan dropped those rocks there. I thought Daddy was the closest to Paul Bunyan you could get.

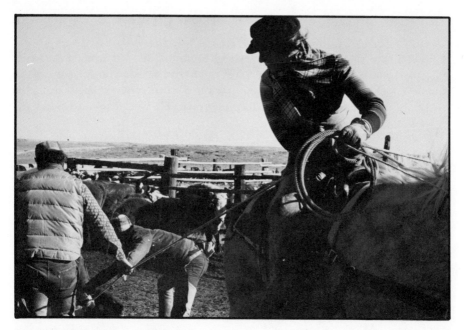

Jennie Mai Bonham, roping steer at cutting time, Iron Mountain, Wyoming, 1980.

When I was about sixteen, Mary and I decided we wanted to go into the cattle business. We each bought fifty heifers. Daddy financed us. We went through the whole process of drawing up the note and everything. Then we had to calve out those heifers. And that was shortly before Daddy died.

We had just moved to Colorado. We sold the place near Steamboat and bought a ranch near West Plains, northwest of Sterling. The new place didn't run the amount of cattle it was supposed to, and it was short-watered. We had to move cattle every day. The day Daddy died, he and I were putting the cattle out. There were two calves Daddy wanted to doctor.

The day before, the vet had been out to vaccinate our horses for sleeping sickness and he gave them bad vaccine. He didn't bring it out on ice. All our horses were sick except for two old, retired horses that weren't worth vaccinating. So that day, Daddy and I were riding these two old horses.

I was riding along, goofing off, and not paying attention. I was practicing heeling [roping a calf by its heels] and I heeled this calf and turned it loose. Daddy said, "Hey, that's the calf we're supposed to doctor!" So Daddy went after it to rope it. He caught the calf, but just then his horse hit a hole and fell, and that was it. Daddy hit his head when the horse fell down. It wasn't the horse's fault. He was old and retired, but he was the only horse we could ride that day.

I went to Daddy and I thought he was dead because he was so still. I turned the calf loose. We were about five miles from home and I rode home on the run. I came onto the hired man—he'd been moving cattle someplace else. I'll never forget that. I didn't have on a brassiere 'cause I didn't have enough that

I needed one. In some way, my shirt had come unbuttoned when I was running that horse. I rode up to the hired man and he kept looking at me so funny. I looked down and my whole front was open. I don't know why that sticks out in my mind. I still can't face that man. He went back to Daddy and I went on and told Mother.

I felt so guilty about Daddy's death, because I didn't see the calf. I had heeled it and turned it loose, and that meant that Daddy had to rope it again. I think I still probably feel bad, but it was terrible for a while. I'm sure that's one of the reasons I hate that vet so, because I don't want to have to take all the blame.

I was sixteen and I was very dramatic. I come from a dramatic family. My sister's horribly dramatic. I think my mother is a little bit too. I know the next time we had to rope I just went to pieces. Jack, our foreman, roped a calf to doctor it and I just fell apart. Of course everybody jumped all over me, and I couldn't figure out why. They thought I was mad because Jack roped the calf. But it all came back. And I couldn't rope for a long time after that. I still can't rope, not like I could before.

Mom and Mary babied me like mad because I started having these horrible sideaches right after the funeral. They didn't think it was appendicitis; the doctor kept saying it was in my mind. But within a month it got so bad that they finally operated, and they caught it just before it ruptured.

Now, that's the reason I got the mare, Margie. I was in the hospital for quite a while. I don't remember that I thought I was that bad, but they thought I was going to die. We had these three full sisters and Mother and Mary divided the horses. They gave me the best mare.

There was never any doubt that we would keep the ranch. That was almost automatic when we discussed it. We affirmed with each other how we felt. That's what Daddy would have expected us to do.

But it was hard. We had just bought the place and nobody knew the boundary lines except Daddy. And because Mother was so lost and we were new in the country, people weren't all that honest. Daddy had leased quite a bit of land and all the leases got snapped up immediately. The people took them back. So we had to buy all the land we ran on. We couldn't get enough land for all our cattle, so we had to sell down our herd.

Mother had to learn everything. But she said—probably even before the funeral—she said, "They're not going to run us off." No, she never was accepted into that neighborhood, and she never worked with many of the neighbors. They were just like vultures. They tried to run her off.

But we were *all* so mean to her. You look back, and even her daughters were mean to her.

Even as soon as they pronounced Dad dead, Mary and I looked at each other and said, "Jack's not going to be on this place." Jack had been our foreman in Steamboat. He was a very strong-willed man. Daddy could control him, but Mary and I didn't want him around because we'd worked with him before. We knew him well enough to know what he'd do to Mother and us.

But the first thing Mother did when we went back to Steamboat for the funeral was ask Jack to come work for us. He treated her like a dog because he thought he knew so much more than she did. And we were mean to her because we resented her getting him when we thought we were qualified to teach her how to run the ranch. It was hard on Mother, I know. And I don't even know all that went on 'cause I went to school. I missed a lot and I'll *never* know what all went on.

I went to school that year in Kimball [Nebraska] and boarded with a family we knew there. Then I went to Stephens in Missouri for a year. Now it's a four-year college, but when I went there it was a high school and junior college. An awful lot of ranch girls went there because it was a place for them to board.

I learned to fly at Stephens. I enjoyed it and at the end of the year they asked me if I would consider coming back and getting a commercial license and then an instructor's. They told me I always had a job there.

I seriously did consider it. I probably would have, but when I got home Mary said she wanted her part out of the ranch; she wanted to go into the ranching business on her own in Steamboat. What with the inheritance tax and all the land we'd had to buy, that really put Mother in a bind. I figured she needed me.

Yet, she wouldn't let me stay home. I went to college at Fort Collins [Colorado. The college was Colorado A&M; now Colorado State University.] I went because Mother made me go. I didn't go because I wanted to.

I took agriculture. Animal husbandry it was then. There weren't too many girls taking it. It was right after the war and the classes were so ungodly big. I'd be the only girl in a class of seventy.

Of course I went through rush week, and I was a pledge. One time Mother called and told me to come home over the weekend to help work cattle. We were supposed to do something as pledges that weekend. I went to tell the sorority I had to go home and couldn't participate. They said, "You can't go. You're ordered to stay here." I said, "Here's my pin," and that was the end of my sorority days.

It was surprising. All the sorority girls quit speaking to me. Not just the ones from my sorority, but the whole Greek community. That was hard on me, because I couldn't figure out what I'd done that was so wrong. To me, the cattle came first.

I took terms off from college to help calve in the spring, and to help show cattle. I probably went four quarters in the two years. I always knew I wanted to return to the ranch. With Mary gone, I knew that Mother had to have somebody to take care of her.

You see, I didn't realize for a long time just how capable my mother really was—and is. Mary and I realized right away that Mother was much stronger than we'd given her credit for. But we didn't give her credit for having any brains.

Right from the moment Daddy died, Mother never went through that hand-wringing "Oh, what am I going to do?" stuff. You look back on it, and it's surprising. But Mother is bright, and she's awfully well read. She's interested in so many things. When I was younger and Daddy was alive, we didn't realize that she had this storage bin up here [in her head] and was always collecting more information. And she retains it. She can call up anything. And I think that's where her confidence came from. I think that deep down she knew she could handle anything. And she knew that from the beginning.

I think she also knew more about the ranch than anybody realized. Now, from things she says, I know that Daddy used to talk to her about the ranch, late at night. Because she has—well, it's kind of a photographic memory. So he would discuss things with her because he respected her memory and knew she would be able to recall it if he needed it. But Mary and I didn't know anything about this.

I don't really know when I realized that Mother was probably a lot smarter than I'd ever be. Maybe I realized it when Mary left, because it was hard to pay her off. I used to go in to see the banker with Mother, to borrow money. And Mother has this great way when she's doing business. She will put on the most stupid face and act dumb. She'd just let me do the talking and she'd sit there and bat her eyes like a bullfrog. But somewhere in there I realized that she was the power behind what I thought *I* was doing. She knew everything that was going on. When the final word came, she would mumble something in a stupid way, to make sure everything was right. But until you got out of there, you didn't realize what an important role she played.

There was an oil boom in that country. We didn't strike oil but we had an awful lot of dry holes on us, and a lot of leases. And Mother always got the best leases in the country. And that's probably when I really realized about that stupid bullfrog look, when I realized that it was an act. Mother knew exactly what she was doing, and she always had.

Really, I probably didn't get married 'til I was older because I always thought Mother had to have somebody to care for her. I realize now that she was always perfectly capable of taking care of herself, but I'm glad it worked out that way. I wouldn't have married Wayne if I hadn't waited.

I think the women's movement is great. When it first started I kept saying that I'd been liberated for years, doing a man's work. That's true, but I hadn't been liberated as far as doing a man's thinking.

Before I got married I had seen too many families where the wife was boss, and I made up my mind that the only way you could have a good marriage was to let the man be the leader, especially on a ranch. I just took it too far. I was *too* docile. And then I started to resent it when I was about forty-five.

That's because I had taken too much of a back seat, and now I can't do anything. If Wayne is gone and something needs to be done, I'll just let it slide until I can ask Wayne how to do it. Even though I know how to do it, and deep down I know it would be all right with Wayne. But I'm afraid to do it. I can't even keep books, and really, most ranch women keep books. I had always had a lot of say before I got married, but I just figured a wife was supposed to stay back. So I did. And the family grew used to that.

I think the women's movement has gone too far. I think there's a happy medium. I still think the family unit needs a head, if that makes sense. But not a completely domineering head. As far as that goes, we know a family where the woman is the head. She has to dominate everything. In fact, what finally woke me up was watching her poor old husband. He'd gotten to be such a vegetable.

And *I* was. I was getting to be a vegetable. I still am, but I'm coming out of it. I felt terrible and I drank too much. I still drink, but I don't drink like I did, because I wasn't allowed to have a thought, or my thoughts didn't count. I could think all I wanted as long as I kept to myself. I think I finally woke up to the fact that it didn't matter whether it was a man dominating the family, or a woman. That no one should be so dominated that they don't think at all.

I spent the first forty years of my life overcoming an inferiority complex.

—Margaret Duncan Brown,
   1926 diary entry, after eight years of running her ranch alone, in
   Shepherdess of Elk River Valley, 1967.

But then, when we got ready to buy a stud, Wayne made sure I went along with him and he made me feel good. Wayne likes the way I love cattle and horses, especially when we worked out together. Course, I don't work out that much anymore—you can tell by my weight I don't. But still, every once in awhile, there's something Wayne or the kids need to know.

I give them a rough time about the eartags. They eartag the cows and they can't train me to read the numbers. I tell them they had to eartag the cows because they didn't have me to tell them what was what. That's easy for me. I can't remember a person's name, but you can point out an old cow to me and I could probably tell you what sort of calf she had five years ago. It's just something that is easy for me. Wayne would probably admit that he's depended on me for that more than anything.

And I do love this life out here. A lot of it's the cattle and the horses. I feel an awful kin to horses and cattle. And it's walking out and seeing what God created.

The other night I heard something at the back door, and when I opened it, there was a big moose staring me in the eye. He was just curious and was looking at the doorlatch, but it sounded like someone knocking at the door. They're such an ugly animal, but

when they run they're graceful and swift. Moose aren't very even in temperament. Lots of people have been charged by them and chased up trees for several hours.

Horses are very frightened of moose. A few years back, we had a yearling moose who was lonely, and he came every day for about three weeks to watch Bob harness the horses. He would hang his head over the corral, and that made the horses very hard to handle. Elk come down here also, but they always run away when they see you. They eat the same things as a cow. Moose eat willow leaves, and the deer and antelope are browse animals. And that is why I like the ranch, there are so many things to see that are interesting. I guess you could call me a bird watcher, a wild animal watcher, a sheep watcher, a flower watcher and a growing watcher.

—Doris Bailey Luman, Sublette County, Wyoming,
from *Spoken Words of Four Ranchwomen,* recorded and
transcribed by Carol Rankin.
© Carol Rankin, 1979, pp. DL/18–19.

3
Cowgirls and Their Men:
PARTNERS ON THE RANGE

*Lucille and
Boots, around
the turn of the
century.*

Carole Horn

Horn Ranch, Middle Park, near Granby, Colorado

Carole Horn on the Horn Ranch, Granby, Colorado, 1979.

I MEET CAROLE IN MID-JULY—HAYING SEASON—AT SUPPERTIME, IN THE BIG kitchen of the old log ranch house. She wears the denim shirt and jeans she has worked in all day; her calloused hands are scrubbed pink. She is surrounded by four of her five children (all high-school age or older), her husband Jack, Jean and Becky Fuchs and Kathy Kennedy* (three rodeo cowgirl-ranch hands who help with the summer work), miscellaneous neighbors, friends, and dogs. Everyone helps with something and the kitchen swirls with movement like a big-city sidewalk at five o'clock. Carole is a bedrock of calm in the boiling chaos.

In some mysterious and imperceptible way, she orchestrates the activity. A

* See Chapter 9.

huge platter of hamburgers, great bowls full of baking powder biscuits, honey, bean salad, mashed potatoes and gravy find their way onto the table. Finally everyone sits down and the chatter calms. In a few moments our initial hunger is sated and the jokes and bubbling laughter surface again.

Afterward, Carole and I talk in the living room while "whoever's night it is to wash up" does dishes. The living room is comfortable, with ranch oak furniture and a casual clutter. The kids' rodeo, 4-H, and horse show trophies line the shelves; photographs of family, horses, and livestock fill the walls.

The first thing that strikes me about Carole is her gentleness. Her movement is slow and liquid, as is her speech. Her soft, steel-blue eyes look deep inside me as we talk.

I grew up on the Blue River. The Blue is one of the prettiest areas in Colorado but it's brutally rugged. The Blue runs very fast and is full of rocks and steep drops; the mountains shoot right out of the ground. The ranches are smaller than here, and the people poorer. We lived real harsh, real close.

The Blue wasn't put on the map until around 1936, but my grandparents homesteaded there in the late eighties. They were some of the first to come down the Blue. My grandfather called it no-man's-land.

We ranchwomen today really don't know the hardships the ladies did then. My grandmother had it really tough. Since my grandfather was a sheriff and a U.S. marshal, she took care of the ranch. She worked in the hay fields and broke all the horses. She raised seven children, lost two of them in the Blue. After most of her children were grown, she took in orphan kids.

All my dad ever wanted to do was ride broncs. He left home when he was in third or fourth grade. He didn't return to the Blue until after he married my mother, a schoolteacher from the East.

I'm the youngest of their five children. I was born in 1932, in the heart of the Depression. My birth was never recorded. Grandma delivered me. Of course, we didn't have a family doctor. The only time you saw a doctor was in an emergency. When someone was born, you told the doctor about it the next time you saw him. Only no one got sick for a long time after I came along, and they forgot to tell the doctor.

Grandpa died before I was born so I never knew him, but we lived with Grandma for many years. Grandma was an iron-rod individual—so brisk and dictatorial that you liked to stay clear of her. She had absolute control over a situation.

When I was a little girl, I remember seeing a team run away with Grandma on the rake. She was thrown underneath. Here she was, in her sixties, being rolled around under the rake. I wasn't even concerned about it, because it was Grandma. Grandma took care of everything. She had that much control over a situation.

Grandma used brute force to control everything, and my father was the same way. He had her ramrod disposition. Dad handled us sort of rough. If we got bucked off a horse, he literally threw us back on.

He was harsh, very harsh. He had a lot of faults, but on the inside he was a beautiful, beautiful person. On the exterior, you wondered sometimes.

It always seemed that Mother was the tender part of our lives. She had come from the East as a schoolteacher. Her family was wealthy and she was educated highly for the time. After she died I found a diploma from Barnes Business College in Denver. We never knew she had gone there. There was a lot she never told us. She lived very close. But she handled us tenderly and she did everything very gently, with a great deal of kindness.

She learned to ranch in three or four years. She just learned from Dad and his brute force, because that's the way Dad reacted to people. She worked out quite a bit, especially when Dad was away. She would take over things, but not with the dictatorial attitude that Grandma had. So you never noticed how much work Mother really did. She would milk the cows, but she would milk them very quietly, very gently.

Dad died when I was about thirty-four. Mother saw him die. She saw him fall off his horse. She caught the horse before she went to him. She knew he was dead. He had never fallen off a horse before.

She called me and took me out to see Dad. I remember just how she reacted. I don't believe that in all my life I've seen such bravery. She rode over to him and took the spurs off his feet and the gloves off his hands. She took care of him very gently, very lovingly. And then she looked at me and said, "I've got to take the reins now." She said it with cool courage. That's what I mean when I say that the older ranchwomen are stronger than we are today. I have never seen such real raw courage since.

I was kind of the apple of Dad's eye because I liked to be outdoors. I was hardly ever in the house. You'd think, being the only girl, I would have been in the house helping my mother, but I wasn't. I was always with Dad.

Dad took me everywhere he went. When I was tiny, he'd set me up on one of the workhorses and we'd scrape out a ditch with the old scrapers they used to have. I think Dad took a lot more time teaching me things than he did with the boys because I was really enthusiastic about it.

Before Alexandra was twelve years old she had begun to be a help to him, and as she grew older he had come to depend more and more upon her resourcefulness and good judgment. His boys were willing enough to work, but when he talked with them they usually irritated him. It was Alexandra who read the papers and followed the markets, and who learned by the mistakes of their neighbors. It was Alexandra who could always tell about what it had cost to fatten each steer, and who could guess the weight of a hog before it went on the scales closer than John Bergson himself. Lou and Oscar were industrious, but he could never teach them to use their heads about their work.

Alexandra, her father often said to himself, was like her grandfather; which was his way of saying that she was intelligent . . . In his daughter, John Bergson recognized the strength of will, and the simple direct way of thinking things out, that had characterized his father in his better days. He would rather, of course, have seen this likeness in one of his sons, but it was not a question of choice. As he lay there day after day he had to accept the situation as it was, and to be thankful that there was one among his children to whom he could entrust the future of his family and the possibilities of his hard-won land.

—Willa Cather,
O Pioneers! 1913.

I started driving the plunger [a horse-drawn machine to stack hay] when I was only seven or eight. That's one of the hardest things to do because you have to back up the team. He built me a little stepladder so I could even harness my own horses. When it came to kindness, he probably exhibited more towards me than anyone else.

This was right in the middle of the Depression. We didn't have a car, so we always traveled horseback. We took a team to town to get groceries. We either went to Kremmling or Dillon. Both were forty miles away. I can actually remember the first time I saw a bicycle, 'cause I thought the whole world moved on horseback or with a team of horses. That's the way we lived.

We rode to school four miles each way. When the snow got really deep, we walked those four miles. I wore a dress and long socks. Life was not easy at all, but we really didn't know it was hard. We accepted it because that's all we ever knew. We'd see other kids with long underwear in the winter and we'd be envious. We thought, "Gee, wouldn't it be nice to be really rich and have long underwear and overshoes!"

We'd find the most ingenious and most dangerous ways to entertain ourselves. In the spring we'd take an ax to school and chop off ice blocks and ride them down the river. Later, when the river was high, we'd climb the alder trees, go out to the end of a limb, and bounce down below that rushing stream and then bounce back up. We'd see which one of us could ford the river first in the spring on their horse. I've had my horse slip on a flat rock in that river. I've been underneath him when he came down, and I've swum out the other side. We played like that all the time, and we had lost two uncles in that river!

When I think back, I actually scare myself with some of the things we pulled. But it was really just our way to entertain ourselves. We didn't have books, we didn't have toys, and we didn't have very much food in the house— you never went into the house for food. We never thought anything about the things we did. I guess we thought the other kids were pansies. They thought we were such little roughnecks that they didn't associate with us very much.

Dad was a good bronc rider. During the Depression, sometimes he would ride to Steamboat—a hundred miles away—to go to a rodeo. And he would come back with money. Mother hated rodeos so bad. She wouldn't talk about it. She wouldn't even watch him ride. But she said there were a lot of times that, if he hadn't been able to win money riding broncs, she wouldn't have known how to feed us.

When I was about eight, construction came into the area. They built the Green Mountain Dam. That was the third largest earth dam in the world at that time. And Green Mountain was the scene of a conflict between the AFofL and the CIO.† They formed this little army and they were shooting people right on the job. The head of the AFofL came and got my father. See, Dad was an excellent shot and a good hunter and he knew the area extremely well. So Dad got involved with the conflict.

The state militia came to our house. I remember my brother and I watched these army trucks come rolling in over the hill. We thought it was neat—we hardly knew what a car was—and we counted them as they came over the hill. Much to our surprise, they pulled into our yard. They confiscated our guns.

They didn't get Dad's rifle, though, and I remember seeing him leave each morning with his rifle in his hand. When he'd come home each night, he'd hide it. He'd tell me where it was. He wouldn't tell Mother or the boys. That's how much responsibility I had, and I was only eight years old.

It's a strange feeling to see your Dad walk out the door and not know if he's coming back. This last winter I read *The Diary of Anne Frank* and I understood how those people felt, because that's how I felt as a child eight years old.

But I also thought it was neat to have food on the table. I thought it was neat to start living like other people again. My brother and I really didn't understand what the conflict was all about until we were much older.

By the time I was twelve or thirteen, my father was drinking heavily. He had always drunk some anyway, but he became almost an alcoholic. Then my brother was killed. He was a timber boy and he was struck on the head with a log. He was seventeen. My two older brothers were in the service. One landed on Normandy Beach [World War II].

---

† Green Mountain Dam was part of the Colorado-Big Thompson Diversion Project to bring Western Slope water under the Continental Divide. Three hundred workers chartered by the CIO at Heenysville, a temporary camp, struck in the summer of 1939 to protest living conditions. After three weeks, a 200-man vigilante force sanctioned by local sheriffs attempted to break up the strike with a midnight armed raid. Governor Ralph Carr had to declare martial law on the Kremmling area and call out the National Guard to quell the violence. The dispute was later settled in labor's favor. See *WORKING IN COLORADO: A Brief History of the Colorado Labor Movement* by Harold V. Knight (Denver: World Press, 1971).

"Little Joe the Wrangler's Sister Nell"

She rode up to the wagon as the sun was goin' down,
A slender little figure dressed in grey.
We asked her to get down awhile and pull up to the fire
And red hot chuck would soon be on the way.

An old slouch hat with a hole on top was perched upon her head,
She'd a pair of rawhide chaps, well greased and worn,
And an old twin rig all scratched and scarred from workin' in
    the brush.
And a slick mague tied to her saddle horn.

She said she'd rode from Llano, four hundred miles away,
Her pony was so tired he wouldn't go;
She asked if she could stay a day and kinda rest him up,
Then maybe she could find her brother Joe.

We could see that she'd been cryin', her little face was sad,
When she talked her upper lip it trembled so;
She was the livin' image, we all saw at a glance
Of our little lost horse herder, Wrangler Joe.

We asked where Joe was ridin', if she knew the outfit's brand.
"Yes, his letter said it was the Circle Bar;
It was mailed from Amarillo about four months ago
From a trail herd headed north to Cinnabar."

I looks at Jim, he looks at Tom, then Tom looks back at me.
There was something in our hearts we couldn't speak;
She said that she got worried when she never heared no more
And things at home got tougher every week.

"You see, my mother died," she said, "when Joe and I was born,
Joe and I was twins," her story ran.
"Then dad he ups and marries and gets another wife
And then it was our troubles all began."

"She beat us and abused us, and she starved us most the time,
Cause she never had no children of her own;
Nothin' Joe or I could do would ever be just right.
Then Joe pulled out and leaved me all alone."

I give the kid my bedroll and I bunks in with Jim
We planned and schemed and talked the whole night through
As to which of us would tell her the way that Joe was killed
And break the news as gently as we knew.

"I'll wrangle in the mornin', boys," she says as she turns in.
"I'll have the horses at the wagon 'fore it's day."
As the mornin' star was risin' I saw the kid roll out,
Saddle up the grey night horse and ride away.

Soon we heared the horses comin', a-headin' into camp;
'Twern't daylight but we plainly heared the bell,
And then someone a cryin' a-comin' on behind,
It was Little Joe the Wrangler's sister Nell.

We couldn't quite console her, she'd seen the horses' brand
As she drove 'em from the river bank below.
From the look upon our faces she seemed to realize
That she ne'er again would see her brother Joe.

—author unknown,
in Katie Lee, *Ten Thousand Goddam Cattle,* 1976.

It was too much for my mother. She had a severe nervous breakdown. I had one other brother at home about a year older than I was. Grandma had moved away, so my brother and I had to take on the responsibility of the ranch. Only, my brother wasn't very good at taking responsibility at that time. He could shun it so easy it wasn't even funny, and make you like him. But I couldn't do that. If there was work to be done, I felt it had to be done. The ditch had to be turned on on the fifteenth of May like we always turned it on—this sort of thing. So in a way, I guess I was the head of the family for a while.

Then, when I was fourteen, this brother and I went to school in town. Mother had prayed from the day each child was born that we might be educated. My three oldest brothers only finished the eighth grade. I've always thought that one cause of her nervous breakdown was her fear that we would never be educated. And coming from an educated and cultured background, that was hard on her.

So my brother and I boarded at an old folks home. I lived there for two years. People died at the breakfast table. This is no joke. They later closed it down because it was so badly run.

There is nothing positive about an old folks home. They hate you if you can walk. There was an attitude there of pure hate, bitterness, and anguish.

I'd get up every morning and think, Boy, can I get up the courage to go down there and sit at that long dining room table with those little old men, or should I go without breakfast? But I learned you simply do what you have to do and you smile about it. You get out in the fresh air and, even if you have to talk to yourself to get through it, that's what you do. But I learned a lot from those old people. I learned I never wanted to be like that, have that complete and utter negativism. There was only a couple of them that I ever wanted to be like. I learned it takes courage to grow old without that negativism. But the courage doesn't start when you get old. It starts way back, somewhere else. If you can take things when you're younger, you might be able to take them when you're older.

So my life never went smoothly when I was young. There was always the adversity, the very adversity. I think I have some real different feelings about things and I think it's because these were all facts, they were real. They weren't something that you read out of a psychology report. I'd look at people who had things relatively easy and I'd think, Why are they unhappy? I couldn't figure it out. I thought if you had money, you wouldn't have problems. But that's not true, not true at all. I learned right then and there, if you can smile, if you can really smile from the depth of your heart, you're all right. And it isn't an escape. It's a blessing from the Lord. I learned, no matter how bad things got, to give thanks to the Lord for the protection he gave us. Because, boy, we needed it.

I think that's why I learned the pure joy of being outdoors. I had always loved the outdoors, but with all this adversity, I really focused on it and saw its total beauty. I really loved the ranch. I was away from it during high school. And I went to college for two years. But I was never really happy if I wasn't on the ranch. The ranch was my whole life.

Dad was going to give me the ranch. He wanted me to have it rather than the boys because I loved it so and I stayed home. I went away, but then I came back and stayed.

I didn't marry until I was twenty-four. I was still on the ranch at that time. I think I would have stayed there forever if I hadn't married. My father didn't come to our wedding. He went fishing. I don't know how he thought for sure. You never knew what he was thinking.

I never would have married a man who wasn't a rancher. I really know that. I had gone with several fellows, but that would be the thing that would always interfere. I just knew that I wouldn't be happy unless I was on a ranch.

The first few years of my marriage weren't very happy, though. I remember when I was a little girl, there was so much conflict between my grandmother and my mother. I was a sassy little outfit anyhow, and I used to tell my mother I would never put up with it. Yet she did, and she never said a word. I never guessed that, down the road, the good Lord was going to give me the same situation, that I would have to live day in and day out next to my mother-in-law, married to her only son.

Now I think that my mother-in-law is my best friend in the whole world. If you said a word against me, she would hate you. But the first few years we didn't get along too well.

I moved into this house with three bathrooms and my knowledge of plumbing was to carry the empty bucket down the hill and the full one up. All I knew was how to push the little handle, no kidding. And electricity—I never knew anything about that. I knew about haying and straps and hames and scrapers, about being outside and the effect a storm had on the disposition of cows, how to stand when you fish and what you look for. I knew that sort of thing. But I didn't know any of the social graces.

They tried to change me for five years, and the more they tried to change me, the more staunch I became about being independent and standing set. I didn't want to stay exactly like I was, but I didn't want to change into what someone was going to mold me.

The Horns thought it was very unladylike for a woman to ride. The first couple years, I never rode. I just stayed in the house. I very nearly lost my mind. I could hardly stand being cooped up in the house. To be raised on a ranch, especially with the total responsibility I had when I was younger, and then to be shoved in with the plates and food all day. It was devastating. I tried everything in the world to satisfy myself—the housework and the cooking, and I raised flowers. But I couldn't stand it.

I remember looking out through the window and seeing this one colt being born. I watched him grow—he'd come tearing down along those willows and then he'd roll right back on his hocks and go the other way at the same speed. He was catlike, he had that athletic ability I liked in a horse. And I thought, When that horse gets to be two years old, he's going to be my horse. Someday I'm going back to riding. Someday I've got to be happy.

So when that colt was about two years old, a girlfriend came by. Mr. and Mrs. Horn didn't know, but we took that horse on the back side of the barn and loaded him into the trailer. I shipped him off to Steamboat and my friend's husband trained him.

Her husband said that when that colt came out of the trailer, it was the meanest horse he'd ever seen. He said he'd never seen a horse turn on him or be as ornery as that horse was the first few times he was ridden. And that's my horse today. He's the most outstanding horse on the ranch.

But I was most unhappy in those years. I fought it. I felt like I was almost a prisoner. In the middle of the night I'd think how I'd leave. Finally I told Jack I had to do something. Then he understood. He had never known how intense I felt because I had kept it all bottled up inside.

He started letting me get out and do things with him, make little decisions. I'd see him coming in with a cow and I'd sneak down there with my broom and help him get the cow in. Gradually, bit by bit, I worked my way into my cowboy position. Jack helped me break the ice. He'd say, "Well, Dad, Carole could really just stand right here and help us turn those cows." Pretty soon I'd help them sort cows. They had never let a woman do that before.

I worked myself in like that, and after I'd been outside for a while, I'd come back to the house feeling so much freer. This joy flooded over me, and it has stayed with me since.

I always wanted my kids to know the responsibility and beauty of animals and being outdoors. I have this theory—I don't know where I got it—but I always told my girls, "I want you to love a horse before you ever fall in love with a man." They could play with dolls or whatever they wanted, but I thought it was very important that they know the responsibility and joy of loving a horse.

Jack and I are very close. You hear all this talk about your liberated woman, but I find real comfort in being a little bit sheltered by my man. I really do. 'Cause I've had the other situation. I've lived without that support. That's probably one of the reasons I appreciate a husband so much. And I really *do* appreciate him. Because he's the head of the house and I know that he has the ultimate responsibility. But he takes it in such a unique way. And I know I'm important and I have influence.

I'm a little western, and I like to see the man hold the reins. But a woman has to be able to take them in a runaway. There is so much responsibility to a ranch, and I think a woman has to be keenly in the harness with her husband to make it successful. They work together.

I'm not the head of the family. I'm just the helpmate. But I can see how much influence I have over the people I'm associated with, just by being a wife and mother. In a lot of ways, if it comes right down to it, the hand that rocks the cradle still rules the world. I'm not in control, but I matter.

I'm a good friend of the Lord's, and I like to think he's a good friend of mine. I have a deep spiritual sense, I think. I can see the Lord working. The Lord's been so good to me, so good. The Lord has taken all my anger and bitterness and turned it into joy. I have so much to be thankful for that I could go on and on.

I don't see how anyone could live outdoors or be in this area and ever doubt there was a creator. You see the raspberries bloom and learn where to get the best gooseberries. We have such vivid changes of seasons here. You feel His presence all the time.

I love to ride real late in the evening. A different feeling comes on you then, as it grows cooler and cooler. You shove your shoulders together and listen to the sounds of the different birds. All you have to do is look around and you know the Lord is with you.

I go to church as often as I can, but I can't always make it. There's the chores, the cattle to be fed . . . But I don't think you really have to go to church all the time. I think it's how you believe, how you treat people. And I have my Christian tapes. In fact, that's my new Bible study program right over there. I have my tape recorder with me wherever I go—in the house, in the car, in the pickup. If Jack's gone, I take my tape recorder to bed with me. And my Bible is in my purse. I just learned to carry a purse in the last five years. I always said, "Why have a purse if you never have money to put in it?" But it's a good place to put your Bible.

About four years ago my horse fell on the ice and broke my leg. Crushed it from the ankle to the knee. The ankle bone came out through my leg and my foot was twisted clear around. The fall knocked the wind out of my horse and he laid on me for a moment or two. When he started to get up, I could see that my foot was still in the stirrup. I reached up and grabbed it out of the stirrup and I didn't get dragged.

While I was laying there on the ground waiting for Jack to come, it was a very spiritual experience. I really felt the presence of the Lord. I said, "Thank you, Lord, for choosing me and letting Jack go." It was calving and we could get along without me, but we just couldn't get along without Jack. It was a very spiritual feeling.

The disaster we most feared was a horse's falling and disabling us. Possibly because this was our most common form of accident. Prairie-dog holes have been responsible for many a broken leg, both of horse and rider. Any rough country is always a menace . . .

But the most nightmarish vision of all was that of having a horse fall, flatten the stirrup, and find oneself caught by a foot when the horse got up again. For this we wore six-shooters long after any other reason for doing so existed. To shoot the horse was the only answer, in all probability. A six-shooter does give one a sense of security. We had a saying, "A six-shooter makes all men equal." I amended it to "A six-shooter makes men and women equal."

—Agnes Morley Cleaveland,
No Life for a Lady.
Copyright © 1941 by Agnes Morley Cleaveland.

Nickie Taylor

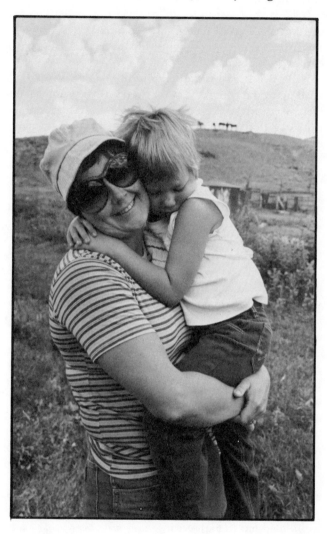

Nicki Taylor and her daughter Brandi, at Taylor Ranch on Blue Creek, near Kaycee, Wyoming.

THE BLUE CREEK RANCH, WHICH NICKI RUNS WITH HER HUSBAND CURT, IS one of the most historic in the Kaycee area. It includes the Hole in the Wall where Butch Cassidy and the Sundance Kid hid out, along with their women friends, Etta Place and Laura Bullion (Della Rose). The headquarters of the Blue Creek Ranch are on Butch Cassidy's homestead. When the law got too close for Cassidy's comfort, he sold his homestead to Curt's great uncle, Jim Stubbs. Stubbs paid for it in gold he had buried in the ground. Since Cassidy did not have the deed with him at the time, he promised to send it within a year. He did.

Nicki is thirty-seven, medium height, heavyset but solid rather than pudgy. She wears a T-shirt, blue jeans, and a patterned cotton baseball cap. When she rides she wears cowboy boots, but today she has on sneakers. She is setting corner posts down at the corral.

Nicki is a hard-working, sunburnt country woman with a ready smile. We head up to the house and wash away the dry summer dust with welcome tumblers of iced tea. Nicki has an infectious enthusiasm and energy, an absolute candor. Later she tells me that she doesn't meet strangers well or make friends easily, but I am struck from the first by her open warmth and hospitality.

Nicki has three children—Quinten, nine; Crosby, seven; and Brandi, five.

Something inside me just has to be free. I can't stand to be confined or stay inside. And I like to be by myself. When I ride I don't want somebody riding next to me and talking all the time. When you're alone the air smells different and you can smell the sweat on your horse's neck. You can listen to the quiet and your horse's breath. This fills a need I have.

I guess this comes from the way I was raised. My folks leased ranches around Arvada and Kaycee [Wyoming], and except for three or four years when I was real young, we always lived on a ranch. I loved to be outside, and my brother and I worked with my dad. We rode and looked after the cattle and sheep and put up thousands of tons of hay.

Dad worked hard and so did we. On the ranch we leased near Arvada, we rode terribly long distances. The house was on one side of the ranch and all the land lay on the other. Dad didn't believe in hauling the horses, so we rode all the way. We left home at a jog and came in at a jog.

Somebody asked me the other day when I learned to ride. I don't know. I don't remember the first time I got on a horse. It's something I grew up with, and it come natural. Dad was always busy and he more or less turned us loose. He wasn't on our case about how we rode. We learned through trial and error.

I was always riding some darn horse I shouldn't have been. When I was in sixth grade we had a crazy horse called Coke Hi. Nobody had ridden him for years. Then Dad rode him a time or two, and I started riding him. One day we headed out to gather cattle and rode over a big cactus-covered flat. You've never seen so much cactus; the ground was solid with it.

One of our neighbors was a pilot and he was out flying that day. He buzzed us two or three times. He flew so low we could practically read his instrument panel. Coke Hi threw one heck of a fit, and he bucked me off.

I guess I did a perfect somersault off that horse's ass, and landed right on my feet! Dad told me later that I looked just like a trick rider. But all I could think about was the cactus. If you've ever been in it, you don't want in it again.

You can get real attached to a horse. When we lived at Arvada I had a colt named Too Late. I'd known him since he hit the ground, and I worked with him and showed him in 4-H. He turned into a good horse. He was so dog-gentle, anybody could ride him. You could do anything on him—rope, or pack a lamb or a calf. He was really something.

———————————————————————————————

> She dashed madly down through the gulch one day, standing
> erect upon the back of her unsaddled cayuse, and the animal
> running at the top of its speed, leaping sluices and other
> obstructions—still the dare-devil retained her position as if glued
> to the animal's back, her hair flowing wildly back from beneath
> her slouch hat, her eyes dancing occasionally with excitement . . .
>   Now she dashed away through the gulch, catching with delight
> long breaths of the perfume of flowers which met her nostrils at
> every onward leap of her horse, piercing the gloom of the night
> with her dark lovely eyes, searchingly, lest she should be
> surprised; lighting a cigar at full motion—dashing on, on, this
> strange girl of the Hills went, on her flying steed.

—E. L. Wheeler,
*Deadwood Dick on Deck; or, Calamity Jane,
the Heroine of Whoop-Up,* 1885.

———————————————————————————————

When I was in high school that horse was more like a person to me than a horse. If I had problems or something was wrong I could talk to him, and he knew what I was talking about. He understood me. He wasn't an animal, he was a friend. I could cry to him if I needed to.

I sold him a few years ago. He was nine or ten years old, and I knew if I was ever going to sell him, I had to do it then. It was hard for me, but I knew he was going to a good home. I had too many horses then, and besides, he had changed. So many people had ridden him that he wasn't the same. But for a long time he was my friend.

I've got a horse now that I really like. He and I have temper clashes, but we understand each other. I don't realize that he does things for me that he won't do for anybody else, but other people mention it. He's a nervous, high-strung person—ahh, horse, or person, or whatever. But I like him. He's a good horse and I can talk to him. Most of the other horses I ride don't make any difference to me. You know, I just ride them.

I've always spent as much time as I could outdoors. Going to school just about killed me. I could stand it in the winter, but I hated it when the weather was nice. In the fall, and the minute spring came, school made me feel like a caged animal. I'd leave my overalls in the barn before I went to school. When I got home I'd go straight to the barn and change. Then I'd ride until dark.

After high school, I went to technical school in Denver and got a degree in architectural drafting. I like drafting, and if somebody wants something I'll do it for them. But I couldn't stand to do it for a living. I'd go crazy working in an office nine to five.

I was lucky I didn't have to do much in the house when I was a kid. Sometimes I'd help Mom get dinner or help her clean, but I didn't have regular household chores because I worked outside so much. Occasionally Dad would have enough men for one of the big jobs, like docking, and then I'd have to stay home and help Mom cook for them. Oh, how I hated that! To this day, I hate to stay in the house. "House" is a dirty word to me. I don't want to stay in it, and I don't want to clean it.

I had a really hard time adjusting to motherhood. I was used to riding and working outside all the time, and I couldn't cope with being tied down with kids. Staying home day after day made me barn-sour. I felt like I was in prison; I felt incomplete.

I took the kids out as much as I could. I rode a lot with the first one. We had an old horse I could lead behind me. I didn't have another gentle horse for the middle one, so I couldn't ride as much. But I've drug all of them from one end of the country to the other in a pickup. Sometimes they would have to stay in the truck for hours while I fixed fence or worked cattle.

I hope that didn't hurt them. The oldest one loves to go. He is quite a hand with a horse, and he's a good worker. And the youngest one likes to go. But the middle one doesn't. I hope I haven't pushed him too hard or hurt him by my selfishness.

But you've got to get out. If you're miserable you make everybody else miserable, and I've done too much of that. My husband and I had lots and lots of fights, and they were usually my fault.

Now I know when I'm getting uptight and I say, "We've got to *do* something about this." Curt will help me. He'll say, "If you want to ride, take the older kids and go ride. I'll work around here or take Brandi in the pickup." At first he didn't understand, and there was no way he would stay home. But he has really turned around on that.

I've learned to cope with having a family, but it has taken me a long time. Now the two oldest are in school and Brandi is five. She's a delight—I enjoy her in a way I missed with the other two because of my selfishness. Something in me finally settled down. I guess I've grown up.

I've always been terribly strong. Too strong, really. I never tried to be, but I was. In high school I had muscles like a man. Girls are supposed to develop the triceps and boys the biceps, but I had both. The guys would even comment on it. We'd be goofing around and they'd say, "Let's see your muscles." So I'd flex them, and the boys were jealous because I had more muscles than they did. But I grew up pitching bales of hay every summer—thousands of eighty- or one-hundred-pound bales—and it made me strong.

This last winter our hired help went to town and stayed drunk for several days, so we fired them. Carl and I fed alone most of the winter. We fed a hundred and twenty bales every day. Carl would throw them up on the wagon, and then I stacked them four high. When the snow started melting, the water saturated the bales and they'd weigh two hundred or two hundred and fifty pounds. Then I only stacked them two high, but I could lift them. You do things like that, and you don't even think about it.

We had all the vegetables we could possibly use, and now Jerrine [my six-year-old daughter] and I have put in our cellar full, and this is what we have: one large bin of potatoes (more than two tons), half a ton of carrots, a large bin of beets, one of turnips, one of onions, one of parsnips, and on the other side of the cellar we have more than one hundred heads of cabbage . . . I milked ten cows twice a day all summer; have sold enough butter to pay for a year's supply of flour and gasoline. We use a gasoline lamp. I have raised enough chickens to completely renew my flock, and all we wanted to eat, and have some fryers to go into the winter with. I have enough turkeys for all our birthdays and holidays.

In all I have told about I have had no help but Jerrine. I have tried every kind of work this ranch affords, and I can do any of it. Of course; I *am* extra strong, but those who try know that strength and knowledge come with doing. I just love to experiment, to work, and to prove out things, so that ranch life and "roughing it" just suit me.

—Elinore Pruitt Stewart,
Letters of a Woman Homesteader, 1913.

A very embarrassing thing happened to me a couple weeks ago in Kaycee. A girl attacked me in front of the bar. Just like that, she came up and clawed my face. I'd never been in a girl fight; I detest them. But when she attacked me I flung her to the ground, doubled up my fist, and beat her head. I hit her about three times and then pinned her with one knee in her gut and the other on one of her arms. There I was, on the ground, face to face with her, and suddenly it all came to me. I was shocked, really horrified. I'm still horrified. I hate to set foot in Kaycee yet, because they are all talking about it. I guess it's better than to get beat up—I wasn't even looking at her and she attacked me. But I am really, really embarrassed about it.

I've never liked town very much, anyway. I was brought up to believe that facts are facts. Things are either true or false, black or white. And you don't tell a lie. You just don't. But the minute I step inside the city limits I feel like I'm being took. In town, you walk into a grocery store or a clothing store and you are being watched.

There are very few people that I really feel comfortable with. And I don't make friends real easy. I guess I've got a shield built up. I was never hurt bad or anything. But I grew up with everything so plain and open, and it's not that way in town.

I am always the same person. What you see is what you get. When I go to bed at night and when I get up in the morning, on Christmas or on Halloween, I am the same. But people don't seem to be that way in town. I don't even like sending the kids to town schools. I believe in country schools. If you don't like the teacher, you can get one you do like.

We all love living in the country. We want to always live here. But they are trying to make this into one big recreation area because of Butch Cassidy and the Hole in the Wall, which is close by. We have Robert Redford to thank for that. He's a nice enough guy to visit with, and he likes history, but he's too much of an environmentalist.

There are too many environmentalists. We get folks from the BLM who come and tell us how and what to do. Yet, they were raised in Boston or someplace, and they have no idea what we do out here. Most of them don't even know where meat comes from. They think it comes from stores. No lie, they've told us that. They think groceries come from grocery stores.

People have an idea that agricultural people are stupid. Farmers and ranchers are the best ecologists and the best economists the world has ever seen. There is no way someone can use the same land year after year after year, and raise more and better crops every year, and be stupid. Inflation takes up everything we make. We get the prices in 1978 that we were getting in the forties and fifties. Yet, we have to pay ten or fifteen thousand dollars for the piece of machinery that used to cost us thirty-five hundred. Year after year, farmers and ranchers run in the red. Yet, they manage to make a go of it, and they couldn't be stupid and do that.

We want to keep this ranch. There is nothing greater than a family out in the country. If we had to, we could do something else. Curt is an excellent horse trainer and we could make a business out of that if we had to. But we don't want to do that. This place may be worth two and a half million dollars, but what would we have if we sold it? Two and a half million dollars. We wouldn't have anything. To us, there is no value on what we have here. This is a beautiful country. We'd like to keep it. We work to do it.

Barbara Davis

Near Cowdrey, North Park, Colorado

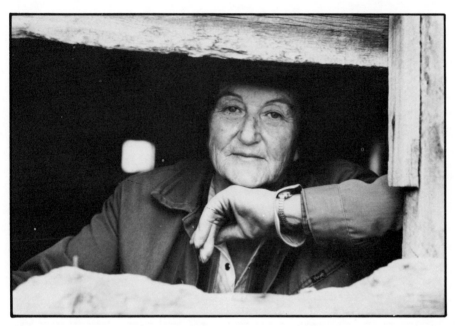

Barbara Davis, Davis Ranch, North Park, Colorado, 1979.

NORTH PARK, A 40- BY 60-MILE VALLEY IN NORTHERN COLORADO, NESTLES BE-
tween the Continental Divide and the Rewah Mountains. In the summer,
North Park might be Eden. The meadows spread before you like plush and
verdant velvet, the bluebells and wild aster bloom, and the spring runoff turns
tiny streams into glistening, diamond-studded rivers. But summer seems to last
no longer than the bud on a wild rose in this valley with a base altitude of 8,000
feet. Winter soon returns with its piercing winds, 40°-below-zero nights, and
paralyzing blizzards. It's hard country, North Park, but good cattle country.
And good cattle country, they say, is hell on horses and women.

Barbara Davis gives the lie to the last part of the adage. She was born in
North Park in 1909 and has lived there all her life. With curly black hair and
crackling, cornflower eyes, she is spry and sparkling.

She married Sam Davis when she was sixteen and they have ranched together for fifty-some years. Well, "together" in a way. Barbara has her herd of
cattle, and Sam has his. Barbara has her pickup; Sam has his. Barbara has her
bank account; Sam has his.

While most ranchwomen today wear T-shirts and baseball caps, Barbara keeps to the old ways. She likes her felt Stetsons, her bright western shirts, and her fringe-trimmed chaps. She also wears mascara and rouge "because it's nice to feel like a lady."

I went with my father right from the start. My older sister would help in the house, but I tagged along with Dad. An older brother and I did a lot of the riding. Then my younger sister and I did too.

My dad was very good with animals. I have a picture of him with a tame woodchuck on his knee. He could tame anything. He had a team of elk that he taught to drive. He's in one of these history books. I guess I might have inherited my dad's way with animals, 'cause it seems to come natural.

My brother and I roped a bear one day. We run him all over the country, up my dad's homestead there. He was pretty well tired time we caught him, but we both had our ropes on him a number of times. Then my brother broke his rope, so naturally he borrowed sister's. But at the time we could either one of us roped him, he was pretty tired.

My brother got the rope around his neck and dallied the rope around a

Barbara Fox (later Davis) (second from left), age fourteen, with her sister Jo (on left), her older brother Ray, and baby brother Casper. Barbara and Ray roped the bear and killed it, 1925.

buck fence post. We weren't too far from a buck fence. I held the bear and he got an ax. Killed him with an ax. I do think I come as near choking him to death as my brother did to killing him.

━━━

The rivalry between [my younger brother] Ray and myself in those first years was keen. His masculine strength was pitted against my two years' advantage in age and corresponding stature. Lora, a frail child, was never a competitor in the tests of bravado which Ray and I felt called upon to set each other. I held a slight edge over him until the day we fought over who should remove the ticks from the calf's ears.

I discovered the wood ticks in the milk-pen calf's ears and set about removing them with a bent wire. Ray insisted that I hold the calf and let him perform the operation. I countered with the claim that, by right of discovery, I should have the morbid satisfaction of digging out the ticks and he should hold the calf. The dispute quickly reached the violent stage and we grappled. I succeeded in getting my arms around his neck from behind and holding his head tight against my chest with the idea of cutting off his wind, while I used my feet further to enforce my point of view. It was a tactic that had proved successful before. But this time there was a difference. Before I knew what had happened, I was on my back and Ray was sitting on my chest. "Give up," he asked—a quite superfluous question under the circumstances —and then with characteristic magnanimity he added, "All right, I'll let you take the ticks out of one ear." After that I never challenged him on his own ground of sheer physical strength, but confined myself to taking him on in matters of skill or cleverness, where I was often no more successful.

—Agnes Morley Cleaveland,
No Life for a Lady.
Copyright © 1941 by Agnes Morley Cleaveland.

━━

My brother said he couldn't have got him without my help. I kept the bear from escaping one time when he went through the fence and headed up Government Creek. I was riding a horse that would jump the fence with the top pole off, and I was just dumb enough to jump it.

Once a team got away with me. The double trees came loose and started hitting the horses, and then pretty soon a tongue would have probably rammed into the ground and tipped the whole thing, so I just rolled over. My folks had always said, "Roll off, roll backwards." So that's what I did. You never light easy, though.

I first met Sam at a dance. I'd heard he was a bronc rider. I'd seen him ride at Steamboat. He never did try to hit the big time, but he was handy with

Barbara Fox,
age fourteen,
with rope and a
set of elk antlers
her father got
years before.
North Park,
Colorado.

*Haymaking in North Park, Colorado, around 1925. Barbara, age fifteen, is on
the rake (drawn by the white horses).*

broncs. As far as courting, I guess it was mostly ride. He worked around a number of ranches, breaking teams and haying. We went to lots of dances. There was a dance every two weeks, sometimes every week. The eight- and twelve-year-old girls were just as popular as sixteen- and eighteen-year-old girls. There wasn't many girls. Boys standing all around.

My dad ran Herefords. He ran about five hundred head at one time. When I was married he gave me two registered ones. I bought two more and started my registered herd with four head. My husband runs a grade herd. [Generally, a registered herd's offspring are sold as breeding stock; a grade herd's offspring are sold for slaughter.] He has a very good bunch of grade cattle, top feeder calves. He likes to pick my herd, get the pick of my bulls. I got him a little spoiled, but that's all right. He enjoys it.

I don't know exactly how we decided to keep our herds separate. He didn't care much for purebreds. He just didn't like that extra work. And you don't

Barbara Davis on Stranger, around 1926. Note the tall, steep heels on the boots.

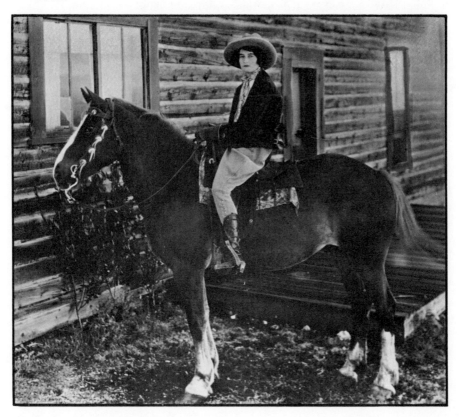

see alike on bulls sometimes, so it just turned out good. Of course, we help each other ride and so forth.

I probably know more about the sires of my cows than some people do their kids! Well, you've got to keep them separate, and know what they are. They no more than hit the ground than I've got a number in their ear. I have to make out papers on them. So there's a lot of bookwork. It's interesting. I love it. I'm just dumb enough to like it. And they've always paid off good so far.

It will be over two years before I can get a deed to my land. The five years in which I am required to "prove up" will have passed by then. I couldn't have held my homestead if Clyde [my new husband] had also been proving up, but he had accomplished that years ago and has his deed, so I am allowed my homestead. Also I have not yet used my desert right, so I am still entitled to one hundred and sixty acres more. I shall file on that much some day when I have sufficient money of my own earning. The law requires a cash payment of twenty-five cents per acre at the filing, and one dollar more per acre when final proof is made. I should not have married if Clyde had not promised I should meet all my land difficulties unaided. I wanted the fun and the experience. For that reason I want to earn every cent that goes into my own land and improvements myself. Sometimes I almost have a brain-storm wondering how I am going to do it, but I know I shall succeed; other women have succeeded.

—Elinore Pruitt Stewart,
Letters of a Woman Homesteader, **1913.**

My daughter bought two bulls from me this spring. She's running a nice bunch of crossbreeds. And Brownlee bought five. You're lucky if you can sell to your neighbors, that's what they say. Because your neighbors know your stock, and they know if any bad characteristics show up. I don't have any trouble selling them. There's been only maybe two years in all the time I've been in them that I had to take 'em to a sale.

The fact that I'm a woman doesn't make it any harder for me to sell my stock. They talk to me with my registered stuff. And I want to do it. I don't want to do the work and then let Sam have the fun of selling them. I like to go out, and if they don't buy, I love to show them my cattle anyway. Course, Sam helps promote my cattle. He likes them. I do his, too. If I find a buyer and I think he's interested in Sam's cattle, I'll show them if he's not around. But he sets his price, what he wants, and I keep still. And I set my price on my bulls.

Sam loves haying. Where calving makes him nervous. Puts him on pins too

Barbara Fox, age fourteen, and her "pard," in North Park, Colorado.

Barbara Davis, age twenty-seven, in North Park, Colorado.

much. But calving don't bother me. Lots of times I'll go down and talk to my calves. My cows are gentle—so far I'm not afraid of one of them. If I am, she soon goes down the road. And I can calve my cows alone. Sam don't like to fence but I like to repair fences. We have good fences.

I don't think Sam and I are competitive. He seems to feel it sometimes. But I don't. He's got a very good eye for stock.

My daughter and I have always been very close. I was pretty young when I had her, only seventeen when she was born. So really we were just like sisters. She would help in the fields. I always hired a cook, so she and I both worked in the fields and did a lot of riding.

We used to show our cattle a lot. Then I'd enter the reining class or barrel race. My daughter and I used to love to enter that. We also did rope spin, fancy roping. We enjoyed that. We performed at Walden, then we went to Steamboat and Saratoga, and around here. I guess we could have went to Denver, but we sort of chickened out. Entertaining wasn't in our blood, I don't think.

My daughter is managing her own ranch now. Her husband got hurt bad in 1972 when a horse fell on him. She could take over and run the ranch; they didn't have to sell it when he got hurt. She's doing fine. It just comes natural to her.

We cut down some after Sam had his heart attack. He used to have around two hundred and fifty head and now he has a hundred and eight. I used to have seventy-five or eighty, and now I have fifty-nine. And we have a boy that helps us feed in the winter. We take more spare time now. We like to play snowmobile. I love it. But we still run the ranch. It's good for us. You know, we could retire. Not bragging, but we could. But what would we do?

I have my own checking account; Sam has his. And I think he needs the lion's share. With my registered stuff, I take in just about as much as he does. Well, like in the house, I built on this room. But when he wants machinery, I'm always for him getting good machinery.

You hear about ranch couples where the man wants a piece of machinery and the woman is mad because he'll spend twenty thousand dollars for a piece of machinery but won't buy her a fur coat. But I think he needs the machinery. I really do. Then the fur coat later. Because I've worked outdoors and I know what machinery is worth. You need good machinery. I have a fur coat, but I didn't get it until I felt like I could really afford it.

Nope, we don't disagree on too much. Oh, little things. Like a friend of mine says, if you don't quarrel once and a while, one of you is just dumb.

I guess I have been an independent woman; my mother always said so. Well, I don't want it too much. I'd rather my husband be the head of the house. Take the lead. What I handle, like my registered stuff, I handle my way. But it's mighty nice to have a husband. I think they still should be recognized. I don't want too much women's lib, really. 'Cause I've been free. I feel very free. And we get along fine that way.

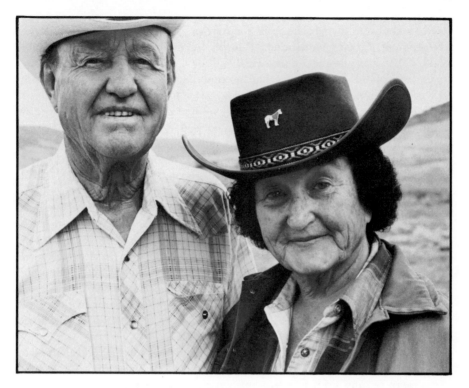

Sam and Barbara Davis, Davis Ranch, North Park, Colorado, 1979.

Barbara and Sam have worked side by side all these years, and it only makes sense for Sam to add his two bits here.

Barbara and I met at a dance down there on Three Mile. She come in with another guy—tall, slim guy—and a half a dozen kids come in alongside 'em. I'd always heard about Barbara being so good-looking, and I thought, "My God, that's not her." So I went on with the dance. Pretty soon I asked, "Is Barbara ever going to get here?"

"Well, that's Barbara over there."

I went over and got a dance with her and made a date for the next night or two, and that's where we got a goin'. We've dated ever since. That's about it, is all I know.

When we first started in, I kept what I made and she kept what she made. Her Dad give her some cows to start with. I think she had two cows and a yearling heifer. Something like that. That's just about as many as *I* had! And so we just got started that way. Oh, them first years were tough. Really tough.

The first few years, I'd go out and buy these skim milk calves from anybody that had a milk cow. [Sometimes people will sell a milk cow's calf so that the cow can continue to produce milk for market.] If I'd hear about somebody having a calf, I'd go give them about seven dollars for it. I had a fellow up in Walden that was running a dairy. He'd call me up and I'd get all of his calves. So the end of the first year, we had around thirty-five or forty head, mostly little calves coming up. That's how we got started.

We had about five or six milk cows, so we had milk to give 'em. We'd give 'em milk in a bucket. We had enough hay to feed 'em. They didn't get the best in the world all the time—we didn't have milk enough for all the calves I was gettin'—but we got 'em by pretty much. They brought in pretty good money, up to 'twenty-nine, before the crash. It got us started.

Then this fellow and I put up some hay down on the Hunter place, here below us. We contracted that hay together. He sold me six-seven more milk cows. He never thought I'd ever get them paid for. But I paid for them in about six months. I let him take all the money from the hay contract on them cows. Then I finished paying for them working on the Big Horn ditches over there. In the middle of winter we was hauling rock and willows, dropping them in there to make dams. They was paying seven dollars a day for man and team then. I finished paying out those new milk cows about four months after I started on those ditches. And then I had that many more cows to feed these baby calves with.

I hauled hay that winter for two dollars a day and my dinner. I'd haul from the Hill place up there, about four miles. I'd haul one four-horse load of hay in the morning, and I'd haul a two-horse load in the afternoon.

Barbara, she'd go out and feed the cows while I was up there. She'd take our team and she'd string some hay for them. That made us a pretty good deal, 'cause I could work for that other man. And you know, that two dollars looked like a million, those days.

I trapped skunks that winter too. I trapped twenty-two skunks and got two dollars apiece for them. Trapped coyotes. Anything to make a dollar.

But Barbara and I have always worked together. She could handle ours so I could work, and we have worked side by side. For years she was right beside me everywhere. We still are. Anywhere you see one of us, you're going to see the other. Everytime. We go to town, we go together. Generally when we're out in the field, we're together. She'd be out there driving a sweep and I'd be stacking or raking or something. Not as much now as we used to be, but heck —I'd ride the fence [fix fence] and she'd be with me. We was. We was together. And Gloria was right along with us. Gloria started driving when her little legs didn't reach that far [gestures to indicate a foot] off the mowing machine seat. She'd make her corners just as perfect as anybody. She's been a real good hand all her life, little Gloria has.

When I was working out, I made enough to support the ranch. We didn't have to take nothing out of what we made off the ranch to keep the ranch a-goin'. So that made it pretty nice. We could use that money to get ahead.

Cowgirls Return:

THE ROAD BACK HOME

Autographed postcard of Alberta Clair, "The Girl from Wyoming," with her saddlehorse and dog. Legend on reverse of card says she was trying to win a bet placed by two wealthy ranchers regarding a trip across the continent.

Marion Trick

Near Cowdrey, North Park, Colorado

*Marion Trick,
North Park,
Colorado, 1978.*

MARION TRICK KNOWS CATTLE. SHE RUNS THE NORTH PARK ANGUS RANCH with three Carls—Carl Carlstrom, her father; Carl Trick, her husband ("Carl Sr."); and Carl II, their son. They were the first to bring the Angus breed to the Park and the first to try artificial insemination. Marion was instrumental in both decisions and both were controversial. Now they are common practice. "Marion knows as much about cattle," says Cebe Hanson, the tall, lanky foreman of a nearby ranch, "as anyone in the Park."

Marion and the two older Carls live in the white frame ranch house that was standing when Marion's father bought the ranch in 1928. I feel at ease the minute I walk in. A jungle of overshoes, cowboy boots, and tennis shoes lines a wall on the back porch. The kitchen is comfortably messy and we share the long breakfast counter with a mountain of magazines and mail, a gallon jar of iced tea, and several bottles of blackleg vaccine. Original art fills the wall behind us, including an oil and several pencil sketches by Raphael Lillywhite, a western artist who once lived in North Park and helped Marion and the Carls put up hay.

Marion—short, a little plump, with curly gray hair—has that curious country trait of moving quickly without seeming to hurry. "Let me think," she says when I ask her her age. "Sixty. I always have to stop and figure it out. Age is relative. You're as old as you feel. It's like these cows—some are worn out when they are six years old; others are sixteen and still throwing big, healthy calves."

This time of year (July), Marion rides several hours early each morning and late each evening, detecting heat (watching the cattle to determine which are ready to breed; bringing them in for insemination). She has time in between to fix the midday meal, at one o'clock rather than noon—"We're on God's time here. The cattle and the land don't understand Daylight Saving Time."

It was a day I'll always remember for no other reason than the sheer beauty of it. Our horses stepped out proudly, exhilarated by the sharp, clear air. The white vapor of their breath came out of their nostrils in regular puffs. Jogging across the soft new snow was like riding across clouds. A gray-winged hawk circled around, then swooped low over our heads to have a closer look at us. The only sounds were the squeak of leather, the occasional snorts of the horses, and the swish of their tails. The acrid good smell of the horses' sweat came out strong in the clean air. Across the trail ran the zigzag tracks of a cottontail. Behind us, the whiteness was broken only by our hoofprints. Smoke from our chimney rose high into the thin blue air. In silence and peace we rode. Into my head came a translation I had once read of a song from the Navajo Night Chant:

> I am walking on the tops of mountains.
> The Gods are before me.
> The Gods are behind me.
> I am walking in the midst of the Gods.*
> > —Jo Jeffers,
> > *Ranch Wife.*
> > Copyright © 1964 by Jo Jeffers.

* *The Pollen Path,* by Margaret Schevill Link, Stanford, California: Stanford University Press (1956).

Marion speaks of the land and cattle with love, enthusiasm, and obvious commitment. Yet, the ranch has not been her entire life.

I always loved the ranch. I loved the area, I loved the mountains, I loved the work. I rode a lot by myself as a child, and I would try to imagine how the Indians must have felt when they came here. This was their summer hunting ground. They'd come up here to kill game and dry it. Then they'd leave in the fall before it snowed.

I loved learning too. I soaked up everything like a sponge. I was interested in journalism, but the only thing I knew I absolutely had to do was learn to fly.

My father knew how to fly, and his brother was a famous pilot. My uncle, Victor Carlstrom, made the first non-stop flight from New York to Chicago and won the Air Club Medal three times. He was killed in 1917 when a wing fell off his plane, but I grew up looking at the pictures and reading the clippings. I had to learn to fly.

I got a full scholarship to Bennington College in Vermont in 1938, but I couldn't take any flight there because it was too expensive. My father had bought this ranch in 'twenty-eight at the high price, and then the crash came in 'twenty-nine. We were struggling to make the ranch pay. I had no money— I rode a bus back to Bennington, three days and two nights, because that was the cheapest way.

I studied South American literature and archaeology. Bennington had no requirements; it was individualized study. If they didn't have the best in your field, you could go anyplace in the world and it would count as if you were at Bennington. So my second year I went to Peru.

A Peruvian girl taught Spanish at Bennington and I lived with her family and studied at the University of San Marcos. A member of her family was in the Peruvian Air Corps, and the Peruvian Air Corps was donating its time to teach people to fly if the people paid for the gas. Gasoline was reasonable, so I went to work at the American Embassy in order to stay and have money to fly. I stayed three years instead of one. I was the second woman in Peru to get a license.

I was never homesick. I think that being raised on a ranch gives you self-reliance. You learn to have some initiative. You love your roots and your ties, but you don't cling to them. You're not afraid to do something new, in a different environment.

Then World War II came along. I applied to a program that was opening up for women to ferry airplanes. I was accepted and came back to the States to go through cadet training. Then I spent twenty-two months ferrying airplanes. I flew all types of airplanes, mainly pursuit aircraft. I was a WASP— Women's Airforce Service Pilot. There were about eleven hundred of us— about eight hundred of us are left now—and Congress and the Secretary of Defense have just determined that we will retroactively get our Veterans benefits.

I met Carl in the service. He was a flyer too, and we got married. I thought I would fly commercially when I got out. My program was deactivated in December 1944. Carl was flying in India, so I came back to the ranch. I thought I would just visit awhile and then I intended to travel around, do my thing, and have fun. But my parents had separated and my father was here by himself. He needed help, and I didn't want to leave when I could be useful.

Carl came to the ranch and liked it. He wasn't raised on a ranch but he had helped on some farms when he was growing up. Then he was in the Cavalry, so he knew how to ride. We wanted to have children, and what better place to have children than a ranch? We stayed.

When I came back here, I had Dad grade an airstrip first thing. But we didn't fly much. We were used to flying such great airplanes, and there was no way we could afford to fly planes like that. Then we were busy, and we had other interests. We had a friend who had a plane and we'd fly occasionally, but we gradually forgot about it.

So many other things filled our days. One time, when the kids were young, we branded some calves and were moving them out to pasture. It was a clear day, just one big old cloud in the sky. It wasn't raining. We were just about to the gate and Carl Sr. started around the herd to open the gate. The next thing I knew, my reins were slack and my feet were out of the stirrups. The air was full of the acrid smell of burning hair. I looked up and my husband's horse was bucking. My son and daughter were draped over their saddles and a friend of my daughter's was sitting on the ground with a vacant look on her face. Right in front of me was a pile of dead cattle. I don't remember hearing any sound. We lost seven mother cows out of twelve, but the calves were all right.

We had to collect ourselves and turn the cattle around and bring them home to the corral before the calves realized they didn't have any mothers. We were sore on top of our heads and on the bottoms of our feet. We felt we were spared because we were spread out. The cows were close together and generated heat that attracted the lightning.

The *Chicago Drovers' Journal,* in an issue during October 1891, contained an item of some length in which was to be found the following words:

"Mrs. Nat Collins, of Choteau, Mont., is here with cattle that sold at $3.65 to $4.00. Mrs. Collins enjoys the distinction of being the first lady cattle shipper from Montana to the Chicago market . . ."

For many years prior to the date mentioned it had been our custom to dispose of our surplus beeves every fall to buyers who came to the ranch and bargained for them.

This practice was quite general with the ranchmen, but just in order to be contrary, I suppose—as all women have the general reputation of being—I at last expressed the opinion to my husband that we were not receiving full value for our stock by practicing this custom, and at last succeeded in inducing him to ship a consignment of beeves to the Chicago market. The experiment proved a most successful one, and the following year found us, as fall approached, again preparing to ship to Chicago.

All went well during the time of gathering and "cutting out" the cattle destined for the long journey, but just a few days prior to the start for Great Falls, from which place the cattle were to go by train, Mr. Collins became quite sick and he dared not undertake the hardships of the trip, and thus there remained but two things to be done—either I must myself accompany the stock or the shipment must be abandoned, for it would be folly to trust to a stranger the handling of the beeves and the large amount of money received from their sale in Chicago. . . .

—Mrs. Nat Collins,
The Cattle Queen of Montana, 1894.

I look back with no regrets. I love the ranch and I love the way of life it gives us. I wanted to learn to fly, I wanted to travel, I wanted to go to college. If I hadn't done those things, I think I would have always regretted it, and always thought about it.

That's why we wanted our children to go out into the world. I think every child, no matter how much they love this country, love the ranching, should go out and know that it's a big world. Get their self-confidence, know what they can do. Then they can come back because they want to come back, not because it seemed the easiest thing to do, or because they were hesitant or afraid to try something else. This makes people strong.

Our son came back. He and his wife love this country very much and they are in on our family operation. But he wasn't sure before he went away.

In flying or riding or anything, I never wanted any dispensation because I was female. I wanted to do these things because I was able. I didn't want to be given a favor of any kind. Maybe I was lucky, but I found that if you want to do something badly enough, you're going to find a way to do it. I don't think you should be given anything because you're female. This is still a man's world, and it really always will be. But if you merit a job, I think in the main you'll end up getting it and being accepted if you want it badly enough, work hard enough.

Martha Gibbs

Gibbs Ranch, Northeast of Buffalo, Wyoming, on Powder River

WHEN I STARTED WORKING THE BUFFALO, WYOMING, AREA AND ASKED ABOUT local cowgirls, one name kept cropping up—Martha Gibbs. I met Martha and her husband, Bob, at their house-in-town in Buffalo.

Martha is forty-five, with curly black hair and flashing brown eyes. She carries an extra pound or two but always moves quickly, energetically, as if she can never quite fit everything into the day. She wears a bright red and white gingham blouse and blue jeans.

Like many isolated ranchers, Martha and Bob bought a town residence when their children outgrew the one-room elementary school near their ranch. (The Gibbs ranch lies two hours northeast of Buffalo. The last twelve miles into their ranch, a nigh impassable dirt road of gumbo and shale, wins my nomination for the worst road in Wyoming.) For the past several winters, Martha and the kids have lived in town during the week, at the ranch on weekends.

The oldest son—John, age twenty-five—recently married, and he and his wife moved into the ranch house on Powder River. Until Bob and Martha decide whether to build a second house on the ranch, buy a trailer, or make other living arrangements out there, they live in town and commute. The recent and temporary nature of this arrangement explains why Martha refers to the ranch in a variety of tenses.

Martha, like many ranch wives with school-age children, has two separate lives—one in town and one at the ranch. The dichotomy sometimes causes problems. Martha has a full and challenging "town life." She is a watercolor artist of increasing reputation and runs the Main Street Gallery in Buffalo with four other women. Yet, her real love is the ranch and she speaks of it with an obvious longing.

All my life, I've run from being a dude. If somebody asks, I say I was raised around Sheridan. I don't mention being born in New York, or tell people I went to boarding school in the East.

I came West when I was eight years old with my mother and stepfather, my sister, brother, and four stepbrothers. My stepfather had been a lawyer on Wall Street and he bought a ranch near Sheridan because he "wanted to get away from it all." Both he and my mother loved the country and my mother had ridden all her life. They thought a ranch would be a better place to raise a family.

I was an addict immediately. I think the whole family was. I had ridden before, and I loved animals. Now I could get totally involved with them. We raised registered Herefords. I knew each cow personally, and rode as much as I could.

I went to a one-room country school. At first, I thought I'd really miss school in the city with all the kids. But it didn't take me long to get used to it. We'd ride to school, seven miles away. We played basketball on horseback. Everything was a thrill, and I loved every minute of it.

I went to the country school through eighth grade and then I went back East to boarding school. I don't mention that very often. I would have much preferred to have stayed out here, but I felt obligated to my family to go.

It was tough, it really was. I went right from my one-room country school-house to a girls' school in Connecticut [Miss Porter's]. They figured I had the equivalent of a sixth-grade education. And I was always wearing Levi's. We weren't supposed to wear them but I'd go to my room, close the door, and jump into my Levi's. Then I'd turn on my western music.

I managed to make some good friends, but I couldn't wait to get back here. In my yearbook, everybody teased me about looking for a cowboy and coming back to my wide-open range. They knew what I had on my mind all the time.

I was going to college in Sheridan [Wyoming] when I met Bob. My family had built an indoor arena and they conducted rodeos on Sundays. Bob came up to rope. We kind of eyed each other for a weekend or two. He came up most every Sunday and pretty soon he began to come up Saturday night. It wasn't too awful long after that that we got married. I was eighteen.

The first two years, we worked for Frank Greenough† and lived on his ranch in central Wyoming. We bought the place we're on now in 1955.

Frank and his wife Doris are like parents to me. I was very young and they taught me a lot. We didn't have running water or a telephone or anything. Those were two very good years. Good for me, because I'd never lived that way. Bob says everybody should live that way for a while, and I agree.

We had our first child, John, about eleven months after we were married. He didn't tie me down, though. We took him with us when we fed cattle in the winter, and we rodeoed with him. If we were branding or going on a roundup or something, my sister-in-law would take care of him, or sometimes Doris. Bob and I just worked things out together because he knew I liked to ride.

I was tied down more, I think, when I had two kids. But then I'd usually get a girl to come out in the summer and watch the kids. Bob felt that it was more practical for him to pay a girl to help in the house so I could work out with him. We've worked together most of the time. Sometimes I'd have quite a few hired men to cook for, but I always tried to get out as much as I could.

Cooking for hired hands and large groups of people was something I had to learn. Bob's mother helped me a lot 'cause I didn't know how to plan, and Doris Greenough taught me a lot. Bob's dad taught me to keep a sourdough jug. It took me a while to learn to organize and plan, but I finally learned and then it became very easy for me.

---

† Rodeo rider Alice Greenough's brother. See Chapter 8.

All the people in the community took pride in their homes and their cooking. I remember somebody telling me that they tried to make every meal a masterpiece. I think I learned that attitude from everybody around me. I've always tried to make every meal something I can be proud of. And Bob always told me that whatever I did, to feed people well. It's better to have too much than too little.

Now I plan enough ahead so that I always have the meat done the night before and the biscuits ready to put in the oven. The freezer helps a lot. I can come in from working outside and have a huge meal on the table in thirty minutes.

I learned to be very efficient so I could get things done and go with Bob to ride, or take part in what was going on. The kids never helped very much. I didn't ask them to. My daughter is a good hand in the house if she wants to be, and we work well together. We can whip up a meal or give the house a lick, spit, and a promise together. But she prefers to be outside. She usually manages to be busy feeding some bum calf or wrangling the horses or something. Now I think my youngest boy helps me more than any of them, just because he doesn't think it's a come-down to help in the house. But the kids really didn't help with the household chores very much.

I never thought that was unfair. I know that sounds funny, but I didn't at the time. At times I was terribly tired and wished I could have some help. I think if I was to start over today, everyone would help more, because everything is so much more shared nowadays. It just never occurred to me, at the time, to ask. I did what was expected, and I didn't resent it. I've always loved to cook, anyway.

Of course, I never had any other idea of being anything else other than a rancher. All I ever wanted was horses and cows, and I thought I would probably be the one to round up the cows. Since I was married ten years before Jonita was born, I helped Bud an awful lot during that time doing what had to be done; dragging the meadows, haying, moving the cattle, feeding in the winter. But after the children came, I've been in the house most of the time. It was awfully hard, kind of confining. You just kind of wanted to go but you couldn't. I don't know if I expected to be the cook and the dishwasher, as it was always my desire to have lots and lots and lots of cows and horses. But you just have to do what you have to do.

—Verla Richie Sommers, Sublette County, Wyoming,
from *Spoken Words of Four Ranchwomen*, recorded and transcribed by Carol Rankin.
© Carol Rankin, 1979, pp. VS/18–19.

The country school near the ranch only went to sixth grade, so when John started junior high, the kids and I moved to town. Bob's and my relationship changed for a while. I became very involved in town with my kids' activities and my own—PTA, women's clubs, classes at the college, all sorts of things. After so many years of hardly seeing the neighbors, not having a telephone, and not getting to town very often, I really enjoyed the activities town offered. Also, I didn't feel as needed at the ranch as I had before, because we had hired a couple and the gal rode.

But Bob would come in and I'd have been living in my own little world. I'd want to tell him about my activities and he'd want to tell me about the ranch. It didn't take us long to figure out that wasn't going to work.

I realized that the ranch was still very much my first priority. All my activities in town shortened my time for the ranch. If Bob said, "I need your help," I didn't want to say, "I can't—I'm busy in here." I wanted to be able to say, "Fine, I'll be right out."

I joined a theater club and I was to have played the part of Gypsy Rose Lee in a musical. At the last minute I had to back out because the [sheep] shearers were coming that particular weekend and I wanted to be at the ranch. I resigned from the club after that, because I knew the same thing would happen again and again.

I had always played second fiddle to a cow, so to speak, and my life in town made me realize how much I liked it that way. My life revolved around the ranch over and above a ball game a child was involved in, a social event, or whatever.

So I narrowed my town activities down to my painting. My family has been a hundred percent in back of my painting. But the ranch comes first for me. Even now that I am involved in the art gallery, the other partners know that the ranch comes first. If I'm needed out there, I'll go.

Life in town could never substitute for life on the ranch. I'm in town a week and I just have to get out there. It's not the air—there's fresh air in town. A lot of times it's just the little things. I love the challenge of bringing a dying calf back to life. I love my garden and my home. I love the thrill I get when I ride over the hill down into the ranch.

We've had so many happy times out there with the kids and without television. We can communicate with them, work with them, play cards with them. It's a closeness you lose in town because they're off and about, involved in other things. Sometimes it's hard to sit down and have a conversation.

I love to bake, especially with sourdough. But I don't do it in town. I don't have the time. I don't *make* the time. There are so many little things that take your time. At the ranch, your life revolves around your ranch activities, planning for the next day. You don't have so many other things competing for your attention.

There's a feeling out there that people in town could never ever understand. One time a gal called asking if I would run for president of the PTA. As I turned her down, I thought, "Oh, if those people only knew what my other life is like." I have a completely full other life that people in town aren't aware of, and I can't describe it to them.

I can put in one hell of a day out there—throw a circle that would kill somebody in town. Or I can get up at dawn and work really hard all morning branding and come in and have dinner ready for thirty people in half an hour because I've prepared it all the night before. During calving, I may come in covered with crud from head to toe, with blood all over my hands. And I love it.

I love any day when we can all go out and ride and work together and drag in exhausted at the end of the day. It's a physical fatigue. You darned sure sleep well. Fatigue is different in town. You can get dead tired but you're all wound up and wide-awake, thinking about the day's problems and events.

A few years ago we were thinking of selling the ranch for coal. The livestock business wasn't doing very well at the time, and there was big money in coal. But you really think about what the ranch is. You think not only of what you'd do, but what you'd be leaving. It's a very intangible thing. While we were thinking of selling, I'd ride up on top of the divide and just think, "How can I ever leave this?" I said to Bob, "If we sell, where will I ride?" That was such a stupid thing to say, but I really felt like this is my country and there is no other place I could possibly ride that I'd be happy.

There are twelve miles of gumbo road going into the ranch, and sometimes when you're stuck, walking down the road in the middle of the night, sloshing in the mud, you think it would be pretty easy to give it up. But those are the things you forget easily. I can't describe what that ranch means to me. It is intangible. But I have a feeling out there of kind of gathering myself together and having time to think, to appreciate what life is all about.

I'm really touchy about my early childhood and my high school days because people peg a person like me with being a rich little dude girl, and they think you always are. But everything Bob and I have, we've made ourselves, including the house in town. The only outside money I have is what I've made on my paintings.

I don't care about being born in the East or going to boarding school, or any of that. I only care about being a ranchwoman, and having proved myself a good hand on a ranch.

Tootie Brocker

Sage Creek Limousin Ranch, near Walden, North Park, Colorado

Tootie Brocker, feeding sheep, Sage Creek Limousin Ranch, North Park, Colorado, 1979.

WHEN TOOTIE SMILES (AND SHE SMILES A LOT), HER NOSE WRINKLES UP, HER lower lip covers her bottom teeth, and she looks like a happy chipmunk. Tootie grew up in North Park. Until she was eleven her father worked for ranchers in the area; then he bought a gas company in Walden and they moved to town. Tootie didn't like living in town, though, so every summer, until she married at the age of nineteen, she worked for a ranch family—cleaning, cooking, helping with the children, cattle, sheep, and haying.

While we talk, two hired men come in to ask her how to start the swather (a piece of haying equipment); the phone rings and a neighbor asks her advice about antibiotics for a sick lamb; and Gordon, her husband, comes in to discuss irrigation water.

Tootie is thirty-eight and has a son, John, fifteen, and a daughter, Kelli, thirteen.

I was always a tomboy. There wasn't any boy that I couldn't beat up. I kicked football for the football team because I was the only one—including the guys on the team—who could kick half the football field. The football players talked about the girls, how they didn't like the girls, but they never included me with the girls.

I didn't wear dresses to school. Not me. For a long time I was very faithful and wore dresses to weddings and funerals, but that was it. Any more, I don't always wear a dress to those! I was a cheerleader for six years, and I wore skirts for that. And I was prom and homecoming queen. You wore the formals, but you still could be the tomboy.

The first prom I went to, I had just started going with Gordon. It was during calving time and one of their cows was having a Caesarean. I'd never seen one, so Gordon and his cousin and this other girl and I all went out to the barn in our formals and watched the operation.

I always thought the biggest thing in my life was to marry somebody who had a ranch. I always said I would never live in town. Gordon had a ranch, and we were in school together. He was really good-looking and he was really popular, so it was a super challenge to see if I could get him. I didn't chase him. I was just always there and always around in the same group. It seemed to work out. We went together six years before we were married. We bought our ranch, though. It wasn't given to us.

Everything we do is half and half. I can do anything on the ranch, and so can Gordon. We each have our areas of expertise, but we can both do everything. There's no hard feelings, there's no bitterness over the fact that it's half and half. Of course, maybe this is a little different here, because I am half owner of this—not because I'm married to him, but because I invested in it. Anything that is signed, or anything that's done, has to be both of us.

It wasn't important to me that I owned half the ranch. It was important that I got to do the work. As far as owning half, I couldn't care less. I always said that if something ever did happen and we didn't get along or got divorced, I didn't want any more than I started with. If I could leave with the horses and the cats, that's all I'd need.

I'm a very stubborn, determined person. I have a mind of my own. Gordon has his ideas and I have mine. Gordon's Irish and I'm Scotch, so one's as stubborn as the other, you know. We have our running battles. Like, we both went to AI school [Artificial Insemination] and I breed cattle one way and he breeds them another. It's best if only one of us goes to the corral at a time. Lots of things like that. But everybody has their say and maybe it's an argument at the time, but the best comes out of it.

I can't imagine a woman living on a ranch and not wanting to know how it runs. If something happened to your husband, you're in for a big surprise and a long ride if you don't know the business. I know from a good example—Gordon's mother. Her husband did everything. He took care of the books, he made all the deals. She never got out of the house. She was a good mother, a good cook, a good housewife. But when he died, she was lost. She had no idea what to do. Consequently, the lawyers took her for a ride and the bankers took her for a ride.

If something happened to Gordon, I know I could run the ranch. I'm a firm believer that you'd better know how to take care of yourself. You better know how, in this day and age. And if you don't, you're out of luck.

This place is worth a million two, valued at right now. It runs seven hundred and fifty cows but we're only running around four hundred head. We owe close to eight hundred thousand dollars on it. We've just been making our payments. We're not going any further under, but we're not paying any more of it off. But I said one thing when we bought this place. I said, "Nobody gave it to us, and either we make it or we don't." Which is the way I wanted it.

When you buy a ranch, you buy a way of life. Maybe in years past, you were buying a business. No way now you're buying a business. Even though the price of beef seems super high right now, the expenses are super high. People don't realize that. They think, "Oh, that price of beef in the supermarket is what the ranchers are getting." How wrong they are! We get a fraction of the counter price. There's the feeder and the trucker and the meat cutter and the supermarket all getting theirs. It just doesn't add up. Ranchers paid for themselves last year, but that was the first year in a long time.

This year is good. Your plain commercial cattle—maybe this year they will make some money. But we have no idea what next year will be like. The only way you make it is to have some specialties on your place. An oil well, a coal mine, sell registered bulls, something like that.

It helps if you have something extra. A lot of people up here go to work at the coal mine up the road. They make twelve hundred dollars free and clear a month. They can work an eight-hour shift during the night and still run their ranch. That's what Gordon did for a while. He may do it again.

Agriculture is what it takes to keep everybody alive, and we're the most walked on business there is. The agriculture people have the least say in anything. We have only five percent say in government. Yet we're producing the one thing that keeps everyone alive.

The one thing that really infuriates me is that we're the prime supporter of the welfare program, and those people sit on their cans and don't work. We work our tails off to support that program. I know the welfare program in town—those people are very capable of working, yet you ask one of them to come out here and help produce the thing that's keeping them alive, and they don't have to work. They have money, so they don't have to work. There's not enough words to say about that!

Probably the only thing that's ever going to help out the agriculture people, farmers and ranchers both, is when there's no food. But it's a little hard to sit with twenty thousand chickens and say, "No eggs." How can you afford to feed them if they aren't laying their eggs to sell? How can you keep a herd of cattle and not breed them every year to produce calves, or not plant a field? If you don't do it for one year, it takes so many years to catch up. You can't just stop. We should have everybody else over a barrel, but they have us over one.

Cattle people have never been subsidized by the government like the wheat people. They've been on their own, and they want it that way. Oh, there have been emergency drought-relief programs and things like that, but nothing on a long-term basis. Which is just as well. The government has their hands in enough things.

I have very little patience with weak people, which is strange to say, because I've taken care of lots of my family who were bedridden and I have lots of patience with them. But when my kids get hurt, I don't want them to be babies. I don't feel I'm weak, so maybe sometimes I'm a little hard that way. But I would rather be too strong than too weak.

When I was twenty-seven, I had a hysterectomy. Of course, everybody said, "You can't do this, and you can't do that." Well, I was in the hospital for seven days, I was home for three weeks, and then I was back doing everything I'd ever done before, including riding a horse. I have no patience and no time for people who sit and dote on being sick or getting old.

If you're outside, you're healthy. And if you feel healthy and look healthy, you put off that glow. If you want to sit and feel sick and old, you look sick and old.

I don't care if you're a hundred—maybe your face looks like you're a hundred, but if you're bubbly, the age isn't going to show. These old ranchwomen around here have the wrinkles from the weather, but that's not what you see.

Dave and Jerri Wattenberg and Gordon and I try to go to Las Vegas together every year. And here sit all these ladies with their really long painted fingernails. You know, no cuts, no scrapes, no stains. And then Jerri and I—this knuckle's knocked off, our fingernails are all short and broke, and there's a little stain here, a little grease there. But it doesn't bother us. And nobody there even notices. That's not what they're looking at. They're looking at our friendly appearance or whatever.

I always said I would never live in town and I still say that. A production company from Hollywood made some advertisements here in the Park for a big supermarket chain, and they offered Gordon and the kids and me the opportunity to go to California and make movies and commercials. Gordon said, "Well, we'll sell this place and move out there," but I said, "I'm not moving. You can go on out but I'm staying here. Or you can buy me a ranch outside Hollywood and I'll run that while you do your thing." I don't really want to leave here. And I won't live in town. I just won't do it.

All I ever want to do is have a ranch and raise cattle and horses and sheep and pigs. I love animals. We have the whole works out here. I take in all animals. I don't care. Right now we have ten pigs for some people who didn't have a place to put 'em. We've got six colts that belong to some other people. I even had a pet fox for a while.

We AI our cows. When we got this place, we had twelve hundred Hereford cows and the Hereford calves weren't bringing all that much. So we started crossbreeding. The first year we inseminated twelve hundred head of Herefords to Limousins. In six years, we've turned the whole herd over to Limousin. Now we have domestic purebred Limousin cattle and we sell bulls.

I always breed the first-calf heifers. They say it's best for women to breed heifers because their hands are smaller. Heifers aren't as big as cows and they put a lot of squeeze pressure on your wrists. My hands are not any smaller than most men's, but it also takes patience. And I think it's an instinct women have. You've got to think like the heifers are thinking. Gordon doesn't get along with them at all.

AI is really interesting. You can hardly wait 'til calving time comes along to see what you're going to get. You feel really proud. It's like being a daddy, I suppose.

> "I'll never forget what Monte said about the cattle business once," Dalt said. "We were riding on the flats that day, and she says to me, 'Dalt, it's like playing God, working with cattle—breeding them, watchin' the blood lines show. It's an art, and it makes up for a lot I've missed in life.'"
>
> —Peggy Simson Curry,
> *So Far from Spring,* 1956.

No, I like animals. I like everything about them. I even like the messy parts. One time I had a cow who was having trouble calving. I couldn't get her, and I thought she was going to need a Caesarean. I called the vet and he came out. We were able to pull it.

He was pulling on the head, and I was pulling on a chain that was on the feet. He was standing behind me, and down a little lower. He just started to tell me to duck because he wasn't sure what all was going to come when we pulled the calf. I didn't duck, and I was right up there. I got a face full of manure. I had my mouth open, too, because you just don't shut your mouth when you're working that hard, and just right directly in line! He was behind me enough he didn't get a drop. Oh, he laughed! Things like that, you always remember.

Nobody *likes* a face full of manure. But manure's not all that bad. There's nothing wrong with it. People bring their kids out here and want to see the animals. They tell them not to step in that poo-poo, you know. Well, that word doesn't quite cut it. No, manure's not bad. It's green, just like money. And to a rancher, it smells like money too.

> Being in the country has also changed my feelings about dirt.
> It's hard even to write this down—for though I feel comfortable
> with my new self, I am still enough the daughter of a good

middle-class mother to feel embarrassed about publicly confessing my unbathed state.

My first discovery about dirt came when I first crumbled soil through my fingers and looked at it closely. There were tiny stones, sand, bits of grass and leaves, but where was the *dirt*? Later came my fascination with manure, another embarrassing confession. Right from the start I liked it—I liked the smell, the heavy sloggy work, the richness of its potential—a fantasy taste of life as a farm hand. But after the first garden grew like a tropical jungle on this cold, foggy coast, then I *really* got into manure. I mashed it in my hands, looked closely and saw—what! There I was with a handful of the most taboo of all dirts, and it was nothing but a bit of grass.

> —Jeanne Tetrault,
> *Country Women.*

When I visited Brockers last, in the fall of 1980, Gordon was once again working graveyard shift at the Kerr Coal Company mine. He added some comments:

We didn't start ranching on our own until ten years ago, and we've accomplished quite a bit in those last ten years. No doubt about it—it's helped that we've both shared in the whole thing.

Tootie can do all the feeding if she has to. Of course, when I come home from working at the mine, I do some. But she does the chores early in the morning and she has all those done by the time I get home.

Last summer I worked through haying. She did the swathing and took care of the hay crew in the afternoons because I'd have to leave about four o'clock [to sleep before going to the mine]. And we get a lot of haying done from four to dark. So she'd take care of that.

And our AI program—if Tootie wasn't involved in it, we couldn't do it. There are days I can't be here. And when we were doing heifers and cows, she took care of the heifers and I took care of the cows. You can't hire a technician to do it, really, and get it done the way you want. Same thing with detection. People have got to be dedicated to do it right.

We couldn't run a ranch this size, we couldn't have made as much progress as we have, if Tootie hadn't helped. She has always helped. And with the mine close by, I can earn a whole other income because Tootie can take care of what needs to be done on the ranch. It makes a whole bunch of difference. You bet.

5

Cowgirls Alone: A WOMAN'S PLACE

The Becker sisters branding a calf, 1894. Fritz Becker and his wife had three daughters and one son. In 1894 the four children conducted their father's big Rio Grande Ranch and handled several hundred head of horses and cattle. Note that the women wear full-length dresses. A few women adopted divided skirts about this time, but it varied between communities. Unlike the rodeo cowgirls who saw each other, ranchwomen had little or no idea of women in other areas. Dress that was accepted in one community might take years to come into another.

Ellen Cotton
Four Mile Ranch, near Decker, Montana

Ellen Cotton and dog, Four Mile Ranch, near Birney, Montana, 1980.

NATIONAL SACRIFICE AREA. THE U.S. GOV'T RECOMMENDS STRIP Mining the Divide North of Here. We Landowners are Opposed . . . LET FUTURE GENERATIONS JUDGE.

The sign, painted in bold letters on a tanned cowhide, hangs in a log cabin on a hill overlooking Ellen Cotton's Four Mile Ranch. The five-room log house was built by Buffalo Bill for his daughter but now serves as the summer bunkhouse for this singular ranch.

No other ranch is quite like Four Mile Ranch because no other rancher is quite like Ellen Cotton. With each of her sixty-five years etched on her strong, aquiline face; her short, straight flaxen hair; faded flannel shirt and jeans; and heavy, lace-up workboots, Ellen might have grown out of this Montana soil, like one of the cottonwoods down by the creek. Instead, she was born and raised in Massachusetts, the granddaughter of Ralph Waldo Emerson.

Ellen visited a Wyoming ranch when she was fourteen and vowed she would return. But first she studied music in Boston and, at the age of twenty married composer Robert Delaney. After he won the Pulitzer Prize for his choral setting of Stephen Benét's *John Brown's Body,* Ellen and Robert moved to a remote area in northern California and lived in an old miner's cabin, fulfilling a mutual dream. Robert worked on a commissioned book of folksongs; Ellen chopped wood, cooked over the fireplace, and washed their clothes in the stream.

One day a neighbor, a Crow Indian woman, told them a fantastic story about big fires. The story's significance escaped them until the next day when they drove to Eureka for supplies. Pearl Harbor had been attacked.

Robert joined the American Field Service and Ellen went back East with their three sons. When Robert returned, the differences in their ages and backgrounds seemed insurmountable, and "this ranch thing was so strong" in Ellen, they decided to split.

Ellen took their three sons to Wyoming and worked as a ranch hand near Sheridan, Wyoming for a year, then found her own small ranch on Beaver Creek.

She met George Cotton, a cowboy eighteen years her senior. They enjoyed each other and he asked her to marry him. Ellen shied away from the difference in their ages and experiences and said no. "Then, I guess you won't be seein' me," he said, and she didn't. For five years. Then, in January of 1952, Ellen saw George in town. The winter had already been severe and Ellen was tired of being alone. "I don't know if you still want to marry me," she told him, "but if you do, I think we could make it work."

They were married. They sold the ranch on Beaver Creek when they found the larger Four Mile Ranch in Montana. They worked hand in hand for fifteen years until George started drinking heavily and they grew apart. They separated and George left the ranch. Ellen was on her own again.

Since that time, Ellen has had a diverse collection of ranch help—her sons, ranch hands from the area, nieces and nephews from the East, college students, friends of friends, free spirits who learned of Ellen one way or another.

The ranch speaks of their various talents. One young cowhand painted a mural on the bathroom wall. The keys on the piano in the living room are yellowed from use. All have contributed to the restoration of the "Big House," the log cabin on the hill. Music, from Mozart flute concertos to Fleetwood Mac, plays constantly on the stereo.

Ellen's boys have grown and moved away and her helpers come and go, but Ellen stays. She loves the responsibility of the ranch, its constant demands. She likes the regularity of the chores, the rhythm of the seasons. The ranch determines Ellen's way of life, her day-to-day activities. And within its requirements, she finds an absolute freedom.

verses from "The Dying Desperado"

Don't pull off my boots and pull off my hat;
You've taken my gun and I s'pose you'll keep that.
I've lived a reckless life, I've fought and killed my men,
And now as I lay a-dying, I think of times that's been:
Of a gal away down in Texas by the name of Pompey Stiles—
She ain't much on the figger and don't give a damn for styles;
Her father was a hog-thief, and her brother was doin' well
Till he went liftin' cattle, was caught and sent to hell.

. . .

But about that gal in Texas, as I had went to say,
She's a shore plumb good un—you don't meet 'em every day.
Could spin the longest windy, could rope the biggest steer,
And ride the wildest bronco that stands upon its ear.

Next time I see Pompey I sort of out and say:
"Come, gal, come git married. Hitch up this very day."
Of course, I knew she wouldn't—I ain't her style nohow,
For how could I support her on one old maverick cow?

—from Blair Boyd, a cowpuncher of the Rocking Chair Ranch,
Texas, in John A. Lomax and Alan Lomax,
Cowboy Songs and Other Frontier Ballads, 1969.

Aristotle, or one of those old ancient guys, said that any country that disre-
gards its agriculture will not survive very long, and that's what I'm concerned
about right now. Nobody's talking about how valuable the land in this part of
the country is. People come out from the East and say, "Goodness, don't worry
about it. You fly over this and see a tiny little coal mine down there in all
those miles and miles . . ."

There *is* a lot of country here, but it takes thirty-five acres for one cow. A lot
of drier parts take more. Yet, this is precious land. A cow can live for sixteen
years on the nutrients in this grass; other places, cows die when they're ten
years old. I keep thinking that our native grass is more valuable than all the
coal or anything else they can take out of the land. Grass will renew itself, but
when they mine they disrupt the air and the water and the land.

It used to be that when people wore out a piece of land, they'd just move
on to something else, but we can't do that anymore. I've seen pictures of
Europe. Everything is clean and there aren't horrible big signs everywhere.
People in Europe have lived there long enough so they really value what they
have. They realize that they've got to protect it and take care of it. But over

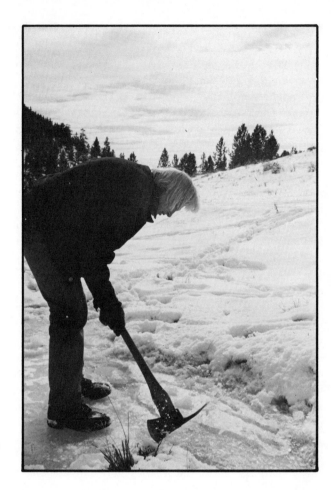

Ellen Cotton chopping ice so the cattle have water, Four Mile Ranch, near Birney, Montana, 1980.

here we've always gone on the basis that if you use something, you throw it away and get something else, something better.

Industry is based on this. They make all kinds of new things just so we can use them up, throw them away, and get new ones. But we're running out of time, and we're running out of land. We've got to have good things and keep them and take care of them. We've got to do that with the land and practically everything we have.

Sure we have to have coal. We have to have coal and learn to use it wisely, just like we have to use our land wisely. We can't grab everything just because we talk about reclamation. The mines are always putting out these doggone things on ecology. I think the Decker Mine is extremely well run, and they're probably very sincere about reclamation. They have signs along the road saying this land was reseeded and reclaimed in 1975. They've reseeded it, but they do not *know* that it was reclaimed. It's going to take a long time to know that. Nobody knows. I've been to a good many hearings and if you pin the mining people down, especially their water experts, about what the mining is actually going to do to the aquifers, the underground water sources, they usually end up saying they just don't know.

It might take many, many years to know whether reclamation works or not. Around Decker, the rainfall is extremely small and the topsoil is very thin. We've gone through a whole series of darn good years, but we're apparently getting into a cycle of very rough winters. We may also get into a cycle of drought. There hasn't been any terrible drought for a long time. Then what? The chance for reclamation will be much diminished. It seems to me that they need to proceed with great care and caution, and take into account how valuable the land is.

The government owns all the coal on this ranch. I don't have any. They can kick me off. Coal comes up in the bathtub. There's a well out by the log house that is only twenty-four feet deep, and coal is always coming into the house from that well. But I don't think the coal right here is as valuable as some other places nearby.

But the coal mines hurt you just by being close. The latest mine is only six or eight miles from here. It's bringing in a whole bunch of construction workers and people who just care about the job. They shoot off the game and run around with snow machines and motorcycles. Even now, all kinds of vandalism and crime is plaguing Sheridan [Wyoming]. Sheridan used to be a wonderful little town. Everybody sort of knew each other and there was a good spirit about the whole thing. Now, you go into town and you can't get waited on, you can't find a place to park. If you forget your checkbook, you can't reach for a counter check. They won't take it. They ask for your automobile license every time you write a check, even in stores where you've traded for thirty years. It makes you mad. You're not a name anymore. You're just a number. It dehumanizes the whole thing.

I don't call this progress. I call it going backwards very fast. The whole spirit has changed a great deal. And I don't think people are any happier than they were. Listen to the old folks who lived through all the hard times. They'll tell you about the things that happened when they were in the old homestead —how it took two days to get from here to Sheridan in a wagon and it was a tough old trip; how they drove to dances in an old sled and used hot rocks to keep their feet warm. The women had it rough in the homestead because they were the ones who usually got stuck. The men could ride and get out and see each other, but the women had to stay and take care of the kids. But all the old people I've talked to look back on the homestead days and talk about what fun they had—the parties and the dances and the visiting. They had such wonderful relationships with all the neighbors. Course, there were always some ornery ones too, but the spirit of the thing was so fine.

God knows, this neighborhood right here is just great. We don't pry into each other's personal affairs or dote on petty gossip and all that junk. We always help each other out and we have a good feeling towards each other. But the neighborhood is changing very fast.

I don't blame people for selling to the coal companies. There are people here who have ranched all their life. They've had to ranch, they never had a chance to do anything else. They worked hard on homesteads and small places or maybe even bigger places. They worked *damned* hard and fought the depression times and bad years. They've kept on plugging and raised families. As they get older, they haven't got much to go on, especially with the inflation. The mines come along and offer them big prices for their land, and you can't blame them if they sell out. If they can end up with something more than they've had, towards the end of their lives, you can't blame them at all.

But I do feel that the coal people have been ruthless about coming in and wanting to take over everything. You think the land is eternal. It should be eternal. But suddenly you find that hills you thought would be there forever have completely vanished. They've just dozed them all away. This is such a beautiful earth. You always think of the country as being here forever. And yet if they destroy it, it may not be. I don't know why people have to be so dreadful. I feel sometimes as if something bigger than us may take revenge and knock this whole thing out.

There are very few ranches that are really making money nowadays. You could probably actually make money here, but boy, you would have had to be absolutely business-minded, which I'm not. I'm not absolutely dependent upon the ranch. I inherited some money, so I've never been in a position where I absolutely had to make good. It wasn't my own choice. It would have been much better if I really had to do it on my own, but I just didn't.

I'm not a business person by instinct, and since I'm not absolutely dependent on just scrabbling along to make my way financially, I think the more good I can do for as many people and critters as I can, the better off I am.

Like almost every other farmer in America today, I'm in debt and hoping for a good season. I'm only at the beginning now, and I know there are many struggles to come and overcome and come again. Someday I too, like my neighbors, will be counting carcasses killed by a marauding dog or watching the spring oats wash away in an "unheard of" late storm. No matter how prepared I am, there is always that vulnerability—to the weather, other animals, disease—that seems to strike when things are finally going smoothly. But inside me there also is this incredible joy. This life is real and good, and it has made me real and good too.

—Sherry Thomas,
Country Women.
Copyright © 1976 by Jeanne Tetrault and Sherry Thomas.

This place has been sort of a haven for a lot of younger people—my brothers' and sisters' kids, friends, friends of friends. They've come out here and worked for me and we've all got along beautifully. I never know who's going to work for me, but somebody always seems to turn up.

Do you ever get lonely for intellectual stimulation?

I'm not an intellectual. I'm not an intellectual at all. I love music and literature and stuff like that, but I couldn't be termed an intellectual. I have all I want. I correspond with people I've known for years and years, and I express my ideas in letters. And there are always people who come in.

One girl who came out here for three summers was a very fine pianist. Her stepfather was one of [my first husband] Bob's best friends who I've known for years. I have a very good old piano, and Christine would come in from working in the hayfields ten hours a day and sit down and play difficult pieces like Brahms intermezzos and Bach fugues. And by God, she'd play them so jubilantly! I'd say, "God Almighty, Chris. How can you come in after working ten hours out in the hot sun and play Bach like that? It astounds me."

She'd say, "Oh, you know, I just feel tired and I come in and get a shower and then I feel that the piano is the one thing I want." She was worried about practicing when I was around. I said, "For God's sake, practice all you want. I lived with Bob for ten years and there was music going day and night and day and night, all the time. When I want to listen to it, I'll listen, and when I don't, I just turn my ears off. You can't bother me." And after I listened to her for a while, I said, "You can't even touch a note on the piano without it sounding good. Don't worry about boring me with your damn practice. It sounds great to me."

When I hear somebody working on a piece, it gets into me. I absorb it much better than if I hear it once or twice. It grows into me and I get to know it very well. That's the way I like to learn because it's awful difficult to understand in the beginning. If I hear it and hear it, it just sinks into me and finally I understand what it's all about.

Another girl who came here played in the Washington, D.C., Symphony Orchestra. Janet Frank. She's a very fine cello player. We went up and sat on the porch of the Big House and she played the unaccompanied Bach cello sonatas, which was something to hear in a house in Montana. We haven't had a lot of music in the Big House yet, but there's time for that, I think.

I'm not strictly business-minded with my critters. A lot of times I ought to sell a horse or something but I'm not sure he would get well-treated, so I'll keep him. When he's too old, I'll just have to put him down. But I know he won't ever get into bad hands. Most people on just a business basis can't think in those terms at all. My old sixteen-year-old cow—most people would have killed her a long time ago. But hell, if she can raise me a five-hundred-pound calf . . . I'm happy to keep them going as long as they can do that.

I had one old horse, a big palomino named Omelet. He was thirty-one, going on thirty-two last fall. We'd raised him and he was a good saddle horse. The kids rode him when they were going to school. They used to ride to school over the hill, about eight or ten miles. He was ridden quite a bit in those years, but since then he didn't do much. He was sort of on a pension.

He weathered the winter before last, but he was pretty thin in the spring. He would have weathered it better if we'd taken him in and fed him, but he didn't want to come in. He came in one time and we fed him and then he began to get that old nervous look. I said, "Well, by God, I guess I'll take you back." I led him from another horse and he strained at the rope the whole time. He couldn't wait to get back out in the old place. I thought he might die that winter, but he didn't. But I said that one winter's enough. That got to him. I didn't want him to have to weather another one.

Last fall, on the eighth of November, I began to have a strong feeling. It was a nice warm day, but I knew something was coming. We went up and got

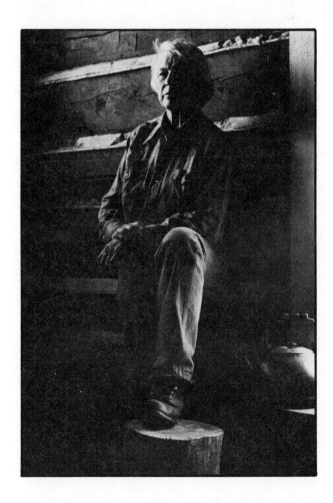

him. He was so proud. He didn't want to get caught. I came at him with a bucket of oats and he did all his big snorting around, a fiery look in his eyes. He finally let me catch him and put a halter on and he got his old nose in the oat bucket. Then we brought him down. We had two colts with him and he had to be ahead of those colts all the way. The minute they came up along his side, he would be furious. He led the processional all the way. It was just marvelous. Then we gave him a big feed of oats and I told the boys to take him up the draw and put him down. I never wanted him to have another night of cold. The very next day the storm broke and we had winter from then on.

I am beginning my ranch and I am loving it. The garden will be superb, and I will have sheep for summer. I love the days I spend working, how quiet and slow yet full they are. The pleasure of being totally tired at night yet not aching or really exhausted—pushed just up to my limits but not beyond them.

—Sherry Thomas,
Country Women, **1976.**

I got old awful quick. Two years ago I had a wreck with a horse and I was unconscious for two weeks. My strength has been very slow to come back. I am just not as vigorous at all. I felt like a great deal of my life got wiped right out. It was a very strange feeling. I felt very lost, like I wasn't there anymore. I never conceived I could feel that way. I'm better now than I have been, but I probably will never gain it all back. Oh, I suppose I might. My mother's ninety years old and she's going strong, so that gives me something to shoot at.

When I had this terrible sense of having my life wiped out, I related it to the coal development. Something I thought I would always have was gone. In my darker moments I thought, What is the use of even living much more? They're going to absolutely destroy this country. But as you grow older, you get wiser in some ways. You don't feel you have to hurry so fast. You value what you can do and what is around you. You grow a little more smart in some ways.

Marie Scott

MARIE SCOTT IS ONE OF THE LARGEST LANDHOLDERS IN COLORADO. SHE OWNS
much of the land from her home place in Ridgeway to the Utah border, and
she built this empire herself. She is a legend in southern Colorado, regarded by
her neighbors with a mixture of fondness, admiration, awe, and a little fear.

When Grace Johnston was asked to write her autobiography
for a community history of Powder River County, Montana, she
summed up her life in the only terms important to her—land.

In 1935 I leased, from the Federal Land Bank, John Waters'
place, but I owned a half section of land I'd bought from Claude
Pease in 1935.

In 1942 I bought from E. A. Moeller a half section; also a
section from John Waters. My father, Fred Engel, bought two
sections of land, one from Cornelius Redmark and one from Joe
Brabant, and gave them to me in 1943. In 1946 I bought a
section from Dave Brindley; a section from Federal Land Bank in
1947 where I built. In 1948 I bought three sections from J. O.

Washington. In 1965 I bought 40 acres from Thomas Preston.
In 1941 I moved a house from the Joe Brabant place and
lived in it until I built a new house in 1964.

—Grace Johnston,
"Grace Johnston Ranch, in *Echoing Footsteps*, 1967.

When I meet Marie, she is sitting in a wheelchair in her kitchen. She has
recently broken her kneecap. She is a diminutive woman, around eighty years
of age. Her short, dyed red hair partially hides the hearing aids in both ears.
She wears a bright red shirt and has slapped a gob of bright red rouge on each
cheek.

Her kitchen is large, simple, and airy. A linen tablecloth covers the chrome
dinette table, and plastic place mats with wildlife pictures protect the linen.
Red towels cover the backs of the table chairs. The only pictures on the walls
are old calendars with the pages torn off that feature color photographs of
Marie's land. We drink strong, stove-brewed coffee from gold-rimmed china
cups.

Sitting there in her aluminum wheelchair, with her red hair, cheeks, and
shirt, Marie reminds me of an invalid robin. She looks so sunken, so old, like a
legend fading before my eyes. But as she starts talking, I realize this legend
hasn't faded yet. She is of an age where a broken kneecap should be her undoing, but "I'm ready to go," she says. "They won't keep me down much
longer."

Marie is, to this day, a hard, almost obsessive worker, and she demands as
much from the men who work for her. One of her neighbors, Peter Decker,
told me a typical story about Marie. Marie hired a crew to put in a section of
fence for her. She told them to set her corner posts four feet deep. (Most
ranchers will accept three feet.) When she visited the job, the corner posts
didn't look quite right. She backed up her jeep, jammed her foot on the gas,
and plowed into a corner post, knocking it out of its three-foot hole. She then
turned to the foreman and told him to pull up the entire new section of fence
and put it in "correctly." Needless to say, she didn't pay for the extra labor or
materials.

Marie has been married once—to a hired hand. The marriage lasted only a
short while, but she kept the man in her employ. "Worst damn husband I ever
had," she says, "but best hired hand."

Marie talks about her decision to ranch full time—at the age of twelve.

I've ranched all my life. I never wanted to do anything else. My mother was
a schoolteacher, and I think she was a little disappointed that my sister and I
didn't want to teach. She sent us to school over in Ouray. When I was twelve
I was there in town and a neighbor pulled his team up and unhitched them. I
asked him, "When are you going back?"

"Oh, not for a couple hours, anyway."

"Well, I'm going with you."

"No, you're not. Your mother would kill me if I brought you home."

"Well, I'm either going with you, or I'll walk over that mountain myself. I know the way all right. And I'll make it in a third the distance!"

"All right. But you'll have to deal with your mother yourself." So he took me home. And then he cleared out quick, 'cause I think he thought something was going to happen.

I walked in and my mother was in the kitchen. There were about ten men at the table. She looked at me and said, "Marie, where did you come from?"

"I graduated," I told her, "and tomorrow I'm going to work in the hay-fields, or I'll go down the road and get a job on my own." I knew I could do that, you see, 'cause I could irrigate and dig post holes and all that. Whatever a man could do, I could do. I knew I could do it, and I knew I could get hired. And I'd rather dig ditches than go to school.

"No, you're not," my mother said. "Tomorrow you are going back to Ouray and go to school."

"I am not. I've never told you I won't do something before, but this time I'm telling you. And you can do what you want. Because I'm either going to work in the hayfield or I'm going out on my own. I've graduated from school."

So the next morning, I went to work in the hayfield. It was hard work, but it was what I wanted to do. And it's what I've always wanted to do, and it's what I've always done.

This is good country, and you can make a living here if you are willing to put twelve hours a day on the business end of a shovel or a pitchfork. Sometimes sixteen hours, sometimes twenty. But it's good country here, just so you're willing to work.

"You'll never be an old woman."

"Sounds good, Kelsey, even if it isn't true."

"But it is. There's the thing in you, like is in my mother—the music, the strong breath of living. That won't die, and because it won't, you'll never be old."

She smiled. "I'll remember that someday—someday when I'm low in my mind and thinking how foolish it is, building up a cattle herd and ranches when there's no son or daughter to carry them on—when there's nobody but myself."

—Peggy Simson Curry,
So Far from Spring.
Copyright © 1956 by Peggy Simson Curry.

Marie died in 1980.

_____

Cleanliness is undoubtedly next to Godliness, but there are
times when I am too ungodly tired to care about either cleanliness
or Godliness.

—Margaret Duncan Brown,
    1932 diary entry, after 14 years of running her ranch alone,
    in *Shepherdess of Elk River Valley,* 1967.

_____

Helen Musgrave

NX Bar Ranch, Northeastern Wyoming, near Decker, Montana

Helen Fordyce Musgrave, NX Bar Ranch, near Sheridan, Wyoming, 1979.

THE AVERAGE HOME IN THE U.S. HAS WHAT? FIFTEEN HUNDRED SQUARE FEET? Add to that the few thousand more square feet that comprise your yard and place of business and you have the quarter acre or so in this world that really concerns you. You can enjoy the fiercest thunderstorm from your window seat, wrapped in an afghan and safe in the knowledge that the chance your tiny space will be struck by lightning is almost nil.

But if you were a rancher in arid country, where forty acres feeds one cow and your "home" consists of forty thousand acres, your attitude would change. A single bolt can set the prairie ablaze and, fanned by a healthy summer breeze, sweep across the plains, charring your summer pasture, licking up your winter haystacks.

Your concern is not only with your own land. Fire pays little mind to fences or surveyed boundaries. A neighbor's problem can quickly become your own. In timber country, the trouble doesn't pass with the storm itself. A struck tree can smolder for hours, even days, before it flares.

The best you can do is spot a fire when it first breaks out. That's why, among the ranchers in the arid prairie and timber ranchland in northeast Wyoming and southeast Montana, fire-watch is a serious thing. You develop an acute sensitivity to sky. The minute clouds start to gather, you, or someone from your ranch, grabs the Jeep and races up the steep divide, to sit for hours on a jagged point, watching the storm, waiting for a bolt to leave a telltale wisp of smoke or flame.

I meet Helen Musgrave, the manager of the NX Bar, in Sheridan. We finish her errands and head out to the ranch, forty miles away, under a still and cloudless late-afternoon sky. There had been no lightning the night before and it looks like there will be none tonight. We decide to stop at the Montana Club, a barnlike roadside bar a few miles from the ranch. When we enter the bar, there is not a cloud in the sky. We come out half an hour later to find the whole sky closed in with heavy, purple, black, and yellow clouds. Suddenly our relaxing afternoon is over.

We careen over the seven miles of rugged dirt road to the NX Bar head-quarters and stop there only long enough to grab a couple bedrolls and switch from the car to the Scout. Then we bounce over miles of cow tracks and prairie roads, heading up the divide. By the time we reach the top of the Badger Mountains, it is nearly dark and the lightning has started in earnest. It is a long way off but nonetheless dramatic. Vast walls of sheet lightning turn the evening into day. Massive, many-fingered bolts splinter the stormy black. At one point, a huge bolt seems to strike backwards, from the earth to the sky. Its image fills a quarter of our horizon and burns a brilliant, naked lightning tree into our minds.

We stay on the divide for several hours. Occasionally, on a distant point, we see the lights of a vehicle turn on, drive a short ways, snap off. Another rancher watching the storm. No fires will start this night, but a tree will be struck on a neighboring ranch and smolder for two days before bursting into flame. The whole neighborhood will respond, but several thousand acres will burn before the fire is brought under control. For now, under explosive skies and over the constant rumble and crack of thunder, Helen and I are free to talk.

Helen manages the NX Bar for her father, Allen Fordyce. The NX Bar is a most unorthodox ranch because of its wildlife breeding program. Along with virtually all colors, sizes, and shapes of cattle, the NX Bar is home to elk, buffalo, yaks, and Ibex goats. The long-term goal of the several breeding programs is to discover or develop the animal that can most efficiently use the native grass—that is, produce the most meat per pound of forage. Short-term goals include hunting and aphrodisiac production (elk antlers are considered an aphrodisiac in the Orient).

The livestock industry is conservative, to say the least, and the various projects at the NX Bar spark controversy. Helen is a controversial figure, herself. In her late forties, dynamic and outspoken, she has unconventional ideas about the role and future of the food production industry.

Helen lives with her fourth husband, Bill Musgrave. He manages his own ranch and is not involved with the NX Bar. Helen has five children, ages seventeen to twenty-three.

Helen is a large woman, warm and maternal. With her thick brown braid, she reminds me of a miniature Mama Cass. Her kind, sad eyes and her strong square jaw signify the conflicts in her nature that have caused her problems all her life.

We're in an energy crisis and we think it's in terms of fuel, but it's also in terms of what we're eating. Calories, nutritious calories, are energy too. I think this point has not been universally recognized in the livestock industry yet. Everybody is thinking about how they're going to manufacture cheaper fuels for tractors and how they're going to get back and forth to town on a cheaper basis. But it goes a lot further than that. When we talk about energy conservation, we shouldn't think only of fossil fuels. We should also think about food.

The American consumer is so outrageously spoiled and unrealistic in the consumption of food. I include myself in this and everybody around me. We demand the most elaborate and expensive packaging techniques. We require fantastic decoration in food outlets. The nicer the store, the more apt we are to shop there. We're utilizing food products that have no real bearing on nutrition and what it takes to survive. And we've become a group of people who just can't bear to put something on the stove if it's going to dirty a pot.

I'm not trying to outrage anybody. I know there are many, many people who go to great efforts to take a bad piece of meat and cook it so that it is edible. But for the most part, I feel that people's nutritional needs in the United States are being met on a totally artificial basis and it's costing us trillions of dollars every year for relatively nothing. Here we are one of the most literate populations in the world, and we don't understand anything about nutrition or the production of food or what it means.

To a large extent, I blame women for this; I really do. I think women have a very valid claim to a lot of things, but I don't think they should try to relieve themselves of the responsibility of providing economical good nutrition for their families. They have tried to relieve themselves from what they consider an unbearable work load and this has developed into a real consumer problem. There is no reason that a woman can't go out and hold down a job—express herself and have a professional life. But at the same time she's got to go back to facing the responsibility to feed her family on the most economical nutritional terms, whether it involves more work or not. The solution probably should be for everybody in the family to take more responsibility for cooking and maintaining the household, rather than blindly or thoughtlessly relying on superprocessed foods. And the women have to take the leadership in organizing their families. If they don't, who will?

We're on the verge of big changes. When it becomes cheaper to cook food at home, we won't go out and buy it in a fast-food chain. Not only cheaper, but so much cheaper that it becomes a necessity. Ironically, it's then that we'll start eating better. I think at the same time, the food production industry has to orient itself towards producing better, more efficient food. For instance, we people who are in the production of livestock, of food off grass, have to be looking for ways to produce something that is nutritionally as good or better for the consumer yet cheaper to produce. We need to look for the animals that will most efficiently turn grass into meat with little or no supplementary feed.

I think we have the responsibility as food producers to educate the public. Not towards what we would necessarily want them to buy or what seems

Helen Musgrave sorting cattle for branding.

Branding at the NX Bar. Helen Musgrave and Dori handle the irons.

most opportune for us to sell, but what is better for us to produce in terms of protein and nutritional efficiency.

Meat has been under fire as an inefficient use of agricultural land for a number of years. It's fine to say that meat is not as efficient as grain to produce protein for human consumption, except that [in the unarable West] we're dealing with land that you can't put into grain production efficiently. Half of the land in the United States is of range character, and something like two thirds of the whole world in unarable land. Its greatest production is not in what is actually produced out of the soil. Rather, it's in what eats what is being produced out of the soil. Food chains. You can't efficiently harvest grass or browse or forage for human consumption. It's too expensive. If you could do it at all, the amount of feed that you could harvest off this very rough terrain would never pay. So you have an animal, a herbivorous animal, that is thrashing or combining it for you and producing another food product. All this land has to be producing something and can be producing something. It's just a matter of finding out what it produces best in terms of energy.

Nutritional efficiency may entail a change in values, like what has taken place in the cars we drive. We're trying now to use cars that don't pollute the environment as much and require far less energy, even though they may not be quite as comfortable to drive. Well, I think food production needs to undergo the same change. We need to rely on food with good nutritional value instead of expensive, empty calories.

In meat production, for instance, fat tissue is going to go out the window.

We're producing huge amounts of fat tissue in our domestic cattle and pigs that have no meaning in terms of nutrition to the consumer. It's being produced because it makes the meat tasty and easy to handle. We'll be relying much more heavily on grass-fed meat. And we'll be looking for the animals that make the most meat out of the forage they consume.

Some people respect me and some people don't. Some people like me; others don't. It's not the average thing for a woman to run a ranch, and there are a lot of people who think that, since it's not being done, there must be something wrong with it. But a lot of it depends on the woman and who she has working for her.

As for getting [a man] to work for you if you are a woman, you are asking for conflict you may have least expected. The female boss is a circumstance man has encountered too recently in history to have adjusted to taking it in stride. It is against his tradition, contrary to his inclination, fatal to his aspiration as a member of the ruling sex, and it takes money applied with tact to make him suffer it. Perhaps enough money might make him like it; nothing else will. Shoving into a composite specimen the run of transient and would-be cowboys who have allowed me to hire them (this excepts the "oldies" who have been the real nucleus of the establishment and have gratefully accepted a woman's place as being better than no place at all), I note regretfully that his response to a command or entreaty is forever evasive and oblique. Before he can comply he has to take measure to counterbalance his masculine complexes.

"Bill," I call, "come here and hold this wrench."

Curious, Bill comes readily. Will he pick up the wrench and hold it in the way and place I indicate? Ha, ha! He has to negotiate and assert. What am I doing and why do I want to do it?

. . . I have nostalgic memories of girl helpers—college girls wanting to stand in for men who had gone to the wars—who followed my lead and let me make my mistakes in peace. Of dozens of men, I can think of only two who have felt obliged to take orders and paychecks from the same source: Wilbur took pains to do things exactly as I directed, and the good Uncle often said, with obvious reservations of male opinion: "Well, if that's the way you want it, that's the way I'll do it."

—Eulalia Bourne,
Woman in Levi's.

It's very hard for a woman to be level and direct in her dealings with some men, especially when it regards business. A woman can't approach a man on a person-to-person basis without getting into a position that threatens her as a woman. Instead of accepting you as what kind of person you are or what kind of manager you are, they deal with you as a woman first and a person or manager second. The fact that you're a woman will influence their final evaluation of you.

I haven't had too many troubles with people over this as long as I am allowed to deal with the people I don't have too many problems with. That sounds obvious, but when I am put in a position where I have to deal with an extremely chauvinistic, hard-line man, then I have trouble. But there are a lot of men who are just as capable as that very chauvinistic man who accept me on my terms. Then we have a human-to-human situation rather than a man-to-woman situation. And I don't have any problems with that.

Helen with Ibex goat.

I'm not trying to negate my femininity or my womanliness. I haven't been the greatest housekeeper or the greatest mother. I'm certainly one of the most unglamorous people that there ever was. But I like doing a lot of things that are considered very much in the sphere of being a woman. I just don't want to be entrapped in that. I don't want to have to be doing only the things that women are "supposed" to do.

I think the thing that all women are really objecting to right now is entrapment. Entrapment into a certain role. I don't think that women should be put down because they take on things other than maintaining the family and the house. It's a form of slavery, simple as that. I've studied the natural world all my life, and I don't think there is anything there which says that a woman is any more or any less than a man. In the natural world, each animal fulfills its endowment. And if a woman is endowed with talents or skills outside the home, she should use them.

I have a vocation for animal science and I have in turn developed skills in things that are related to animal science. And I don't think it has a goddamn thing to do with me being a woman. It just happens to be the kind of person that I am. Yet, there *is* a problem for a woman running a ranch, because people don't accept things on those terms.

I'm not saying that the things I've failed to do have been due to the fact that I am a woman. Rather, they've been due to a lack in myself—a lack of nerve, lack of ability, or lack of understanding of the problem. Sometimes the things that I *have* been able to accomplish have created personal problems for me. I am very dynamic. I may give and give and give up to a point, but there's a point where I just can't give it up anymore. I think that, in the end, all you have is your creativity, no matter what sphere it's in. You've got to do as much as you are able.

UPI writer Richard H. Growald ran across 73-year-old Pearl Tompkins—the woman called Horse—in Big Arm, Montana in 1978. "Pearl Tompkins is beautiful," he wrote. "A Mixmaster might have done her gray hair . . . Her figure is Henry A. Kissinger off his diet."

Growald hunkered down with some coffee at the Big Arm Restaurant, General Store, and Post Office and listened to Pearl Tompkins. It didn't take him long to figure out why they call her "Horse."

Don't call me Miss or Missus. I'm just plain Pearl Tompkins.

I was born back in the North Dakotas and came out here forty-some-odd years ago. I came with nothing. Worked myself up to eight hundred acres.

I've had Quarter Horses, Thoroughbreds, American Saddlers.

I've had all the horses, but ahh, the Walkers. A Walking Horse will do anything any other horse will do but will do it better. A Tennessee Walking Horse is not smart; it's intelligent.

Some folks bark about last winter. But remember 'sixty-one. So much snow that even the bulldozers got stuck. My horses were in the fields of snow, three quarters of a mile from feed. They couldn't make it any closer than a quarter mile to the barn. So I had to crawl out there in the drifts and under the barbed wire and I reached old Annie. Good horse. I got atop old Annie and led the rest of the horses out to where the hay was. I got over a fence and pitched the feed over to them. Other horses had it bad in the snow. Mine got through fat.

Old Blue. My first horse. Now, I don't want to brag, but there was a time when I would have put Old Blue and myself up against any horse and man. There wasn't anything Old Blue and I couldn't done.

I loved Old Blue. He was thirty-two when we finally had to shoot him. His teeth were ulcerating bad through his gums. Maybe some wouldn't understand you have to shoot something you love. But you shoot a Blue because you love him.

And old Tony, who nudges the cattle so nicely. I was up in the pasture this morning and there was old Tony. He's twenty-six. I guess he knows that horses fetch forty cents a pound now. Old Tony shook his tail.

I reached up and patted him. I told him, don't worry, don't you worry, Tony, about that forty cents a pound. You're with Pearl Tompkins. Don't you worry.

> —Constructed from quotes in "She's as Tough as the Country—Rugged Western Royalty," by Richard H. Growald, UPI, *St. Louis Post-Dispatch,* August 27, 1978, p. 101.

Mildred Kanipe

Near Oakland, Oregon

To find Mildred Kanipe's ranch, you turn right at the feed store and drive three or four miles to a fork in the road. Turn left and in another mile the road forks and you hang left again. Pass the old white frame schoolhouse and Mildred's ranch is the second on the left.

I arrive in the afternoon. The morning fog has lifted but a gentle mist hangs in the air. I stop at the wire gate across the road leading into Miss Mildred's ranch. It is padlocked. The road into her ranch sweeps gently to the left towards an old ramshackle unpainted house that has been in the family for over a hundred years. On the right is a large barn with a new tin roof, a milk shed on one end, and a maze of corrals. The buildings are below the road, by the creek, and nestled beneath giant, guarding oaks.

I fiddle with the lock and realize I can't get it. As I wonder what to do, Miss Mildred comes 'round the bend in the road.

Miss Mildred wears gum boots, black rubber pants, and a black rubber coat. A green gingham scarf wraps her wispy white hair and ties under her chin. She tops this with a low-brimmed black leather cap with red plaid earmuffs. Her walk, shaped as it is by "art-ritis," is slow and shuffling, yet steady and determined. She comes out of the mist and she might be a schoolboy shuffling, a little unwillingly, towards school, daydreaming and whistling at the ground.

"Used to be we never owned a lock," she says as her bent, calloused hands undo the gate chain. "But the very ground you're standin' on would disappear these days. How do. We'll sit in your car."

I am not to be let through the gate. But then, I am a total stranger, only a voice she has heard on the phone. She sizes me up—slowly, unobtrusively. At that stage, I have no idea how well she can see, but later she tells me how tall I am and comments, "You look like you can ride a horse." Those words of acceptance, of kinship, are the most sincere handshake.

Mildred's life is etched on her face. A life of sun and occasional wind, long winter nights and hot summer days. Most of her front teeth are missing, and years of tight determination have shaped her thin blue lips. She feels she is a woman who has worked and who has lost any beauty of youth that a life of leisure might have preserved. She won't allow a photograph, even after she seems to trust me. "It would ruin it for them," she says. "They'd say, 'Why, that poor crippled up old thing couldn't do all that.'" Yet her eyes, her big faded sky blue, mountain pool eyes, twinkle with an unquenchable light. The sides of her mouth turn up in a childish grin of pure delight as she recounts the events of her lifelong love affair with the land. Mildred Kanipe—half hob-

bit and half boy—is one of the most beautiful women I've ever been privileged to meet.

I was my daddy's only boy. He taught me everything I know. I say I learned from an expert, 'cause boy he was.

I must have been around eighteen when I bought the first land. I wasn't even grown yet. But I wanted land. I had to have me some land. And I finally got a chance to buy a piece that was pretty close, about a mile away.

I worked for some of the neighbors—I rode for them and broke horses. I saved all I could of what I earned. I stayed home and worked while the other kids were going here and there. You know, playing and having a good time. They thought I was crazy. "Why don't you come with us here?" they'd say. "Why don't you come with us there?" But I'd stay home and hang onto that money. Finally, I got enough to buy it.

I was walking on air when I got it. Wasn't much of a place—a hundred and sixty-seven acres of creek bottom land, full of brush and trees. Most everybody told me, "If you'd cut that timber, you would have some grass and you could keep something." Well, I cleared a lot of laurel brush on it. But I wasn't going to cut those trees, those fir trees. I was always crazy about trees. Land and trees, grass and stock—that's my interests. "Nope," I said, "I ain't gonna cut them trees." But I plowed it up and worked it good, and when I got through, it raised lots.

Mildred was about twenty-five when her father died and she took over the home place—about two hundred acres. A few years later, she added seven hundred acres that joined the two pieces. "To pay for it," she says:

I ran a grade-A dairy for eight years. Let me tell you, don't ever get a dairy, unless you want to work yourself to death. Because it don't make any difference. If you died, you'd have to get up and milk those cows. They got to be milked every morning and every night. Three hundred and sixty-five days a year. And three hundred and sixty-six on leap year. It wouldn't be so bad if you had two people. But I done it alone for eight years. And no matter, if I got sick or I got hurt, I had to milk those cows.

I got the flu once, and I couldn't stand up for more than two or three minutes at a time. I had to go out there and milk the cows. I'd have to get down on my knees and lean against a cow to keep from falling over, and get the milkers on and all.

Another time, a horse rolled over with me—crushed my shoulder and tore up my knee. So I hobbled around on crutches to milk the cows. I couldn't use one arm and a leg for a long time after that. I had to drive to Cottage Grove every day, about thirty miles away, to deliver my milk. To drive, I'd reach down and get ahold of my boot top, pick my foot up and set it on the clutch. The weight of my foot would put the clutch down. I'd have to let go of the steering wheel, of course, while I was doing that. Then I'd reach down and pick up my foot and set it off. Yeah, it was hard. But you have to be strong. After all the time you've spent doing it, you couldn't just quit and lose everything. So you hang on and hope it will get better. And it finally did. I finally sold the dairy. I accomplished my purpose with it when I paid for the big place. Then I bought a Cat [Caterpillar tractor] and went to logging.

I done quite a bit of that myself, too. Which people don't do. They don't log alone. "It's too dangerous," they say. "You have to have somebody there." There are very few people who have ever worked alone. But I done a lot of it by myself. Those were long days. I'd start in the fall, soon as haying was over. I'd get up in time to do all the chores and start logging at seven o'clock. I'd get home after dark and I'd move the irrigation pipe by moonlight. It's silver, you know, and shows up in the moon so I could see to find it. After I'd move it, I'd do the chores. So I didn't have too much time off. More than I did, though, when I had the dairy. When I had the dairy and was haying too, I was doing good to get four hours' sleep a night.

There was an old gal, name of Louise Richtor, ranched up the mountain. I think she was an old maid—anyway, she lived alone. You didn't see her too often, but she was an interesting old gal. Rawboned. Used to wear a black net over her hair, and a beaver hat.

She'd come to the fair every year and race horses. I remember when she'd come to the grocery store to get groceries, she'd bring a pack string of three or four pack horses. She'd tie them in the alley behind the grocery store and she'd get the clerks to help her pack them. They all hated that—some of the horses weren't too gentle.

One spring we had to work over the telephone line—all the ranchers in that area got together. We ended up with the job of digging post holes. At one stage, the rest of us were stringing wire and putting up insulators and Louise was digging the holes by herself. At noon we had to jump in the truck and go way, way up the canyon to catch her—she was outdigging us pretty bad. I'll never forget that. She was right down on her hands and knees digging those deep holes with a shovel. Worked just like a man.

—Bob Gibbs,
Gibbs Ranch on Powder River, Wyoming.

How'd I keep going? Just tough! That's the only thing I can see. I don't know. But I did. Not just a few days. It went on for weeks and months, working like that.

Vacations? Ha-ha! A rancher don't take vacations. No, the only vacation I had was a year ago last fall when I got sick. I was in the hospital for near a month. I guess you might call that a vacation. Anyway, I was lucky enough. I had some real good friends, neighbors, that came and took care of the place.

I've only been outside of Oregon once. I haven't even seen all of Douglas County. Course, it's a pretty big county. But I went to California once, clear down to Los Angeles. I took a load of Christmas trees down there. I had a trailer on behind my pickup, and took four and a half ton of trees. Before I went down there, people that had been there said, "You can't go to California! You got to drive seventy-five miles an hour or get off the road. They put you off." "Well," I said, "they'll have to put me off then, because my pickup won't go but sixty-seven miles an hour." I knew, 'cause I tried it out when I first got it, and that was the fastest I could make it go. And I said, "I ain't going to be going that fast, pulling a trailer. I guess they'll put me off." Well, I drove about forty miles an hour, pulling that trailer. And I didn't have any trouble at all. I stayed over there on the outside where the slow traffic was supposed to go, and I got along just fine.

That was quite a trip. The people I was delivering the trees to told me to stay on Washington Boulevard. Washington Boulevard, twenty-seven miles long. I didn't even know where I was going, but I found Washington Boulevard, and I stayed on it. They was supposed to been down there to stop me, you know, show me where to go. And I went and went and went. Finally I got down in the main part of the town, where the big factories and things were. I knew then I was in the wrong place. So I turned around and finally found the place. It was quite a deal, not knowing anything.

When I got back, somebody wanted to know, "What did you think of Los Angeles?" I'll tell you, if I had to live there in order to have it, I wouldn't take the whole city of Los Angeles as a gift. Why, I never saw such a rat race in my life. Oh, the cars—go, go, go, go. Nobody walks anyplace. If I was going to go someplace two or three blocks away, I walked. Oh, that was the funniest thing. They'd look at me—"Why don't you drive?" They thought I was crazy. But to get out in all that mess of stuff when you could walk that little distance? Boy, it's silly to me.

But nobody walks. They're all in them cars. Going just as hard as they can. They skid to a stop. When the light changes, BRRRRR, go just as hard as they can go.

I could understand why, after I seen it, they all look like they did. They all got such a—oh, I don't know what you'd call it. A worried and sour look. And nobody ever smiles or nothing. But where they lived, no wonder they looked like they did.

It took me a long time to get home from California. I come back up through the redwoods. It took me a long time to get through there. Boy, I'd have to stop and look at those big beautiful trees. Oh boy. They sure are pretty. I said, that is the only part of California I'd give two cents for, is the northern part, and it was so much like Oregon.

Did you ever marry?

I didn't have time to marry! Didn't have time to be lonesome, either. People come out here—in the spring it is all so green and pretty—and they say, "You sure are lucky to have this place. You sure are lucky." Well, they can call it luck if they want. I call it something else.

I'd like to go around, over more of the country. Just to look at it. I don't want to stay, I know that. I don't ever want to stay anyplace, only here. But I'd like to *see* more of it. And I'd appreciate this more when I got back. Ahh, there's no place like home, I guess. 'Specially when you've lived there all your life.

A lot of people, home is nothing to them. They live here and they live there. But I've always been here. I'm like these old oak trees. I'm rooted down in here so deep that I don't think there is any moving me. It makes a lot of difference all right. I can see why, if they aren't there very long, they don't care anything about a place. A lot of people don't care anything about the land or the trees. Some of them don't care anything about the stock. All the stock means to them is the money. And I suppose I look at it a different way. I figure the stock is mine and I'm responsible for it. I better get out there and take care of it. I don't think about whether I'm going to make two dollars or ten dollars. I just figure they've got to be took care of, and it's up to me to do it, because they are mine.

Same way with the land. I figure I ought to take care of it and not destroy it or damage it. So I've built it up quite a bit. And I never overgraze it. I don't kill *my* grass! And I don't run all over it with a tractor or a pickup. That's why I go afoot. I don't want it all cut up and rutted. So I walk.

It's pretty hard, when you think of what I used to do and what I can't do now. If I could do half of what I used to do, boy, I'd just be doing fine. But I'm all crippled up now, can't do much. I guess I could have retired. But I'd probably been dead before now. All of my neighbors got old and sold their land and moved to town. And all of them, ever' one of 'em, died within a year after they sold their land. So I guess I'll hold onto mine!

No, I like it awful well here. I was born here. I've lived here all my life, and I'm never going to leave. This is where I'll die.

I am pretty far out [of town], but Progress will catch up someday. When I am bumbling around in a wheelchair, a sharp real estate salesman will drive up to offer to buy and sell my outfit. Not for cash, of course. Who would want to give an old woman cash? How about trading for peace and comfort in some nice clean house in town with a porch and a rocking chair?

"Young Lady," he'll say (that's what you get called when it no longer applies), "you can't make it here any longer. Your fences are down. Your corrals are falling to staves. Your pipeline has rusted away. Your trees are dying for lack of care. Your house is too much for you. You cannot cope with a place so large. I'd like to see you resting easy. You could have a little house in town and be comfortable. No hard work to do. No insoluble worries. Let me have your little ranch for my client and you . . ."

"Just a minute," I'll interrupt. "This nice quiet home you want me to trade for. Is it located where I can hear a cow bawl?"

"Oh, no. It's near the doctors and the hospital and . . ."

That's the moment I'll lower my ear trumpet and sic the dogs on him.

—Eulalia Bourne,
Woman in Levi's.
Copyright © 1967 by Eulalia Bourne.

Cowgirls from Outside:

THE DUDE EARNS HER SPURS

Calendar cowgirl,
photographed by
William Henry Jackson,
1903.

Linen Bliss

Bliss Ranch, Powder River County, Montana

Linen Bliss, lifting feed sack, Bliss Ranch, near Otter, Montana, 1979.

LINEN BLISS LOVES THE LAND—COMPLETELY, INSATIABLY. ON DAYS WHEN she has time after the ranch work is done, she runs across the sagebrush plains and up the steep divide, five miles, six miles, seven. "I set a goal. I will run to the end of that pasture, climb that hill, reach that tree. The whole ranch becomes a personal challenge. When I climb a hill, it's mine in a way it wasn't before. It's part of me and I'm part of it. Running makes me very aware of the things that grow here; it makes me feel like I'm one of the growing things."

Last summer Linen bicycled alone to Sheridan, Wyoming—seventy-five miles over rugged dirt roads. This winter the first snowfall welcomed her cross-country ski tracks among the usual paw, hoof and claw prints.

Forty-one years of age and the mother of four children (eleven to twenty-one), Linen is slim and athletic, iridescent with energy. She radiates a sense of pure joy and it is easy to believe her claim that this isolated ranch is the perfect place for her.

Linen was not born to the land. She grew up in Short Hills, New Jersey, and Dorset, Vermont, the daughter of a successful stockbroker. Groomed by country clubs, boarding school and women's college, she married her childhood sweetheart—a Yale graduate and stockbroker—in 1957. She was nineteen. After five years they realized that the marriage they were "bred to" didn't work and they separated. Linen had three children under four years of age and a nervous breakdown; her first husband had an alcohol problem.

In 1966 Linen came West to vacation at the H F Bar dude ranch near Buffalo, Wyoming. She fell in love with the area and made a snap decision to move West with her children for a trial year. She met Dave Bliss at a rodeo. They were married in 1967.

I guess I am a classic case of "dude comes West, meets handsome cowboy, marries handsome cowboy, rides off into the sunset, and lives happily ever after." That has happened many, many times, and it darned sure happened to me.

When Dave and I got married, we didn't have any plumbing or telephone. There were no cattle guards on the road, so we had to open seven gates to get in here. The road was gumbo, and if we had a drop of rain we couldn't get out.

I was on a real pioneer spirit high. Everything we did was the hard way. We were seventy-five miles from the closest town and had so few of the modern conveniences I was used to. I was completely taken up with learning to rough it, and with conquering my new occupation.

It took about four years for me to really feel confident. Those first four years, I still felt like I was kind of intruding on my husband's bachelor life, or perhaps it was more like intruding on a very masculine domain. There were so many things I had to prove to myself as well as him, and I suppose the community. I had to totally divorce myself from all the things I had relied on in the past as being me—my education, or rather schooling, background, "family heritage." If I was going to be a successful western ranch wife, I had to forget everything I was. Of course, it wasn't a successful ranch wife that I had to be. I just had to develop a "me" that was me on my own rather than live up to a pedigree with none of my own signature on it.

I knew little about horses and nothing about cattle. But Dave was great. He expected right from the start that I would learn it, and that I would work with him. It never occurred to him that I wouldn't be able to do it. I was a ranch wife married to him and we were going to do ranch work together, and there was nothing he didn't expect me to do.

As an example, when Scott was five weeks old, Dave went to rope steers at the Denver Stock Show. He drew up badly. He was supposed to rope his first steer on the first day, and his second one ten days later. Then the weather turned and Dave couldn't get back here between the two go-rounds. It was twenty-four degrees below zero, and I had two hundred cows to feed by myself with a five-week-old baby. The only way I could load the hundred-pound sacks of cattle cake onto the tailgate of the pickup was to drop them off the top of the cake pile onto the freezer and then slide them into the truck. Our freezer still has a big dent in the hood. But Dave expected me to handle the situation, and I could.

Dave wasn't taking advantage of me. Some people judge Dave for working his wife, but it's not that way at all. He always treated me as an equal. He thought I might consider it an insult if he had somebody come over and help me, because he would be saying, in effect, "You can't handle this." But he doesn't say that. He lets me handle things. And I treat him the same way. He can handle the domestic chores.

"I'm going over to the barn to see if Ramón has got back yet," I said as [my husband] came back to dress. "If he hasn't, I shall have to help Tio Maximo with the morning chores and you can get breakfast."

He agreed without expressing any surprise. We have always been used to exchanging jobs inside and outside, and since he had not been helping with the feeding, it would be much better for me to do it.

"What lovely biscuits!" exclaimed Mrs. Mellott, when we were at breakfast.

"I made them while my wife fed the cattle," responded Charlie. Her blue eyes widened with amazement.

"I'd so much rather work in the corral than in the kitchen," I explained placidly.

I could see that she did not know whether to believe me or to conclude that I was the most down-troddenest and put-upon woman she had ever encountered. A gleam came into her eye that hinted of a desire to emancipate me, to set my feet on the right path—leading to a life of luxury and ease. First she must rouse in me the spirit to break the chains, or the riata, that bound me to the corral.

"I should think you would find it so hard to cook on a wood-stove," she began commiseratingly, as she enveloped herself in my largest kitchen apron and helped me by wiping the breakfast dishes. "I have an electric range—and a cook."

"We have no electricity," I replied.

"Oh!" That was hard to get over. She wiped the cups.

"I must remember to fill the gasoline lamp that went out last night," I remarked, "and the coal-oil ones too."

"What a nuisance!" she cried indignantly. "If you simply must live on a ranch and go into barns and places like that, you should have every convenience in the house. I don't see how you stand it!"

I made no comment.

"I have an electric refrigerator," she continued; "the little ice cubes are so cute! I have an electric washing-machine—and a woman who comes to work it on Mondays. I should think you would want electricity more than anything else in the world!"

"That's because you don't know me," said I, laughing. "More than anything else in the world, I want an inch of rain."

—Mary Kidder Rak,
Mountain Cattle.
Copyright © 1936 by Mary Kidder Rak.

The kids were determined not to be dudes, and they never were. They were tough pioneers. They rode horses to school. The schoolhouse is eight miles away by the road or five miles across the hills. You wouldn't believe the weather those kids took off in. Every morning they'd saddle up, get into the cow trail, and ride single file over the hill, still sort of sleepy and mesmerized.

Our daughter had a wreck coming home from school when she was nine years old. The kids got in a fight and split up, and she came home a different way. She saw some cows that were out and decided to move them back into the right pasture. Her horse fell into a coulee and threw her up against the bank. When he climbed out, he stepped on her chest and his hoof hit her eye. She had a compound skull fracture and lost the eye.

She rode home. She crawled off and opened two gates on the way. She even closed them after she went through. When she arrived at the barn she fell off her horse. Her head was swollen and there was blood everywhere. You couldn't recognize her.

Dave was in Pendleton roping, so I called Big Horn Airways. We had a telephone by that time. They picked us up and took us to Sheridan. The hospital sent us right to Billings. She was in surgery there for a long time and in intensive care for a couple of weeks, but she was all right. She had no brain damage. We were so lucky.

I was really strong through all this and I stood up to it until it was all over and she was home. Then one day, after she went back to school, I really broke down and fell apart. You know, for a while you're so glad that somebody's alive that you don't worry about the cosmetic part of it, or the loss of her eye. Suddenly all that sunk in. But Dave really snapped me to. He said, "Now look,

Linen. You've got a healthy, normal, wonderful daughter, and you can make her into a cripple by the way you treat her." He was absolutely right. She has done really well with it all along.

The accident upset me but it didn't make me doubt my decision to move out here. My parents had always worried about how far away from a doctor we are. Well, I think you can get from here to Sheridan and then to Billings faster than you could get treated in a crowded emergency room in New York City. I mean, you can get *lost* in an emergency room. It just didn't take that long.

Dave and I worked side by side and I learned about ranching. In time I found that I could handle most everything here. My confidence started coming when I could recognize areas of our business that Dave was less enthusiastic about than I was. Calving heifers was one of those areas.

Dave hates calving heifers, but I love it. It makes me feel so important, and I just love to feel the life come into those calves. I get very involved spiritually and physically in the whole schmeer and I'm terribly conscientious. Overly conscientious, really. Dave kids me about it. He says, "Now, are you sure your babies are going to be all right?" But he could see how conscientious I was and gradually he turned more and more of it over to me. Now the heifers are my department and I'm very confident with them.

We usually calve out about sixty heifers, which isn't very many, but it's the right number for me because I really get to know each one. I talk to them when they're calving. I say, "Come on Momma, push a little harder." Dave, on the other hand, is gruff and says, "Come on, you dirty son of a bitch." I say, "Dave, you can't talk to them that way. If you'd been through this, you'd know how much you can't talk to them that way." I think women have a real advantage in that department, particularly if they've had children.

They are my family in the spring. I really get a thrill out of calving them, and then when we turn them out in the lot, the calves all run around with their tails straight over their backs, charging here and charging there. It really tickles me. I go down there and watch them for hours, and I sketch them a lot.

The other thing I really like to do is winter the yearlings. When I had kids in high school, I had to live in town during the winter so they could go to school. We have a small place in there that puts up enough hay to winter about two hundred and fifty yearlings, and I took care of them.

I had an old 'fifty-nine GMC four-wheel drive named Brutus. I'd load Brutus every night and then about seven o'clock each morning Brutus and I would head for the feed ground. My dog would gather the cows and then I'd put Brutus in compound and get in the back and feed the bales. I'd turn Brutus loose, and it looked just like somebody was driving him. He'd drive himself in a snake pattern. He'd head one way until he hit a bump and then he'd head another way. Sometimes he'd head right for a snowdrift and I'd have to jump off and straighten him out or he'd bury himself. I'd have little competitions from day to day. Getting off twice and straightening him out was a really good day. Every once in a while I could feed the whole forty or forty-five bales without getting off. But sometimes Brutus was ornery and I'd have to jump off five or six times.

The first year, the calves got pneumonia and I had a lot of doctoring to do. I spent a lot of time just observing the cattle—the way they walked, lay down, held their heads and ears. I got to where I could spot when they were getting sick before they were really bad. This turned out to be the key to wintering calves and in six years we only lost three calves.

"Listen, young fella," she said, "a cattleman's life depends on noticin' things. When you ride anywhere on a ranch you see everything. You gotta see if a ditch is runnin' high or low, if the outlets are washed or plugged. You gotta look at cattle and see what shape they're in—thin or fat or ailing. You gotta see fences—if they're up or down or about to fall. And you always check the grass, notice if it's greenin' or still hung over from winter. Young fella, you gotta learn to keep your eyes open if you expect to work for me!"

Kelsey sawed at the tough steak, his face smarting. The meat tasted like sawdust. Then he heard the curt, husky voice again. "I come in from the flats this afternoon. I seen three cows, two of 'em dry, up in that country you were supposed to be ridin' over. By lookin' across the upper meadow, I could tell by the shine of water the ditch was carryin' a full head and the outlets filled. I seen green showin' on the hills north of the ranch and lots of green under the spread ditch. Those three cows are bound to have been along the ditch where it was greenest and left their tracks and their manure plain for anybody with eyes to see."

. . . He shook his head, torn between humiliation and disgust. A woman, a woman talking about things like cow manure! It was—well, not proper at all.

—Peggy Simson Curry,
So Far from Spring.
Copyright © 1956 by Peggy Simson Curry.

This ranch is something we all do together, and that is really different than the way I was raised. There was always the proverbial joke back East—"What would you do if your husband came home for lunch?" But we live and work together day in and day out, and we respect each other's competency in different areas. Dave is so much better at doing some parts of the ranching than I am. I don't think I'm *better* at any of it than he is, but I like to do some things that he doesn't and won't take as much time with.

I once had a visitor, a dainty, little town-body she was. "All right enough, I guess, but pretty much of a light-weight mentally," was [my husband] Charlie's opinion of her.

One evening I had to go over to the corral to separate some cows and calves, and she walked over also, staying outside the gate to watch me. I was having some trouble with them, and all at once my guest came in with me and began dashing about among the cattle in a most efficient manner. Charlie came home just in time to see her running around the corral, forgetful of her white kid shoes. We learned then that she had spent much of her childhood on a ranch, and how Charlie's attitude did change! He told me sometime afterward that he believed the husband of my friend owed much of his business success to his having married an exceptionally intelligent woman. And all because she could shoo a few cows away from their calves.

—Mary Kidder Rak,
A Cowman's Wife.
Copyright © 1934 by Mary Kidder Rak.

Our kids work right with us, too, and I feel that the life offered on a ranch does a lot for the children as well as for the parents. Sometimes you lose patience with your loved ones before you would with an outsider. But you learn to recognize each other's limits and strengths and work around those. And you learn to respect each other for what you can do.

A lot of families are only together for recreation, and sometimes it's hard to have fun playing together. I look at people stuffed in station wagons, a thousand miles from home, broken down with a flat tire. The kids are hot and their popsicles are melting all over the back seat. I wonder how that could possibly be fun. I think you learn a lot more respect for one another working together than you do playing together.

And our kids really understand their father's business. Eleven-year-old Scott knows exactly what we do because he does it too. My own father was a stockbroker and my mother used to comment that the brokerage was a real gamble. So when I was in fourth grade and had to fill out a form with my father's occupation, I said he was a gambler! And I really believed that he was. I knew nothing about his business, and to tell the truth, I still can't have an intelligent conversation with him. He treated my mother and me as if, "You don't have to worry your pretty little heads about that."

Ninety percent of a man's life is involved with his business and it's fantastic if you can be part of that business too, because the rest, that 10 percent, isn't enough. You have no way to understand your husband's preoccupied mind.

Dave is preoccupied all the time with the cattle business. Everything in the news relates to the cattle business—whether it's the President, or oil and gas, or whatever. But when my father would read in the news about some stock or Boeing 707s or something and be thinking how it would affect him, my mother didn't have a clue what was on his mind. I think it's great when you can know enough about each other to take up more than the 10 percent left over after your work.

I see Dave as my partner, and I like to see him as my boss. I'm old-fashioned in that. Even if we're doing the same thing side by side, I like my husband to be the boss. I'd rather be his "hired hand." I think you're challenging something a bit more complicated if you overstep those bounds. Your man is your man, and I like it that way.

When I lived in town during the winter and took care of the yearlings, I was the boss. I took full responsibility for them. But Dave would come in and ask me, "What do you want me to feed the calves today?" and I didn't like that. It made me uncomfortable when Dave asked me for instructions. I want to be boss of whatever it is that I have to do, but not boss of Dave, ever. There is only one boss on this ranch and it's Dave. I want to keep it that way.

I've got it easy. I get to do the things I like, be conscientious in my best areas, without the burdensome responsibility of managing the whole outfit. Spoiled? You bet, and I love it! That's not to say I don't do a lot of things I'd rather not, like run the chain saw or grade roads or something, but I don't have to worry about getting things done. I just do what Dave wants. I'm my own boss in the good areas and a "slave" in the bad areas. Actually, we cover well for each other's weaknesses.

I really love ranch life, even when it's hard. And sometimes it's brutally hard. This last winter was the hardest winter in anybody's memory, even the old-timers. It started to snow on November eighth and it just snowed all winter long.

We turned the cattle onto winter grass, but there was so much snow cover that they got into the pine needles by the last week in November. Cattle will eat pine needles if they can't get grass, but they can only eat so many before they abort their calves. You never know where the balance is. You know they're eating the needles, but you can't afford to move them right away because you can still keep them out in the pasture if the weather breaks. As it turned out, we had a whole patch of winter grass that was never used last year because we had to bring them onto the feed ground so early.

We gathered the cattle around December first and brought them down to the feed ground. The snow was terribly deep and it was slow going. The cows were weak, particularly the three-year-olds, and some of them were trapped in snowdrifts. It took us ten hours to gather around two hundred and twenty-five head and it was dark by the time we trailed them home.

We had a full moon that night. It surrounded us with a warm, yellow glow and was so bright it cast perfect shadows. It was terrifically cold and we led our horses most of the way. The trail is very narrow, and the cows strung out, single file, over the top of the divide. The cows all knew where they were going. They walked very peacefully, sort of like tired soldiers walking home. It was gorgeous. I was really turned on by it all.

[The ranch wife] has learned to live with herself and like it,
because she has no alternative. Being on a ranch, twenty miles or
more from the nearest town, she has found joy in simple things.
She is aware of possessing an almost sacred knowledge of the
living things around her. She suspects, although she may not
admit it, that there is nothing on earth more pleasant than
working all day at something you love, eating a simple supper,
washing off the dust and grime in a hot bath, and sleeping soundly
between fresh sheets, listening to the wind rustling the cottonwood
leaves outside the window.

—Jo Jeffers,
Ranch Wife.
Copyright © 1964 by Jo Jeffers.

So we got them gathered, and that started the great feeding process. Dave
and I and two shiny hay hooks fed four hundred tons of hay this winter. By a
lot of people's standards, that's not a lot of hay. But to feed it by hand, and
with all the hard weather, it was plenty.

When the snow got too deep to feed with a pickup, we used a team. We
have a two-horse team of Belgian horses. They weigh about eighteen hundred
pounds apiece and have big feathery legs. When they get sweaty, each one of
the hairs frosts immediately and they get big icicles coming out of their noses.
That is sad for them, but they are beautiful when they get frosty all over.

Each morning we'd harness the team and drive them across the hay
meadow. Often the temperature would be around thirty below zero and the
wind would howl across that meadow. We would put a couple of bales on the
front of the sled so that we could crouch down behind them. One day the
wind was blowing about thirty or forty miles an hour. The snow came straight
at us, and our eyelids would freeze almost shut. Dave would drive for about
three minutes and then have to get down behind the bales. Then I'd drive for
three minutes. That was all we could stand before our faces would freeze. We
alternated that way all the way to the feed ground. I don't know how the
horses stood it.

We fed like that all winter. We'd get white spots all over our cheeks and get
frostbitten and itch. We worked day in and day out. We'd finish feeding
around two o'clock, come home for a bowl of soup, and start right out to get
Scott from school. Then we'd load up for the next day's feeding. But it felt
good. It's hard to explain how some things that are so miserable at the time
can be appealing. But the livestock is dependent on you, and they are your responsibility. It's a challenge, and you've met the challenge. You haven't gone
back into the house for another cup of coffee and said, "Well, the cattle probably wouldn't want to eat today anyway 'cause it's storming too hard."

Ranch life is sometimes terribly busy, like last winter, but other times you
have a lot of free time. This is an isolated existence, and it can be lonely. Then

it's extremely important that you have something that gives you satisfaction. The winter months are long, and if I have extra time I ski outside or I draw or read or run on the packed road or anything. I don't mean in a frenzied way, trying to fill up all the hours. But you've got to learn to use your time so you're not bored with yourself. As soon as you bore yourself, you are boring to others, and that's a real bummer.

I really love the ranch, and I feel awfully lucky to have this kind of life to lead. It is easy to be snide about the East versus the West, but I appreciate the East. It is a fabulous place with terrific opportunities, particularly culturally. It just happened to have a stifling effect on me. I think my parents felt this and were a little hurt by it, although I love them and never intended to throw rejection at them. I will always be grateful for the broadening experiences and opportunities they gave me. I was lucky enough to be able to make some choices that were pretty important to me. And this rugged country has made me discover a strength in myself I had never been forced to find in the East.

When the Earl of Dunmore decided to venture into ranching in Montana in 1880, he needed help to choose which of his thirty thousand head of Scotch cattle would fare best in Montana. He found an able adviser in Miss Middy Morgan, a Montana cattle expert who caught the fancy of *The North British Agriculturalist* and was described in it in detail:

. . . There are strange characters to be met with in America, and Middy Morgan is one of the strangest. The daughter of an Irish gentleman, well born and well educated, left dependent on an uncle already overburdened with a large family of his own. Not a moment did the brave girl hesitate in her choice between idleness and dependence, or liberty and work. But the prejudice of birth is still great in the sister island, and poor Middy durst not seek employment amongst her friends, so she started for New York in quest of a situation as governess, with the idea that, with her accomplishments, she would find it easy to obtain.

But she was deceived; the New York ladies, who have to suffer from the tyranny of Irish cooks and housemaids, object entirely to Irish governesses, and so Miss Morgan was fain to do as so many emmigrants from Europe had done before her—to "go out West." Here she found no prejudice against her Irish birth, but much against her "accomplishments"; and after having sought in vain for a "genteel" situation, and "one that was not menial," she was glad to accept the post of a hired girl, to a farmer.

So completely did she identify herself with the change in her position, that in a short time she had acquired so much skill in the breeding and rearing of stock that the farmer, perceiving her value, admitted her to a partnership in the farm. Soon did her fame spread abroad, and at every fair and cattle market in the West was her name familiar. Gradually this fame has travelled East, and indeed no reputation is so widespread over all the Union as that of Middy Morgan.

At every great fair or market may she be seen, with broad-brimmed hat tied down beneath her chin by a bandanna handkerchief, a thick frieze coat with many capes, short skirt, ingeniously gathered into high leather boots, something like knickerbocker costume. With a long cowhide whip in hand, wending her way with skill between the droves, now stooping low to examine the hoofs, now standing on tiptoe to examine the head of the beast brought to her for valuation; and so great is the reliance placed by the farmers on her judgement in these matters, that none would ever seek to cheapen the animal after Middy Morgan has pronounced her verdict . . .

—*The North British Agriculturalist,* June 30, 1880, p. 412, col. 2.

Gwynne Fordyce

Wagonhammer Ranch, 60 miles northwest of Gillette, Wyoming

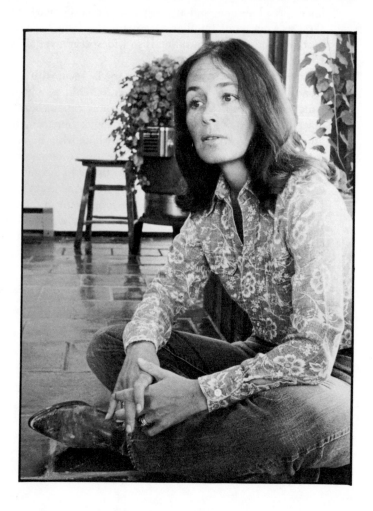

THE EXPANSIVE DECK ON THE SOUTH SIDE OF THE FORDYCE HOUSE LOOKS OUT
on twenty-nine thousand acres of rolling plains, broken here and there by steep
ridges and deep gulches, dotted with sagebrush, Ponderosa pine, and gnarled
cedar. Visitors often find the landscape desolate, but those who live here feel
the same awe at the vastness that a sailor does for his endless sea.

Gwynne hears me drive up and greets me at the door. Petite and athletic,
she has large hazel eyes and thick, shoulder-length brown hair. She wears a
navy T-shirt, and blue jeans held up by a belt with a silver buckle bearing her
initials. Around her neck hangs a thin gold chain. She grew up in Virginia and
South Carolina and met Ike, her tall, pipe-smoking husband, when she waited
tables at a Wyoming dude ranch after high school.

The ranch house is elegant and modern, a showcase for Gwynne's interest in interior decoration and Ike's in architecture. The glassed front opens onto the deck. Beveled glass side windows cast rainbows of light across the white tweed sofa and love seat in the living room. Navajo rugs are scattered on the gleaming oak floor and their reds and grays and whites blend with Williamsburg apple-patterned chairs. Ike's collection of Borein etchings fills one wall; a spiral staircase leads to the bedrooms on the lower level. Through the modern kitchen you can see the sunny recreation room with its carved-wood pool table. Ike and Gwynne did most of the work on the house themselves, with help from their two daughters—Shirley, twenty-two; and Lolly, twenty-one.

Gwynne and Ike differ from most ranchers because they have moved from ranch to ranch. They leased a ranch after they were married but soon bought Teepee Lodge, a historic dude ranch, from Ike's parents and ran it for twelve years. They also ran cattle, and when they sold Teepee they continued in the cattle business. Since that time they have owned three separate cattle ranches.

In the past few years they have developed ranches. They buy a ranch and run cattle while improving the water and irrigation, fences, corrals, etc. This has given them a greater degree of mobility than most ranchers and they have spent the last few winters off the ranch, first in Aspen, Colorado, and now in Santa Fe, New Mexico.

Ike sits in on the interview and later adds some comments of his own.

I was brought up in a household where the wife stayed home and raised the family and took care of the house and the social activities. We had a lot of colored help. I was brought up by a nanny and we always had a cook and someone to do the laundry and housecleaning. I was never in the kitchen and I never learned how to cook. I didn't learn how to sew or do laundry.

I always thought that I would follow in my mother's footsteps and be a suburban wife, living the same sort of southern white life. I figured I would have a maid who came in periodically to clean. I would entertain and have cocktail parties, I'd go to a ladies' bridge club every week, and I would probably have a horse or two that I would show and hunt. I never imagined, in even my wildest dreams, that I would be a ranch wife in Wyoming.

I had never been west of the Mississippi until I came to work at Eaton's Guest Ranch as a waitress after I graduated from St. Katherine's boarding school in Richmond. I had no idea that cowboys existed outside of the movies. The first time I saw Ike, he was standing in the middle of a corral with his hat and boots and Levi's, and he was cracking a bullwhip.

Western men are different than eastern men. The first thing that hits you is that they are just more masculine than someone who dresses in a suit and sits in an office. They give you a feeling of being able to handle more situations. They work outdoors, and they are part of the land.

I was impressed with the number of things Ike could do. He rode bucking horses and roped calves, he knew how to work cattle and fix fence and fix plumbing. He had been to Middlesex [boarding school in Massachusetts] and

I felt that he had an extremely good education. I could talk to him on an intellectual basis.

Ike and I spent a lot of time together that summer. Then I went to Stephens College in Columbia, Missouri, and he went to Colorado A&M [now Colorado State University]. We corresponded during the winter and were married that spring in June.

I realized that life on a ranch would be very different than what I was used to. I knew there wouldn't be any maids or ladies' bridge clubs. I felt that the West offered a much more wholesome kind of life than I had been leading. People who I had met in the West were down-to-earth and honest and hard-working. I had been caught up in a very social, superficial kind of life—boarding schools, debutante parties. I thought if I was ever going to fulfill my potential, I needed to be challenged, and I saw the West as a challenge.

Looking back, I realize that I had no idea what actually took place on a ranch. To me, it was all very glamorous. I loved the country, and I loved horses. I didn't realize that there was a tremendous amount of hard work involved in ranching.

It was tough, very tough! It was almost like moving to a foreign country because I really didn't know what was expected of me. Ike was trying to rope calves on the rodeo circuit and run the ranch and make enough money for us to live on. I missed my family, and I missed the ocean. We had a couple of bad drought years. I had a tough adjustment.

We had children right away—two girls, eighteen months apart. I had to learn to raise children and cook and take care of the house and do the laundry. Sometimes we had to haul water because the well didn't work. I had to learn how to work cattle.

We leased a ranch fifty miles from Sheridan [Wyoming], and I felt very isolated. I didn't know anyone my age, and I was pretty cut off since we lived so far from town. People are very reserved in the West, and they don't particularly accept eastern people. The neighbors didn't make much of an effort to come down and include me in anything, even though we were trying to be a part of the community. They never came down and said hello, and they never introduced themselves when I was at any sort of community gathering. I made the effort to get up and introduce myself, but I also sat in the corner from time to time.

I hadn't experienced that before. The South is casual and warm, a very easygoing place where everybody comes up and says hello. I just assumed that it would be the same out here, but it wasn't. For the most part, people who live in isolated communities are reserved. They don't get a lot of social conversation and they are not trained that way. Maybe they feel uncomfortable around strangers, but I didn't understand that. If I had had a little more experience traveling and living in different areas of the country, I probably could have handled it more maturely than I did. But I developed a sense of inferiority. I thought there was something definitely wrong with the way I handled people and projected myself. This made me shy and withdrawn until I realized that there was nothing wrong with what I had been doing.

I think a great many people here will always think of me as a dude, even though I've lived on a ranch for twenty-three years now and can work cattle with most people. I resent that a bit. I've never been anyplace else that took so long to accept you. I feel now that it's O.K. I'm happy with what I have achieved and it doesn't really matter whether I'm still viewed as an Easterner, or whether I'm finally accepted as a ranch wife. But when I was younger it was pretty important.

I had one really good friend—Martha Gibbs.* She and Bob lived on Powder River, about two hours away. Martha was from the East but her family bought a ranch out here when she was quite young, so she had been out here quite a while. I think she sensed that I was lonely and isolated and didn't know anything about ranching or how to cook for help. She made a big effort to be a friend, and she's been my best friend ever since I moved into this country.

Neither one of us had a telephone, so the only way we could see each other was to drive over and hope the other was there. We didn't see each other much. Maybe once a month, Ike and I would go over there and have dinner, play poker, and spend the night, or Martha and Bob would come here. That was about as often as we could manage to get away.

I've found a lot of other ranchwomen to be without much scope. Basically, all they can talk about is the children and what is going on at the ranch. I was interested in so many things besides that. And it's fun to find somebody I could talk to about other things.

The other thing that got me through that tough period was that Ike had sense enough to say, "I will hire somebody to take care of the children if you will help me with the cattle work." I didn't know anything about working cattle but I was sure willing to learn, so I got out of the house in the summertime.

The only way to learn cattle is to get out and work them. It takes a lot of time and a lot of miles. Ike would say, "You get that bunch and we'll meet at the bottom of the draw." Every time I would make a mistake, Ike would tell me what I'd done wrong and tell me how I should have done it. I made a lot of mistakes! But after you've made the same mistakes so many times, you decide you don't want to make them anymore because your horse is so tired you're practically afoot and you're so mad you're in tears.

Cattle can be terribly frustrating. Baby calves will break out of the herd and run back on you, and they are terribly hard to get back in the herd. Yearlings will scatter, and you almost kill your horse trying to get them gathered and headed in the right direction. There have been many, many times when I've felt like, "I am never going to do this again for the rest of my life. This is the most frustrating work in the world." But you know the work has to be done. There's a certain amount of stubbornness in me; there's that challenge. I'm ca-

* See Chapter 4.

pable of doing it; I know I can do it; I'm just going to get out there and get it done. Besides, you know there isn't anybody else to do it, so you get on your horse and try again.

Then you have days when everything works perfectly. You get where you're going without any problems and you get the gate open and everybody else gets there at the same time with their cattle. Those are very rewarding days.

The one advantage I had was that I'm very comfortable on a horse. I didn't have to worry about riding. I don't even think about it when I'm working cattle. I really enjoy riding good horses, and Ike has always given me good horses.

I feel I've led a more productive life than most of my friends who are still in the East, with the exception of the ones who have jobs. When I go back there, most of the women I know talk only about their children and their neighborhood and their social life and their next trip. I would have been extremely bored with that kind of life.

Living on a ranch, you learn to handle a lot of situations. You don't get too upset when there's an accident or the electricity or water goes off. If you cook for six or eight people every day and you only get to the grocery store every two weeks, you learn to think that way and make do with what is on hand. You become very much at ease around machinery and livestock and horses and all different kinds of people. You get mentally stronger because you have to cope with things most women never encounter.

Viola McCrorey came to southeastern Montana with her parents in 1912. She was nine. Six years later she married rancher Kenneth McKenzie. He died in 1939 and Viola continued with the ranch.

One summer I herded our sheep part time while the herder helped with the work at the ranch that was too heavy for me to do. I carried my bed tied to the back of my saddle and slept beside the sheep when they bedded down at night. I kept them on my own range and told my children to be careful they did the same when they were caring for the sheep.

Early one morning when my sheep and I were leaving camp, the foreman of a large ranch appeared. He accused me of watering my sheep at one of his springs. I did not know where the spring was and told him so. He called me a liar; for a few minutes I wished I were a man.

That afternoon he rode down by the creek where my sheep were lying in the shade of the banks and bushes after they had filled up on a good drink of creek water. He apologized for calling me a liar. I did not look up at him or give an answer. I was still

angry because he called me a liar. My thoughts would not have
been becoming to a lady if I had spoken them aloud. Neither
would they look good on paper.

—"Viola McCrorey McKenzie Sieler and Family" by Viola
  Sieler,
  in *Echoing Footsteps,* 1967.

Everything Ike and I have done, we've done together, and I feel I've contributed more to what we have accomplished than most eastern women. A lot
of them, and my mother's a good example, have absolutely nothing to do with
their husband's business. They live totally separate lives. They see their husbands in the evenings and they go out socially, but they don't share in his business concerns.

Ike and I have always worked together in every business we've been in—the
dude ranch, and the cow business. We have the same goals. In all the business
we've ever done, we've sat down and talked about it. Whenever we've bought
a ranch or a big piece of property, we've discussed whether we could handle
the payments, whether we wanted to make the sacrifice and so forth. And I
think that has made a big difference.

Also, I've done more than just run the home. When I cook for help or work
cows, I know I've contributed to the support and income of the ranch. If I
didn't do this, we'd have to hire somebody. I don't think my mother felt she
contributed in any way to the income that was coming in.

Unless I had my own career, it would be very difficult for me to live with
someone who went to work at nine and came home at five and never discussed
his business with me. I don't feel that Ike's and my marriage is traditional in
any respect. Consequently, I feel like I'm a more liberated woman than most
of the people I grew up with.

I admire tremendously the women who have careers, but I think that I
would have felt unfulfilled had I not married and had children, and been a
part of my husband's business. I think I probably would have done pretty well
if I had gone into something on my own, like interior decorating, because I
have a certain amount of determination to do things well. But I think you
have to make a decision somewhere along the line—am I going to develop myself and let it go at that? Or am I going to contribute to other people's lives? I
made my choice. I feel that being a ranch wife and mother is much more demanding of me as an individual than a career would have been. Certainly,
raising children is the most demanding and rewarding thing I've ever done.

I have wondered from time to time if I should have had a career of my
own. Up to the time the girls left, I had so much work that I didn't have time
to think about being bored or unfulfilled. But after they left, the transition period was hard for me. I wondered if I had wasted my life, if I should have

built my own career. I was dissatisfied and it was very hard on Ike. I took a lot of my frustrations out on him. I was going through a period where I thought I hadn't realized my potential. But that's not true; not true at all.

Now I'm interested in having more free time to learn new things and go new places, meet new people. Ike and I bought a place in Santa Fe and we are both going back to college. No, I have no regrets. I feel I am the source of what happens to me, and I have no regrets about the fact that I didn't go out and have a career. I feel like I have had an enormous career for the last twenty-three years.

Ike: Gwynne is mentally much tougher—way, way tougher—than she was when she first came out here. Then her first reaction to a problem was to do nothing. Doing nothing was part of her background. Now she always reacts, she always does something. She makes decisions. And she's usually right. She is able to decide because she *must* decide.

Gwynne started working cows with me because she was interested in doing it and that was the only way she could learn. A ranch is something you have to learn by repetition. And if she wanted to learn it, there was really no reason not to.

Cattle can be frustrating, there's no doubt about it. I had been raised around people who knew livestock, and it took me a long time to figure out that this really was totally foreign to Gwynne. If she fell apart or burst into tears, I didn't react very well. I probably increased the pressure on her. We had some drought years and some bad cattle markets, and that increased the pressure too.

Gwynne adjusted much more quickly than she says, and she is also a much, much better hand than she will admit. The fact is, she can do anything I can do that doesn't require more brawn than she has. We don't ask her to dig post holes, for instance. But anything else she can do.

When I married, I never thought about whether or not Gwynne would work outside with me. She looked pretty good, but I don't think I ever asked myself if she'd be a good cowboy or not. I wasn't smart enough to think about that, I guess. Gwynne's insistence on working out surprised me—not just getting on a horse and going for a ride, but actually working out.

But I didn't feel threatened by it. There was no reason to. One thing—when I was growing up, we sold a lot of horses, and we had used girls on horses a lot. We had become aware of the fact that, for the most part, girls handle young horses better than boys do. My sister† is an excellent horsewoman. So I wasn't surprised that Gwynne rode well and knew how to handle a horse. I think I was less involved with the macho cowboy thing than most men my age would have been at that time, because I'd seen girls who were good with horses.

I was glad to have Gwynne with me. She was feeling very isolated—she

† Helen Musgrave. See Chapter 5.

missed her family and the ocean and the trees and the whole works. Psychologically, it was extremely hard on her. It helped her a lot to get out—she liked to ride, and she was good with a horse. It helped me because she kept my rope horses in shape. I was on the rodeo circuit and she was good with rope horses. Also, if you live as isolated a life as we did then—we had no telephone and we didn't go to town or see the neighbors very often—it's nice to have your wife around doing things so there is somebody to talk to. It was partly economic too. We always worked for ourselves, so it was a question of getting things done as best we could and getting the banker paid.

We simply wouldn't have done as well if Gwynne didn't work, if we had to hire someone. The mobility we have now is due in large part to the fact that Gwynne has worked all these years.

And this is true of most of the younger women on ranches now. They are getting out and they are riding. They are more a part of the visible side of the ranch. They've always been important, but they weren't as visible as they are now simply because you see them on horseback.

Ranching has changed a lot over the years. It used to be that there were a lot of homestead families who needed work and a rancher could hire day labor. Ranchers' wives, for the most part, rode socially, but they didn't work out.

My mother was in the middle phase somewhere and never did anything outside. She kept the books and knew how to cook, and she had a flower garden. That's not to take anything away from her. She was part of a time when women were not very involved. They didn't need to be, and their husbands didn't want them around some of the men they had to hire.

Now we've got a situation where ranches are of necessity quite large and they've become mechanized to a certain extent. Labor, if you can get it at all, is very expensive. And women do have conveniences—refrigerators and mixers and microwave ovens—that are a tremendous help. It's now possible for a woman to get out, and she's needed much more than she ever has been. Every rancher I know who is my age uses his wife unless they have very small children. With the exception of that period in time, women do an awful lot of work. They are directly involved with the business and have an interest in it. This is a relatively new thing.

It's been very fortunate that Gwynne and the girls could help. The girls are excellent hands—I would put them up against any cowboys I know. Yet, it's not a macho thing with them. They'll take the time with animals that they need to, and sometimes boys don't.

I think eighty percent of all the cattle work we've done in twenty years, we've done ourselves. This is not a tremendous outfit, but it is fairly big. If you don't know the country, you might as well get off and walk. Gwynne and the girls know it and they know how it works. I can get more done with them than I could with six men hired on a day basis. We really miss the girls now. There are some things we wait to do until they come back to visit.

WE SIT AT A WELL-SEASONED WALNUT TABLE IN THE KITCHEN OF A WHITE frame house. The house is simply furnished but alive with healthy, voluptuous plants. A few canisters and a sourdough jug sit near the sink.

Donna has wispy, shoulder-length blond hair and big blue eyes, deep and liquid, like a doe's. She has a deerlike shyness as well. I have the feeling that she would bolt and disappear at a loud sound or sudden movement. She is petite and thin, fragile. Yet, in a few moments I realize this frailty is deceptive, like the tensile strength of tempered steel thread.

Donna was born and raised in Colorado Springs, Colorado, and received her B.A. in Political Science from Colorado State University. She had ridden but knew little about ranching until she married Corky eight years ago, when she was twenty-eight.

Corky had ranched all his life but lost his land near Pinedale, Wyoming, to the divorce settlement with his first wife. Corky and Donna leased land near Pinedale for several years and recently bought the North Fork Ranch. Like all who buy agricultural land today, with price set by real estate value rather than agricultural use, Donna and Corky have a lot of lean years to look forward to. They have two children—Eric, seven; and Leta, four.

When I married Corky, I knew ranching was a lot of work. Since then, I've found out exactly how much.

Right from the beginning, I wanted to learn every aspect of the life—spring, fall, winter, and summer. The first few years were rough because I didn't know anything. It takes a long time to learn, and I can't say that Corky was patient.

He got very irate when I wouldn't do things right. I wish he had more of a sense of humor sometimes, but he feels that if you go out there, you are supposed to do your work and do it right. Oh, well, I have learned since.

When we came to live on this ranch, I had absolutely no knowledge of cattle. Moreover, I was terrified when the mildest cow even looked my way. If I could have acquired the knowledge I needed as quickly as I got over my fear, I need not have asked all the questions that I now hear asked by others. Like Little Joe the Wrangler, I "didn't know straight up about a cow," and no one seemed to want to tell me anything.

"Watch—and see for yourself," was the best I could draw from my husband. I did watch and saw a lot, but that only whetted my curiosity. It was by no means enough to see how things were done; my inquiring mind demanded to know "Why?" Finally I hit upon a desperate ruse and it worked admirably. I would start for the telephone, saying to Charlie, "If I can't find out what I want to know about cows from you, I'll ring up Mr. Moore. He'll tell me!"

"I don't want any of the neighbors to know what an ignorant wife I have," was Charlie's flattering response to that, but he did relent and answer my questions. Little by little I learned about a cow, and now I fear that I have, along with that knowledge, a little of the supercilious attitude of the small boy who "always know'd."

—Mary Kidder Rak,
A Cowman's Wife.
Copyright © 1934 by Mary Kidder Rak.

I really like to work out, even though sometimes it is hard to keep house and cook at the same time. Corky is real considerate. He doesn't actually cook or scrub or anything like that, but he'll pick up his clothes and he doesn't make a mess any more than he has to. He's real careful not to come in if he has manure on his feet—things like that. I think I almost do better at my housework when I don't have much time, because it's a challenge. I don't like to leave a messy house. It's not too clean, but it passes.

I'm afraid I don't feel the same about cooking, especially during haying when I cook for six or seven people. Corky has always told me that I don't have to work in the hayfield since I cook, but I want to. Sometimes I wish I could forget the cooking—especially the night meal. I work as hard as anybody else all day, and I don't like to come home tired and have to get a meal. You can work out in the field under a hot sun all day, but somehow you never get as hot as you do standing over the stove. But somebody's got to cook. Tell your man to cook! [Laughs] You get a lot done ahead of time and freeze it. It's kind of a solution.

Sometimes I resent the domestic work. When we take our cows up to summer ground in the forest or bring them home, we get a lot of people to help us ride. It is a really enjoyable day, just trailing the cows, and it's fun. But I usually have to fix the lunch and then bring it along in the truck. I would rather be out on a horse.

I've learned the least about the mechanical aspect of ranching. We have an old John Deere tractor and I made it a point one year to watch just what Corky did about oil and the grease job. I even wrote it down in a book so I would know what weight to put in the engine and the transmission. But I haven't mechanicked a lot and that is probably my weakest point. I change the oil in my pickup and that's about it.

I don't know why I haven't learned more except that we do most of our mechanic work right before haying. We've just hired help and Corky wants to put them to work. That's always one thing the guys know how to do. And they know so much that I'd feel kind of funny standing out there, asking questions. I'd like to learn more. It's part of the whole thing.

I realize that a lot of ranchwomen don't work out. They spend their life in the kitchen and just take care of the kids. I guess most of the older women don't get out except when they have to. I think they miss out on a whole lot of things, like the calving and lambing in the spring and dragging the meadows and fencing and haying. They probably haven't learned how to drive a team or break a green horse. They've sat in the kitchen and said, "Well, I have my kids to take care of." But I believe strongly that you've got to be able to do both. Where there's a will, there's a way. You can get your kids out and you can do both if you want to.

You figure out how to work a tractor with a kid in your arms, or how to ride a horse and leave your kids at the truck and have them stay there when they're just two or three years old. Your kids learn to live out in that hayfield. They learn not to bawl or need a nap at a certain time, and they've gotta be about as versatile as you are.

There are some women who will condemn you for this and say that's no way to raise kids. But I disagree. I think the kids enjoy being out. You don't abuse them, certainly. I know a lot of women will send their kids off to preschool or something like that so they can get out, and I don't really think that's right, either.

When Eric was a baby, I would have to leave him in the house alone sometimes. We can't afford to hire help all year round because it's hard enough to pay for the place. In the winter, there were some things Corky can't do alone and I had to help him feed and drive the team, and break workhorses. It was too cold to take Eric out, and I left him for hours in the house alone, which was a bad thing. I worried continually. I was smarter with Leta. My father built her a little insulated box the size of a bale of hay. It could fit right in front on the sled and she would go with us and stay warm, even in twenty-below-zero weather.

I remember once when Eric was about three. He was riding on the back of the sled and fell off into the deep snow. We didn't miss him at first. Then we happened to look back. Here were all these cows gathered around, staring at something. Corky said, "That's Eric." He was back there bawling and all these old cows were staring at him and sniffing. It was the same with Leta. If we'd leave her in her box while we made the circle on the feed ground, those old cows would come over and wonder what she was.

I think kids are a big part of ranch life. I think they should learn that way of life, so when they get big enough to decide if they want to ranch, they know how to do it. Eric, even as small as he is, can do lots of things. He can drive the rake tractor, he has his own horse, he goes out to feed. He can even milk a cow. There is so much he can do. He's out with Corky all the time.

I love my kids, and I would never think of not having them. Corky loves kids. I never think about not being a mother.

I think the women's movement has a point. A lot of ranchwomen won't say that, but I do. There is a lot of male chauvinism in ranching. I don't really know whether it's chauvinism or just custom. But when I first started shearing sheep, Corky's dad gritted his teeth and said, "What are you doing shearing sheep?" That was a no-no. Corky's mother was the same way. I mean, they lived on a ranch all their life and she's raised all kinds of bum lambs. Yet, she's never sheared a sheep and she says, "No, it's not a woman's job." So this thing is in with Corky. They don't like you doing certain things. Maybe they just don't like you getting too capable. You know, it's their male ego. Or maybe they think the neighbors will say, "Look! His wife's out there shearing sheep. He should be doing it." I don't know what it is. They seem to have this old attitude that a woman is supposed to stay home and cook and only get out when they need her. They don't realize that the wife wants to do it and likes to do it, and it's her thing.

[One] day we rode the upper river pasture. The San Pedro flows northward, lazily at that time of the year, the current shallow and purling contentedly. We had been quiet, ourselves. [My husband] Dan always was, and my chatter had been stilled as we rode along, enjoying the cool breezes from the distant Huachucas and keeping a sharp watch for straying cattle. At least Dan was watching for cattle, and occasionally watching me.

"Why do you keep looking at me?" I asked, thinking of the unbridelike battered Stetson, and windblown hair. "You couldn't

be entranced by my sunburnt nose, so what are you thinking
about?"

"I'm thinking you ride like you'd been riding all your life," he
answered, surprisingly . . . The sky was bluer, suddenly, and the
birds in the willows were singing louder, or maybe the music was
in my own heart. My agonized endurance of all the miserable
hours in the saddle was justified. Dan thought I could ride.
Moreover, he had said so! The range horses probably thought it
an entirely silly proceeding, but they reluctantly allowed
themselves to be persuaded closer together, and then I learned
another range technique, and that a kiss from the saddle can be
very satisfactory.

—Elizabeth Ward,
No Dudes, Few Women.
Copyright © 1951 by Elizabeth Ward.

Corky's first wife and his mother stayed in the kitchen and cooked for haying. Cooking was a full-time thing. I don't know as Corky wants me out in the
field. Well, he does now because when you're a help out there, he can't quite
say, "Stay home in your kitchen all day." He doesn't say that.

Have I changed Corky? I don't know if anybody changes a man or not. But
yeah, I guess he realizes that women are going to do what they want. He says,
"No use telling you what you're going to do, because you'll do what you want
to, anyway."

Ranch life can be pretty frustrating. It's hard to make the payments. I guess
it is a littler easier if you had a ranch passed down from generation to generation. But I think the debt weighs heavily on Corky. I just figure that somehow
we'll make it, 'cause you gotta think positive. But it's quite a thing to have to
make these payments.

Corky had another ranch when he was married before and his former wife
just about took it away from him. He got the cows and equipment and she got
the ranch. The way the economy is, you can't split a ranch like that and each
of you come out with enough to really continue. She sold the land, so she came
out pretty good. But Corky had to kind of start from scratch. It's been hard
for him because he had it made once.

There are times when you wonder why you're doing this. Particularly in
those years when you lose about twenty-five dollars a day and you're paying
hired help twenty a day. You wonder—why in heck? And sometimes lambing
and calving is terribly frustrating. You'll sit with a little calf for a month, trying to get it to suck and then it will die. Or you get a spring storm and it kills
off a lot of little newborn calves. You've got them all in warm water in the

bathtub, trying to get them to come to, but you lose some. I don't like to see things die. When you do all you can and it just doesn't seem to be enough, you really feel frustrated, like, What's the use?

When I was a secretary, my work was over at five o'clock. But here you're not done even if it's four in the morning and you've been up all night. You want to go to bed, but if a heifer is ready to go, you've got to go out and wait 'til she's ready to pull. I let Corky sleep at nights. His work during the day is more demanding than mine, and he's gotten to where he can't do both.

I remember one night there were two heifers calving. I went out and I thought one would be O.K. I went with the other one. They both had their calves at exactly the same time, and the one I thought wouldn't have trouble did. The calf hung up on the lungs and died.

Another time, we had our heifers in the pen out here where we could look out the window and see what they're doing. One day we butchered a beef and were cutting it up. I had been up all night with one heifer and I was tired as the devil anyway. But I hadn't taken time to walk out through them. I had just looked out the window at them, and I didn't see anything ready. Later, we found one hiding in the corner with a calf stuck in her. We lost the calf. That makes you really mad because you didn't take the time to look. It would have taken two seconds to walk out there.

When you lose one, there's always that feeling of utter frustration. You think you could have done something else. That's when you want to give up.

Have I ever considered quitting? Oh, I think everybody does occasionally. You almost give up sometimes. But there are all the good times too. You lose one, but the next one is healthy and strong and there is nothing that makes you feel so grand. I can't think of anything else I'd rather do. This is our way of life. It's the only thing Corky knows; it's the only thing he's ever done.

What keeps me going? Probably the challenge of it all, really. Certainly not the money; it couldn't be the money. [Laughs] And I wouldn't be happy in a city. Here, there is something new to learn all the time, every day. I want to learn as much as I can. You're forever learning. It's a good thing you never learn it all. It's what keeps you going.

The thing we are trying to do [pay out the ranch] may not seem worth doing, but the urge to do it drives us on. It seems at times sordid and trivial, someone else before us has done it much better. It seems useless to struggle toward the mediocre, but nevertheless we go on and perhaps learn as we go. Perhaps that is what we are here for—for our objective just to learn. . . . There are always times in any undertaking when one only longs to quit, times of profound discouragement, of stress of circumstances that

seem too great to cope with. But quitting is usually the hardest
way out. . . . It makes me wonder if people instinctively cling to
their own self-made crosses, after a problem has been too difficult
to solve. Yet you still feel that it is individually your own problem,
and you struggle on with it.

—Margaret Duncan Brown, 1917 diary entry,
in *Shepherdess of Elk River Valley*, 1967.

7

Cowgirls on Contract:
WOMEN RANCH HANDS

Edith Kendall, 1922.

Maggie Howell

Miller Ranches, south of Daniel, Wyoming

MAGGIE STUMBLED INTO RANCH WORK. A MAYVILLE, WISCONSIN, WELDER'S daughter, she visited friends in Colorado on her way back to college in Mexico. She liked Colorado so much she decided to stay. She found a part-time job at Buffalo Park Ranch, a horse ranch in Evergreen, Colorado. Three years later, she married a schoolteacher-carpenter.

After four years of marriage, she and her husband decided to separate. Maggie traveled to Nepal and spent several months at Mount Everest base camp. She grew homesick for the West. When she returned to Colorado, she and her husband decided to make their separation permanent, and the Buffalo Park Ranch was about to sell out to development. It felt like the time to move on to Wyoming.

Maggie worked short, fill-in stints for two other ranches before finding her present job at the Miller Ranches, a group of twelve ranches in the Pinedale area, run by Mildred Miller and her son Jim. With that job, Maggie felt a firm commitment to her career as a ranch hand.

"I guess I didn't realize for a long time that I might be able to work on a ranch as a full-time job," she reflects. "But it was something I never could get enough of. I just wanted to do it more. It became—oh, not an obsession, but just something that grew stronger and stronger, something I felt I had to get out and do. I was going to do it."

Maggie finds her work as a ranch hand is also her recreation, the love of her life, much as it is for athletes who turn pro to finance their sports—skiers, surfers, tennis buffs. With her strong, sunbronzed jaw, her blunt-cut brunette hair, and the impalpable aura of the well-traveled, Maggie emanates an easy, athletic goodwill. I could as easily picture her instructing ski students at Vail as bucking bales on this ranch south of Jackson Hole, Wyoming.

At 7 A.M., we head out with the team to feed. The sun, just risen, streams very pure and bright, almost horizontal, through the snow crystals that hang like weightless diamonds in the thin, subzero air. The hay bales are a deep golden-brown; the horses, iridescent in their blackness; the fat Hereford cows and calves, an auburn so rich it is almost magenta. Like early technicolor films, the colors are too rich, too deep to be believed. But they are real.

I was looking for a job when I learned that Miller's needed a night-rider for calving. I came to talk to Jim Miller. I told him I had never night-rode before and he said that was O.K. I asked him if he minded hiring a woman and he told me he'd hired them before; they seemed to make pretty good night-riders. I said, "O.K., I'll take the job." I came to work in March and started calving.

Maggie Howell, feeding hay, near Daniel, Wyoming, 1980.

I had never calved before. It was all new to me. Sid Skiver, an old cowboy who'd been with Miller forty-three years, was kind of running the calving operation. He had been here so long, he had taught everybody around here, all the young fellas who manage the Miller Ranches. He had been their teacher and he became mine.

He taught me a whole lot. We'd go out together and he had such an eye for everything. I'd say, "Sid, tell me a little more," and he'd start explaining some more things. I know he wanted to use the words that most of the guys use, like —oh, I don't know if I could say it [laughs], but words for the female anatomy—but he was always so polite with me. He'd say, "Maggie, I want to just use these words but I can't quite say them to you. But you'll figure it out."

Sid broke me in and I started night-riding. Then Sid would come up to the calving sheds about five in the morning when I was finishing my last ride of the night. He'd pick me up and we'd go through them again. After we'd come back, he'd bring out his little bottle of Yellowstone he had stashed somewhere and he'd say, "Here, have an eye opener." About five-thirty in the morning, a shot of that old Yellowstone . . .

We calve up on the hill. We have about forty acres up there, you can kind of see it from here. Our calving sheds are up there and then we've got two big

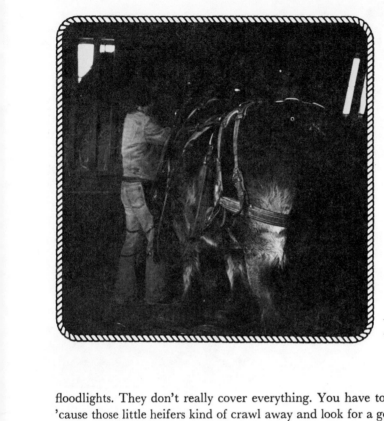

*Maggie Howell
harnessing.*

floodlights. They don't really cover everything. You have to be on the lookout
'cause those little heifers kind of crawl away and look for a good hiding spot.

Every couple hours, you ride through with a lantern and check every heifer.
If something's really close to calving, you put it in the pen. I had a walky-talky
in the shed, and if I had any trouble I'd give Robin a call. He's my foreman
and he'd come up and give me a hand. If it was an easy pull, I could handle it
myself, but if there were complications Robin was always there.

I remember the first time I ran into trouble. I was just starting my first ride
of the evening and I had a heifer that had gotten into the ditch over on her
back. She couldn't right herself and the calf was already starting to come. The
cow was just about gone. I kind of panicked at first 'cause I wasn't expecting
to find a heifer all four sneakers up. All I could think was, "Oh no. I don't
want to lose a heifer." I got some help and we got a rope on the cow and
turned her over. Saved the heifer but lost the calf.

From then on, things like that happened all the time. That whole spring, it
was one after another. We had a heifer with a lumpy jaw. She was kind of
poor anyway and they were thinking about shooting her but they never did. I
came across her early in the morning and she had started to calve. The head
was out but there was a foot behind and she couldn't handle it. She was just
too weak to calve. We tried to push the calf back in so we could get the foot
but the head was too swollen. We had to dismember the calf and pull it out in
parts. Pretty gruesome. Had to do that several times since.

We calved out about eight hundred heifers that spring. Calving—a lot of it is just experience. Getting out there and looking and looking and looking. All of a sudden you start tuning into it and you get a finer tuning the more you're out there. That's why Sid, working for Miller's over half his life, was an expert. I think it takes almost all your life to learn it. I'm by no means an expert, but I know a lot more than I did when I came here.

After I hired on here, I found out that they had been trying to decide whether to send me to one place or the other. I didn't go to the first place because the fellow there wasn't willing to have a woman work for him. He didn't think I could feed hay and buck bales and pretty much do a man's job. So I went to the Todd Place. [Each of the twelve Miller Ranches carries the name of its original owner.] It all worked out fine because Robin, my foreman, was willing to see it work out. At this point, I don't think anybody has any doubts.

At first, I was kind of on the bottom of the totem pole. I usually got all the old horses and the old harness—they didn't have anything else to give me. After I'd been here awhile, two fellas came up with two different workhorses. Another came driving in one day with a harness—not a new harness, but a nice one that wasn't all pieced together. Somebody else came up with some parts I needed to fix my hames. They were all sort of contributing to make it a little easier for me because they knew I was working with old stuff. That felt nice, felt like they were acknowledging what I was doing.

I had a lot of support and cooperation from everybody I was working with. All of them were real willing to share what they knew, and that's good. I feel very much at ease with the men I work around. I respect them and they respect me. I do my share of the work, they do theirs. And they'll still open a door for me, which is nice. I wouldn't want to be one of the boys.

Sid would always say, "Maggie, haven't I always been a gentleman toward you?" and I'd say, "Yes, you have." "Well," he'd say, "you've always been a lady toward me."

The skill I probably lack most is mechanics. I'm not much of a mechanic and I don't like to do it. I don't like to drive the big equipment like the backhoes and the Cats. That's fine with Robin because that's kind of his area. He's really good at the backhoe, he's good at the Cat, he's an excellent mechanic. It's kind of a nice balance between us because he doesn't like to ride a whole lot anymore. He was in a critical accident about seven years ago and his balance is way off. Yet riding is one of the things I prefer to do, so it's an even deal. Works out good.

I don't mind tractors, but that's probably 'bout the biggest equipment that I'll drive. My tractor bucked me off last year. We have one three-wheeler tractor. They're kind of dangerous anyway, and I wasn't too crazy about driving it. I had a post pounder on the back and I'd come across a ditch. My right rear tire hung up on the ditch and it spun me around. The post pounder caught in the ground and pivoted me right around. It held the tractor straight up in the air. That post pounder made kind of like a tripod. If it hadn't been for that, the tractor probably would have come clear over on me. When it came around like that, it threw me off. It threw me off real good. Scared the shit out of me.

I always have had bad luck with machinery. One day I was on my way up to cow camp. I had the big stock truck and I had all my horses in there ready to go to the roundup. Had six horses in there. I was coming up to the highway up over the top of that hill. I shifted down and started to hit the brake and realized I had no brakes. I kept hitting the brake but nothing was there and I was coming onto the main highway. I tried to shift down once more, but I was afraid I would lose the gear that I was in to begin with, so I went back to third. I'm starting to really barrel down that hill and I looked out and there's a car coming. I thought, Oh my God, I'm just going to have an awful wreck. All I could think about was my horses and my dogs.

I came barreling onto the highway and I hit the barrow pit, came back up, was on the road, and just missed the car that was coming down the highway. They kind of swung off and hit the barrow pit themselves. They were cursing me, shaking their fists at me.

I just kept going. I still didn't have any brakes, but I was on the highway and I was headed for a flat stretch of road. I didn't get the stock truck stopped until I got to Daniel. I got out and said, "That's it. I'm not taking this truck an inch further."

That was probably the scariest moment of my life, thinking of wrecking with all those horses. And I didn't even have a horse go down. They were all standing when I got them to Daniel.

Course, you can get into a jackpot with horses too. I had a runaway last year. I was coming out of a gate and I was off the rack closing it. My team wasn't tied all that tight, but I didn't figure they needed to be. They decided to take off and head for home and kind of left me behind. I finally caught up with them and jumped up on the sled. Then I realized that my mare had rubbed off her bridle. I couldn't control anything from on top of the sled, so I jumped down. I didn't think fast enough that my mare didn't have her blinders on anymore, and she saw me jump down. I came up behind her and she kicked my hand. Broke a bone in it.

Then they really took off. They were coming back to the barn, and they were coming into where I parked. I thought, "Oh great. They're just going to stop at the usual place." But instead, they continued on and went into the barn with my sled on. Kind of reshaped my sled a little bit.

I got a couple horses that if they get too much of a load on, or if they get in a tight spot, they're going to balk. They balked for about five hours one day. There was nothing I could do to move them. It was forty below zero and the wind blowing like a son of a gun. I was pretty much of a screaming maniac out there. Finally, I just kind of gave up and I was about ready to walk back to the house. I thought, "Well, I'll try one more time." They just moved it out like nothing had happened . . .

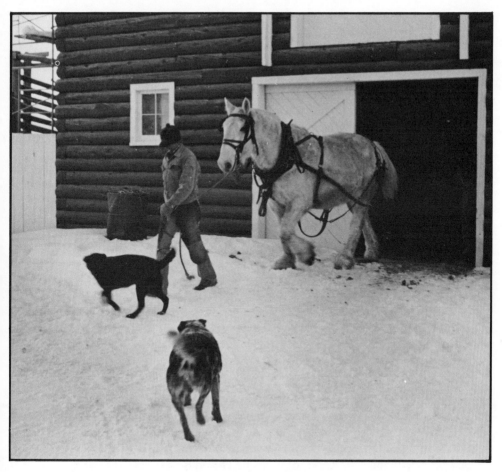

Maggie leading a horse out to hitch up to the sled.

Last winter was so severe. I had double the cows that I have this year. I feed three hundred and twenty-five this winter, and last year I had close to five hundred and fifty. It was such a nasty winter. So much snow, so much wind. For three weeks it never got above twenty below. So last fall I was considering —maybe I should go South. Find someplace in Arizona to work for the winter, a feedlot or something. But Robin said, "Well, listen. That winter was a tough one. It's going to be easier, believe me." I said, "Well, I don't know . . ." But he was right. This was an easier winter. I don't know—I'm probably a little more competent than I was last winter. But this winter I don't have too many complaints at all.

I have been trying lately to think of myself as working for
someone else at this job and find it stimulates and gives me a
different outlook. I am very thankful to be able to be out of doors,
to work by myself and as the very old say, "to have my faculties."
I am often driven and wish I had time to live more graciously.
But I suppose one can cultivate a poise in business as well as in
social life. One thing I know: I have passed another milepost. I
have quit being lonesome. I stop and wonder about it sometimes
and have the same reaction I have had in realizing that I am
recovering from an illness—a sense of restfulness and peace with
yet the memory of what lies so immediately behind me.

> —Margaret Duncan Brown,
>   diary entry, around 1920, two years after her husband died
>   and she decided to pay out the ranch alone,
>   in *Shepherdess of Elk River Valley*, 1967.

I get lonely out here. Sure. Of course. God, yeah. But that's part of the price
of this kind of work. I prefer loneliness to crowds of people in big cities. It has
its drawbacks, especially in the winter. The summers aren't too bad, but the
winters are rough. You can get real lonely. But I think everybody has to deal
with that, no matter where they are. I don't feel that alone.

> When fate in the form of a younger, fairer girl de-spoused me, I
> sought a substitute teacher for my little cowpunchers and became,
> for a time . . . solely a woman-with-a-little-ranch; actually, a
> woman-about-to-lose-a-little-ranch. The odds were overwhelming.
> No help, no capital, no credit and—the greatest of all
> handicaps—no rain. But when everything is against you, when
> you haven't got a ghost of a show, the injustice of the battle
> enrages you to superhuman endurance and fighting strength.
>   When I read *Gone with the Wind* I was greatly touched by the
> pluck of Scarlett O'Hara, determined to save her beloved Tara,
> the plantation where she was born, with her bare hands. In my
> case, "Tara" was a little rawhide outfit that added up
> economically to nothing but hard work and hard luck.
> Sentimentally it totaled more. It was the home of my cows and
> horses and dogs; my own roots had dug in there for seven dry
> years. I couldn't abandon it.
>
> >   —Eulalia Bourne,
> >   *Woman in Levi's*.
> >   Copyright © 1967 by Eulalia Bourne.

My attitude toward work has changed since I've been working on ranches. I guess when I got out of school, I didn't have a motivation in me to really work. Work didn't mean a whole lot to me. Now work is such a part of my life. It's almost the love of my life. I enjoy my work, and when I don't have anything to do I start climbing the walls. Usually end up at the Daniel Bar. So my work is important.

I visited my folks over Christmas in Arizona. They're in a retirement place down there. The thought of being old and retiring from your life's work is almost disgusting to me. I see a lot of bored, unhappy older people. I feel that I never ever want to retire.

It's very enlightening to me to see somebody in their seventies just jump on their horse and do an amazing job, cutting and working cows. You can see in them that that's their life and that's their work and they still love it. Sid was that way. Mildred Miller's another. She's an incredible lady. A hell of a hand and a very unassuming woman. For the outfit that she has, you'd never know it.

My father says, "Well, you can't do this the rest of your life." Maybe he's right, but for now I think it's all right. It feels good to me. Miller has just told me I can start running my own herd, which is nice. That's kind of an exciting thought. I mean, who can plan out any of their future?

Ranches don't provide a retirement program. At least the ranches around here don't, that I know of. Sid was a good example of that, being with Miller's forty-three years. He did have a Miller ranch of his own, but he started drinking pretty heavily and lost that. He was still always Miller's top cowman. But you could see him getting that feeling, "What am I going to do when . . ."

I could see a lot of pain in Sid. He wasn't able to do a lot of the physical work anymore. You could see he was very, very worried about not being able to do the job. His work was his whole life. He would still ride a horse sometimes when he couldn't even walk. [Sid died in 1979 when the lodge he was staying in burned down.]

My mother's not so worried about my ranch work as she is concerned about me finding a man. I guess she worries about me a lot, being alone in my work and alone in my life. Not having a husband and not having a family. I don't quite fit into the pattern she wanted.

I don't know if I'll marry again. At this point in my life I don't know who'd even have me. It would have to be . . . I don't know who it would have to be. Certainly somebody who's had more life experience than Sublette County. I don't know. I'm not really looking, but I'm not really *not* looking, either. Right now, I like my single life.

I'm thirty-one, and I bet I'm stronger than I was when I was twenty-one. I'm in better shape physically and probably mentally, too. It seems the older I get, the fitter I get.

Maggie married Jerry Hermansen in August 1980.

Early-morning feeding, Maggie Howell and friend.

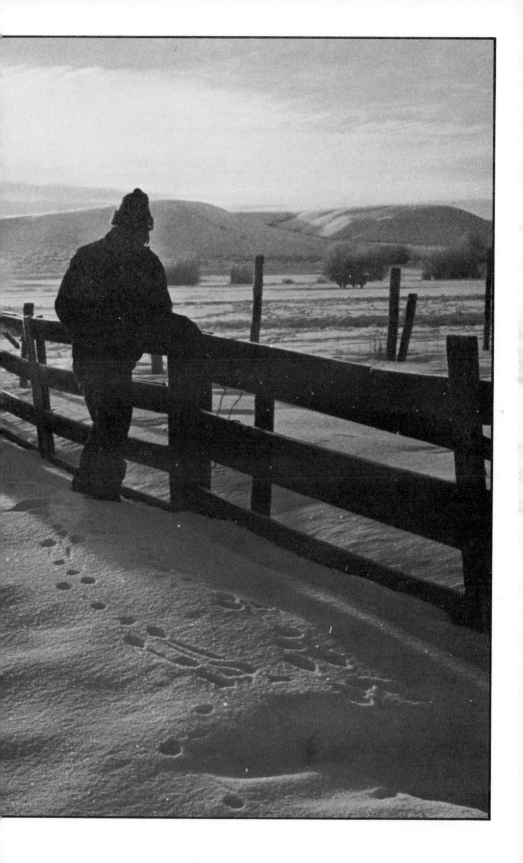

"A lot of women helped their husbands drive cattle of their
own," wrote Thelma Kimmel of her friend Vivian Thorp
McClarey, "but Vivian did the job for a living. Life's 'silver
platter' was usually a tin one in some cattle or harvest camp, and
often she cooked the food that went on it."

Vivian was the granddaughter of the first settler in the Yakima
Valley of the Washington Territory. Old Fiddling Mortimer
Thorp would have been proud of his granddaughter—small and
wiry, she knew horses, cattle, and the expansive Washington
country east of the Columbia. Her father died when she was
young and she had to fend for herself. She turned to the skills she
knew best and "worked for any cattle drive that would hire her."

———

All of us Thorps were born in the saddle—us older ones. My
mother, Harriet Hattin, was fourteen when she married my
father, Bayliss Thorp, and she helped him drive cattle all over
Washington Territory—babies and all. There were six of us and
many's the time she hid out in the swamps with us when
unfriendly Indians were about.

I grew up in a big, raw country. My father died young, leaving
my mother with six children to raise, so we all had to go to work
early.

I guess I drove more cattle, broke more horses and ran more
races than any woman I ever knew. But do you know, when I
rounded up and drove cattle for Frye and Company they
wouldn't list a woman's name on the payroll? I got my wages,
though.

Cattle and horses were about all I knew except cooking in a
chuckwagon if I had to. Not my choice of working for a living,
but I had to eat. One thing I always had was a good horse of my
own. That was something all the Thorps took the greatest pride
in—their Kentucky-bred saddle mounts.

I felt much better on a horse than cooking. I learned to pick
out racers; I've forgotten how many races I rode in—clear to
Montana sometimes. I wore a big hat and boots and a riding
skirt.

What was the most exciting moment in my life? I guess it was
Halley's comet. No, I think maybe it was when they chased Harry
Tracy, the bandit, and caught him over near where I was working
in Creston.

Wait a minute—I know! It was when my horse beat Maude

Lillie's in a race. Because you just didn't beat Maude Lillie in anything. Maude was a beautiful, educated, part-Indian girl whose mother owned much of the town of Toppenish.

Well, Maude used to ride with the cowboys just for the fun of it. She had fine horses. Later she got an airplane and flew from Canada to the cattle camps for the thrill. So naturally there was money put up on that race, though I don't think anyone expected me, who had to ride for a living, to come out the winner, much as Thorp horseflesh was respected. It wasn't a very joyful time for the Toppenish Queen, though she really had a heart of gold.

—From quotes in "All of Us Thorps Could Ride!"
by Thelma Kimmel, *True West,* January–February 1974.

Vivian Thorp McClarey died in 1970.

Marcia Brazell

Spring Valley Ranch, the Black Hills near Pringle, South Dakota

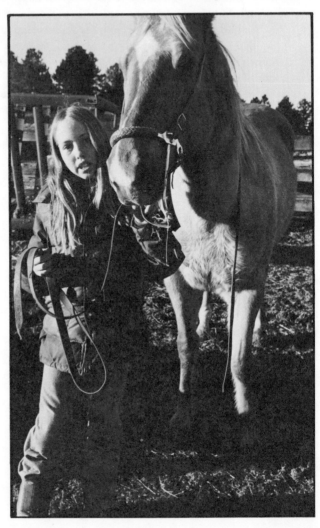

Marcia Brazell's daughter, Susie, Spring Creek Ranch, near Custer, South Dakota, 1979.

MARCIA AND I MEET IN FRONT OF PRINGLE'S ONE-ROOM SCHOOLHOUSE ON AN unseasonably warm and sunny February afternoon. We talk in the cab of her pickup until school lets out and her three children—Shirley, twelve; Susie, eleven; and Casey, nine—jump in the truck. Then we drive the seven miles to Spring Valley Ranch headquarters, weaving through a maze of side roads which, in this forested area, all look the same. Now I understand why Marcia suggested we meet in town rather than directing me to the ranch. On the way, we pass Marcia's trailer, snug in a stand of Black Hills pine.

Marcia has known her employers, Ned and Doris Westphal, almost from the time they moved West from Minnesota and bought this registered Quarter Horse and commercial cattle outfit in 1970. Marcia's husband Larry helped the Westphals build their barn and later worked for them from time to time. Marcia helped out too, and has worked at Spring Valley full time since 1975. When Marcia and Larry divorced in 1976, Marcia and the kids stayed on.

Marcia is the Westphals' only full-time employee, and the three of them are more like an extended family than traditional employers and employee. Marcia helps with everything—the cooking, cleaning, and washing as well as the work outside. Her children come back to Westphals' house after school. The two families usually eat together. If Marcia is tied up, Ned or Doris will pick up the kids or take them to an appointment. Discipline is shared, and when the children are home, they are as likely to go with Ned or Doris as with Marcia. They each have chores around the ranch.

Marcia's financial relationship with the Westphals is untraditional, as well. Marcia does not receive a set wage. Rather, Ned and Doris see that she has enough for her needs. They recently set up a profit-sharing program to provide for her children's education and she is named in their will.

Marcia is soft-spoken, a little shy. She speaks slowly, as if weighing each word before it comes out. Her ash-blond hair, shagged on top but hanging to the middle of her back, makes her appear younger than her thirty-one years.

I dreamed all my life of being on a ranch or a farm. I was raised, mostly, in Rapid City [South Dakota]. My mom was raised on a dairy farm in eastern South Dakota and my brother Johnny was always sent to the farm in the summertime to help my grandparents. Us girls were not allowed because that wasn't really the place for us. Besides, both my parents worked and I knew I had to be home and help.

I never argued about it. I guess I always learned to do what my parents said and stay out of trouble. My mom had a cafe and my two sisters and I were either down there helping or at home taking care of the house. I spent a lot of time babysitting. It was nothing to have ten kids around. But I always wanted to be on a farm, a ranch. . . .

Has there been, in the last hundred years, a boy born who did not at one time or another want to be a cowboy? Hero of the Great American Dream, most inexorably Western of all Westerners, his way of life and code of ethics are familiar and enduring. Enchanted word—"cowboy." Visions of fast horses, wide-open spaces, and the desire for freedom that is in the heart of every boy. Every boy, and, once in a while, a little girl.

At the age of five, I was the two-gunned scourge of Brown

County, Minnesota. I gulped down Ralston every morning
because it sponsored Tom Mix. On the radio and in the comic
strips, I followed the Lone Ranger and Tonto ("Hi ho, Silver,
awaaay!") in their relentless pursuit of the Bad Men. I spent
those dreadful mornings in kindergarten thinking about the next
Saturday afternoon Gene Autry movie. My favorite book was a
dog-eared volume called, simply, *The Book of Cowboys*. Many
were the days and nights I spent in bed, gasping with asthma and
wheezing merrily as I read my cowboy book and one called *Little
Rose of the Mesa*. During the long, northern winter nights, with
the snow piled up against the window, as I lay restless, choking
for breath, honestly fearful lest I might die before morning, I
promised myself that one day I would be strong and healthy. One
day I would ride horses and walk in clean, sunlit air. "When I
grow up," I thought to myself, "if I ever do, I shall go to Arizona
and be a cowboy."

—Jo Jeffers,
Ranch Wife.
Copyright © 1964 by Jo Jeffers.

I dreamed of it quite often. In fact, in high school I dated a guy that
worked on a ranch. Our dream, his and mine, was to get married and have
kids and have a big ranch. That's how we spent our weekends in the summer,
either on the tractor in the hayfield or checking cattle. That was about the first
taste I really got of doing anything like that. But our plans kind of fell
through. He went one way and I went the other. [Laughs]

I got out of high school and went to beauty school and then I got married.
As I look back on it now, I was too young, really. I always thought, If I have
to take care of my mom's home and babysit all these kids, why not have a
home and family of my own? I met Larry and we got married.

Larry's folks had a ranch. We were going to buy into the ranch but it just
didn't work out. It wasn't a big enough ranch and there wasn't enough profit
to support two families. They had talked about incorporating it, but I think
they saw at an early stage of the game that that wasn't going to work either.
There was enough work for everybody but it just wasn't profitable enough.

So we came to Custer [eleven miles from Pringle]. I worked in a nursing
home, I worked for different motels cleaning rooms, I was a cook at a little
drive-in, I was a dispatcher for the Sheriff's Department. Just odds and ends,
you know, whatever I could pick up.

We met Ned and Doris because my husband worked for the man who built
their place. Larry was working on the timber and doing carpentry work. Ned
and Doris were going somewhere and asked us to come down and look after
the place. My husband was to do the chores and then go about his timber
work. I'd be here during the day to watch things, and after a while, I was the
one that did all the chores.

It was a relief for me to come down here. We lived in a little tiny trailer. This is a small house, but it seemed like a mansion to me. [This interview takes place in the Westphals' two-bedroom bungalow-off-the-barn.] And I loved doing the chores outside.

Now and then, Larry helped Ned and Doris put up the hay and different things. They told us we could move our trailer onto their land. We decided to because this was the type of life Larry had always had and the kind he really liked. That was in 1975, I think, and that's when Ned asked me to come full time.

That was in the summertime and we were trying to put up hay. They had a camp going at the time, had a bunch of youngsters here from the YMCA in Minneapolis. I did a lot of the cooking and cleaning, running errands, driving tractors, changing oil. You name it, I did it. They even nicknamed me "gofer."

Dad taught us quite a bit, because we were his helpers, his hired hands. We were more like gofers. We'd go for this and go for that. Everything he taught us, it saved him that much time.

Like if we were working on some machinery. If he could get us started on something, then he could go ahead and do something else. We'd get it done that much quicker. One time he was custom haying for somebody and my sister and I showed up with some parts that he needed. He just told us to go change them. There was this gentleman there, he couldn't believe that us girls were working on the machinery. But to us it was fun to be able to work around things like that. It took the place of Tinkertoys, I guess. Same with the horses and cattle.

I must have been about thirteen the first time somebody hired me to do some cow work. Before that, it was always just going with Dad and it was more a pleasure than to be hired. If you got to go, it was really something. But long about thirteen, I started working for an older guy. He'd call me up on a day basis and I started riding for him off and on, as an extra hand. He paid me something like five dollars a day and I probably thought I had me a bunch.

I started working for Fuchs off and on in about 'seventy-seven. Holly [Mr. Fuchs] would hire me to move cattle or something. And then last year his kids were all going to be gone [Becky, Jean and Ethan—see Chapter 9] and he asked me if I'd work full time. I helped take care of the cattle and worked with the horses, the breeding program, and everything.

Now I'm working heavy equipment because the money is pretty good. You can't really complain about it. I'll go back to ranching sooner or later. I know that. I'll never stay completely away from it.

It's hard for a woman to get a job as a ranch hand. They don't
think you're as capable of handling everything, and it's kind of a
trick to find a job. But just before I came up here I was asked to
help in a calving situation. Felt pretty good to be asked. I don't
think I'll have too much trouble finding a ranch job when the
time comes.

—Debby Kenton, age 24, Thedford, Nebraska.
At the time of this interview, February 1980,
Debby was working on a road crew in Scotts Bluff, Nebraska.

Larry got to where he didn't want to be around doing the ranch work and
he went back into the timber. I don't know what happened. This ranch wasn't
his, and I don't know if that kind of bothered him or what. But the whole ten
years we were together, it seemed we grew farther apart rather than closer.

We divorced in 1976. I kept the kids and stayed here. It wasn't hard for me
to adjust to being a single parent. For a family situation, I always was the one
to make the decisions, so it wasn't hard for me to adjust to that. In fact, it was
easier in a way. It was kind of a relief from the tension. Even now it doesn't
bother me that I'm alone down here with the kids. It seemed like I always had
to do a lot of things on my own. Even when I was younger it was that way,
with my folks gone a lot and me home doing housework.

I have always felt at home down here. Ned and Doris have always made us
feel like part of the family. We spend holidays together when we can. They
have taken the kids on as if they were their own too. It's a very healthy environment, especially for me being a single parent.

The kids are with me when they're off from school—on the weekends, in the
summertime. If I was working in a job in town or something, there would be a
babysitter. This way they're with me and we have made them take on some responsibilities. They know how to do the chores. If we've had to go out and do
something with the cattle and we've left the kids here, come chore time they'll
take care of things.

Susie and Casey have adjusted quite nicely. Susie loves anything to do with
horses. She rides all the time. She wants to be a jockey when she grows up, and
I know she'll end up doing something with horses—riding on the racetrack,
jumping, training, something. This is the perfect place for her. And Casey—all
last spring and summer he would ask to stay in the bunkhouse. He wanted to
be with the boys. He would get up with them at six o'clock in the morning and
work all day like he was eighteen or nineteen years old, cleaning the barns,
running the bobcat [a small multipurpose tractor], hauling hay or sawdust.
This fall Doris asked him what he wanted to be paid for the summer work he
had done and he said, "That's O.K. I don't want anything."

Shirley Brazell.

It's harder on Shirley because she's more feminine and she'd rather be where she can do more city things. She loves attention. She just thrives on it. I've tried to make it so she is involved a little bit. She's getting to the age where she does some cooking and different things. She always wanted to play the piano, so she's taking lessons in that. And then she got involved in ballet dancing. I think that has helped. She's learning now that she doesn't have to do without that stuff just because she lives down here.

My duties here aren't that hard. I do a lot of the running for parts and feed. Some days it's nothing for me to go to Hot Springs and Custer both. Sometimes I clean house, sometimes I cook. I do all the bookkeeping and get everything ready for the C.P.A. at the end of the year. I help clean the barns. About three years ago, I even scraped and painted the barns. I had some help but I did most of it myself. I fix fence. I drive the tractor. I change the oil in the vehicles.

When I first started working here, I hauled water a whole lot. Water in this area is very scarce, and in the summertime we have the cattle out on open-range Forest Service permits. The only water they get is what we haul to them. Now we've got a 1,500-gallon tank, but before we had only a 350-gallon tank. It was nothing for me to haul eight or nine loads. Sometimes I'd even be hauling water at midnight. The animals needed it, you know.

I have never had a basic salary, really. It was never, "You get so much a month," or anything like that. I have always felt that money isn't everything. Ned and Doris give us our meat and we eat a lot of meals with them. We have a place to park our trailer and our utilities are paid. They buy my work clothes. If there's a special thing coming up, like a birthday or something, Ned and Doris help out. Like one year, Ned said that the kids needed a stereo and bought them one.

When they go to Denver during the National Stock Show, they always take me down. We've taken the kids to Colorado, through the Rockies, a couple of times. There would have been no way I could have done that on my own.

It's always been what I need, when I need it. I had an old car that needed repairing very bad, so one Christmas they fixed my car up for my present. Last year, I got more than what I have in the past because both the girls had orthodontist work done and I had to have a lot of dental work too.

I think nowadays we should go back to more of this instead of "You give me this much and I'll do this much." I think we should go to more of a bartering system. I think that's why we've grown to be more like a family than employer and employee.

Now we're going to change this a little bit. Ned and Doris are working out a profit-sharing program with me so that the kids will have something for their college education and all that. And they have me signed up for health and life insurance.

I'm here every day of the week. I don't get any days off, unless the kids have something special going. Then I know I can have that day.

The other jobs I've had were not very satisfying. Cleaning homes and motel rooms, cooking at a drive-in, working as a dispatcher. Well, there just weren't many rewards. I liked the nursing home because I was helping people. But you see these people that are nothing and you know once they were very energetic. You get close to them, and then they die. It's hard.

This working on a ranch, there's so many challenges. You never know from day to day what you're going to be doing, if you're going to be hauling horses to the vet or pulling a calf. I love to work with animals and see the babies born. If they need your help and you can keep them alive, it's something fantastic.

Melody Harding

Bar Cross Ranch, near Cora, Wyoming

Melody Harding and dog, Bar Cross Ranch near Cora, Wyoming, 1980.

5 A.M. MELODY SQUATS ON AN ANCIENT T-STOOL, MADE FROM TWO SCRAPS OF two-by-four, and milks the cow. Already she has chopped the ice in the water tanks and fed the horses and cattle in the corral. The barn's thin walls break the whorling February wind but offer little insulation against the cold, and Melody leans into the cow for heat. The rhythmic pull on the warm, greased teats sends streams of steaming milk into the pail. Against the galvanized aluminum each jet resonates, musical and clear.

Melody finishes with the first cow and pours half the milk into a couple dented metal plates. The barn cats that have been waiting, yellow-eyed and patient in the corner, swarm the plates as Melody turns to milk the second cow.

When she has stripped all three cows, she carries the bucket to the porch and separates the milk. Then she walks to the horse barn and harnesses her team. Her small but calloused hands fasten the various pieces of harness with a practiced assurance. Finally, she is ready for breakfast and fixes it for her husband Richard, and herself. By 7:30, as Richard leaves for his job as a road

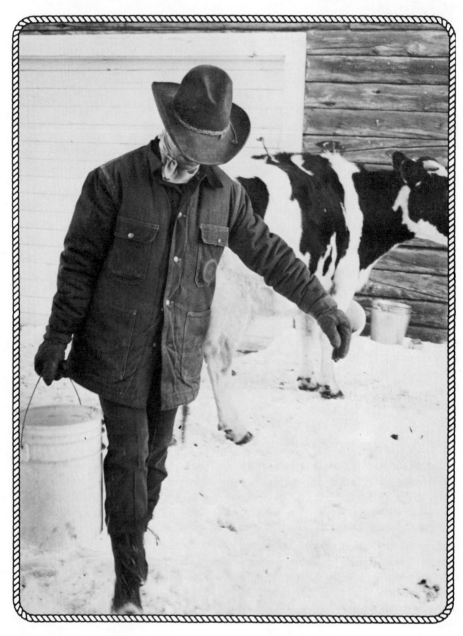

Melody Harding done with the milking.

equipment operator for Sublette County, Melody has her team hitched to the hay sled and pointed toward the feed ground.

Each day, the chores are the same. Yet, Melody never tires of them. Regular and rhythmical, they are pleasant in their familiarity, like finger exercises for a concert pianist.

Melody has worked on this thousand-cow outfit for ten years, been foreman for six. She grew up on her grandparents' ranch near Lander, Wyoming, and ranch work is the one and only thing she has ever yearned to do.

Melody chews (yes, tobacco), and the pocket of her denim jacket has the familiar circle worn white by her can of Skoal. But Melody is hardly rough and tough. With blond hair hanging about her tiny waist, a broad smile, even, white teeth, and a flawless complexion, she looks more like a model than a twenty-nine-year-old woman hardened to the land.

Melody is a very private person. Except for rodeos in the summer, she rarely leaves the ranch. Aside from her folks, she seldom has company. Her husband, dogs, horses, cows, and cats are enough company for her. Her world is complete within the confines of the ranch.

Melody's husband, Richard, came originally from New York. They met when Richard hired on at the ranch in 1973, and they were married two years after.

Getting along with animals is a gift. I've known people who have been around cattle for years and years and they just don't seem to have that special knack. I can get along with a lot of horses that other people can't. It's not that I'm so good or that I have so much experience. Some people are gifted to play the piano. They don't even have to read music, they can play anything as long as they've heard it once. To a certain extent, it's the same with animals.

It's just a little rapport we have between us. Maybe I'm real close to their mentality or something. [Laughs] We understand each other. But I don't feel like it's all my own doing. Roping and shoeing are obviously things that you've got to practice on to be good. But I think the other—working with horses and cows and doing a good job with them—is partly a talent or a gift.

I've always loved cattle and horses. My dad wasn't a rancher. He quit ranching when he got married. Said that was the end of his starvation. He was going to get into something that he could keep the family on real well. He's a carpenter, and apparently he's never had any desire to go back to ranching. He doesn't miss it at all.

But I was raised pretty much on my grandparents' ranch. Mom and Dad and I always lived real close and I spent most of my time with Bap and Pa. That's what we called my grandparents, Bap and Pa. Mom spent a good deal of her time there too, because they had a huge garden and she was always helping with that. We hayed with horses, and she helped in the hayfield, driving the buck rake or whatever. Dad helped in the evenings, mostly by building things like a chicken coop, a corral.

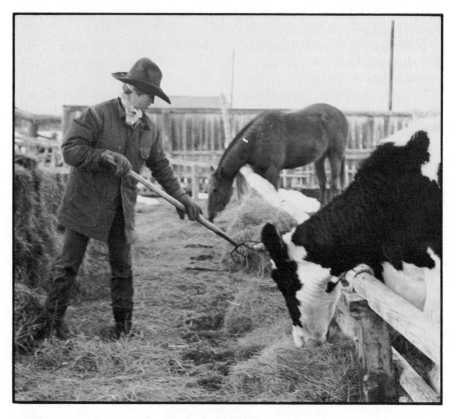

Melody Harding, feeding in the corral.

The ranch was pretty small. We had a hundred and fifty cows and probably two hundred sheep. But it was adequate to make a living on, something a small family could keep track of.

Pa was a real neat guy. He was real calm and he had probably the greatest faith of anyone I've ever known. He never tried to change people, just accepted everyone the way they were. He very seldom said a bad word about someone, even though they might do him dirt. He just figured that, no matter what they did, there was a reason.

He had a lot of patience to put up with me. When I was little he had me with him all the time. Even when I was tiny, he would take me in a blanket on his horse. He had me riding my own horse by the time I was a year and a half.

Pa loved teams. He didn't allow any sort of tractors or mechanical equipment on his place. We did everything with horses, which I thought was great. We'd go to the cedars and get posts with a team and wagon and spend a whole day out there. Or we'd go to the creek for cement. We had a log house and it had to be daubed every fall. We'd take the wagon where there was a sandbar. We'd throw gravel against a huge screen to screen out the sand, then throw it in the wagon and haul it back home to make cement. I don't know why that intrigued me so much, but it did.

We didn't have any plumbing. We had a well that we carried water from. No problems.

A ranch across the road came up for sale and we got in on that. We moved over there because it had a much nicer house. It had plumbing and all. But Pa wouldn't move. He stayed in the log house. Bap and Mom and Dad and I moved, but not Pa. He'd come over for dinner and sometimes supper, but he wouldn't live over there full time.

Later on, we moved to another ranch. Bap and Pa had leased their ranch with an option to buy, but when the owner died, it got sold out from under them somehow. It all turned out for the better, because the next place we went was a better ranch.

The new ranch was surrounded by the Indian reservation, and that was a real interesting experience. Leo, the man who had the ranch before, was an Irishman and he was a little bit of a racist. He was a real great guy, but he had it in for the Indians. He didn't have a very good communication line to them and they really hated him.

When we moved there, he said, "They'll steal you blind," but they never did. Oh, some kids might have stole eggs out of the chicken house or something like that, but nothing malicious. They saved our house from burning down one night while we were gone. They could have just sat at home and watched it burn. They not only put the fire out, they made an attempt to clean up the mess after they were done.

But Pa had a very early understanding with them. Right after we moved there, we ran short of pasture. It was a real late fall and we didn't have any snow. Rather than feed hay, Pa said, "I think I'll just rent a pasture from one of these Indians, 'cause they all have land that is theirs to rent."

He made a deal with George, the nearest Indian. Pa paid him, and George took the money and grinned and walked home. He didn't tell Pa he had also rented the pasture to another man.

The next morning, we drove our cattle all the way from their old pasture to the new one, only to find cattle already in there. Pa said, "Gosh, the fence must be down."

He went to George's house to ask about the fence. Well, turns out George had leased the pasture twice. Leo was with us and he said, "Yeah, you'll never get your money back." Pa told him, "I'm going to take these cattle home, but I'm going to get my money back." Leo just laughed.

As far back as I could remember, Pa was real mild-mannered and easygoing, but Bap told me that he had been a real fighter in his younger days. He liked to brawl and he was always the one out back of the barn dance, fighting. He was an old man by the time we moved to that ranch, in his early seventies. But he was real healthy and robust for his age.

We turned the cows around and started back with them. Pa went on up to talk to George. This Indian was a fairly young man, fairly big. But Pa got him right by his collar and started banging his head against the wall, just whiplashing it. He said, "Now, we're heading home with these cattle. You better have that money to me before we get there, 'cause if I get home and get unsaddled and have to drive back here, I'm really going to be mad."

We got just about a quarter of a mile from home and George drove up. He had all the money. Leo was just amazed. He said, "I just can't believe it. These people spend the money as fast as they can get it."

And after that, George became one of our best friends. We leased his pasture for years after that and he never did that again. He always came down to help us if he could. The Indians turned out to be great friends, but Pa let them know early that he meant what he said.

It never occurred to me to want brothers and sisters, to want someone to play with. There was always so much to do. Pa was always training a new team and we'd drive clear into town in the buggy. Or he'd have cattle to work. He always had something going on. I enjoyed working at home. I liked milking in the morning before school, and I liked coming home to do the milking in the evening. I never felt like I "had to do the chores." It was a real treat to me to be able to do them. Anything besides going to school.

Sometimes school friends came out to the ranch, but they usually only came once. [Laughs] The first little girl that came out fell off a horse and broke her

Melody Harding with team.

arm. She hadn't ridden much, probably not at all. I was used to tearing around bareback just wide open. I figured everyone knew how to ride that way. I did get her a gentle horse, but we got way up in the field where there was a straightaway where I would always race. Her eyes got as big as saucers and I thought, "Boy, what a baby." We got going along there and she fell off and broke her arm. Her mother wouldn't let her come out anymore. I don't think she wanted too, either!

So it was usually a one-day stand for my friends. Either they would get hurt or they would be so tired when they got home that their mothers would say they couldn't come back.

I hated school. I always did. I never enjoyed anything about it unless it was recess. I felt like I was wasting time. I would sit in school and think, "If I was home I could be out riding and having a good time . . ." And I hated cities.

But I did go to college. That's when Pa decided to sell the ranch. Bap was getting to the point where she really didn't want to be there anymore. She wanted to go and spend time with my mom. So it was just Pa and me there and he was eighty by that time. He wasn't able to do real hard work all the time. He asked me if I would like to go to college, and like a dummy I said, "Yeah, I'll go to school." He sold everything. And that was the end of that.

College [The University of Wyoming in Laramie] was probably the closest I'll ever get to hell, unless I die and go there. That was really a bad time for me. It seemed like people were always trying to provoke me into doing something I didn't want to do. I didn't like dating especially, and I didn't like running around in cars with other kids. It just seemed like I was always a lot different than everyone else.

For the first part of the year I came home every weekend. Thursday I was packing, getting ready to go home, and Tuesday I was just getting unpacked from being home. I never could really get into the swing of school.

It wasn't all terribly bad. I made a couple real good friends, girls from the same background as me. And I got a job at a western store. Then I exercised a horse for a lady while she was gone. That kept me going. But I just really didn't like college.

When summer come around, I knew I wanted to get back to a ranching situation. We had sold all the cows, only kept a few horses. The only connection to a ranch I could think of was my uncle Red, who was foreman of this ranch at the time. I decided to call him, but I really didn't expect much.

I didn't know how Red felt about women. His brother Marvin is a bachelor and he believes that a woman's place is in the house. I remember as a little girl, if I'd come out to the barn when a cow was calving, Marvin would throw a fit. He would say to Pa, "Get her out of here. She has no business out here. What are you doing, letting that kid be in the barn? She's a girl." I figured Red would feel the same way and just say, "You're a girl!" But he knew my background and he knew what I was capable of doing. He told me to come on over. I went. And ten years later, I never got away.

When I first came here, I made only two stipulations. I said, "I will not cook, and I will not work in the yard." John's mother [John Barlow is the owner/manager of the Bar Cross], Mim, was here at that time and she was real proud of her garden. She would have you get fresh horse manure at a certain temperature for her sweet-pea beds. That sort of stuff. I'd been around here one summer for a few weeks and I'd seen that go down. I knew I didn't want to get in on it. I avoided that. I did end up doing a lot of cooking, but that was O.K. because I combined it with my outside work.

When I first came, I went to work for a hundred and fifty dollars a month. Now that's nothing, but I was just eighteen or nineteen and gosh . . . Also, I had several horses at home. They weren't broke so I'd bring them over one at a time and break them and sell them, so I thought I was doing O.K. for money.

I got my wages raised to two hundred and I thought, Wow! What a big deal. The next thing was to get a car. I didn't have one. I bought a red El Camino and I thought that was pretty terrific. Then I bought a red horse trailer. I started going to rodeos and I really enjoyed it.

That first summer, I did everything. I irrigated, I helped move cows, I peeled, sharpened, and creosoted posts. Everything. Then haying came around and I hayed.

I hate machines so bad. If they hayed with horses, I'd go right after it. Horse-drawn machinery can be noisy with the mowers and sickles going back and forth, but you're not sitting up there on this motor. Horses always start, they never run out of gas, they're never low on oil, you don't get greasy. There is just something about working with flesh and blood as compared to working with a hunk of metal.

After driving that tractor all day, my back hurt so bad. God! I lived with Red and Maxine [Red's wife] and I'd spend my nights in their big recliner chair because I could not lay down. I think they thought it was my imagination 'cause I hated machinery so bad. Then I had an accident with a horse and had x-rays taken of my back. It turned out that I had a vertebrae that had never been in line. The vibration of the tractor was enough to really kill me.

That winter Red wanted me to stay. It was hard to get someone that wasn't a drunk who was happy to stay here the winter. Red was chariot racing at the time, so I could fill in for him when he was gone and cook for Maxine and pick up loose ends. He propositioned me to stay by saying I could break horses. I did some of that, but as it turned out, that was the least of it. By the time I got through with everything that had to be done when they were gone, there wasn't much time to break horses.

I started really helping Dad when I was about twelve years old.
I'd go out and gather the cattle that were coming down from the
summer mountain pasture, and put them in the fields for him.

During my Christmas vacation when I came home from high
school, I'd gather horses off the desert and bring them in for the
winter. And in the spring I'd go back to the desert and gather the
mares and put them in with the stud horse. I don't think I started
haying until I was thirteen years old, but when I did I drove a
team because tractors weren't being used then. It took us about
forty-five days to do all of the haying, so we'd have to use two
teams a day. I'd harness one team and work it in the morning,
and then at noon I'd change teams. This kept the horses fresh so
they wouldn't play out on us before the haying season was over. I
never drove a tractor until I was married, and I still can't drive a
tractor.

—Verla Richie Sommers, Sublette County, Wyoming,
from *Spoken Words of Four Ranchwomen*, recorded and
transcribed by Carol Rankin.
© Carol Rankin, 1979, p. VS/9–10.

That next summer, I was offered a job on a dude ranch. The owner said,
"I'd love to have you come up and wrangle and pack, 'cause I can't get people
who are real good with horses." I told Red, "I'll work for you up until haying,
but I refuse to ride tractors and hay again. I'll go up and work on that dude
ranch for the summer and then come back this fall."

Red said, "Well, really we need someone to ride up on the forest. The cows
come down and get in the corridors. The Forest Service gets mad, and everyone else is too busy haying to take care of it. Besides, cows or calves get sick up
there and no one ever knows about it. They just aren't attended to. You can
do that."

I started doing that, and I've been doing it every summer since. I really
don't see how they got along without someone before, because it is sure a full-
time job. In the summer I also keep the horses shod, and I shoe some for
neighbors. I keep the sickles sharpened for the mowers 'cause I'm the only one
who likes to do that. If they lose someone in the hayfield I'll sure pitch in and
help for a day or two, but I try to stay clear of that.

After I had been here about four years, Red left. I was sort of the only person around for the foreman's job. It was the natural thing to do. It just
evolved.

I thought the older men might resent my being foreman, but when we've
had older men work here they were perfectly happy with the situation. I think
as long as I don't give an order like a direct command there is no resentment.
When I ask someone to do something, it's almost like I'm asking them to help
me personally. It seems people are always more than happy to help.

Most of the time I work quite independently here, anyway. In the winter we
usually hire one man and he usually goes with John. I really prefer to feed

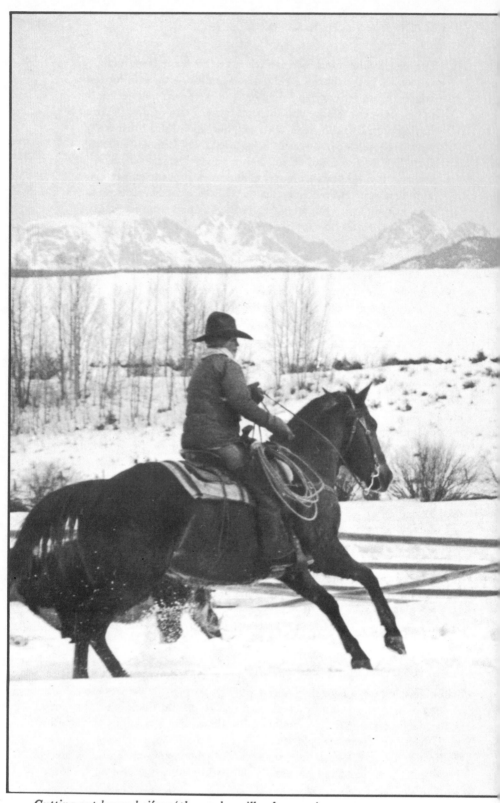

Cutting out heavy heifers (those who will calve soon).

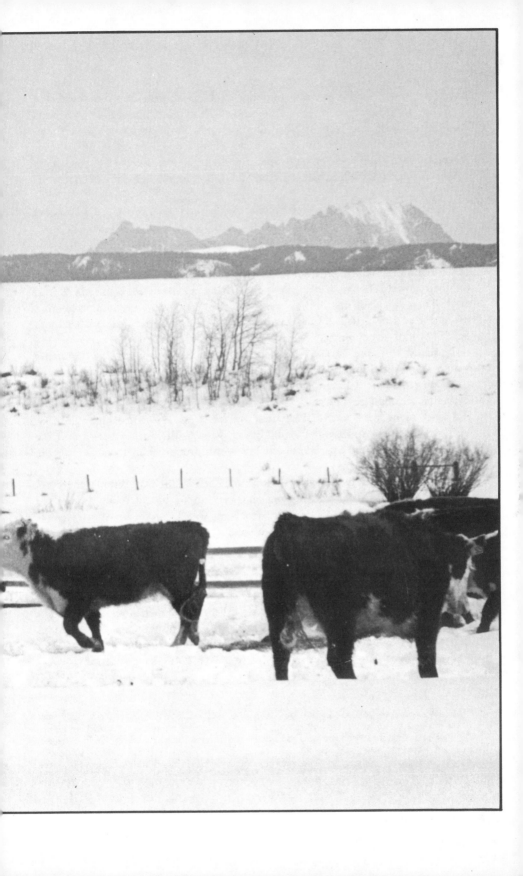

alone. I want to go in the morning and I'm very impatient. I don't want to have anyone else under pressure thinking, "Oh, I suppose she's out there tapping her foot, waiting to go . . ." Also, if I'm going to be on the rack [haysled], I want the responsibility of the team. Yet I feel bad when someone else goes with me and they have to get off and open the gates, be the dog. I would much rather get off and open my own gates and drive my own team —get the good and the bad all together—than make someone else be my lackey.

Besides, it's a challenge to feed alone. At the end of the day you know you did it all by yourself. I was an only child, and I guess maybe I'm selfish in everything I do. I want to do it by myself, and I want to have full credit for it.

But it's such a neat feeling when the cows come up out of the willows and they're humped up with the cold and they've got ice on their faces and icicles on their noses. They're frosty along their back and they look miserable and cold. Then you load up the hay and feed them and they wrap their tongues around it and drag it into their mouths. It's a really nice thing to watch them eat. They look so contented. That's the best part of feeding to me.

I usually keep the barns clean myself. Most people who work on ranches would rather ride than do the other work. I do almost all the riding, and since I get the good part, I hate to turn around when it comes to the bad parts, like shoveling out manure, and say, "O.K., now I need your help."

I work alone a lot, and I like it that way. I enjoy my own company. I like visiting with other folks, but I really like to work with just my horses and my dog. My schedule and attitude about life is so different than the other people here.*

To me, every day is the same. I don't care if it's Sunday. I think the cows like to eat at eight o'clock in the morning on Sunday just as much as they do on Monday. The horses like a clean barn. This way I can do my share when I feel it is best, without trying to run everyone else's lives. But when someone else owns the place, you can't say, "Now, this is the way you're going to do it."

I make four hundred and fifty dollars a month. I just got a raise. That doesn't sound like a whole lot, but I also figure that I've got my horses here. It's expensive to buy feed for four horses. We get our own house and we get our utilities. We get meat and milk and cream and butter and all the things that come from the ranch. When Richard isn't here, I eat with John and Elaine, so a lot of my groceries are covered. We don't have many living ex-

---

* Melody and her boss, John Barlow, are very different people. Where Melody has never wanted to do anything but ranch, John has traveled all over the world and only decided to return to Wyoming and take over the family ranch in 1972. He has varied interests—among other things, he writes lyrics for The Grateful Dead—and still travels frequently. When he is at home, he and his wife, Elaine, frequently have company.

penses, so we can save most everything Richard makes. We've got a real good deal. Most of all, I'm getting to do what I like most.

One woman who just visited Barlow's asked me what my motivation to work was. I said, "Mostly, I work to make it easier for the cattle. I want to see them have good calves. I want to see them be the best possible herd they can be." She said, "Yeah, but that doesn't benefit you." Not personally, not monetarily. But I'm still proud that I'm involved with them. They don't have to be yours to be proud of them. It's like a grandmother being proud of her grandchild. It's not her own child, but she's got quite a bit to do with it.

The woman told me, "I don't see how you can keep any interest here at all. You're going to get your wages one way or the other. I feel like a person should have a personal interest in order to do their best."

She's not the first. Several people have mentioned that and said, "God, what a fool you are. It's just stupid to take as much responsibility as you've got, at such a little wage, not to think about the future." It's not that I'm a blundering idiot. I hope they don't really think that I'm that bad off, that I just go along thinking, "Oh well, the sun's going to come up again tomorrow." I think about the future but I don't worry about it. I have faith that if you do your best you will get your reward.

I may be a freak, but when the day's done I get a personal satisfaction out of knowing I did the best I could. Sometimes that's not enough, but at least I did the best I could and that's all anyone can ask. I can feel good and get a good night's sleep. I'm doing what I love and the money is not that important.

The only thing that I would be interested in money for is if there was a real close possibility of buying a ranch of my own. Then I would be very grasping and eager for more money. But since that's a dim light way, way back, as long as I've got money to buy the things I need, money is not one of my biggest worries.

I have dreams of having a ranch of my own. Dreams are good, they keep you going. I know I'll never own a ranch this size, unless we have a total depression and everyone comes out with just the boots on their feet. Then I feel I could work just as hard as anybody else. But I've always said I didn't care how big or small it was, I'd be happy with anything that would grow a cow or a horse.

Richard would like a ranch. He said if we could get a place, I could take care of the ranch and he'd be perfectly willing to work at something else to help support it. That would be great and we might even be able to pull off something like that. Who knows? At some point, if we just don't get too anxious, if we just keep saving money. . . .

Richard is a pretty remarkable person. I think he's probably one of the few people I could ever be married to, because he doesn't worry about what people might think of him in relation to me. I don't think it should bother anyone, but most guys don't want to feel like their wives might be more competent than they are in any respect. Richard doesn't resent my work here at the ranch or resent the fact that I might know more about this situation than he does.

He doesn't mind helping out, like stopping for groceries if I can't go into town. He really asks very little for himself. He doesn't demand that dinner be on the table at seven o'clock sharp. He doesn't have any strict rules that he tries to force onto me. If the tables were turned, I'm not sure I could handle it nearly as well as he does.

I don't want kids. I really don't have the temperament for them. I get so nervous. Course, everyone says it's different if they're your own. But I feel like I can be much more productive doing what I'm doing than I can be as a mother. There's plenty of other people to raise families.

Before I married Richard, I made sure he knew that I had no incentive to have children and raise a family. I made sure he realized that he wasn't going to change my mind later on unless it would be a real accident. I have a hard enough time taking care of my dogs and horses and cats and Richard and me, to want children.

This ranch is around seventy-six hundred feet altitude, and the winters are cold and long. I suffer a lot. I have rotten circulation. Even while I'm in the house, my hands and feet are cold. When I'm outside, sometimes I wonder. I could be sitting in a nice warm house doing something different. But then at the end of the day I wouldn't have done as much. To me, it's not enough to say, "Well, gosh—I mopped the kitchen floor, I cleaned the closet, I did the washing and ironing." I mean, so what? So many other people do that, but not many women do this. My life is something a little bit special.

Cowgirls and the Crowd: The Early Years

WILD WEST AND RODEO, 1885–1941

Mabel Strickland, after roping and tying a steer. Late 1920s.

Women in Rodeo 1885–1941

A Brief History

Cowgirls, around 1920.

"WOMEN IN RODEO" REALLY GOT THEIR START IN WILD WEST SHOWS. THESE shows, such as Buffalo Bill's Wild West Show and Pawnee Bill's Historical Wild West, were rather like cowboy circuses. The shows traveled from town to town with salaried performers. (As compared to rodeos, where the contestants paid entry fees and competed against each other for money and titles. In fact, at times the distinction between the two is hazy, for rodeo producers sometimes paid contestants to appear.*)

Little Annie Oakley was the first female Wild West star. She joined Buffalo Bill in 1885, just three years after he started his legendary show.† She was a crack shot and not a cowgirl—when she joined the show she couldn't even ride a horse—but she captured hearts both here and abroad. The unprecedented wave of adulation that swept over her demonstrated the public's appetite for a woman who was feminine in appearance and manner but the master of "male" skills.

By 1887 Buffalo Bill had added other women—more truly cowgirls—to his

---

* Joyce Gibson Roach, *The Cowgirls* (Houston: Cordovan Corporation, 1977), p. 84.
† Ibid., pp. 84–85.

Pawnee Bill's Historic Wild West Poster, around the turn of the century.

cast, including Mrs. Georgie Duffy, "Rough Rider from Wyoming," and Miss Dell Ferrell, a Colorado equestrienne. Emma Lake Hickok trick rode.‡

Buffalo Bill's closest rival, Pawnee Bill's Historical Wild West, followed suit in catering to the public taste for beautiful but daring ladies. Pawnee Bill's wife, May Lillie, developed into a gold medal sharpshooter. She won contests in Philadelphia in 1887 and in Atlanta in 1889 and later appeared in the show. Pawnee Bill (Gordon Lillie) made increasing use of women in his program and in 1906 hired a Colorado cowgirl who had already made her name in rodeo as a bronc rider, Bertha Blancett.*

By the time Bertha joined Pawnee Bill, cowgirls had been riding broncs at rodeos for ten years. The first cowgirl bronc ride this writer could find mention of was at Fort Smith, Arkansas, in 1896 when Annie Shaffer rode a wild one.† After 1901, rodeos began to feature cowgirl bronc riding contests with some regularity.‡

‡ Ibid., p. 86.
* Ibid., pp. 86–87.
† Milt Hinkle, "Cowgirls—Rodeo's Sugar and Spice," *Frontier Times*, Oct–Nov, 1971, p. 40.
‡ Roach, op. cit., p. 88.

Prairie Rose Henderson, early 1920s. The crowds loved the cowgirls' wild daring, their verve, their romantic beauty.

Bertha Blancett rode broncs at Cheyenne in 1904 and 1905, and when she joined Pawnee Bill in 1906 she demonstrated the exchange of talent between rodeo and Wild West shows that continues to this day.

By 1920, rodeos regularly featured three cowgirl events—ladies' bronc riding, trick riding, and, at the rodeos with a race trace, cowgirls' relay race. In the bucking event, ladies rode saddle broncs. To score, they had to stay on board eight seconds (the men rode ten) and they could ride with two reins (the men rode with one). Like the men, they rode one-handed, and if their free hand touched the horse they were disqualified.

Most women bronc riders rode with hobbled stirrups—their stirrups were tied together, which supposedly made the horse easier to ride. At times, the hobbles could be dangerous:

> *Velda Smith remembers watching Bonnie McCarrol receive fatal injuries at Pendleton because she could not free herself from her hobbles. Bonnie drew a rank horse and she was tied too tightly in the stirrups. During the violent ride, she lost hold on the ropes. Unable to grasp mane or horn, the rider's body was whipped and snapped over and over again. Finally her feet came loose and Bonnie was flung violently to the ground. She died eight days later from her injuries.* *

The men and women rode different horses. The women's string had showy buckers, but the real outlaws went into the men's string. That was the idea, at any rate. In reality, horses moved back and forth between the two strings as expediency required, and women saw their share of outlaws.

Ladies' bronc riding was dropped as a contest event after 1941. There were never more than fifteen to twenty women bronc riders at any one time, and their numbers were dwindling. In addition, as the war situation in Europe worsened, rodeo stock grew scarce and transportation resources were limited. Rodeo producers found it increasingly hard to maintain two strings. The women were in the minority, so their event suffered.†

---

* Ibid., p. 118.

† Occasionally you hear that one reason cowgirl bronc riding was dropped was that a few of the cowgirls would raise Cain if they did not win (Roach suggests this, pp. 125–26). Almost certainly, through the years there were sore losers among the women contestants. There were among the cowboys—and the contestants of any sport. Women came and went in rodeo and only a few stayed with the sport and made names for themselves. The top contestants, like Lucille Mulhall, Tad Lucas, the Greenoughs, and the other women mentioned in this brief history are almost universally remembered with the greatest fondness and respect. In fact, the cowboys stood up for the women's bronc riding event. One reason the Cowboy Turtle's Association (precursor of the RCA and PRCA) went on strike at the Fort Worth Fat Stock Show Rodeo in 1939 was that the rodeo had cut the cowgirls' bronc riding. (Foghorn Clancy, *My Fifty Years in Rodeo,* San Antonio: The Naylor Company, 1952, pp. 221–22.) I suspect that an occasional demonstration of poor sportsmanship on the part of the cowgirls sticks out in people's memories more clearly than a similar act by a cowboy simply because there were so few women involved in rodeo. One poor sport stands out in a field of twenty more clearly than ten in a field of a thousand.

Cowgirl on stretcher, hurt in the relay race at Pendleton Roundup, 1910.

In trick riding, contestants made up tricks to be performed on a horse running at full speed. The tricks consisted of stands, drags, vaults, and anything else the rider had nerve enough to do, including going under the horse's belly at a gallop. Each trick was judged on the basis of the ease, gracefulness, and skill of its execution; the number of straps used (straps were used for hand or toe holds; the more used, the lower the score); the speed of the horse; and the degree of difficulty of the stunt.‡

Since the tricks were graded on the basis of their difficulty, the cowgirls tried to make up ever more complex and dangerous tricks. In the mid 1930s trick riding was dropped as a contest event and continued on a contract basis—that is, trick riders were hired by the rodeos as entertainers. Since their income was

‡ Roach, op. cit., p. 122.

guaranteed and the element of competition removed, the trick riders had little incentive to continue the most dangerous stunts. Still, the good riders liked to give the audience a thrill.

Relay races were held at large rodeos that had race tracks, like Cheyenne and Pendleton. Each cowgirl had three racehorses. She would circle the track on one, then change to the second, then the third. Vera McGinnis invented the flying change—jumping from one horse to the next without hitting the ground —a stunt that increased the speed and excitement of the race. Usually the cowgirls did not own the racehorses but rode for rodeo producers.

The war put a damper on women's relay, like it did on their bronc riding. With purses down and transportation at a premium, few owners could afford to maintain a relay string and the relay race gradually died out.

Cowgirls demonstrated other skills in the arena as well, sometimes in competition but more often as an exhibition. Lucille Mulhall's fame as a roper spread worldwide. Once she even roped a wolf—at Teddy Roosevelt's request.

Jeanne Godshall doing a Russian drag on her fast-running Quarter Horse "Strip" in 1955.

Vera McGinnis, 1923.

Fox Hastings bulldogging at Pendleton, 1928.

Fox Hastings wrestled steers and Mabel Strickland roped them. Tad Lucas and Alice Greenough rode bulls and steers.

These rodeo women were stars, celebrities, their names well known nationwide. They were wined and dined in every city, and the top magazines and papers gave them lengthy coverage. These "little wisps of women" who could tame the wildest bronc or hang upside down over the hooves of a galloping steed, but who still dressed in silks and satins and loved to preen for men, charmed an America long in love with the Wild West.

But this glamorous era came to an end. Nineteen forty-one marks the turning point for women in rodeo. That was the last year the Madison Square Garden Rodeo featured a cowgirl bronc-riding contest, and other rodeos followed suit. Relay race was dead or dying. Trick riding continued on a contract basis at a reduced level. In large part, women's rodeo was a casualty of the War. When it was resurrected a few years later, its personality had changed.

The final cowgirl featured in this section, Fern Sawyer, really straddles the two eras, for she competed between 1932 and 1947. But Fern's main event was cutting. (A cutting horse is trained to work a cow out of a herd and put it through a gate with no guidance from its rider.) Although many rodeos have cutting contests, the American Cutting Horse Association is separate from both the Rodeo Cowboys Association (later the Professional Rodeo Cowboys Association—PRCA) and the Girls Rodeo Association (later the Women's Professional Rodeo Association, WPRA) and its history does not follow the same pattern. Besides, in background and attitude, Fern is closer to the old-time "Wild Bunch" than the "New Breed."

A race at Rockingham Park, around 1939.

After that race at Rockingham Park. Left to right: Margie Greenough, Polly Mills, Tad Lucas, Alice Greenough, Vivian White. You can sure tell who placed where in the race.

Pearl Mason

California

PEARL SAYS SHE WAS THE WORLD CHAMPION BRONC RIDER IN 1918. IN FACT, there was no world championship at that time, but Pearl won several major contests. I learn about her from another cowgirl and drive down the town's main street to find her shop.

No shingle hangs over the door. I drive past the tiny shop several times before I search out the small semicircle of letters that spell out the store's name on a window. I open the door and, when my eyes adjust to the light, I realize I am face to face with an elderly woman seated at a sewing machine on a raised platform, looking out through the window display. This is Pearl Mason,* and she sits and sews and watches the town pass by; greets it when some part of it should enter.

The shop is only about three yards wide, but goes back a long way. A counter runs the length, and a narrow walk space separates it from a wall lined with saddles on sawhorses. Headstalls, bits, crops, chaps, and spurs hang above the saddles. The aroma of leather fills the long, dark shop. Bright square-dancing dresses and handmade Navajo dolls hang from the wall behind the counter. Way up (the ceiling must be 20 feet high) hang old Indian rugs and newer Mexican ones. But back to Pearl.

Pearl sits at her sewing machine and misses nothing. I introduce myself. She is unimpressed. "No," she says, "I have nothing to tell you. I won't talk to you. Why? Those days are past. That was a different world. You wouldn't understand." She turns away, spits a mouthful of tobacco juice into a green-bean can, and returns to her sewing.

She wears a bright-purple homemade dress, with a white nylon store jacket. She is an attractive woman, still active and energetic in spite of her eighty-plus years. The bulldog set of her jaw indicates she has never been one to mince words or temper her opinions.

No. I'm not going to talk to you. I'm not going to talk to you because I am not a women's libber. I have no time at all for women's lib. And it's all women's lib right now. In my time we were ladies, and there weren't no time for this women's lib. The girls now are all so different. Spend all their money on five-thousand-dollar horses and all their time with their fannies up in the air, chasing barrels.

I didn't even go to the all-girl show here. Haven't gone in ten years. What

* For privacy, this is not her real name.

would it be like if I went? I'd introduce myself and say, "I was the world champion bronc rider in 1918," and they'd look at me and laugh and say, "You were what?" No, I'm not going out there.

The girls today are content to compete in these silly all-girl shows. The men won't let them compete in their shows. But I'll tell you—if I'm going to ride, I'm going to ride with the best. I'd want to ride in the men's shows. 'Cause this girls' association is nothing compared to the men. And this idea of the men having their shows and the girls having theirs—what a bunch of hogwash! When I was rodeoing, we were right in there with the men. We helped put the shows on. And the people came to see us. If the girls would ask me, if they'd listen to me, I'd tell them how to go about it.

Of course I was delighted to have a home, but this wasn't my dream log cabin. This was just a house to live in between rodeos, not a place to grow roots. The rodeos had become a compulsion I followed blindly, without questioning where they would lead.

—Vera McGinnis,
Rodeo Road, 1974.

You know what happened to put the girls out of the rodeo? Well, the girls did it themselves. A few of them did. A few of them, if they didn't win, they'd get out there in front of the grandstand, with a bullhorn, and start yelling the dirtiest, filthiest, rankest language at the judges. They were whores, chippies, nothing but dirty little sluts, that's what they were. And a few of them ruined it for all of us.

Some of the girls only rodeoed so they could be around the men. In those days, you know, we'd all be staying in the same rooming house. And about two or three in the morning, or maybe you'd get up to take your shower at five, you'd see these chippies come out of a judge's room, smacking their lips. Smack, smack. And you'd know what they had been doing. How old are you? Twenty-three? Well, then, you know.

And in the show we'd ride together, and I'd get first money. And they would be mad! They hated me. Oh, how they hated me. Because I was always a lady. I was nice to the judges, and when they gave me first I would always go up and thank them. But I never slept with them. And they respected me for it. And they were a whole lot more likely to give me first because I hadn't slept with them.

Now it's different. You can sleep with a man and he don't think anything about it. But in those days a man could take a bath and clean up and the next day he was a good man. But not a woman. She was ruined. She could never regain her name. And you can't tell me it's all that different now. A man still don't respect a woman who sleeps around.

I'm not saying I never slept with no man. I was married. I'll tell you—I have my boyfriends yet. But I'm not going to marry them. I might live with them. But I'm not going to marry them. Or, if I did, it would be *my* way. Because no man is going to tell me what to do. If I married and some man said, "O.K., you go home now and I'll take care of the store"—no sirree!! This is my store and I built it and no man is going to tell me how to run it.

Oh, what a family I came from! My mother was so religious, and my father wasn't. God, God, God, that was my mother. She was a slave. All women were then. The Negroes and the Mexicans and all that talk about being slaves. But I'll tell you who the real slaves were in those days. They were the women. My father wasn't just so dumb, you know? And he could see what was coming. He'd say, "She's going to learn to do for herself. She is going to grow up and no man is going to tell her what to do."

And my mother said, "Oh, no . . . she must grow up and marry and raise a *family!*" But the old boy raised me different. He raised me to do for myself.

My sisters hated me. I have a sister and we haven't spoken for twenty-five years. And down south there, my sisters are still turning over every rock, every goddamn rock, to see where I buried all the babies I had before I was married. Because they figured, since I rodeoed, I was bad. And I must have had a bunch of babies before I was married. Huh!

I made saddles for years. And I made some of the best saddles in the world. But I don't make saddles anymore. I'm too old. But almost all the purses, and all the dresses and the dolls you see here, I made. See this dress? I just made it. I think it's awful pretty. See all these dresses? [She points to a rack as long as the shop.] They are all pretty. This is part of my life. I go out and see the material, and I know just how it will look when it's made up. I sew all the time. It's sort of a hobby with me. And these dolls. You see their faces? From here, it looks like they are painted on. But those faces are beaded. And each one is different. So don't look at one and say, "I want a face just like that one," because I never make the same face twice. All the chaps, and most of the headstalls here—I made those too.

That coat? It's made of rattlesnake hide. Mostly diamondbacks. Those skins came from California and Nevada and New Mexico and Old Mexico. I killed some of them myself. And some of them were given to me. Some of them are over six feet long. I wore that coat for years. But now it's getting stiff. I've tried all types of oil, but I can't seem to keep it soft.

Someday I'd like to write the story of my life. My lawyer comes in here and says, "Pearl, I'd like to read the story of your life. If you write it, I want to read it. I bet it's something!" Well, it's something, don't you think it isn't. And someday I'm going to write it. I feel good now. But you never know. Bam, you're gone. But someday I'll write about my life. And that will be left.

Tad Lucas
Fort Worth, Texas

*Tad Lucas in her old
rodeo gear, 1978. Women
in rodeo enjoyed their heyday
in the 1920s and 1930s. Most
rodeos featured women's bronc riding
and trick riding, and if the arena had a racetrack, women's relay. The top
names enjoyed a celebrity near that of movie stars. But better than fame, if
you were good enough, was the money. Tad Lucas brought home over
$10,000 a year during the Depression—not bad for a "girl!" Alice Greenough
was another top money winner.*

TINY TAD LUCAS WAS BORN TAD BARNES IN 1902, THE DAUGHTER OF THE
first white settler in Cody, Nebraska. The youngest of twenty-four children
and the only one in the family with an interest in rodeo, Tad went on to become the greatest trick rider of all time. She won the largest women's trick-
riding contest—at the Madison Square Garden Rodeo in New York—eight

times during the twenties and thirties and brought home trophies from hundreds of other rodeos in the United States and abroad.

Tad was a champion bronc rider and relay-race rider as well. In a good year she could win between ten and twelve thousand dollars. Not bad for a woman, especially during the Depression.

When Tad was going under her horse's belly in the trick-riding contest at the Chicago World's Fair in 1933, she slipped. Caught up in the horse's galloping hooves for several seconds before she could roll free, Tad broke her arm severely. The doctors told her she would lose it and, even if they could save it, she would never ride. Within a year, Tad trick rode again, using only her good arm. Her left arm was still in a heavy cast. Within two years she was back to bustin' broncs.

To this day, Tad cannot bend her wrist, lift her little finger, or turn her arm over. Because of the several bone grafts the arm required, it is an inch and a half shorter than her right.

Tad married a bronc rider, Buck Lucas, in 1924. Their daughter Mitzi (now Mitzi Lucas Riley) started trick riding at the age of four. Tad and Mitzi often performed together, and Mitzi made a name for herself in her own right.

Tad was inducted into the Cowgirl Hall of Fame in Hereford, Texas, in 1978. Her trick-riding saddle and many of her trophies are prominently displayed at the National Cowboy Hall of Fame in Oklahoma City.

Today Tad lives in the Fort Worth, Texas, house she and Buck built in 1933. She is still tiny, still spry, and bubbling with years of happy memories.

I rode all my life. I can't remember when I didn't ride. I rode three miles to school and back every day. I always had horses and rode all day long.

My dad raised horses and he traded horses back and forth all the time. My first horse was an old Indian pony and he hated Indians. Oh my, he hated Indians. They would steal him back a lot. You could hear the Indians coming to town before they'd ever get there 'cause they'd be whooping and hollering and running their poor little horses. When my pony would hear them coming, he would run and get on our porch and he'd try to get in the house. Every time they'd steal him, he would get away and come back. He was coal-black. I called him Black. That's always been my favorite horse, a black.

During World War I, every Saturday there would be bucking horses and bulls on Main Street [Cody, Nebraska]. No corrals or anything. People would ride them for hat collections and give it to the Red Cross. That's how I got to riding broncs.

They'd brought this bronc in. Now, my brother, he thought I could do anything. He said, "Tad'll ride him." So somebody threw an old saddle on him. The stirrups didn't fit me or anything. I climbed on him, and of course he bucked me off. My dad hadn't known anything about it and he come around the corner. He didn't like it much. He said, "Tad, you get home." [Laughs] But I rode our own green colts. We always had horses to break. I guess I was about eight or nine.

Tad Lucas
on Juarez,
Salt Lake City, Utah,
1924.

I was in my first contest when I was fourteen. I started galloping racehorses for some neighbors and they took me to the fair. Mildred Douglas [another famous cowgirl bronc rider of the era] was there and she wanted to ride steers. Somebody asked me if I would ride too, so we could have a contest. She got bucked off, so I won the contest. Well, that ruined me, right there.

Soon after that I moved to El Paso and lived with my sister. We moved around Texas some and ended up in Fort Worth. For a long time I just went to little shows. Then in 1923 I went with Colonel Frank Hafley's Wild West Show. His daughter Rene [later Rene Shelton] got me started trick riding. We went to Mexico and worked in the bullrings for three months. Then we went back East and worked all the big eastern fairs. We went into New York that fall.

New York was my first big rodeo. That was at the old, old Madison Square Garden. I rode a Brahma [she pronounces it bray-mer] stag at every performance. I'm the only girl ever rode Brahma at the Garden.

I entered the trick riding but my horse hurt his leg and I had to take out of that. I won second in the bronc riding, though. They had great big Canadian horses, the big, strong bucking horses that you seldom see anymore.

There were an awful lot of rodeo people here in Fort Worth at that time. Some of the other cowgirls were Bea Kiernan, Rene Shelton, Ruth Roach, and

Mabel Strickland. There were no horse trailers at that time, so we had to ship our horses to the rodeos. We would ship them by train and go to the shows together. You got a car for horses for each twenty-five tickets so we'd have a carful of horses.

Those train rides were fun. We would play cards from here to New York. The girls would play together, just penny ante and dimes. We never bet over a quarter, I'm sure. Course the cowboys played for big money.

We'd be on the road several months each year. You'd have to take so blamed much stuff! You'd wear summer clothes when you left and you wouldn't get back until it would be getting cold in places like Montana, so you'd have to take coats and jackets too.

We all had lots of clothes. We always wore our best clothes, no matter what we were doing. If we had to ride a bull or a bucking horse or anything else, we wore our best clothes, we sure did.

This year's crop of rodeo cowgirls sets a new high standard of good looks and it takes more than an outlaw bronc to make one of the cuties forget her mascara.

Tough as any ranch hand when it comes to riding, the girls spend as much time on their makeup as any chorine in Rainbeau Garden. One rides with a fresh gardenia over one ear, and they all touch up with perfume.

Their tack rooms in the rodeo barns back of the Coliseum are fully equipped with mirrors. No cowgirl would think of coming out in the arena without powder, rouge, lipstick, eyeshadow and mascara.

Their costumes are practical, but ultra feminine. Most of the girls who sew as well as they ride broncs, make their own. Vivian White of Ringwood, Oklahoma, champion bronc rider for the past two years, has a sister who makes her costumes. Grace White, the heavyweight cowgirl last year, remember?

The cowgirl costumes, braided and embroidered and worn with bright blouses, are all made of pastel flannels and tailored—the girls hope—to stand up under the toughest wear. That's quite a trick of tailoring, considering the way the clothes fit. You may have noticed what happened to the breeches of a cowgirl trick rider Monday afternoon.

She was very embarrassed.

—Bess Stephenson,
"Cowgirl Cuties Just Girls A-foot Backstage" *Fort Worth Star-Telegram,* n.d.
From Tad Lucas's scrapbook.

We had such gorgeous materials. We bought just about all our material when we were back in New York, enough for the next season. There wasn't any such thing as a western shop then. I used to try to get dressmakers to make trousers but they never could fit them right. So when I broke my arm so bad, and there were so many things I couldn't do, I thought, "Now I'm going to make riding breeches. I know it just can't be all that hard."

I bought a lot of cheap material to practice on. I had a time cutting it out because of my cast. I'd lay the cast over on it while I cut. But I learned to make them fit. So from then on I always made my own.

My husband was a fairly good artist and I could tell him what sort of thing I wanted for trim. He could draw the pictures and then I would cut them out of leather or felt and trim our suits.

People were wonderful to us at the rodeos. They were always wanting to meet us. Like in New York and Boston—Boston especially. I love the people there. They'd do so many little kind things for you. Even strangers would want to take you out to dinner. They'd bring you gifts. I've had handmade quilts brought to me. Sometimes they'd bake you something and bring it to the hotel.

We had a lot of fun among ourselves. We were always playing jokes on somebody. Like in Boston. We didn't work on Sunday in Boston, so that was our day to frame people. We'd call some of the cowboys or cowgirls and tell them we were publicity men. Of course, you were supposed to go out and do things if you were called on. We'd tell them to get all dressed up in their best clothes, that the publicity men would meet them at such and such a place for photographs.

We would have just picked an address out of the phone book where they were supposed to go. They would get all dressed up and maybe travel for a long, long way in a taxi. And when they got there, nobody would be waiting for them. But oh! We did all those mean things. [Laughs] That was our Sunday fun.

Had this one old fellow from Aberdeen, Texas. Oh, he'd really dress up. He always wore a white suit and he had a huge hat that come right up to a peak. He was always loaded with badges. I don't know what all those badges were. We all called him "Sheriff." He just loved to rodeo, and all he come for was to just ride the grand entries. He had lots of money, I guess. Of course, they always had a beautiful white horse for him. In fact, Buck and I had a beautiful white stallion and we'd sent it back East just to let him ride it.

We thought it would be funny to frame him, so we had this fellow call him and tell him that this family had seen him ride in the Grand Entry and they would like to invite him out to dinner and hear a little about his life. We picked this number out of the phone book. Lord knows where it was in Boston. He got a taxi and went way out there. He walks up to the door and those people had no more idea who he was! Oh, that was awful.

I thought, "Well, believe me, they'll never get me!" I'd helped play so many on everybody else, I thought I was wise to it. But one morning somebody

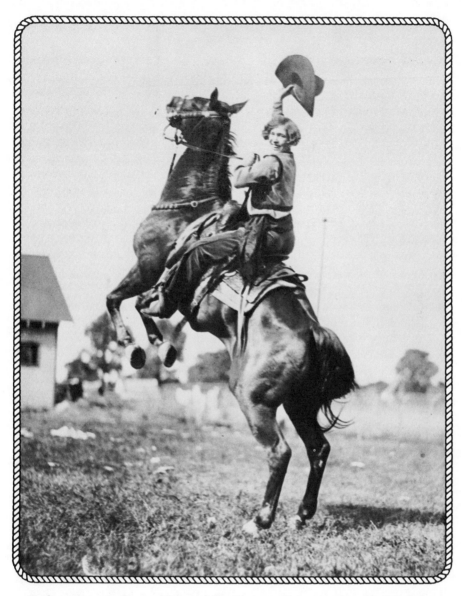

Tad, age twenty-five, on Tony while three months pregnant with Mitzi, in 1927.

called me (of course they'd got somebody who I couldn't recognize their voice) and said, "This is Mr. Didley." Mr. Didley was the manager at the Garden. "Tad, I want you to be over at Jack Dempsey's for some pictures."

Well, Jack Dempsey's restaurant was right close, so sure enough, I get dressed up in my best clothes. [Laughing] I get over to the restaurant and I don't see Jack anyplace. There is another girl with me, so we sit down and have some coffee. We sit there and we sit there. Nobody shows up. Pretty soon

I look out the window and here goes Harry Knight and Tom Johnson and Hub Whiteman, going by the window and peeking in. They were just laughing! I thought, "Well, they finally got me."

At the big rodeos in Boston and New York we'd stay in hotels. But traveling in the summertime we'd usually camp. I was the one who wanted to camp rather than stay in a hotel, when we rodeoed in places like Cheyenne and Sheridan and Belle Fuche. I had to be on the racetrack by daylight each morning to gallop racehorses, and it was difficult when you were staying way off someplace. Especially when Mitzi was a little girl, it was a chore. So we had a tent, bigger than this here kitchen, I'm sure. [This interview takes place in Tad's medium-sized kitchen.] It even had a floor to it and we had it fixed up real comfortable. It was right there where the horses were and I could get up and gallop my racehorses. After that, of course, I had to work my trick-riding horses. Buck would take care of Mitzi. Then I'd get in and fix breakfast. By that time, it was time to rest a little while and get ready for the afternoon show. Camping was so much easier than living off someplace you had to drive to. Besides, it was fun.

I met Buck at a rodeo here in Fort Worth. He was a bronc rider. We got married and had our honeymoon on the boat to England for Tex Austin's Wild West Show. Over a hundred of us went over on the same boat. It was an old freighter and we went right with our horses.

That was a great show. We put it on in Wembley Stadium and it was a big success. The stands were packed every night; everyone treated us like royalty.

But when we went back to England in 'thirty-four, it was very different. We worked in White City Stadium that year and they were having dog races. Seemed like they were having dog races every other night or something. The crowds would really come to the dog races, but when we'd have our rodeo, there would be nobody there at all. Course, they fussed about with the events. Humane [the Humane Society] wouldn't allow bulldogging, so we had to change it where the cowboys would pick a ribbon off of the steer, which didn't amount to anything. And they wouldn't allow the flank strap on the bucking horses. By the time they got through, the show didn't amount to much.

No crowds come at all, so it lost a lot of money and we didn't get paid. We didn't all come back on the ship together like we usually did. Some of them stayed over there thinking they could get their money, I guess. They did get their way paid back eventually, but we were so disgusted we just paid our own way and come back ahead of time.

The first year, the Britons were wonderful to us. They entertained us all royally. We went out all the time and oh, they had some wonderful parties for us. But in 'thirty-four we were invited out very little. We did take trips every day to see what we could see.

The worst, of course, was Brussels in 'fifty-eight. The World's Fair was going on then, but we weren't associated with that. Our show was promoted by some Californians. The location was the worst I ever saw. It was right down in a big hole. Used to be a gas plant or something. Nobody knew where it was. We were supposed to have an inflated tent to cover the whole thing, but the tent wouldn't work. It was huge and it would have made a wonderful arena, but the gosh darn thing wouldn't stay up. So we had no top and it rained, rained, rained. We were down in that mudhole and nobody knew we were there. I never could understand why it wasn't promoted. Nothing was right, nothing at all.

We were there several weeks. We stayed because you just kept thinking things would get better. What could you do? I had enough money because I used to never leave home unless I thought I had enough money to last me for a few months. But a lot of them were plumb broke. We were supposed to be paid by the week and they were expecting their money.

I think we were supposed to get a hundred and sixty dollars a week and the promoters were supposed to see that we had fine living quarters at a certain price. That was supposed to be all arranged and ready for us. When we got over there, they had nothing for us, nothing. We had to get out and find our own places to live. That took two or three days just looking around to find a place. This girl and I roomed together and we found one. It was a brand-new, beautiful building, but it had no conveniences. We had an apartment up three flights and we had to carry our trunks up. It was a room about the size of this kitchen and it had two hard cots in it. There was no clothes closet or anything. We paid seems like a hundred and twenty dollars a week. Pretty soon there was thirteen of us stayed there. We had one bathroom, so I used to get up about five o'clock in the morning and run in there to get my bath.

At the end, the show owed for horse feed and they owed for this and that. Everything was attached. Some of us girls had our saddles down on the grounds but they wouldn't let us in there to get anything. So we rented a little old Volkswagen. We got somebody to get the attention of the boy on the gate, and we went down in there and loaded up our saddles and got out of there in a hurry. We stole our own saddles.

The government paid our way back. There were supposed to be return tickets over there for us when we got there, but there weren't. We went over with champagne and the most wonderful food; we come back with old ham sandwiches on the worst-looking old plane you ever saw. It was a plane they had been carrying Hungarian refugees in; it was a terrible-looking old plane.

Gene Autry had had a lot to do with the show and he met us in New York. He took everybody to dinner and I think the cowboys ordered everything on the menu for vengeance. Then he paid our way to Denver.

The cowboys were trying to get up a petition for us all to go together and sue Gene, but I wouldn't sign it. I've seen that sort of thing happen too many times, and there's not a thing you can do about it but try to forget it. I heard since that I was about the only one that sent the money for my plane fare back to the government. A lot of them never sent a dime. I don't know if one of the promoters paid it or not. I darn sure paid mine myself.

I loved to ride bucking horses, just loved to ride them. And I never ever had any fear of one of them, I never did. I wouldn't have ridden if I'd felt afraid. I would have quit right then.

You do get in some awful wrecks, though. One time a horse bucked me off that I'd ridden dozens and dozens and dozens of times before. I don't know how come he bucked me off. The whistle had already blew, but he was one the longer you rode him, the harder he bucked. He bucked me right over his head and I lit just sitting up on the ground. He was kicking, of course, and he hit me right between the eyes with his foot. If my head hadn't been coming back, why I guess it would have took my head off. But he just hit me hard enough to black my eyes. But oh! I had the blackest eyes.

—————————————————————

. . . The mention of Ruth Roach recalls to mind one Sunday afternoon at the Garden two seasons ago. She came whirling and twisting out of Chute Number Three on a wicked devil-inspired bundle of steel muscles and tough horse meat called Domino. He reared just outside the chutes and Ruth went down to earth. Domino speared at her wickedly with his flying hooves, to be driven away by the fast-riding [pickup men], whose duty it is to take off the riders when their seven seconds of trial are over.

Ruth climbed gamely to her feet. Shook back her blond curls and walked unassisted to the gate leading back of the chutes. It is one of the fundamental rules of the rodeo arena that only the dead stay down.

Once through the gate, she crumpled down in a heap in the dirt. But with a clean shirt—the one she had ridden in was half torn from her body—and a fresh make-up she was back in the arena again in a few minutes, gay as ever.

But, out there, trampled into the stirred-up dirt where she went down under the thundering feet of Domino, lay a shining lock of golden hair, sheared off her head as neatly as by a barber's shears, by those terrible flying hooves.

—George Brinton Beal,
Boston Sunday Post, **November 3, 1935.**

—————————————————————

Another time, in New York, I was riding a new horse. They'd just brought him in from Montana, and I guess he'd never been in a building before. I guess he just didn't see the wall at the end of the arena. He hit it head on. It killed him dead, broke his neck. I was under him, but he wasn't hurting me because he was dead. The pickup men were off in a minute and pulled me out from under him. But Humane was so strong up there, and instead of just dragging the horse out, they had to come out and shoot him. He was already dead; there wasn't any sense in shooting him. And then they dragged him out. I was so mad because the blood got all over my reins and the saddle and everything.

I had a racehorse fall on me in Deadwood, South Dakota. I was riding for a stranger. I never knew him; he just wanted me to ride his horses. And there was nobody up there I knew who had racehorses, so I rode relay for this man. The race was on the hardest track I ever saw. It was shale. It was just like riding on cement. It was a dangerous track.

I was on my second horse and I was way out in the lead. About the second turn that horse broke his leg, just broke it clear off. He turned over with me twice and turned right over the top of me. He was laying right across my waist. I wasn't hurting at all. The only thing that hurt me was that my head hit the ground. But I looked up and saw that poor horse's leg broke off. He was still alive but he was sort of knocked out. I knew if he started scrambling or anything, he would hurt me bad.

The cowboys had to run clear through the chutes from the arena, which was a long way. This was a half-mile track. They got him off me. I thought they'd shoot him right there, but they tried to lead that poor horse off, his leg just hanging by one little thread and everything. It was awful. And then they shot him.

But the worst wreck I ever had was when I was competing in trick riding at the Chicago World's Fair. I had been going under the horse's belly for eight years. It was a simple trick for me. It always seemed real difficult for everybody else and they never wanted to do it. But when we were contesting, somebody had to do it. The other trick riders hated it so much they would even buy me things so I would do it. It just didn't happen to be hard for me, and I didn't mind at all.

I had worked in Sydney, Iowa, just before going into Chicago, and I kind of hurt my back. The first day of the show in Chicago, I thought I'd go under my horse's belly. He did run awful fast, and just as I got underneath him, I dropped down too far. He caught me in his foot and jerked me clear down. I was right under him so his feet were turning me and turning me, over and over and over. It just shattered my left arm all to pieces.

My arm was in a cast for three years. Infection went into the bone. I had something like seven operations on it. They took bones out of both my legs.

The infection in my bone was osteomyelitis. After I finally got well, I started reading a little about it, and not many people live with it. But I didn't know that! One doctor said, "They will probably have to take your arm off." I said, "Oh no, you won't take my arm off." I said, "I'll certainly never allow that. I'll die before I get an arm taken off."

They told me I would never ride again but I didn't believe them. I was riding in no time, with my arm in that shape. I had a huge cast on it and it was awful heavy. But I was trick riding again within a year. I just had to do tricks I could do with one arm.

Who's to Blame

Into a ward of whitewashed walls,
Where the sick and suffering lay,
Crushed by a man-killing bronk
A cowgirl was carried today.
Somebody's darling young and brave
Smiling in spite of her pain.
Gathering courage, she whispered,
"Don't worry, I'll soon be riding again."

Somebody's tearfully waiting
To clasp her to his heart,
While there she lies silently suffering
Waiting to make a new start.
"Blame not the Bronk," this cowgirl did say
It's all a part of the game,
When fortune smiles we are heroines
When she frowns, then who's to blame?

—Frank I. Morse,
    dedicated to "TAD LUCAS,"
    the girl with the rippling laughter.

Of course, I had always rode broncs [held the bucking rein] with my left hand. Most people do. I had to switch to ride with my right hand and that was the hardest thing I ever tried to do. That was a lot harder than trick riding with one arm. It just seemed like I didn't have the same balance. I don't know why it was so difficult.

My arm finally did heal. My wrist won't bend and my arm won't turn. I can't handle this one little finger. I used to tape these two fingers together because I was always catching it on something and I was afraid I'd break it off. But my arm is strong, awful strong.

About a year after I broke it, I was asked to come to Pueblo, Colorado, and trick ride. I hadn't tried to do a thing since my arm was broken, and I tried to figure out some tricks I could do. I told the rodeo folks, "Well, I know there's at least two I can do. I don't know whether I can do more than that, 'cause I haven't tried anything with my broken arm, but I bet Mitzi can do some."

Mitzi was only five years old, but she had been traveling with us since she was five months old. I used to take her in the grand entry when she was a tiny baby. We bought her a little Shetland when she was two.

I had one real gentle horse. He was littler than the horse I usually used and

*Tad holding
daughter
Mitzi.*

Mitzi rode him all the time anyway. She had been wanting to learn some
tricks.

It took just about a week and she was doing four or five tricks. The little
paint horse she used just run like the dickens and it used to scare me. She was
so tiny and that horse looked so big under her and he run so fast. I'd try to
hold him until she got her little strap and she'd say, "Turn him loose, I want
to run!" [Laughs]

She'd do two runs and I'd make two runs. Of course, she was the one that
got all the applause because she was so tiny. I dressed her up in little shorts
and a little fancy blouse, and the crowd just loved her.

I never really competed in trick riding again after I broke my arm. Right
about that time, the rodeos quit having it as a contest event. They would have
it as an exhibition event. I don't really know why they had the change, but it
was very fortunate for me. There were a lot of tricks I could do with one
hand. I could do a sit stand and a back drag, I could do a shoulder stand, I
could do lots of good exhibition tricks. But I had learned all that when I had

two arms, so it wasn't too difficult for me to do them with one. But it would have been hard to learn new contest tricks. When trick riding was a contest, we were very competitive. You just practiced all the time, trying to come up with new, more daring tricks.

Of course, your trick-riding horse was very important. You needed a horse that would run fast but straight, that wouldn't shy. I've always said trick-riding horses are born, not made. The finest horses I ever had just worked right away, it didn't take long. But I've seen people work with them and work with them and work with them and never be able to trust them. A good trick-riding horse was very hard to find. You were very fortunate to find one your size with a good gait and color.

My favorite horse was my little black horse, Candy Lamb. He was the finest horse I ever had. I was crazy about him, Candy Lamb.

I bought Candy Lamb in Cheyenne from a bulldogger. I hadn't ridden him and I thought I'd ride him in the parade. He was a real nervous little horse, just dancing and prancing all the time. When the parade was over, he'd rear up and I had to break him of that. When we started back from that parade, he run off with me. I seesawed him and I done everything I had ever done on any horse to try to stop him. He got the bit over to the side of his mouth and he run all the way to the grounds, which was about three miles. I was so mad when we got to the stable that I got off and said, "Well, I'll just never ride him again. I'm just never going to ride that horse again!" [Laughs]

But the horse I had been using was so ornery. You couldn't depend on him, and he was liable to buck me off while I was trick riding on him. We had just bought him in a hurry and he was a horse that you could never trust. So we went to the rodeo in Rawlins, Wyoming, and I knew I was going to have to use that little black horse. We fixed the bit where he couldn't get it on the side of his mouth, but the first time I trick rode on him he run clear around the racetrack before I could even stop him. After that, I kept working 'til I finally learned how to get him to stop. I'd run him into the fence or anything to stop him.

He was a great little horse to trick rope off of, because he would never slow up and he wouldn't shy. And oh, the trick ropers just loved him. "Will you let me use Candy Lamb?" And then he'd run away with them. He run off with every cowboy that ever rode him. But he was a wonderful little horse.

He was awful tall for me. I could just barely reach the saddle horn. We did a lot of ground work in those days and it was really hard for me because he was so tall. *Too* tall, really. I could double-vault him easy, but there were other tricks, especially where you had to hit the ground, where I just couldn't reach him.

So we bought another little horse named Country Jack. I just called him Country. He was an ornery little devil, but an awfully cute little horse. He was just about the right size to practice on. I could check him down where he wouldn't run away with me. Candy had only one gait and that was as fast as

Tad Lucas with trophies, 1930, Fort Worth, Texas.

he could run, but I could check Country down. When you fall off a fast horse, it can really hurt you, but off a horse that doesn't go so fast it doesn't hurt you near as bad. So I done most of my practicing on Country, and I could use him to do contest tricks that I just couldn't do off my black horse. But he wasn't the showy horse that Candy was.

Oh, Candy was a wonderful little horse. I got him when he was six and he died when he was about twenty-eight. That would have been in the early forties. I trick rode on him up to the time he was twenty-five years old, but I could tell his legs were weakening. He would never slow up, but I could tell his legs were going, so I knew I had better retire him. Never had another horse as good.

I retired from rodeo myself in 1958, after I came back from Brussels. My old trick-riding horse was getting real old and I sure didn't want to start breaking another one. The rodeos weren't using trick riders so much anymore. Like now, a trick rider would starve to death if that's all he did. So I figured it would be a good time to quit. I worked one last rodeo, at Huntsville, Texas. I always loved to work there. And then I quit.

Alice Greenough Orr

Tucson, Arizona

Alice Greenough, age thirty-three, in 1935.

ALICE COMES FROM ONE OF THE MOST FAMOUS RODEO FAMILIES OF ALL TIME. Her father, "Packsaddle Ben" Greenough, was a Brooklyn orphan who made his way to Montana in the early 1880s and won the first bronc-busting contest in the state. Five of Ben's eight children rodeoed—Turk, Bill, Frank, Alice, and Marge. To this day, Red Lodge, Montana, bills itself as "The Home of the Riding Greenoughs."

Alice and Marge were two of the greats among the lady bronc riders of the thirties and won titles from one end of the country to the other. Some of Alice's most proud trophies came from Boston Garden in 1933, 1935, and 1936; Madison Square Garden in 1941; and The Cowgirls International Buckjumping Contest in Sydney, Australia, in 1934 and 1939.

Marge, the younger of the two, married Heavy Henson, a bulldogger, in 1930. (Their son, Chuck Henson, was named Professional Rodeo Clown of the Year in 1978.) But Alice stayed single and foot-loose, free to travel with Wild West shows all over the world. She did not marry until 1958—to Joe Orr, a lifelong rodeo friend.

During the thirties and forties, Alice coupled her vigorous rodeo career with occasional ventures into journalism, and some of her insights into rodeo are excerpted elsewhere in this book. She also worked in Hollywood from time to time, with small parts in several movies, including *The Californians* in 1937.

Some director along the line required she dye her brown hair blond. When she was asked about it by a reporter, she said bluntly, "It looks like Hell."† She could have continued in pictures but preferred to return to rodeo, where a brunette could stay that way.

Today Alice lives in Tucson, next door to her sister Marge. Both women are widowed now, but never lonely. They regularly work in movies and television programs filmed in Tucson including "Little House on the Prairie." They usually drive teams. Some of their many rodeo friends are always passing through Tucson and never miss a chance to see the "Greenough girls."

Rodeo was a different world when Margie and my brothers and I competed. Rodeo boys were wild and tough, I'll tell you that. Those boys were ranch boys. I mean, they didn't sack groceries at a grocery store and go to Little Britches rodeos. They were boys who, during the slack season, went home to their ranch or worked on a ranch for somebody else. They were a different type of boy than is on the road today.

These boys today are trained athletes. They learned to ride from Little Britches on up through High School Rodeo and College Rodeo. It's like an education. And today they have every type of rodeo school—bronc-riding schools and bull-riding schools and roping schools. Our boys learned the hard way, because they had to. They learned on the ranch.

We sure did. We grew up near Red Lodge, Montana. Our dad had been an orphan in New York and ran away from the orphan home when he was only fourteen. He lived in cardboard boxes in back of stores and sold newspapers. He sold newspapers while they built the Brooklyn Bridge. Then he got a job outside New York City, riding a horse that pulled boats up and down the river. He made enough money there to get out to Minnesota or Michigan or someplace. There he worked for the railroads, carrying water for the railroad men. He finally got to Miles City, Montana, when he was sixteen and worked as a little porter boy. He did the same in Billings, and finally he hired out as a cowboy.

He rode for every big cow and horse outfit in Montana and Wyoming. He rode horses, he drove stagecoaches, he carried the mail, he punched cows, he packed in the mountains, he was a hired guide. He spent the rest of his natural life with cows and horses. He couldn't even turn a key on in an automobile.

He was an old-timer, all right. He batched with Liver Eating Johnson for a while, and their cabin's still in Red Lodge. He lived around old Calamity Jane. She took care of him as a boy and he'd cut wood for her to haul into Billings for the hotels. He'd sell the wood and then give her money to get drunk on. He'd save enough to buy groceries for her so she wouldn't go back to that cabin of hers out west of Billings and not have anything to eat. He'd have to hide from her then because he knew she'd get drunk and want the rest of that

† *Red Lodge, Carbon County News,* Friday, June 4, 1937.

money to drink some more. But she never could find him. He'd hide in hay corrals and everyplace.

Dad lived with old Curly, the Crow Indian scout that escaped the Custer battle. They batched on the banks of the Little Big Horn River, and there is still part of that old cabin there. Curly taught my father the Crow Indian language, both sign and verbal. Dad could talk five different languages fluently and he was a great friend of the Indians. He traded horses with them regular.

He always had a lot of horses around—two, three hundred horses. A lot of them weren't even halter-broke. He'd got them from the Indian reservation or gathered them off the range. He'd look at 'em and he'd say, "Well, Frank, take this. Alice, you take that. And Marge, take that one." One of his famous expressions was, "If you can't ride 'em, walk." That's how we learned to ride. We rode to school, we learned to drive teams, learned to handle horses. We learned to hunt right, and we learned to pack in the mountains. We learned to do a lot of things. It was a good teaching, a good background.

Mother was a shy little woman, raised in Illinois. Her daddy was an old Civil War veteran. He come from the war very ill and passed away shortly after. So Grandma had to start a boardinghouse to raise her family.

Dad used to ship horses into Illinois and Indiana and sell 'em to the farmers, have auctions. When they'd take the horses back, Dad and my uncle Bill and some of the cowboys would go, and they'd stay at Grandma's boardinghouse because there was no hotels. That's how Dad got acquainted with my mother. She was a milliner by trade.

They corresponded five years before they made any plans to get married. Finally, my dad asked her, would she marry him? But he was always too busy. He wrote her, "I can't come back to Illinois and get you, but you come to Billings, Montana, we'll get married there and go to the home ranch."

So that poor little thing—we're all such big old wild Indians, but she was a little tiny thing—she packed her trunk. All of her friends knew the Indians was going to scalp her. They could just see her massacred. But she arrived in Billings with her little trunk and her clothes and gifts and they were married.

Then they took the train to Red Lodge where Dad had left a wagon. He hauled her the five miles to the homestead. He had a little log house already built for her right on the bank of Rock Creek (pronounced "Crick"), and that was her first home. When she arrived, all these old cowboys come out from the barn just a yellin' and a hollerin'. She said later she was frightened spitless. She'd never seen anything like them before.

My father had to leave her alone a lot because his work was in the mountains. His horses and cattle were way back in the mountains where there were only trails. It was a three-day horseback trip to the top of the mountain. He'd go in and stay a month and she'd be down on that ranch by herself, just scared to death half the time.

A lot of Indians used to come through that country. Of course, back in Illinois they'd heard these awful stories about Indians. For the first two or three

Alice Greenough,
about ten years old,
in Billings,
Montana.

years, Mom was awful afraid. They'd come to the ranch to see my dad. She couldn't tell them that Dad might be back or that he was gone. They might hang around and camp all night. I can just imagine the fear she'd have until she finally learned that the Indians weren't going to harm her.

Course, then she started having babies. There's just a year's difference in most of our ages. The eight of us were born over a ten-year period. She never went to the hospital with a baby. She hauled her own water, chopped her own wood, did the washing. And she was so tiny. Couldn't have been five feet tall, and I doubt she ever weighed a hundred pounds. But she was strong and wiry.

In the evening, we'd come home from school and take off our school clothes, put on our overalls. Mom would get the washboard out and wash our clothes and then hang them by the stove to let them dry so we'd have clean clothes each day before school. We didn't have a change, you see. I remember waking early in the morning and seeing her standing there ironing our dresses, making sure they were dry before we put them on. By the time us kids got up, she'd have ironed our clothes, fixed our lunches, and cooked our breakfast. And she'd have her bread already punched down. What hour of the morning that little woman got up, I don't know.

This went on every day and every day until summertime when we went on vacation. In the summer, Dad would take us older ones with him to help with the camps in the mountains.

We'd go way up around Bear Tooth Lake. Then he'd go into the mountains for a month or so and leave us in the camp by ourselves with no living human closer than three days' trip horseback.

I don't think I was ever frightened one day of my life. He never left a gun with us. He left a fishhook and some line, and we fished. We killed grouse with rocks. I can't think of a day in those mountains that we didn't have fun. If nothing else, we'd have contests to see who'd catch the most fish. We'd see who could climb to the top of a mountain first. We climbed every mountain in that whole range. We always found something to do.

In 1917 my dad took a rural mail route out of Billings. But he had so much to do at home that I was his substitute. I was only fourteen years old. I was supposed to be eighteen to be bonded to carry mail, but I carried the mail route out of Billings thirty-seven miles horseback every day for three winters and two summers. Every day, even through forty-below-zero weather in the winter.

During the war, a rancher came over home and asked Dad if he could hire my brother to help him put up his hay. He couldn't get any help. Dad said my brother was already working but he could hire me—I'd work just like a man. So I worked all spring doing that. I'd drive six or eight horses on the gang plow.

In the twenties, Margie and I worked for Dad, and we worked for the ranchers around. We could do most anything. Sometimes everybody would get together for the Fourth of July or a celebration and line up their cars to make an arena and we'd have a rodeo. Margie and I rode lots of relay races. Sometimes we rode broncs for an exhibition. First time I rode bronc for a crowd was at Forsythe, Montana. These cowboys decided I ought to ride a bucking horse, so they brought over a gray bronc and saddled him and turned me loose in front of the grandstand. I didn't buck off.

In 1929, Margie and I got ahold of a copy of *Billboard Magazine* and saw an advertisement for this outfit that wanted bronc riders and trick riders. We wrote the guy a letter—it was Jack King with King's Wild West Show, the IXL outfit—and it wasn't very long 'til we got a telegram back telling us to be sure and come, to meet them in Ohio.

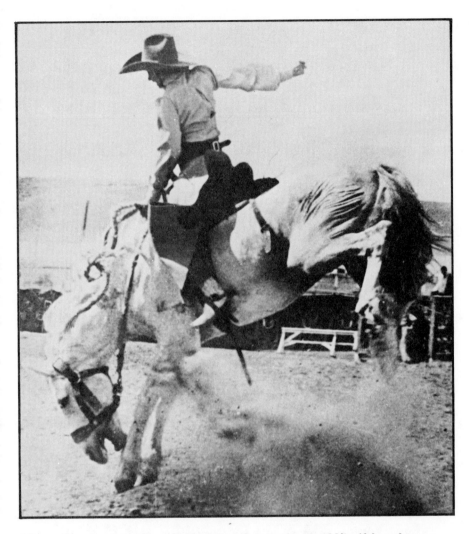

Marge Greenough on Great Falls, a Leo Cramer horse, 1937. Although most considered the women's bronc riding the most daring and most exciting for the crowd, the cowgirls also rode in races (both relay and flat), and trick-rode. A few cowgirls trick-roped, roped steers, and bulldogged. In these last events, the cowgirls usually performed as an exhibition rather than in competition—there simply weren't enough entries in the events to make a contest.

So Margie and I got all ready. We went to tell my mother and father that we were going to go rodeoing. It hurt their feelings to think we were going to go away from home and leave the ranch. But Dad said, "Well, that's all right. You have more guts than good sense, anyway. When you go, take Old Willy with you." Old Willy—that's what he called willpower. He wished us well and

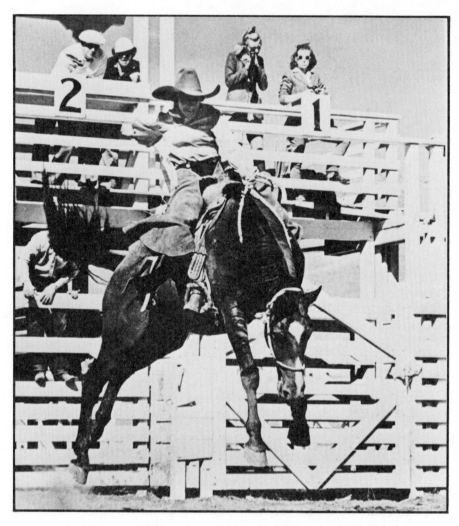

Alice Greenough on a bronc, Iowa's championship rodeo, 1935.

said, "You write to Mom and Dad and let us know where you are and what you're doing." And I'll tell you one thing, we never had to write home for five dollars, either.

So that was the start of our rodeo career. We slept in tents most of the time. There were no motels then. And the hotels were not too much in some of those little towns. They were usually full before we'd get there, anyways. So we had our own bedrolls and we had our washpan or water bucket and coffeepot. All the cowboys did.

We lived off our winnings. Lots of times it was just day money—twenty or thirty dollars if you won first place. Moneywise, it didn't sound like very much, but it bought a lot more than it buys today, so we lived just a good life. Everybody helped each other. There weren't so many people in rodeo as there are now, and we were all so close.

If one fellow had ten dollars, you had five of it. The cowboys sort of had their own banking business, their own loan business, among themselves.

Like if you were out of money and needed a tire for your car. If some old boy had fifteen or twenty dollars, he'd come and say, "Now are you all right? You better use this to get yourself a tire." You didn't have to ask. They'd come to you.

One of our favorite rodeos was the show at Madison Square Garden every year. We'd drive to New York and it took days and days and days at that time. We'd stay at hotels near the Garden.

The Garden was a big rodeo. One year they had fifty-six performances, and then we went right to Boston and put on thirty shows.

They kept all the saddle horses and the stock they were going to use that day in the basement of the Garden. When we had spare time, like after breakfast if we didn't have a morning show or didn't have any shopping or sewing to do, we'd all go down to the basement and sit around on bales of hay and visit. On days that there were rodeos, we'd get dressed and go down there an hour before rodeo time.

The New York people were very friendly to the Westerners at that time. The Garden would be filled every performance. The same way in Boston. And they just screamed when you rode a horse. They appreciated everything we did.

But those New York people, they thought that cowboys that showed up on the street ought to have a pistol. "Where's your pistol, Cowboy," they'd say when they'd see us. "Where's your horse." And of course, a cowboy comes to New York and he can't carry his gun on the street.

We had such wonderful friends in New York and Boston. Old Jack Dempsey, Mrs. Chrysler, Cornelius Vanderbilt. We were invited into their homes for dinner. If we were between the shows at New York and Boston, they'd invite us to stay the night.

Nineteen twenty-nine was my first year at the Garden. I didn't get to go in 1930 because I broke my ankle at a rodeo in El Paso, Texas. I hung up on a bucking horse and like to twisted my ankle off. I lay in the hospital there for about nine months. The bones wouldn't calcify. They were going to amputate my leg, but a German doctor came through El Paso and heard about my case. He talked to my doctor and said, "Wait a day or two." They operated again and that German doctor showed him how to use ivory pegs to wedge the bones together. I still have that ivory. I was called "The Girl with the Ivory Ankle." I wore a boot-shoe and rode broncs for years that way. It's hard to tell how many head of bucking horses I rode after I had that serious accident.

Out West they might not go in for city ways, psycho-analysis and the like, but Western women are happier, I believe, because they have to be tough—and that means strict rules of physical and mental health.

You don't see hysterical, dull-eyed women in the saddle. Cowgirls learn early that wants of the soul and body are first controlled by the mind. They are taught that beauty to be outside must be inside.

Cow-people believe that mental poise comes from physical health—that every muscle in your body must be educated in the work of health. Each muscle finds its response in the mind—and the mind cannot have an ill-used muscle to control, or when riding a bronc it's impossible to stick to his back. A horse's mind is quicker than a human's anyway, and it takes the best that's in you to stay on a bronc.

My Dad told me to stick on a pony's back as soon as I was old enough to climb on a saddle. He also taught me it was wrong to wear any garment which bound my body. These were my first lessons in muscle development and body posture.

In strengthening and toughening your body, which to the cowgirl is another way of saying beautifying your mind, you wear no heels to unbalance your structure. Heels and pointed toes cramp your viewpoint. It is believed that city women's dread of childbirth is mainly due to the unnatural position continual wearing of high heels has on the inner organs.

A cow-woman takes no coddling, gets no martyr complex just because she is going to have a baby. She rides in the show up until two months before she expects the child—and she is back in the saddle bronc-riding in contests not later than six weeks afterward. This is the reward of developing strong backs, erect posture, educated muscles.

A cowgirl would no more think of wearing spike heels, a tight girdle, a binding brassiere, than she would drink poison. It is not that a cowgirl does not want to attract the masculine eyes, but we know cowboys. They like slimness, line, grace—but they want it natural. . . .

If a girdle or corset is needed to hold muscles which have been allowed to grow lazy and inactive, the cow-people believe that a girl has allowed her mind to grow ugly—she has sinned, broken health laws.

Daily routine of cowgirls is both mental and physical training. . . . She learns to take care of a horse—and as some girls learn to love dolls the small Westerner learns to love an animal and thus to appreciate natural beauty.

She is taught early that a good rider cannot drink or smoke. She is taught, too, that necking and kissing are not to become habits.

Yes, city women whose nerves are strained and whose systems are shot could learn much about poise and nerve health from natural Western women.

Women with curved spines and swayed abdomens, with half the muscles in their bodies wasted from lack of exercise and use, who fear childbirth because they have not kept their bodies natural enough to accept the most natural experience in the world, wonder why their lives are not rich, full, vital—yet they never dream that the violation of natural health laws is the cause of everything. . . .

—Alice Greenough,
"What Cowgirl Wants from Life," *Physical Culture,* **May 1937.**

I was back in New York in 'thirty-one, but I didn't ride broncs because my foot wasn't in any shape to ride. I did ride grand entry and quadrilles [square dance on horseback]. In 1932 I was at the Fort Worth show when an impresario or a promoter from Spain came looking at some of the cowboys and cowgirls. He picked me out to go to Spain to work in the bullrings for a year.

I went to Mexico and had my first experience in a bullring there. Then I sailed to Spain and I worked in thirty-two of their largest bullrings. I worked in Madrid twice, Barcelona twice, and all of the big bullrings.

Every fighting bull that I got on, they killed. I come out of a little old steel-constructed chute, and I'd ride the bull. Then they would go ahead and use him in a bullfight and kill him. I also had a trick-riding horse and I trick rode at all the shows.

When I was in Mexico City they told me that the Spaniards were very temperamental. If they didn't like what you were doing they were likely to throw bottles at you and get real excited. Try to run you out of the country, really. The Spaniards liked my riding. If they hadn't, I would have left Spain in a hurry. But for some reason or other, they accepted me all over Spain. And I worked in the south of France too.

At that time it was very unusual to see a girl alone in Spain. The unmarried girls were all escorted; even when they went for walks they had a chaperone. The men didn't try to court me. They were very friendly, but they were a little shy. I had two or three of them see me on the street and ask me if I was a French girl. I was very indignant. I said, "No!"

Of course, it's different in Spain now from the way it used to be. I remember one morning I was walking around with my pants on. I had my bridle and I was going out to work my trick-riding horse. I came across a whole group of little girls going to school. The nuns teach the girls, and the bishops teach the boys. When the girls saw me, the Sisters made them turn around and cover up their faces. They weren't supposed to look at me 'cause I had pants on. Course, the little girls giggled and peeked through their fingers. They wanted to see me anyway.

That year in Spain was one of the best I ever had. Then I went to England with Tex Austin's outfit in 'thirty-four. I went to Australia in 'thirty-five and stayed over there eighteen months. I won their International Buckjumping Contest. I went back in 'thirty-nine and won it again. I won Boston Yard in 'thirty-three, 'thirty-five, and 'thirty-six. And I won New York in nineteen forty-one. Those are the big ones. Marge and I worked in every state in the Union but three—Maine, Vermont, and New Jersey. They just didn't have rodeos then. It's hard telling how many shows we won.

Margie and my brothers and I were really well known. We had a lot of fans. Little kids in school would pretend to be us when they'd ride their stick horses and play cowboys and Indians. Instead of pretending to be Tom Mix or Hoot Gibson or something, they would pretend to be us. People would tell us, "My girls play like they're Alice Greenough," or, "My boy plays Turk Greenough. He wants to be a cowboy." Makes you feel kind of good.

Alice and Margie Greenough at Madison Square Garden, 1938.

Packsaddle Ben's mantel at the home ranch at Red Lodge, Montana, 1941.

'Forty-one was the last year they had girls' bronc riding in New York, and I think that was probably the end of the long career of girl bronc riders. At one time New York had something like seventeen girl bronc riders entered. After 'forty-one, a few shows had exhibition girls bronc riding, but that just about ended the competitive era.

I don't really know for sure why they quit the girls bronc riding. There weren't so many girls to ride anymore. We were all ranch-raised. There were still girls off ranches, but they didn't come up the hard way like we had. And the war changed a lot of things. Transportation was hard and the producers couldn't transport as much stock.

So in 1941 I went into the rodeo business with my old friend Joe Orr. We put together a rodeo outfit. We started right out with nothing, but every time we'd have a little money we'd buy a bucking horse. We put together a good string of bucking horses and we'd send them to the Garden for the rodeo. After about two years of that we decided we'd keep our own good bucking horses and put on our own shows. We produced rodeos until nineteen fifty-nine.

We furnished stock all over Idaho and Montana, Wyoming, Calgary, Dakota, as far east as Milwaukee. I ran the office myself. I didn't even have an adding machine the first two years. I did it all on paper. I took care of all the books and ran the arena and paid off all the cowboys myself. And I rode broncs as an exhibition.

I never married until real late in life and then I married Joe, my lifelong friend. After we sold our rodeo outfit, I think he thought, "What's going to happen to me? I'm just a lonesome old cowboy." So one day he said, "Why don't we get married? You don't know anybody else and I don't want anybody else."

I said, "Sounds like a good idea. I've known you all my life. I know all your faults and you know mine."

So we got married and built our house in Tucson and made a home for ourselves. That was the first home he ever had. We got along very good. Just no problem at all. We shared everything—our work and what little we saved. My friends were his friends and his friends were my friends. It wasn't a new life at all.

That rodeo life was a good old life. We were all so close-knit. It's a friendship that we created over the years. And it's still the same. You go down in that hotel lobby [I interviewed Alice during a reunion of old-time rodeo hands during the National Finals Rodeo in 1978] and everybody's so happy to see you that they can't hardly sit still. There's not an old man with a big hat here that don't know who we are. God bless 'em. They all think we're pretty great, I think. And we think as much of them.

We all keep in touch. Anytime anybody comes through Tucson, they stop and see Margie and me. You can look on my back porch from eleven o'clock on, and if there isn't five or six cowboys sitting there drinking coffee, something is wrong somewhere. They still come together at our house because we are the two old cowgirls in the rodeo business there. And if they want to stay all night—pull their camper in the back lot, or keep their horse out back—they're welcome.

We're still all very close. When Margie's husband passed away, and then when mine did, you never saw so many friends. Old cowboys, ranchers, boys from the stockyards, the brand inspectors. Flowers and telephone calls and messages. You'd think the President of the United States had passed away.

We came from a great era. We call ourselves the Wild Bunch. It's all different now. Now you have the New Breed. They're great athletes, but it's not the closeness like we had. No, our era is fading away. We have a big long panoramic picture, about twenty-four inches long, took of all of us at Madison Square Garden, and you can just go down the lines . . . he's here, he's here, this one's gone—just right down through. 'Bout every third one's already passed away. So there's very few of the old-timers left. That's the reason we have the Wild Bunch, our reunion, so the few of us left out of the cowboys that really started rodeo can get together.

It's like the First World War. There's very few of those veterans left, and they are still very close. The First World War, and the Second World War. But I think the Korean War and this last war, they are another breed. They could care less about a fellow that fought the First World War or the second one. It's just a different world, and it's too bad. And rodeo is the same way.

Fern Sawyer

Nogal, New Mexico

Fern Sawyer on her ranch near Nogal, New Mexico, 1979.

IT IS THE EVENING OF THE MISS RODEO AMERICA PAGEANT AT THE 1978 National Finals Rodeo in Oklahoma City and Fern is a little late getting to her seat in the judge's box. She has come through the rows of coliseum seats instead of using the normal access through the pressroom, and a four-foot railing plus a drop of about three feet separate her from her seat.

I am sitting next to the judge's box, in the press area. I had met Fern earlier in the day. She recognizes me and says, "Now tell me, honey—how in hell am I 'sposed to get down there?" I start to tell her about the route through the pressroom but she interrupts with, "Oh hell, this little old rail ain't much." She puts one hand on the rail and pops over it. You should know—Fern Sawyer is sixty-two years old.

Fern lives hard. She works hard, plays hard, drinks hard, smokes hard. She looks Indian, with chiseled features, dynamic coloring, and thick, pure-black hair that reaches her waist. She has the figure of a sixteen-year-old—she wears size eight jeans—and dresses with an elegant and unself-conscious élan. Color-ful silk shirts, tailored pants, coordinated Stetsons and handmade cowboy boots with high, steep, riding heels and her brand— 5⌐—worked into the design on the tall stovepipe top. If it's cold, Fern wears one of her many fur jackets. Always, she wears Indian jewelry most museums would give their eye teeth for. Tonight, for instance, her turquoise belt buckle is about half the size of Texas.

Fern is the quintessence of cowgirl chic, an ultra style based on the romance and perquisites of the range that has been picked up by New York's top designers in the past few years. Fern has always dressed this way.

(Later I visited Fern's ranch near Nogal, New Mexico. Her house, a show-case adobe, mirrors New Mexico's light and space. After taking me through the living area, the bedrooms, the several sunken baths, the patio with its ex-pansive pool, Fern said, "Now you've got to see the best room in this house." She opened the door on a closet that ran the length of the house. Racks and racks of clothes, drawers from floor to ceiling, around 150 pairs of handmade boots and Stetsons in a rainbow of colors. "Of course," Fern says, "when you do as many things as I do, it takes a lot of clothes.")

Fern's father, U. D. Sawyer, was a pioneer cattleman in New Mexico. Al-though he never held office himself, he was intimate with governors and sena-tors of the state. Fern's mother was Democratic National Chairwoman from New Mexico for twenty-five years. Fern has been a delegate or alternate to nearly every Democratic National Convention since she was twenty-one.

Fern rodeoed in the thirties and forties and today is in great demand as a judge. She was a hand at all events and nigh unbeatable in the cutting on her famous cutting horse, Bélen. Fern won several major cutting contests and was the only woman ever to win the huge cutting contest at the Fort Worth Fat Stock Show. She was inducted into the Cowgirl Hall of Fame in 1976.

Fern lives full-throttle and always has. She minces words with no one and her conversation is peppered liberally with "goddam," "hell," and "son of a bitch." Feral and unquenchable, she embodies the exotic self-indulgence of an F. Scott Fitzgerald heroine gone West.

I have a great philosophy of life. Do all you can as fast as you can. If I had it to do over, I'd do the same thing, only a little more of it.

I always drive fast. I get lots of tickets if I don't know the cops. At home I know the cops. I always have had a fast car. I just can't stand that fifty-five miles an hour. Drives me crazy. I'm not interested in doing anything if I can't do it in thirty minutes.

I don't play golf; it's too damn slow. But I play lots of tennis. Just took that up recently. I went to Manzanillo, Mexico, and won a tennis tournament, men and women. Of course, I was handicapped, but that just tickled me to death to win over all those twenty-year-olds. I'm sixty-two years old.

I'm real lucky, I guess. I'm real healthy. For my age, I feel like I'm pretty young. I try to keep my body in real good shape. If you're roping and riding and skiing and playing tennis at my age, you have to be healthy. I'm a pretty good athlete, always have been. They say it's all downhill from here, but I never think of that. I'm always looking for tomorrow. My sister says there's only one alternative to birthdays, and that's to die.

I'm always going to have a good time. I have never been bored in my life. Everybody says, "Don't you ever get lonesome when you're out there alone on the ranch?" I've never been lonesome a day in my life. Ever. If I get lonesome, I'll go find somebody.

I've always worked. From the time I was a year old, I worked—riding, helping men, branding, everything. I still do. I rope ever' calf that's branded on my ranch. My daddy always said, "Even if you've got a million dollars, you don't have a penny if you don't work. If you've got too much idle time, you're in bad shape."

I can't imagine people getting so bored with theirselves and their life that they stay drunk or take pills or smoke dope. All these women taking Valium, all these funny things—I have never had anything in my life except allergy pills. I'll go to a dance and drink and have more fun than any human—but the drinking is not necessary for me. When I'm home alone, I never do that.

You asked me how come I won so much in rodeo. I'll tell you why. 'Cause I had a daddy that was the best cowboy that ever was. He's dead now, died in 'sixty-six, but I was with him all my life on horseback.

He could see a calf born and never see it again 'til it was grown, and know which cow was its mother. That just has to be natural. I asked him, "How do you do that?" He said, "Well, it's just a flesh mark. It's just like knowing people."

I can't do that. Now, I can see a calf and pick out its mother in a big herd, mother them up. But to see it born and never see it again 'til its grown, and *then* tell you which cow it belongs to—no way! My sister could have been that good. But she wasn't interested. She didn't like to ride and she didn't like cows. And I'm in the business, and I should have had that ability. But I get along just fine.

I was on a horse from morning 'til night, growing up. Daddy always told me, "You don't have to ride. You can either help me, or you can go help your mother in the house. That's your choice. But if you go with us, you are going to be treated just like one of the cowboys. You don't quit. You are just one of them."

And if that's the choice I made, I was never sorry. Sometimes I thought I was—it would be cold out and you had to get up at three o'clock in the morning to ride—but I was always glad I went.

My daddy was a real good man, and a real kind man. I did pretty much what I wanted to do, except around the cattle. That he was going to make me do right. He taught me to cut, he taught me to mother-up cattle, he taught me everything I know. I wouldn't have ever learned if he hadn't taught me so well. You know, being a girl, you wouldn't have learned those really technical things if your daddy didn't work with you. Every day and every minute of the world. Because there really is a lot to know in the cattle business, and it really is hard.

When Daddy died I thought I'd go crazy. I had my ranch at Nogal. I'd always call him on the telephone and say, "I'm going to sell these yearlings today. What do you think I ought to get for them?" He'd tell me. And I always had him there to do the thinking.

I thought I could do any damn thing there is to do on a ranch until he died. But when he died I was the most lost human. I thought I'd cry the first time I branded. You know, without him there to say, "You do this, you do thåt, you do this." He always did all the thinking, and I was just there roping. Then I had to get the branding together, get the vaccine, organize everything. Same with everything on the ranch. It took me about three years before I could get it all together.

I started rodeoing when I was about fifteen, in about 1932. I worked cutting and roping and I did a little of everything. I went to the first all-girls rodeo they ever had, in Amarillo in 1947. Nancy Binford and Thena Mae Farr put it on, and it was a good rodeo. [Nancy's sister Barbara also helped produce it.]

The stands were packed every night. I competed in tag races, cutting, barrel race, roping, team roping—everything but the bronc riding. I won just about everything and got the all-around.

I wasn't entered in the bull riding but one night they didn't have anybody to ride a bull 'cause everybody was hurt. I told them I would do it because the crowd deserved to see a bull ride. I had finished my events and Dad said, "Let's go put the horses up." I said, "No, I'm going down to the chutes." "What are you going to do?" "I'm going to try to ride this bull."

Well, Daddy just had a fit, but I went down there and got on that bull. The last thing I saw was Daddy peeking through the fence. He said, "Well, if you get on him, you damn sure better ride him." I did ride him, but I broke my hand in nine places. I didn't get bucked off. I broke it gripping so hard.

I didn't say anything about my hand, just went and drove my horses home. Pretty soon my hand got about as big as my leg. 'Bout a week, they had to fly me to Lubbock [Texas] and put all those bones in place.

I'd got seven dollars mount money to ride that bull. That wasn't prize money because I wasn't entered. That's just what they paid me to ride him. Daddy didn't think I'd made very much with that ride because he had to spend about a thousand on my hand.

I went to the rodeo at Madison Square Garden after they cut out the women's bronc riding. I came in right on the tail of that. After 1941, the girls were contracted. They called us glamor girls or something and they hired us for color. We rode barrels and rode in the grand entry. And we were paid to do it. I thought it was real silly. I liked the bronc riding.

I felt real bad because Tad Lucas and Florence Randolph and all those

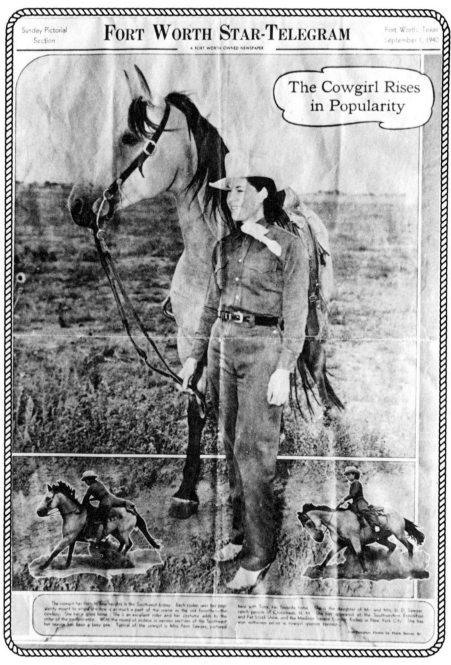

Article about Fern Sawyer, 1940.

great cowgirls I admired so much were back there. They were my idols. They weren't too nice to us at first, because they felt we were amateurs. Some of the glamor girls could hardly ride. Here the rodeo knocked out a good event to bring in a bunch of little old girls who weren't supposed to be anything. I don't blame them; I would have felt the same way. But they were always nice to me. I could ride real well, so they accepted me. They've been my friends ever since. I just love 'em all. Later I rodeoed with Mitzi, Tad's daughter.

Rodeo is a good deal different now than it was back then. We rodeoed because that was what we did on the ranch. We don't have any real cowboys anymore. We have athletes, trained athletes. Rodeo hands come out of cities. Some of them are ranch-raised, but a lot of them aren't. There's cutting-horse clinics, queen clinics, roping clinics. Little Britches Rodeo, High School Rodeo, College Rodeo. These rodeo hands today are trained as much as Olympic athletes.

I went to Texas Tech to college, and they were going to kick me out because I went to a rodeo. Now they give scholarships so kids can rodeo. I go back there and judge their college rodeos. How about that! I blazed that old trail for these rodeo kids, for college rodeo. I really did. And I fought every step of the way.

I rodeoed because I couldn't do anything else. I knew how to ride a horse and I wanted to prove to the world I could. I got real serious in the cutting, and I had a pretty good horse. I was winning second, but this other horse was winning first. Belonged to Barry Hart, a bronc rider from Texas. We were at a rodeo in Texas and Daddy was down at the arena talking to me. I said, "I heard Barry price that horse." Daddy said, "How much?" I said, "A thousand dollars."

Well, that was like a million dollars in nineteen forty-one. Daddy said, "Why, I wouldn't give a thousand dollars for any damn horse I ever saw." And he went back up in the grandstand.

In a minute my mother said, "If she's going to rodeo, she's got to have the best." So Dad come down to me. I didn't have a car, and we had been talking about getting me one. He said, "Which do you want? The car, or the horse?"

I said, "I'll take the horse."

He said, "Will you promise not to get married for five years if I buy you that horse?"

"No, I probably won't get married, but I won't promise."

"Well, O.K. We'll take it."

So we bought him. I'd never ridden him, I'd just seen him. The man who owned him rode in the trailer with him for five miles and patted him. He was real sad.

Bélen was the best cutting horse that ever was, but he was a mean son of a bitch. He would have killed me 'til the day he died. But he was so good it didn't make any difference.

One time in Denver, he bucked me off higher than that damn grandstand.

Here I was, just amazed out there in the arena. I said, "You old son of a bitch!" and it just rung out! Homer Pettigrew, one of the bulldoggers, was on the side and he said, "Go get him. You can still win." I went and got back on him, and he worked better than he ever did. I won the cutting that year.

Bélen and I won lots of cutting contests. I was the only woman to ever win Fort Worth. Won out over about a hundred and fifty men in nineteen forty-five. I won Pecos four times in a row, and that was one of the best cutting contests ever. I won thirteen or fourteen saddles. Then the war came along and they started giving war bonds. And after that, they usually gave award buckles. I was sick, because I wanted to see how many saddles I could win. You get a thing about it, you know.

Bélen was seven-eighths Thoroughbred. His mother was on the track, a running horse. He wasn't a Quarter Horse—that's what delighted me! I beat all the Quarter Horses! He really was unusual.

Bélen could really run. One year at Pecos, a bunch of cowboys wanted me to run him in a race. I said, "No Way!" They said, "We'll give you a thousand dollars to run this race." And you know, a thousand dollars was a thousand dollars then. But I said, "You can ruin lots of horses, but you are not going to ruin a cutting horse."

He was a hard bucker, and he was just plain mean. Like I say, he would have killed me 'til the day he died. But I'd love to have another horse like that. If I ever find one, I'm going to get him, even if I have to sell the ranch to do it.

I was a founding member of the National Cutting Horse Association. They weren't going to let me in because I was a woman. I said, "You know if I had a sorry horse, you'd be delighted to have me. But I have a good horse, so you are worried about it." I said, "I think we ought to take a vote." We were all out behind the stock show, sitting on bales of hay. There was only about twenty of us. I went around and talked to everybody on those old bales of hay, and I won that vote. I won Fort Worth right after that.

Rodeo's a real close world. If you've ever rodeoed, you are one of them. If you haven't, you are just out. It's like all them kids down there tonight [at the National Finals Rodeo].They just accept me because I was a rodeo hand. Maybe their parents knew me; maybe not. But if you was ever in that circle, you're in. Rodeo people are real clannish, to tell you the truth. And I was too. When I rodeoed, I didn't give a damn what was going on in the rest of the world.

I didn't get married until I finished rodeoing.‡ I quit when I was thirty, in nineteen forty-seven. Nobody made me quit, but I thought that was a good time to quit—when you are on top, not when you are on the bottom.

‡ Fern married and divorced twice and has no children.

I've always been involved with politics. My mother was the Democratic National Chairwoman from New Mexico for twenty-five years. I was County Chairman for eight years. I've been a delegate or an alternate to nearly every Democratic National Convention since I was twenty-one.

Jack Kennedy was a dear friend of mine. I don't like Ted and I didn't like Bobby, but I sure did like Jack. I've still got letters he wrote.

I met Jack when he was a senator. I had to pick him up at the airport in Albuquerque. He was going to be the speaker at our state convention and I was a delegate. I had an old El Dorado convertible, so Senator Montoya and I went out to pick him up.

I thought, "He's just so smart. I'm not going to talk." So I didn't. But Montoya said, "Jack, did you know that Fern used to rodeo?" Jack said, "Do you know Casey Tibbs?" [Casey Tibbs is a legendary bareback and saddle bronc rider who won nine world championships between 1949 and 1959.] I thought, "Boy, there's one subject I can talk about." Jack said he admired Casey Tibbs more than anybody. I thought that was something. I had to call Casey and tell him that. Casey should have gone to see Jack. That would have been like the President coming to see us, for Jack.

Ted rode a bareback horse in Tucson. He was campaigning for Jack. I couldn't believe it. He'd never seen a bareback horse before. He got up on the chute and said, "Where's the saddle?" They put him on and they said he made a pretty damn good ride. He was just a kid then. I really did like Ted, but he's gone off the deep end. I don't know what the hell's the matter with him. Wants to nationalize medicine. He's a crazy liberal.

Since I was twenty-one I never missed a time of voting. I think it's your duty and your privilege to vote. Some of these kids preach all this wild liberal stuff, but they won't do a thing about it, they won't even go vote. It makes me furious. Here I am out there working and trying to keep a conservative sort of government—you know, where you can live—and they won't even vote.

I went to McGovern's convention and had a fight on the floor. It was the worst thing you ever saw. We had this hippie-type kid who had a master's degree. He was filthy dirty and had an old hairy chest and no shirt—he just looked like hell. We were having a courtesy vote for Senator Montoya for Vice-President. It was strictly a courtesy vote to show you appreciate your senators. This hippie told me he wouldn't vote for Joe Montoya. He voted for Cesar Chavez from California. I said, "What did you vote for Cesar Chavez for?" He said, "Because he is a fine gentleman."

I said, "He's a card-carrying communistic son of a bitch is what he is. Everybody knows that."

Bruce King was governor then and he said, "Come on, let's go. I'm on your side, but we can't be on TV."

That was in 'seventy-two. You saw what happened to McGovern too. They put up with stuff like that and got a Republican elected. That's all they did.

I've worked a lot in politics. I was appointed to the New Mexico State Fair board for fifteen years. I never worked so hard as I did on that. That's why we got a good rodeo at Albuquerque, 'cause that was my part.

Jack Campbell was governor and he called my daddy. He said, "What do you think about me putting Fern on the Fair board?"

Daddy said, "Jack, she's liable to tell everybody in the state to go to hell," and Jack said, "Maybe that's what we need."

He called me the next day and put me on. Sure did surprise me. I didn't even ask for it. But I worked like a dog and spent many a dollar. And enjoyed ever' minute of it. I believe I was the first woman that was ever on the fair board anywhere in the United States.

I don't believe in women's lib. When I started cutting, a woman had to do double good to get the same marking. But I don't believe in preaching women's lib or hollering about it. I believe action proves more than words. I wanted to prove to them that I could do it and I did. Maybe I'm a little egotistical, but I have never failed at anything I tried to do.

The people that are really independent and do things, they don't like women's lib. Take old Bella Abzug—I can't stand her. I went to her meeting on women's lib at the Democratic convention in Miami, just to listen. I have never seen so many crazy people. Bunch of lesbians is all they was. I got up and left. I didn't want any part of that. It made cold chills go up my spine, the things they were saying!

And here I was supposed to be the big liberal. I was smoking a pipe at that time. Later I saw an article in some magazine that said this woman from New Mexico who smoked a pipe and wore a lot of Indian jewelry had the *audacity* to get up and leave during Bella Abzug's speech. Huh! I don't feel comfortable with those kind of people. They're nuts. They're not doing any good, it looks like to me. All they're doing is raising hell and putting women in the draft and a bunch of crap that they shouldn't be doing.

I believe you prove what you can do. If you're good enough, you'll get there. You can't tell me that in America, if you're good at your job, you won't make it. I've seen too many of them make it. And without no women's lib.

Cowgirls and the Crowd: The Recent Years

THE GIRLS RODEO ASSOCIATION, 1942–1981
(*now* WOMEN'S PROFESSIONAL RODEO ASSOCIATION)

Deb Leatherberry on a bronc, Hereford, Texas, All-Girls Rodeo, 1978.

Women in Rodeo 1942–1981

A Brief History

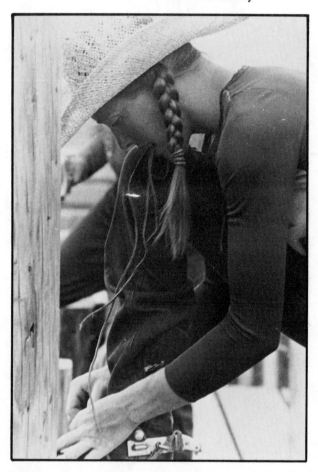

*Judy Robinson,
1978 GRA
All-Around
Champion Cowgirl,
tying down her
spurs, 1978.*

IN 1942 THE MADISON SQUARE GARDEN RODEO REPLACED THE COWGIRL BRONC riders with "sponsors" or "glamor girls"—girls chosen from the western states to ride in the grand entry and barrel race. The rodeo regulars complained that the girls were chosen more for glamor than talent, that some of them could hardly ride.

But the event is significant because it signals the beginning of barrel racing's acceptance on the professional rodeo circuit.* Although girls had been barrel

---

* Professional rodeo producers had a logical reason to want the barrel racing in rodeo. Each barrel racer has her own horse and requires no other stock. Barrel racing is the only rodeo event that does not require the producer to supply stock. Thus, it is a "cheap" event. Yet, it generally ranks right behind bull and bronc riding as an audience favorite.

racing (running a cloverleaf pattern around three barrels—shortest time wins) for some time in the Southwest, the Garden in 1942 was the beginning of its acceptance on a national scale.

Very little happened in women's rodeo over the next few years. Rodeo-goers grew used to seeing barrel racing on the program. Women who wished to compete against each other in other events did so only on a local jackpot basis.

Then in 1948 three ranch cowgirls, Nancy and Barbara Binford and Thena Mae Farr,† organized an all-girl rodeo in Amarillo, Texas, the first of its kind.‡ Cowgirls from Texas and neighboring states converged to compete in calf roping, bull and bronc riding, barrel racing, and other events. At that rodeo a dispute arose over a calf-roping contest, and since there were no standard rules, it led to a heated argument. The cowgirls at the rodeo decided they needed to organize. As they set down rules and regulations, the Girls Rodeo Association (GRA) was born.*

In 1948 the GRA had seventy-four members and staged one rodeo. In 1979 it had close to two thousand members and sanctioned fifteen all-girl shows. In 1981 it changed its name to the Women's Professional Rodeo Association (WPRA). (For simplicity's sake, the term WPRA will be used to denote both the original organization and the present one.)

Official WPRA events are barrel racing; bareback bronc riding; bull or steer riding; team roping (one roper ropes a steer's head; the other, its heels); steer undecorating (the women's version of steer wrestling. The mounted contestant snatches a ribbon off the steer's neck instead of jumping off the horse and wrestling the steer to the ground); goat tying; and calf roping (both breakaway, where the end of the rope is tied with a piece of string to the saddle horn so that it "breaks away" as soon as the calf is caught; and tie-down, where the rope is tied "hard and fast" to the horn and the cowgirl jumps off her horse as soon as she catches her calf, throws it, and hog-ties it).

But of the two thousand members in the WPRA, only a fraction of them compete in all-girl rodeos. Most of them barrel race on the PRCA† circuit, for most PRCA rodeos feature WPRA barrel racing. The WPRA approved 652 barrel races in 1980, and most of them were held at PRCA rodeos.

Within the WPRA there are two groups of barrel racers—those who compete in other girls' events and barrel race at the all-girl shows; and those whose only event is barrel racing and who hit the PRCA shows. Although the second group can compete at the all-girl shows, they rarely do because the purses are so small.

---

† The 1979 GRA Annual mentions only the Binfords; but Fern Sawyer, who won the all-around at that rodeo, recalls that Thena Mae Farr also helped produce it.
‡ Faye Kirkwood produced what she deemed "The World's First All-Girl Rodeo" in Bonham, Texas, earlier that year, but hers featured exhibitions rather than contests, so it really was a women's Wild West show rather than a rodeo.
* 1979 GRA Annual.
† Professional Rodeo Cowboys Association, formerly the Rodeo Cowboys Association, RCA.

The difference in potential winnings between the two groups is astounding. In 1980 the WPRA All-Around Champion Cowgirl, Gloria Paulson, competed in all WPRA events except bull and bronc riding and earned $8,100. She had the highest earnings of any all-girl rodeo competitor. The 1980 World Champion Barrel Racer, Martha Josey, won more than $48,000 in her one event. In that year close to $800,000 was awarded in prize money in the WPRA and the bulk of it went to the barrel racers on the PRCA circuit. It's not surprising that over 75 percent of the WPRA members keep their horses turning those barrels.

To understand how the dichotomy in the WPRA evolved, one needs only go back to that barrel race at Madison Square Garden in 1942. By the time the WPRA was formed six years later, rodeo crowds were used to seeing barrel racers at PRCA rodeos. The WPRA barrel racers had a national circuit ready and waiting for them. The other events were not customary at the men's shows, so a new circuit had to arise to accommodate them. The WPRA barrel racers could enjoy the benefits of the PRCA's much larger structure—its audiences, promotion, and purses. The all-girl shows had to create their own structure from scratch. Perhaps if the "glamor girls" had roped calves instead of run barrels at the Garden, we would see women perform in a different capacity at PRCA rodeos today.

The look of women's rodeo has changed significantly since the era of Tad Lucas and Alice Greenough. In their day, rodeo was as much a daring entertainment—like a circus—as a professional sport. The lady bronc riders were great athletes and competitors to be sure, but they were also show people. They dressed in vivid costumes designed to please the crowd.

But today, with close to a million dollars up for grabs, women's rodeo is most definitely a professional sport. The women see themselves as athletes rather than celebrities and they dress accordingly. They wear neat, bright clothes (the WPRA has a rule that barrel racers cannot wear blue jeans in the arena), but not costumes. Ironical, perhaps, for the descendants of the glamor girls.

Barrel racing is growing fast as a women's professional sport. Each year the WPRA approves more barrel races and each year the purses grow. Although some PRCA rodeos do not give the barrel racers equal money (that is, not as much money is added to the purse after entry fees), their number is decreasing and the goal of equal money at all PRCA rodeos is in sight—meaning even higher earnings for the WPRA.

The picture for all-girl rodeos is not so rosy. In 1977 there were twenty-four all-girl shows compared to twelve in 1980. They are scattered all over the western states—from Texas to Montana and California to Oklahoma. The purses are small and skyrocketing gas costs make it impractical to haul a horse five hundred or a thousand miles for a hundred-dollar rodeo. The sheer economics involved are making all-girl rodeo an expensive hobby rather than a profes-

Annette Pollard on a bronc, Hereford, Texas, All-Girls Rodeo, 1978.

*Suzy Thomas, bull
and bronc rider and
calf roper, at the
Littleton, Colorado,
All-Girls Rodeo, 1978.*

Jocko Jonckowski on a bull, Hereford, Texas, All-Girls Rodeo, 1978.

sional sport. The only things that can turn it around are aggressive promotion and major corporate sponsorship. Once again, as in 1941, high transportation costs and few competitors jeopardize the traditional events in women's rodeo.

Shari Korff

Huntington Beach, California

*Shari Korff,
barrel racing at
the 1978
National Finals
Rodeo,
Oklahoma City,
Oklahoma.*

IN BARREL RACING, MORE THAN IN ANY OTHER EVENT, SUCCESS DEPENDS ON your horse. Most barrel racers will tell you that at least two thirds of the credit goes to the horse; some will attribute as much as 80 percent.

In the WPRA, the toughest barrel racing circuit in the world, runs are usually measured in hundredths of a second. Often, less than three tenths of a second separate the top six barrel racers in a contest.

A good horsewoman can get more out of her horse than a poor one can, and training is very important. But there is a point beyond which you cannot go. If it takes a 16.9 to win and the best your horse can run is 17.5, you are not going to make much money going down the road. It takes an extraordinary horse to win at barrel race on the professional circuit. It's as simple as that.

For that reason, barrel horses are the highest-priced performance horses in rodeo. A price of $20,000 is not uncommon; some go as high as $40,000. The horses you see at the top in the professional circuit are almost always proud, powerful Quarter Horses whose good breeding shows in every muscle.

Once in a while you find an exception, a mongrel horse from nowhere who

*Shari Korff's
trophy buckle
from the 1978
Salinas Rodeo.*

has barrel racing in his blood. Shari's Geronimo is such a horse. Shari raised the chestnut gelding out of a $125 mare. Among his pedigreed counterparts, Gerry looks like a runt. Yet, the little mutt is a barrel-running fool. Gerry and Shari made the Finals their first year in the WPRA, 1978, and ranked twelfth overall at year's end. They ended up seventh in the World in 1979.

Gerry has become a sort of cult hero. Every old-time cowboy who was around in the days of cowponies, before anybody bothered to note who a horse's mama and papa were, gets a charge out of Geronimo. Anyone who has ever rooted for the underdog is on Gerry's side. And Gerry has earned the respect of all the other barrel racers as well.

Shari is a bit of a renegade herself. The top barrel racers tend to be a rather serious lot. There are fewer variables in barrel racing than in any other rodeo event. In roping, it matters whether your calf or steer runs straight or dodges. In the bucking events, half your score depends on how hard your horse or bull bucks. But in barrel racing, there is very little "luck of the draw." The condition of the ground makes some difference, but within reason, it is the same for all contestants during a round. Since a few hundredths of a second may mean the difference between win, place, or lose, a barrel racer must be at her best. If she is the least bit tired, the least bit distracted, she can jeopardize the absolute oneness of horse and rider necessary for a perfect run. With the need for such complete discipline and self-control, it's no wonder barrel racers aren't much to party.

Not so for Shari. Although she doesn't drink much herself, she loves the camaraderie of the bar after a rodeo. She is always greeted with enthusiasm when she walks in. Tiny and blond, with a sunny and irrepressible smile, she hardly seems the serious sort. Yet next day, in the arena, she is as serious as they come. She focuses entirely on the job at hand, and it shows in her results.

I always had horses, but my parents didn't want me to rodeo because they thought the world of rodeo wasn't the best place for a young lady. I was never permitted to run barrels until I was married. Then my father-in-law gave me an outstanding young horse. I trained him to run barrels. I started rodeoing.

I love horses. And I guess I'm a competitor. And if you're female and want to compete on horseback, barrel racing is the way to go. So that's the way I went.

—Carol Goosetree,
1978 GRA Champion Barrel Racer,
1979 World Champion Barrel Racer.

I like the professional circuit 'cause I just like making the money. [Laughs] It's a little bit easier than working your nine-to-five job. And I like being my own boss. If I don't want to go to a rodeo, I don't have to go.

I'd just run barrels around home, gymkhanas and things, until about three years ago. One day a girlfriend of mine said, "There's a rodeo in town. Why don't we try running the barrels?" I ran. I was the first one out in my first rodeo and I was settin' first until the second-to-the-end girl beat me by a couple hundredths of a second. I won a hundred and sixty-eight dollars, and ever since then I got the fever.

I went IRA the first year [International Rodeo Association, an amateur circuit]. Rode for about six months and made twentieth in the nation. I decided I'd like to go to the Finals in the IRA, so I went a full year IRA. But I just couldn't make enough. There wasn't enough rodeos to go to in California.

I had run against the GRA girls and they were tough, but I found that I could beat them occasionally and win some money that way. I decided there's more rodeos in the GRA, so I went GRA this year. [This interview was conducted in 1978 at the National Finals rodeo.] My object was to try and go to the Finals and I made it.

I've been to sixty-nine rodeos this year. My truck sitting out there has about thirty-eight thousand miles on it and I've had it seven months. Before that, there's no telling how many miles I drove.

I usually haul alone except for Gaiter, my Doberman. I was traveling with a cat called Fuzz Buster for a while as well, but somebody stole him at Albuquerque. And occasionally there's a bull rider or a bareback rider or a team roper, calf roper, somebody who needs a ride I'll take along. I've traveled to a couple of rodeos with other girls. But mostly I haul alone.

It prevents a lot of hassles to haul alone. I enjoy having somebody's company, but you get on each other's nerves sometimes. I've had a couple of trips where I just about couldn't have made it if I didn't have somebody with me, but I've gone a lot of miles by myself too.

You have some crazy runs sometimes. One run I drove fourteen hours to Townsboro, Washington, ten hours to Winnemucca, and ten hours to Lancaster. This is all in a matter of three days. When I pulled into Winnemucca, the rodeo had already been going two hours. I come hauling up in my truck and jump my horse out and ask if the barrels had been run yet. Somebody tells me it will be about a half hour before they run, so I have a half hour to warm up my horse and get ready to run the barrel race. I ended up winning fourth in that rodeo, but it was hectic.

Another time, I was on my way to Imperial, California. I thought they meant Imperial Beach. Somebody told me it was by San Diego and there I was, flying down the road in my camper. That was at the first of the year and I hauled my horse in a three-quarter-ton pickup. We had converted it. It had an overhead camper on the back of it. It was just a shell; there was nothing on the insides. We reinforced the sides with three-quarter-inch plywood and put bars over the windows. The whole back end would unsnap, and we built a ramp. I could just leave my horse in the back of the pickup and it looked like a camper on the outside.

I go buzzing off to Imperial Beach. I was a little late, and I missed it. I drove by, and ended up in Mexico. I come back and was trying to go back across the border. The guard wouldn't let me across, not without looking in the back of that camper. I said, "If I open up the back of that camper, that horse is liable to come out on top of us both." He said, "Really! There's a horse back there?" He told me it was his job to check in the back, but he finally said, "Well, go on. I don't want to look, go on."

So I drove back to Imperial Beach. I didn't know where the rodeo was, so I stopped at a liquor store. You know the way these cowboys are. So I ask, "Where's the rodeo?" The man at the counter says, "Rodeo?" Like, what's a rodeo? I said, "You haven't heard anything about a rodeo?" and he says, "No." So I says, "Well, what would you think if somebody said 'Imperial' to you?"

This man standing in line behind me says, "Imperial? Hell, that's where I'm from. That's a hundred and sixty-nine miles away."

I decided to try and make it. I wasn't really sure what time the rodeo started. When I had phoned in my entry the line was bad and I couldn't understand what they said very well. Sounded like the barrels would be run between twelve and two. I had figured I'd just try and get there by twelve.

Well, I pulled into Imperial Beach at twelve o'clock, and it was something like one-thirty when I left. I got all the way over to Imperial by three-thirty. I don't even know how fast I was going. But I made it in record time.

So I come pulling in and the guard says, "You with the rodeo?" I say,

"Yeah. Do you know how long the rodeo's been going?" He says, "Oh, only for about maybe a half hour. You a barrel racer?" I said yes and he said, "Well shoot, just go back over there . . ." He directed me. I just go flying into the place.

I pull in and a friend comes running over to me. She says, "Shari, we didn't think you were going to make it." We unload my horse, and my hands are shaking so bad she has to fasten my reins for me. As it turned out, I had over an hour to warm up my horse 'cause they were just on the calf roping.

I don't know how long I got teased about that. I was living in Yucca Valley at the time and Imperial was only a two-hour drive away. Somehow I converted it into a six- or seven-hour drive. We won second at that rodeo, I think it was.

I was in Coleville, Idaho, and was going to drive to the rodeo in Myrtle Point, Oregon, with this bronc rider. We had only five or six dollars between us, this bareback rider and me. I don't even think I had a full tank. We got a flat tire on the way and had to pay to get it fixed, which cost us eight dollars. He managed to get a check cashed for that somehow, and we made it to Myrtle Point. We didn't eat a thing all day long. We rode in the rodeo and he won first in his event and I won first in mine. We went to a restaurant and just porked out. I mean, I had french toast, three eggs, and bacon . . . I just chowed that all down and he's over there chowing down. We literally stuffed our faces, we were so hungry.

Geronimo is my horse. I call him Gerry. He's just a mutt. He's Welsh Pony, Saddlebred, and Quarter Horse. We had a mare we'd paid a hundred and twenty-five dollars for, and we bred her to the stallion next door for twenty-five dollars. That's how I got Geronimo.

He just seems to love running barrels. He seems to look forward to it. There's quite a few horses come into the arena, you can tell they hate it. They don't like running 'em, but they do it because they have to. But Gerry, the second he walks in the arena, he's all charged up. He's looking for that first barrel, ready to go. He really, really enjoys it.

He loves the people. When the fans are yelling and screaming for him, he just eats it up. Afterward, when they have their introductions and stuff, he'll come in and tuck his old head and start prancing.

He's got all the personality in the world. He'll come up and nuzzle you. I'll roughhouse with him, like I'll sock at him, and he'll bite at me and kick at me and stuff. He'll smile for you, come up and put his head on your shoulder and give you a hug. For play, he's worse than a Doberman pinscher. But if somebody were to come up to me and try to hurt me, I think I could tell Gerry to get them and he'd kick them.

Gerry's eleven years old, and I don't really have another horse in the hole. I know where his half brother is, and if I really got desperate I think I might try and buy him back. He's even more of a mutt than Gerry 'cause he's Welsh

Pony, Saddlebred, Quarter Horse, Thoroughbred, and Appaloosa. He has a lot of heart, but at the time I sold him, all I ever wanted was Gerry. I didn't think I needed another horse.

There is one horse I'm looking at that is pretty high-powered. But the prices these girls are paying for horses nowadays . . . Here at the Finals, this guy bought my horse in the calcutta for two hundred and sixty-five dollars. [In the calcutta, contestants are auctioned off and the money put into a pool. If the contestant you buy wins, so do you.] He came up to me and told me he had two hundred sixty-five riding on me. I said, "Hey! That's twice as much what I paid for my horse." He just kind of turned green.

It's funny how you sort of get your fans. I won the Salinas [California] rodeo, and then a gal came up to me at the Cow Palace [rodeo in San Francisco] and says, "Shari, you don't know me, but I've been following you all year long. There's quite a few of us from the Salinas community who're really rooting for you. We're really hoping you make it to the Finals. We pick up the *Rodeo News* [*ProRodeo Sports News*] and they say you're getting higher and higher in the standings and we just think it's wonderful."

Then another gal came up to me here at the Finals. She told me she was sitting in the stands at the Cow Palace and these people were making fun of my horse. They were saying, "That little scrawny horse down there is going to run against all these high-powered Quarter Horses?" They thought it was a big joke. Well, this gal turned around to them and said, "I'll tell you what, I have a hundred dollars on that horse says he'll win." She told me she won three hundred and twenty-five dollars off them at the rodeo. She said she'd take me out to a steak dinner sometime.

They say rodeo cowboys are the most pursued men in the world. I don't think there is anybody who chases barrel racers around. Like last night at the rodeo, there was a girl up there in the stands, just literally screaming, going out of her brain over Denny Flynn [a bull rider]. Well, I don't think there's any guys up there screaming their heads off over the barrel racers. They treat you good, kid you about your buckle, but they're not going to chase you around.

Cowboys treat you different if they know you're in rodeo. Like if I walk into a bar without my buckle, some of the cowboys will treat you really bad. They think you're just somebody hanging around, you're a buckle bunny [rodeo groupie] or something like that. Then they find out that you travel with the rodeo, and it's completely different.

This year I've been able to support myself pretty good with the barrels. I usually don't stay in motels. The whole ten days I was in Cheyenne, I stayed in my truck and trailer. There's usually somebody that has a room and I can use their shower. Or I can stop at a gas station and wash my hair in the rest room, use a KOA shower, or something.

I've spent some money pretty foolishly. I made close to two thousand dollars at the Cow Palace, and the next weekend I made five hundred. When I got here, I had only about five hundred left. Kind of blew some of it. Bought some clothes, a pair of boots, a jacket so I wouldn't be cold when I got here. Things like that. But rodeo supports me O.K.

I haven't thought too much about the future. I just hope to keep on going down the road for quite a while. I don't know how long I'll be able to do it, but as long as I can. I hate to say it, but I can't think of a better life. I wouldn't trade it for the world.

Round and Round She Goes
(The Barrel Racer)

On a cold Montana morning
   On the road to Idaho
I watched her order hot and black to go.
Don her boots and spurs and bluejeans
   And the lonely in her eyes
Told me just how much she loved the rodeos.

I asked where she was headin',
   She said, the Boise show.
   She took a third in Butte just yesterday.
No, she never has been married,
   And she probably never will,
   'Cause silver buckle dreams
     Don't leave time for standing still.

CHORUS: Round and Round and Round she goes
       Where she stops nobody knows.
       The miles are gettin' longer,
         And the nights they never end.
       Old rodeos and livestock shows
         Keep the lady on the go.
       Lord, she loves to run those barrels,
         And it's the only life she knows.

For nigh on fifteen seasons
   The circuit's been her home,
   And at times she misses kids she never had.
But she wouldn't trade a minute
   Of the years that she's got in it,
'Cause she's had herself some happy,
   And she's learned to take the sad.

When I looked up from my coffee
  I saw Boise on her mind,
  And she had that look of leavin' in her eyes.
As she drove into the morning
  It slowly dawned on me
How hard it is to tell a dream goodbye
  (You just can't tell a life-long dream good-bye.)

—S. LaPrade Riddell,
Pointed Star Music,
recorded by Chris LeDoux.

Jan Edmonson

Ponder, Texas

Jan Edmonson tapes her cracked ankle before the bullriding at the Littleton, Colorado, All-Girls Rodeo, 1978, while Jocko Jonckowski looks on.

JAN RIDES BULLS, BRONCS, COWS, STEERS, AND—AS THE SAYING GOES—anything with hair. She is five feet two inches tall, 115 pounds of pure gristle and guts. At thirty-five, she is one of the oldest rough stock riders—men and women both—in the country. (The average age of bull riders in the Professional Rodeo Cowboys Association is twenty-four; in the WPRA it is even younger.)

But rodeo has been Jan's whole life. Her father produced rodeos in Idaho, and Jan has competed as long as she can remember. She has been an active member in three different rodeo associations—Northwest Rodeo Association, an amateur association; the International Girls Rodeo Association, no longer extant; and the Women's Professional Rodeo Association.

For women in the WPRA, Jan is the "mother of rough stock." She has helped nearly every other rough stock rider get into the sport. She goes to every women's rodeo and watches every ride, supercharged by the excitement, barking out advice and encouragement non-stop, hardly taking time to ride her own stock.

Age and an almost unbelievable list of injuries have not slowed Jan down in the least. She ended the 1979 season ranked second in the world in women's bull riding (beaten only by her eighteen-year-old daughter, Tanya), sixth in bareback, and eleventh in all-around.

For pure guts—the ability to ride through pain, to bounce back from injury, to live completely outside fear—Jan is the single toughest woman I have ever met. Yet, she is not mannish and she seldom swears. As she says, "My daddy always told me, 'You can be tough, but when you start being rough, you're through.'"

I have seven kids and every one of them rodeos, right down to the little baby. Tye is five and he rides calves and he's in barrel racing. He's been doing that for three years. They all started young. They've all come right up with it. I try to encourage them. Anytime I can help them in any way, I do. We'll take off from work if we have to. If there's a rodeo, we'll get there.

When I was a kid, I had encouragement from my daddy. I grew up working on the ranch, and if I worked really hard my daddy would always take time off to take me to the rodeos. That's the way we did it. My mother used to say, "There's nobody works harder than your dad, and nobody plays harder either."

I had been rodeoing for nearly twelve years before I ever went to a rodeo without my dad. He'd just always take me. One time I asked him to take me to a rodeo and it was just before hunting season. He was an outfitted guide at the time and he said, "Boy, babe, I don't really have time." So I said, "Daddy, if you will come to the rodeo, I'll be sure and help you." So he took me.

I had a real nasty cow. Cows are real bad in the chute. You know, bulls can't compare with a cow for just being stupid in the chute. They bang you around; they won't hold still.

My dad's always been one to just drop right down on their head in the chute and hold them still for you. He'd do this not just for me, but for all the girls up and down the line.

Well, this old cow I had, she was jumping all over. He just sits on her head and she runs forward and falls down. Bent both of his knees backward and we had to pack him out, put his knees back in.

I'd told him I'd help him, you know. So I had to go with him and shoe fifteen head of horses that next week, pack out camps, and everything else. But that was part of the deal. He'd help me if I'd help him.

I'll tell you about my first rodeo. As you can well see, I think an awful lot of my daddy. And this was the first [all-girl] rodeo my dad was producing. He went and leased some of this stock from a friend of his. Then he rode every one of them out because he wasn't going to put the girls on them until he knew what they did for sure.

I was twelve. I rode my first bareback horse at that rodeo. Name was Meathead. And Meathead went out there and he just kind of crow-hopped out across the arena. I rode him and there was only four of us covered [rode the required eight seconds]. Well, I was setting third and, boy, I was proud as punch. Real big head, you know. First horse I ever rode and I was winning third place on him.

I went down to the other end of the arena and I was untying calves and this girl come along and said, "Jan, you got a re-ride." Course, I'd been raised around rodeo. I knew what a re-ride was. And I thought, "Oh, good. Now I'll win first."

Before I rode, I had a little time and I told Momma I had a re-ride. I imagine I was playing pretty hotshot, pretty big stuff. I told her I was going to ride Basher Boy. I didn't know the horses, 'cause I hadn't been with Dad when he tried them out, but Momma had. Basher Boy was one of the top horses, and he was rank. Momma said, "Your dad better not put you on that horse." I said, "Oh, Mom, I can ride him!"

I went up and Daddy had my rigging on this big, stout sorrel horse. I got on and Dad said, "Now, watch this horse, babe. Don't let him get you back off that riggin'. He's pretty stout." Well, if my dad will warn me about anything, it's time to look out, but it still didn't put a dent in me. I just came out on that old horse and about the second jump, I'll tell you, he popped me back off that rigging. I ploughed a furrow in that arena you could have planted corn in. I couldn't close my eyes, couldn't close my mouth, they were so full of dirt.

What had happened when I'd rode old Meathead, somebody back behind said, "Oh, that's the producer's daughter. She gets an easy horse." Well, Dad wasn't going to have them say nothing like that, so he put me on the roughest horse he had! That's the way he is. It helped. It took the bigness out of my head in a hurry. I found out right quick I couldn't ride just anything.

Now see, I don't agree with this rule the GRA has that the rough stock riders have to be sixteen. I don't agree with that at all. My best years of riding were from the time I was twelve to sixteen. I have argued this with them before— there are some good girls that they are turning down and they shouldn't.

I've got a little gal, she will just be twelve and she is ready to start. I'm sure the board won't turn me down because they know she can do it. She rides steers, and she does a good job on them. I won't start her on the big old bulls, because they are too stout for her. Tanya started on cows. She rode cows two years before she got into bulls. She didn't think she'd ever ride bulls. But they are her favorite event now.

Tanya was not sixteen when she started in the WPRA. She is just seventeen now and this is her third year.

Tanya's the best traveling partner I ever had, and I had to raise her! Yeah, Tanya and I are awful close. We do just about everything together. We work together. We insulate houses for a living. We rodeo together. And when we get done, we go dancing together. There isn't much we don't do together. Of course, she don't take me on her dates. I don't know what's the matter with her, but she won't take me out on her dates.

We spend an awful lot of time in the pickup, driving from one rodeo to the next. Mostly we talk about rodeo. Tanya has had a problem starting her horse. [A bronc rider must "start" a horse by spurring from the point of each shoulder the first jump out of the chute. Failure to do so penalizes the rider five points per shoulder.] She didn't used to have that problem; it's just lately. She's getting overanxious. She did it today. So we try to work on that.

Tanya is one of these who has to do a lot of psyching up. I don't know, I guess I've just been at it so many years, I just stay psyched up. I don't worry about it for me. But Tanya is one that needs a lot of psyching, and we'll work on that. She gets started on it when we're driving down the road talking about her problems. She'll work on them, sorting them out. She's been in quite a slump, but she is coming out of it now. This dislocated shoulder doesn't help a bit.

She dislocated it at Big Sandy. Won the bull riding, and I don't know if she did it while she was ridin' the bull or when she got off or what. She had a beautiful bull ride, really a good, solid ride. The judges were really impressed —said they didn't want her to enter no bull riding against them! But she dislocated her shoulder and she didn't ride at Gatesville. This is the first time she's tried it, since.

She's got to learn to cope with that arm being tied down. It's getting to her mentally more than anything else. I've never seen Tanya blow a hand on a bareback rigging. [Girls are allowed to ride bareback broncs using two hands on the rigging. If they "blow a hand"—that is, lose their grip with either hand —they are disqualified.] And she did today. She didn't blow the bad arm. She blew the other one. Just because she wasn't thinking about it. She was thinking about something else.

When you ride a bull, there's a certain spot you look at. Some people watch their head, but I don't. A bull can be deceptive with his head—move his head one way, and then spin another. I watch just above the point of the shoulders. If you watch that point, you can tell if the bull drops his shoulder to go into a spin. You watch that spot, and you don't ever take your eye off it. If you take your eye off, where you look is where you're going to land.

You concentrate on relaxing. You keep telling yourself, "Relax, relax, relax." Because if you relax, you're going with the bull. If you're tense, you are really fighting the bull, and you're not helping yourself any. You concentrate on relaxing, and then

everything comes into place—moving your arm to keep your
balance, moving your feet to score points.

For a long time we couldn't figure out what I was doing wrong.
Last year [1977] I went on the circuit. I hit twenty-four rodeos.
Jan [Edmonson] was trying to help me, but she told me she just
couldn't figure out why I wasn't staying on my bulls, because I
was moving my arm right and everything.

Then I drew a great big strong bull at Duncan, Oklahoma. I
went out on him and he took about four jumps, and man! He
started to turn, and I went off the back of him. Just then he lost
his balance and his hind end hit my back as I was going down. It
was like a pile driver bashing me into the ground. It knocked the
wind out of me, but I got up and went over by the chute. I was
trying to catch my breath and Jan came up to me yelling, "I
know what you're doing! I know what you're doing!" She told me
that after I got out on the bull, I tightened up and didn't stay
loose. When I tightened my hand grip, I tightened my whole
upper body. And you can't do that. You have to keep your grip,
but your body has to be relaxed.

For my second bull at Duncan, I drew a big white Brahma. He
was a hard bull to ride because his skin was really loose. Sitting
on him was like sitting on a raft out in the middle of the ocean.
His skin was just rolling all the time. We pulled a lot of his skin
out from under the rope so that the rope wouldn't be moving
around on him. And I took a really, really tight rope.

When I went out on him, it was the fifty-second time he went
out. He's only been ridden to the gun once before. I concentrated
on relaxing. And I rode him! That was the first bull I ever
covered [rode to the gun]. I was thrilled. It made me feel really
good to ride that bull. It was something fifty people hadn't been
able to do, and I did it.

—Jane Kruse,
GRA bull rider.

So we'll talk about that, going down the road. We go over every rodeo all
year, what we did right, what we did wrong, just riding along.

You've had some injuries yourself.

Oh, last year, all I had—I had a blood clot early in the year, which I had
all year. And then at Miles City, Montana, a pickup horse ran over me and
landed on me—broke four ribs, one of them twice, and dislocated my shoulder

and broke my collarbone. So I was off three weeks with that. I was supposed to have been off quite a while with my blood clot, but I thought a week was long enough.

This year they are getting to me already. I hit heads with a bull at Duncan and broke my cheekbone and had to have it operated and set in place. I've got a wire up over my eyebrow now—that's what this scar is here. Then the Fourth of July, my cinch broke on my bareback rigging and I hit the fence and cracked my foot. That's something you just don't hear of happening very often. I've broke a couple of bull ropes, but I've never broke my bareback rigging before. I laughed. I said, "My daddy always told me to sit on that rigging, don't worry about the horse. I took it to heart. I landed and I was still sitting on my rigging. But I didn't have any horse."

. . . [When you have been thrown] if you are not at least dead, get out of the arena. Die behind the chutes. It looks bad to the crowd to lay out there, roll around, then get up. It has been proven—crowds don't mind seeing hairy-legged boys get hurt, but they don't like to see women get hurt!

—Sue Pirtle,
All-Girl Rodeo Director,
in *GRA News*, Girls Rodeo Association, May 1978.

I guess one of the worst weekends for wrecks was Spring Creek, Nevada, in 1975. That was just one big wreck. I started out by hazing in the steer undecorating and this little gal I was hazing for, she got her ribbon, but then—I don't know what. She made a mistake in judgment and turned her horse right straight in front of mine and the steer. She cut the steer off and he put his head right between my horse's front legs. There wasn't no place for us to go but down.

That peeled and bruised me all up—didn't hurt me bad. And then I had my bull. I was the last bull rider out, and they had the horses loaded for the bronc riding, which was next. I slapped heads with that bull. I come down on him, had a horn hit me in the face. Broke *this* cheekbone in three places and broke my false teeth. But my bareback horse was in the chute when I got hurt. Joe Alexander and Gary Laffew were judging and I said, "Can you hold my horse 'til my head gets cleared?" 'Cause I was so dizzy. Joe said, "We'll hold him for you 'til morning because we still got slack in the morning." [When there are too many contestants to all compete during the regular performance, they compete before or after the show, in "slack."]

So the next day I had two bareback horses and a bull to ride. I placed on my bareback horses. I didn't win, but I placed. I bucked off my bull. Then I went

home and had surgery on the cheek and lifted it back to place. I guess I've
been hurt a lot of times, but never too severely.

. . . The inherent chivalry of not only the public, but the
cowboy, makes them shrink from witnessing injury to a woman.
This was evidenced by Skeeter Bill Robbins after Brown Eyes fell
and rolled on Peggy Warren's foot; crossing half the arena in
about three leaps to rescue her, he then rubbed his sleeve across
his sweaty forehead and remarked, "I sure do hate ter see a *girl*
git hurt."

—Charles Wellington Furlong,
Let 'Er Buck, 1921.

Tanya and me, we compete between the two of us, but it's like we say. If one
of us has got to be beat, we'd rather it was the other one of us that did it. We
try darn hard to beat each other, anyhow. I'm sure neither one of us has ever
held anything back.

I've always said I was going to keep rodeoing 'til Tanya beat me, and then
I'm going to retire. But I may have to retire this year if I say that. She's ahead
of me right now in the bareback, but I'm ahead of her in the bulls. See, last
year, we don't know for sure who won. I can play on a technicality. Last year,
come out in the bareback, and we are not sure which one of us placed second
and third. There was just a few cents between us, and the Association doesn't
know whether the final figures are accurate. There was a mess-up in the payoff
at Duncan, and they sent me an extra twenty-five-dollar check. They don't
know whether it's on the books or not. If it's already there, then Tanya beat
me by about three dollars. If it's not, then I beat her by about twenty dollars.
So we just say we split second/third in the bareback last year. That way I
don't really have to quit. She didn't really beat me!‡

Actually, let's be facing facts. I'm too old to be doing this. But we're just
about to have our first National Finals. I said, "I've worked for it all my life,
and I'm not quitting now. This is what I've worked for all the time, and I'm
going to be there when it comes off. [The GRA held the first National Finals
Girls Rodeo in San Antonio, Texas, in November 1978.]

I'd like to see the Girls Rodeo Association changed to the Women's Professional Rodeo Association. Especially in this day and age, I believe it needs the
"Professional" somewhere in there. We are professional athletes. And the Girls

‡ This interview was conducted during the 1978 season. At the end of the year, Tanya
beat her mother in bull riding, coming in second to Jan's fourth. Jan ranked third in
bareback over Tanya's fourth. In 1979 Tanya was world champion in both events, with
Jan placing second in bulls and sixth in "bares." Jan is still riding.

Rodeo Association sounds like just a bunch of gunsels decided to try something on a jackpot deal.

I have an ex-mother-in-law who's not exactly on the closest of terms. And she says to Tanya when she was home, she says, "Don't they have an age limit on that Girls Rodeo Association? Your mother isn't exactly a girl anymore." [Laughs] Yeah, I think it's time they change it to "Professional Women."

The GRA was changed to the Women's Professional Rodeo Association in 1980.

Kathy Kennedy

Channing, Texas

Kathy Kennedy, telling stories while working on the Horn Ranch, Granby, Colorado, 1979.

IF YOU'VE BEEN LOOKING THROUGH THESE PAGES FOR A WILD AND CRAZY COW-girl, meet Kathy Kennedy. She loves to gamble, to party, to drink. She will spend her last fifty dollars to buy a calf roper in a calcutta; go down the road playing liar's poker to pay for her gas. She separated her shoulder a couple years ago—not at a rodeo but in a bar. At different times of her life she has lived just one step ahead of the banker.

It's hard to describe Kathy. One time she'll have on her aviator glasses and her old broad-brimmed straw hat, looking like a cowgirl version of Fearless Fly. A few moments later, she'll be clowning around behind a Groucho Marx mask. But you just might catch her when she has curled her shoulder-length, white-blond hair, looking, in her words, *"Almost* like a respectable human being."

But now meet the other side of Kathy. The side of discipline, of immense and varied talent. She, along with her traveling and team roping partners, Jean and Becky Fuchs, rank among the five top women ropers in the nation in anybody's book. Kathy was GRA Team Roping Champion in '78, and National College Rodeo Association Breakaway Calf Roping Champion the same year. She has won more buckles in both associations than she can count. In addition, she regularly ropes in jackpots and mixed ropings [team ropings where men and women rope together. Teams may be two men, two women, or mixed.]; sometimes over top-ranked PRCA team ropers. Most everything is a joke to Kathy except her roping. About that, her dedication is complete.

Kathy is also a gifted sculptor. Carole and Jack Horn [see Chapter 3] sponsor Kathy's work and help her get it cast. Her first, a study of a bronc rider, stands proudly in Horn's home. Kathy is quick to point out what she feels are flaws, but the sculpture has that quality of motion and life, of absolute kinetic frenzy, that many sculptors spend a lifetime trying to achieve.

Kathy also cartoons. Pen-and-ink sketches fill her letters and the scraps of paper crumpled up in·the cab of her truck, with an unkosher and amusing chronicle of cowgirl life.

Kathy is the more remarkable in light of her background. Her natural mother died at age twenty-three of breast cancer. Kathy lost her twin sister and aunt to cancer as well. In 1979, at the age of twenty-three, Kathy discovered a lump. It was malignant. In September she had a radical mastectomy on her right side.

Kathy ropes with her right hand. Three weeks after the surgery she won a mixed roping. She learned to throw a low sidearm loop, so she didn't have to raise her arm above her head.

When her college rodeo club at Chadron State in Nebraska staged a benefit roping for her on Thanksgiving day, Kathy looked so good and roped so well she worried that everybody might think "this was just some big con deal I'd rigged up." And now, even after a year of chemotherapy, Kathy is the same—still laughing, joking, roping well.

Kathy overflows with energy, courage, humor, talent, unbridled *joi de vivre.*

Kathy Kennedy and Jean Fuchs, team roping at Hereford, Texas, All-Girls Rodeo, 1978.

I get more satisfaction out of roping than anything in the whole world. I can rope a dummy, not even be on a horse and just rope a dummy, all day long and not ever want to quit. I don't ever get tired of roping.

I hang around a lot of people that rope, like Jean and Becky [Fuchs]. The main thought with them is just to be a better roper. If you're around people like that all the time, it's your whole life. You strive toward it. It's kinda hard to explain.

It's just like when you watch tennis players. You know how much they practice and how much they put into it. They deserve to win because they're the ones that concentrate on it more, practice and think about it more. It's the same with rodeoing. The ones who sit around and maybe practice every now and then and go to weekend rodeos, they're in a different class than those who sit and practice and think about it *all* the time. Those who put a lot into it, they're going to win. They deserve to win. It's only right.

I'm not a very serious person, but I don't have any trouble getting serious about my roping. If I'm roping good, I can make a lot of money. When I'm roping good, I usually catch them the right way—rope them right and tie them right. But if I'm roping bad, I might catch or I might not. I'd like to be where I roped good most of the time instead of just half the time. I'd like to be really consistent.

A lot of it's practice. When I practice I rope better. Like this winter, we were snowed in all winter, we didn't get any practice. But last fall, I roped better than I had probably ever roped in my life, and that's because we had practice calves to rope every single day. It's work. You have to work to do it. But I like to practice.

Concentration is so important. You can't let other stuff in your life affect your roping. Say you were married and you were having trouble in a marriage —you can't let that affect you when you compete, which is really hard. I've never been married. But I have a lot of trouble roping if I'm going with a guy and he shows up at a roping and I didn't know he was coming or something. Especially if I don't want to go with him much more.

You have a hard time concentrating on what you're doing and still being decent to other people. When I rope, I like to just sit down and not pay attention to anybody else except for ropers. I have a hard time because I like everybody and I like to know what's going on. But you have to keep stuff like that out.

Each time, before I run the barrels, I psych myself up. I get a little nervous. Usually I get real quiet. I say a little prayer that everything will go all right—that Missile won't get hurt and I won't hurt myself. Then I try to get my concentration started.

I think mostly about my hands. I'm bad to put my elbows out. Sometimes I feel like I have all these loose hairs floating around outside me, and I try to pull everything inside, get together in a knot. I try to put myself in one place.

You've got to concentrate on that will to win as much as anything. I think the will to win is most important. If you're mounted, you've got to sit back there and say, "I can win if I want to, if I give it my best shot . . ." You've got to concentrate like that run after run after run.

> —Lynn McKenzie,
> 1978 World Champion Barrel Racer,
> 1979 National Finals Rodeo Champion,
> 1981 World Champion Barrel Racer.

The whole thing is having enough self-control to where you don't get too excited. If you have to beat like a seven [seconds, in team roping], you don't get excited and throw really quick at the heels when you don't have a shot. But if you stand up under that pressure and make a good run and go ahead and win —there's nothing in the world that feels better than that.

I like to rope against men. That's quite a challenge and it's a lot more fun. 'Cause nothing's worth doing unless it's hard. If you want to accomplish something. Like to be a really good roper, it's hard. I get a lot of satisfaction out of it because it's a long haul.

The men accept you pretty well. In team roping they do. They respect you as a roper. If you're good, it doesn't bother them to ask you to rope if you're a girl. And it doesn't bother them to be beat by you either. Depends on which girl you are probably. But after you've roped around men for quite a while, they accept it pretty easily. They just think of you as a roper. They invite you to come and practice with them all the time.

"I really like to [team rope] against the guys," Sammy [Thurman] told a reporter. "I'm pretty accurate but not real speedy. If I win the boys tease each other. But I think they're kind of tickled."

—Lynn Haney,
Ride 'em Cowgirl! 1975.

I'd like to go PRCA. [Professional Rodeo Cowboys Association. A woman can buy her permit in the PRCA and fill it by winning $1,000 in team roping at PRCA permit rodeos. She then becomes a full member and can rope at PRCA rodeos, qualifying for the National Finals Rodeo if she is good enough. Although several women have bought permits in the PRCA, as yet no one has become a full member in team roping.] But I have a lot more work before I'm good enough to do it. I'm not even close to good enough now. But if I find a place to practice, I think maybe I could do it. Sure like to try it, anyhow.

My dream is to rope at the National Finals. I'd like to do that a whole bunch. I don't know if I ever will. But I think a person can do anything they put their mind to. All it takes is determination.

People put up their own mental blocks by saying they can't do something, that it's unreachable. Nobody ever told me a girl couldn't rope. Like when I first started roping, girls didn't rope that much. But my mom and dad never told me girls couldn't, so I went ahead and did it.

You hit a dry spell, you get discouraged. Like Kay Parker. She was broke and she got really mad. She cut up all of her ropes and quit and now she's making a whole lot of money in Las Vegas dealing cards. I never ever thought about quitting. I just like to do it more than anything else.

Rodeo is a special sort of friendship. You work together, you play together, you get awful close. There for a while, everybody we ran around with had nicknames. There's "Pantyhose" Parker. Comes from when you rope a steer around the hips, they call it pantyhosing him. She pantyhosed a steer one time, and everybody started calling her Pantyhose Parker. Becky was called "Reba the Sheba." Reba is short for Rebecca, and the Sheba just rhymed with Reba. Bonnie Pleasant was Bonnie "Unpleasant" 'cause the GRA secretary got mad at her one time and told her she should be called Bonnie Unpleasant. We picked it up. Amy Iverson was Amos. I was Bobo 'cause I reminded someone of a dog named Bobo.

It's funny the things you get into. Like the time we flew to the rodeo in Jackson, Wyoming, from Hereford, Texas. We all went to the all-girl rodeo in Hereford and they were having an all-girl rodeo in Jackson the same weekend. We competed in Hereford and then I rigged this thing up so we could fly to Jackson.

I was going with Bill, this guy who was a great airplane pilot. I think he flew in the Navy or something. He had a good deal on a plane, so all I needed was some other people. I got Jennifer [Haynes] and Bonnie [Pleasant] and Twyla [Rutherford]. That was four of us and him that were going.

So this is a four-person plane and five of us were in it. Bonnie and Jennifer had to strap themselves in on the same seatbelt. The weight limit was really strict because we were close anyhow with one extra person. All we could take was one rope and one rope can. Bill was real strict about it, and whenever Bill's cautious about those things, I get nervous.

To take off, we had to take the rope can out of the back of the plane and put it in the front so that we could get off the ground. When Bill first told us that, everybody got pie-eyed. They were all scared to death. See, I'm always getting these bargain deals rigged up, and everybody was scared that they were taking their life in their hands on one of my bargain deals. I have to admit, it was one of the few times in my life I've ever feared death. I wondered what I'd got into.

We left about eleven o'clock at night because we didn't want to fly over the mountains in the dark. It's pretty flat around Hereford. Everybody stayed awake because we were afraid to go to sleep. Bill is a really good pilot and he's really conscientious. But he'd lost a lot of sleep coming down to Hereford. I don't know how he stayed awake on that trip to Jackson.

We had to stop here and there to refuel. It all went pretty well until we got up around Denver. Then we started running into some storms and they really rocked the boat. Twyla and Bonnie were especially scared. They would hardly look out. They were white as a sheet.

But we got past that. We were in the air twelve hours, packed in like we were. Every time we took off after we refueled, we had to pass that rope can forward. It was quite a deal.

We got to Montana and everybody was dead-tired because we'd all been too scared to sleep. We stopped at Dillon, Montana, right before we were supposed to hunt for the arena at Jackson. We hadn't had anything to eat and we bought some macaroni and pop and called the rodeo. We told them to have a sheriff waiting out at the airport to take us to the arena because the arena is out at a ranch seventeen miles from the Jackson airport.

We were going to have to land on this dirt strip in Jackson. All we'd landed on so far was pavement, so we were all scared anyhow. Then we took off again and one of the doors didn't get all the way shut. We were way up in the air and Bonnie looks down and sees this door open and it just scares her to death. It wouldn't fly open, probably, but there was a crack in it and the wind was blowing and she goes, "That door's open. Is that door *supposed* to be open?"

Bill goes, "Send those cards and letters to Jesus, that's Jeeeesus, Del Rio, Texas," like on the all-night radio station. Everybody just cracked up.

So we circled in the mountains, looking for this place to land and we all got sick. Except Bill, I guess he's used to it. I couldn't hardly stand it. I was praying we'd find it soon.

It was time for the rodeo to start and everybody is usually really concerned about being late, but we were all so sick we didn't even care. I was in the front with Bill. I had my glasses off and I was slumped down. Everybody else was trying to sleep or something so they wouldn't be sick.

We were just circling and circling. Poor Bill, he was looking for the arena. Finally he goes, "Kathy, you've just got to put on your glasses and help me." So I put them on and pretty soon we think we see it. Sure enough, there it is. We fly down and they're already having the grand entry. We fly really low so they'll know that we're coming. Then we fly to Jackson to the airport, and there's nobody there. What do we do?

We decide to fly back to the arena. So we fly back there and there's the sheriff, watching the rodeo. They're roping calves by then and we were up in the roping. So we flew really low so they'd know it was us and they all knew it was.

There was this highway about half a mile from the arena and Bill was circling around. He goes, "Well, girls, what do you think about landing on the highway?"

Bonnie's eyes got really big and she goes, "Are you sure it's safe?" She was petrified anyhow. I said, "Well, I am sick of being in the air, so let's land on the highway." Besides, I thought it would be kind of cool. We had this big long debate. We had to check out where the power lines were and everything. Bonnie kept going, "You really think we should do this?" We landed on the highway and this guy comes out in a pickup and we jump in the back. We can't even sit up, we're all just like rags. Bill pulls the plane off the highway and goes to sleep in the plane.

We get to the rodeo and they'd already had the calf roping, but they kept our calves for us. We all made a little bit of money. Jennifer and Twyla did really good. And the rodeo just loved it. It was a neat rodeo—just ranchers coming and they all sit around, you know. They were really tickled that we flew up there.

As soon as it was over, we went back out and rolled the plane back onto the highway and climbed back in it and flew back. When we got back to Cheyenne and landed, Jennifer and Twyla got out and snuck across the runways and climbed this little fence and hid out there—the plane was leased for only one person, so the whole thing was pretty illegal. Then we all got together and caught a bus to go back home. It was pretty wild. Probably wouldn't have paid anybody to fly up there for a little rodeo like that, but it was pretty wild. I wouldn't do it again, though, that's for sure. After it was over, I felt like I would never get in another plane again.

So many things happen to you in rodeo, and they make pretty good stories. I've had a lot of funny things happen. And I've heard some really funny stories but I wasn't there. Like there's this one story Sheila Bussey told me about a barrel racer. You know how they run up those alleys. [Many arenas have "alleys," lanes the barrel racers can run up to get their speed before they enter the arena.] Well, there was this lady in Texas. She's a little big and she always rode these great big old high-powered horses. They're about half outlaw anyhow. You know, she used chain tie-downs on their heads and stuff. Well, she finally got him pointed up this alleyway and she's running. There was this guy just anciently walking across the end of the alley, where the arena was. She hollered, "Look out!" and he turned around and saw her coming. So he throws his hands up and she hits him. He caught his arm on the breast collar and she dragged him all the way to the first barrel. You know how most people would stop and be concerned. Well, she beat him on the back with her crop all the way to the first barrel because he was messing up her barrel run. Then, after it was all over, she went over and chewed him out.

I wasn't there at that. I just heard it. You know, every time you hear about it, it gets more exaggerated, depending on how much beer you've had when you tell it. Like for instance, if I'd had a little beer it could really turn into a big story about how she beat him on every single barrel, then roped his legs, tied him on, and drug him across the pasture . . .

I think my life philosophy is not to have a philosophy. The way I figure it, most people get really concerned about a lot of stuff. You know, like being broke. Only if you look at it, it doesn't make any difference anyway. It might to some people. But things could sure enough be a lot tougher than what they are.

I just think how lucky I am. I'm pretty lucky because I've got everything I want in life. I've got a pickup that runs, a good horse, and a good horse trailer. I've got rodeos to go to, and right now I've even got the money to go to them. I have lots of good friends, and a pretty good conscience. And that's a lot.

The only people I've ever hurt is banks. I was never really rude to an individual or anything, and I got a lot of friends. Like if I was to die tomorrow. If you figure like you're going to die tomorrow and you could die saying, "I've lived a good life," then you couldn't ask for more.

I'm really careless with money. I had a hundred-dollar bill in my pocket at this team roping for luck. I won the team roping but I lost my hundred-dollar bill. I don't know what happened to it. I do stuff like that.

Last summer I thought I was really broke so I was working for Horns, painting and stuff. I washed this pair of pants and I put them on. I felt in the pocket and there's this wadded-up piece of paper in there. I opened it up and it was a check for eighty dollars, which seemed like a fortune to me. I was really ticked because I probably wouldn't have been working if I'd known I had money.

Another time I was going to a rodeo. I didn't have enough money to go, so I cleaned out my camper and found sixty dollars. Just a twenty here and a check there. I'm really careless that way. But I have a savings account now. I'm independently wealthy. [Laughs] I'm doing pretty good for me.

Usually every semester at college I end up staying in my camper 'cause I go broke. [Kathy has a shell camper on her pickup. It is just a shell. You can't stand up in it and it has no facilities. At this time, she went to college at Torrington, Wyoming, which is not known for its warm winters.] If you're rodeoing, you're never there anyhow, so it's kind of ridiculous to spend the rent. I like staying in the camper a whole lot, because ever since I was a kid, I just wanted a camper and a pickup and the freedom to hit the trail.

It gets pretty cold every now and then, but usually I know enough people where I can stay the night if it gets too cold. And there are some really good fringe benefits to it. Soon as word leaks out you're staying in your camper, people are always inviting you over for dinner. So you eat better than when you're in an apartment. Instead of TV dinners, you eat Swiss steak at people's houses.

Last winter, I'd set my little alarm clock and wake up early to feed my horses. Then I'd go to the Vo-Tec building and take a shower. I had an eight o'clock class, art history. I knew the teacher really good. I'd go in with my wet hair and let it dry during class. Always looked at slides in the dark, anyhow. It would be dry by the end of class and I'd go plug in my curling iron and curl my hair and look fine the rest of the day.

I had it really good. I kept my horses out at another teacher's place. Whenever I was gone, his kids fed my horses. I paid them good because they are really good kids. When their dad found out how much I paid them, he never charged me rent.

Then I gave a guy some wax one time and showed him a little bit about working it [for sculpture]. He and his wife and I all got along really good and she was a bartender, so she'd give me free drinks pretty regular. They'd invite me over for dinner, and he gave me a bunch of hay one time. Then the rest of the hay we picked up at night from the feed barn. [Laughs] So I had a pretty good little arrangement. I didn't have any horse rent. I didn't pay any rent myself. I had hardly any grocery bills. I didn't buy hay. All I had to buy was grain. And the college rodeos were paying really good, so I had it great.

If you had a million dollars, what would you do with it?

Make a down payment on all the money I owe. No, I don't owe quite that much. I don't know. That's a lot of money. I could probably rope it out pretty quick so I wouldn't have to worry about it. I'd buy a really nice outfit. Buy a little land. I think that would be really nice to have a little place all your own. You could sculpt up there and have a nice practice pen, and practice. If you wanted to see somebody you could, and if you didn't you wouldn't have to. You could have all your friends come out and practice all the time. Not to have to worry about working.

I don't even particularly want a million dollars. I'd just like to not have any debts. But even they don't really bother me all that much.

Kathy died of cancer in 1981.

Becky Fuchs

Thedford, Nebraska

Becky Fuchs, breakaway calf roping at the Hereford, Texas, All-Girls Rodeo, 1978.

BECKY FUCHS (PRONOUNCED FYOOSH) AND KATHY KENNEDY HAVE RODEOED together for over five years. At first glance, they are so different it is hard to understand the basis of their long and lasting friendship. Becky is taller, darker, quieter than Kathy. Becky never gambles and is not the partygoer Kathy is. But the biggest difference is their attitude toward money. Becky always has some. Kathy seldom does.

"I don't like to be dirt-broke," says Becky. "I like to stay pretty secure financially. As far as being rich, I have no great goals that would take a lot of money, like having a really nice house. But I like to keep enough money laid back that I could buy another pickup if mine went out. I never buy anything on time."

Becky bought her first pickup and trailer when she was a sophomore in high school and paid cash. She earned the money winning rodeos, gymkhanas, and Quarter Horse shows, as well as through her various enterprises. She held her first roping clinic (to teach others to rope) when she was sixteen and started training horses for other people that year as well.

Becky, now twenty-four, has since held roping and training clinics all over the country and she is highly respected both as a roper and trainer. One of her own horses, Topsy, has three times been named Super Horse of the Year. (The Super Horse is the horse in the WPRA who wins the most money with three different contestants at five designated Association rodeos. To win this, a horse must be a superb performance horse who will work for others besides its owner/trainer.)

In the last couple years, Becky has become quite a horse trader as well. People tell her the sort of horse they want, Becky finds a horse with potential and trains it, and then delivers it.

Where Kathy's nonchalance about money is famous, Becky is a natural businesswoman—a major difference in attitude, but not so important in light of what they share. Both are completely committed to their roping and they both have high goals. Perhaps most important, they are both absolutely self-reliant. If their world turned inside out tomorrow and they came out with only the boots on their feet and the shirts on their back, they would both survive in style.

They would approach the problem from different directions. Kathy would "rig up some sort of deal" where Becky would start a clinic or find some horses to train. But they both would find a rope—even if they had to braid it themselves from hemp—and someone to contest.

Here Becky tells about the nightmare of all rodeo people who haul—rolling a trailerload of horses. The story is a telling portrait of rodeo life "in the fast lane," where true champions ask a lot of their horses and even more of themselves.

We were driving all night, on our way to the all-girl rodeo in Salt Lake City. It was about three o'clock on Friday morning and we were on those Three Sister hills about thirty miles out of Evanston. I was asleep and Kathy was driving. We hit an icy bridge and the pickup started jackknifing both ways. She couldn't get it straightened out. The pickup and trailer went opposite directions and then they ripped apart. The pickup rolled to the right and the trailer rolled to the left.

We landed upside down. As soon as everything quieted down, I asked Kathy if she was O.K. She said, "Yes, are you O.K.?" I said I was and then she goes, "My hand is pinned. I can't get it out."

I jumped out of the pickup—I could get out pretty easy—and ran around and crawled underneath. There was broken glass all over the place, but I could get down there. It was snowing and the wind was blowing and it was really cold. I tried to get her hand unpinned but I couldn't do it because it was really snapped down in there behind the steering wheel.

About that time, some truckers saw us and slowed down. In about five minutes, this guy comes and says, "We got a crowbar." They got Kathy unstuck.

While they were doing that, I ran back to where the trailer was. It was lying on its side. I couldn't hear a single noise and I thought all the horses were probably dead. I got the back gate open pretty easy because all I had to do was throw the back gate up. Topsy was standing up and Channing was laying down. They both had been tied. It was real easy to get Topsy out, but Channing was tied to the side that was next to the pavement. That's why he couldn't get up. I got his halter rope unsnapped. He didn't exactly want to get up, but I pulled real hard and got him up. So I got the back two horses out really fast. By that time, somebody had come along and helped me hold them.

Then I tried to get Sissy out. There was no way I could open the middle gate. The latch to it was down on the pavement and I couldn't reach it. She was tied next to a tackroom that I had built on one side of the front. This tackroom was a homemade deal made of expanded metal. I had four saddles in there, all the bridles and blankets and everything I owned. The trailer landed with the tackroom to the highway and Sissy was on top of the expanded metal. It had caved in because it's not that stout.

Sissy was stuck. Her back foot was stuck between what would be the ceiling, which was the side then, and the top of this expanded metal. And the other foot was down over the front of the manger. Then the rest of her body was kind of laying on this sagged-down metal. So she couldn't stand up, she couldn't do anything.

There was nothing I could do but wait until something came that could get her out. In the meantime, a lot of people came by and asked if we needed help. These truckers were trying to get ahold of a wrecker with a cutting torch.

I just kept standing there, trying to calm Sissy. She would fight every ten minutes for about thirty seconds. She would try to stand up. I'd say "Whoa," and push on her real hard. Then she'd quit fighting.

When we first wrecked, I looked her over and she wasn't hurt that bad. But every time she fought she got hurt just a little more. Her cuts got deeper and she started losing more blood. And she really started bashing her head a lot up in the manger. There was a lightweight metal door up in the front that she broke out. She got cut on it, it was real sharp. So she was bleeding in about three places—on her hind leg, her front leg, her head . . .

It took the police about forty-five minutes to get there. I had on a trench coat, which was lucky or I would have froze to death, because it was really cold. People kept telling me they were worried about me, that I should go sit in the truck, but I kept saying no because I was scared for my horse. I thought if I went in, she would really hurt herself.

And Kathy—they had got her out right away. She was kind of hurt but she just stayed with me. They kept trying to get her in. She really was in a lot worse shape than I was, and they were afraid she was going to go into shock. They told her she better get where it's warm. So she'd get in the truck and then she'd come back out. It was wild. But she felt so bad, she was really upset.

Finally the ambulance came and she wouldn't leave. They looked at her arm and thought it was broken and they wanted to take her to the hospital. But she said, "No, I can't leave Becky out here." Finally the ambulance guy came over to me and said, "Would you please convince your friend that it's best for her to go to the hospital? She's not going to do any good out here and she might go into shock." So we had a little talk and I said, "Kathy," I said, "you go on in. Everything will be O.K." She really didn't want to go, but they took her away.

That was about an hour and a half after the wreck happened. The wrecker showed up in about thirty more minutes and the vet arrived about the same time. By then, Sissy had been fighting for a long time and she was getting pretty tired. They decided they would have to cut things up with a cutting torch. The vet looked at Sissy and decided to tranquilize her so that she wouldn't fight with the cutting torch.

They had to cut everything off the trailer. If they could have cut some of it off earlier, she would have had enough life left in her to struggle the rest of the way out. But by that time she didn't have an ounce of fight left in her. They cut out everything, and then we had to drag out every saddle, everything underneath her. It took about two hours.

Finally, the only thing left was her laying on this piece of metal. The vet said, "If we don't get her out in five minutes, she will be dead." Her tongue was sticking out and she looked absolutely dead. So they pulled her out by hooking her halter to the tow truck. They pulled her back over herself and she almost did a flip. Then, all of a sudden, she got about halfway over and she kind of came to life.

When she got up, she had the whole inside of the trailer because everything was cut out. She was really staggering and she bashed her head on both sides of the trailer. We got her up and stepped her out of the trailer. That cold wind hit her and she really started shivering, her whole body was quivering. She reached over and she bit me, really hard. Because she was completely under drugs and she was quivering so bad.

She was bleeding bad out of a hind leg, a front leg, and out of her head. They thought she might bleed to death. They had to get a bunch of IVs in her real quick to keep her alive in that cold wind.

Somebody had brought a trailer and the other two horses had been loaded in the front of it. She jumped right in the back and they took her to the vet clinic at Fort Bridger. They operated on her for about six hours that morning.

I didn't go. I stayed there and helped clean up the wreck. It was about nine o'clock in the morning before I left the wreck, and this had happened at three.

The police took me to the hospital in Evanston where Kathy was. Her arm wasn't broke but it was all wrapped up and in a sling. We picked her up and they took us to a motel room.

We needed to make some phone calls and there was no telephone in the room, so we went to a cafe. I was really cold because I had been outside all the time. My hair was a mess. I usually tie it back because it is so long, but that night it had been loose and just whipping around in that wind. It was all matted and caked with blood, and my trench coat had blood on it. Kathy had her big sling. Everybody in that cafe just stared.

This was Friday and the first performance at the rodeo was that night. We were supposed to be up and we had to get them to schedule us for the performance the next afternoon. We called the insurance company. Then we tried to rent a pickup and trailer to get to the rodeo. We couldn't find anything but we got ahoid of Jennifer [Haynes] and Jan [Howell] at the rodeo and they said they'd come pick us up. Of course, they couldn't leave until the rodeo was over that night.

We decided that Kathy would go ahead to Salt Lake City on the bus. She took a bus out about four o'clock in the afternoon. She made it to Salt Lake City just about at the end of the rodeo. She was in really bad shape. We'd both been up since Thursday morning, and we hadn't had any sleep at all. When Jennifer and Jan saw her, they just put her down in bed and said, "You stay here," and came back and got me.

By this time I had been back out to the vet clinic. Sissy's whole head was swollen. Her eyelids were so swollen that when they were open you couldn't even see her eyes. And her ears—there was only one way they could go and that was sticking straight up. They were maybe a half an inch thick everywhere. Her whole head—she looked like a mongoloid. Three of her legs were taped clear up to her stomach. She was cut under her legs and on her neck. Boy, she was a mess. She would stand up and just sway back and forth. But at least she could stand up. That was about the only good thing.

Jan and Jennifer came in the middle of the night and we took one horse. We had Topsy because she was the least hurt of all of them. She was skinned up and she was really stiff, but we could Bute her [Butazolidine, a painkiller used frequently with horses] and use her at the rodeo.

We got to Salt Lake City Saturday morning. Then Kathy and I called all around trying to get an outfit rented to take to Riverton because we were entered in a college rodeo there the next day. We tried all morning up to the time of the rodeo but we couldn't find anything.

We did really good at the rodeo. There was an afternoon performance and then the finals that night. We placed in quite a few things.* Kathy's back was really hurting her, she could hardly ride a horse. If you've ever hurt your back, about one of the most painful things to do is get on a horse and ride it, especially at a trot. And of course, her arm. But she placed in the tie-down calf roping. Of all things to place in, in the condition she was in.

We finally found an outfit. One of our friends knew this girl who lived in Salt Lake City. She didn't know us at all, we were complete strangers. And she loaned us her pickup and her trailer to drive to Riverton, Wyoming, as tired as we were, and after having just wrecked one outfit.

By the time the rodeo was over and we picked up our checks and got the outfit and got the horses loaded, it was about 1 A.M. We took off and drove all night to Riverton. Riverton is a long way away. Her outfit didn't pull too

---

* Becky placed third in tie-down calf roping and Kathy placed second. Becky placed fourth in steer undecorating and Kathy placed third in team roping.

good and we couldn't go too fast. Then we took a wrong turn and went over a hundred miles out of our way.

We got to Riverton about eleven o'clock the next morning and the rodeo started about one. We had just enough time to clean up before the show. We unloaded Topsy from the trailer and she was really tired. I was scared to Bute her again because you're not supposed to Bute horses two times in a row like that. So we gave her a bunch of other shots, just to kind of pick her up and keep her from getting sick.

That was one of my best rodeos all year. Kathy and I were second in the team roping. I got on a horse of Kelly Yates's and Kathy rode Topsy to heel on. I ran barrels on Topsy and if we hadn't hit a barrel, she'd have placed in that. She was really hurting when she ran barrels. You just can't believe how much "try" that horse has. And I won the breakaway on her. It was really freaky because it was one of the best runs I had all year. I won the all-around.

We had to get the outfit back to this girl in Salt Lake City before Monday morning at eight o'clock because she had to go to work. So right after the rodeo, we picked up our checks and got in and drove all night long. This time we had two outfits to drive back because a friend of Kathy's had brought Kathy's outfit to the college rodeo at Riverton. See, Kathy was supposed to go on to the Feedlot Roping Finals [Feedlot Ropings are held for anyone who works in a feedlot or has a family member who does] in Spring Creek, Nevada. I couldn't go because I had to get back to school at C.S.U. [Colorado State University at Fort Collins] Before we ever had our wreck, we had made arrangements to have Kathy's outfit meet us at Riverton.

Kathy drove her outfit and I drove the one we'd borrowed, which means that each outfit had one less driver for all those miles. We drove all night long. I was so tired, I just kept weaving all over the road. I'd pull over and wait for Kathy because her pickup wasn't running very good, and then she'd come by and we'd take off. This was Sunday night and I hadn't been to bed since early Thursday morning. Kathy had had those few hours' sleep in Salt Lake City and that was all. We were both just thoroughly exhausted.

We stopped by the clinic in Fort Bridger where the horses were. It was about three o'clock in the morning. That was absolutely one of the most touching scenes . . . We unloaded Topsy from the trailer and Sissy heard Topsy. Sissy nickered and Topsy nickered. They just went crazy.

We turned Topsy loose in the corral and she went and lay down. She was so physically tired that she couldn't even stand up to eat. She just lay there. Kathy and I went and sat down in the dirt next to Topsy. We held her head and petted her. And she was just so tired. I've never seen a horse so physically tired in my life. So wore out she couldn't even get up. And we had won a little over thirteen hundred dollars on her that weekend.

After we decided she was going to be O.K., we loaded Channing, because it had been a couple days by then and he was healing up O.K. We went on to Salt Lake City and got that girl's pickup and trailer to her by about seven-thirty. We made it by half an hour.

We tried to pay her for the use of her outfit, but she absolutely would not take one dime. I said, "At least take something for changing the oil . . ." But she wouldn't take a cent.

She didn't have a tape deck in her pickup, and when we were in Riverton that morning before the rodeo started we bought her a tape deck and speakers. We were going to get it installed but we didn't have time. We hadn't told her about that or anything when we were trying to pay her. So finally we just said, "We left something for you in the truck." She was thrilled. But you know, it still wasn't enough for letting us use that outfit. It's so amazing she ever loaned it to us, the condition we were in.

About ten that morning I caught a plane for Denver. My sister picked me up and drove me to Fort Collins and I was in class that afternoon. I was sitting in class at three o'clock Monday afternoon going, "Wow, man, I don't believe this." But at C.S.U. it's pretty hard. You can't miss too many classes.

Kathy went on to the Feedlot Roping Finals and she won that. That was about eight hundred dollars. They gave her the Hard Luck Award because of the wreck, and I think they paid a hundred and fifty dollars or something. Then she was in a matched roping with somebody and won that, so she won over a thousand dollars at that Feedlot Roping. But she did get a day in there to sleep before she did all that. And believe me, she took the whole day too.

I counted up one time and we went something like a hundred and twenty-two hours with only seven hours' sleep. We had gotten up Thursday morning and didn't get to really lay down and sleep until Monday night.

Of course, while we'd been on the road, I had called the vet about Sissy several times. They told me she had a 10 percent chance to live, because she was bleeding internally. In fact, for ten straight days, they only gave her a ten percent chance to live. But she lived. It was over a month before I could pick her up. But she healed O.K. She was fine the next summer. And this last summer ['79], she was better than she was the summer before.†

"You know what happened the other day?" Denise says. "I used to work in a western bar. I ran into one of my customers. We were very good friends. I told him I planned to ride bulls at Loveland. He got red in the face. 'You're ruining rodeo,' he said. He turned his back and walked away."

Denise reflects, "Some people call me a women's libber. I sympathize with some of the women in the movement. I buy a lot of their ideas, but I rodeo because it's fun. It's making me grow. I like being a woman. I like being soft and feminine. But God gave me a good strong body and I'm going to use it."

—Lynn Haney,
Ride 'em Cowgirl! 1975.

† Sissy ended 1978 ranked fourth in the Super Horse Contest. In 1979 she ranked third.

Epilogue

The country fosters a kind of woman who seems never to have been bothered about who she was supposed to be, maybe mainly because there was always work, and getting it done in a level-eyed way was what counted most. The men can all cook just fine for themselves. Getting the work done, on horseback or not, and dicing their troubles into jokes. These women wind up looking 50 when they are 37 and 53 when they are 70. It's like they wear down to what counts and just last there, fine and staring the devil in the eye every morning.

*—William Kittredge**

The question remains: Why, in an America fascinated by the cowboy and his Wild West, have these vital women remained invisible? The first and most obvious answer is that historically their numbers have been few. Yet fewer still were the bandittas, desperadas, and wild women of the West, and every schoolchild knows of Calamity Jane and Belle Starr. But those women actively sought notoriety; it assured the place they had found for themselves as novel renegades, forever on the fringes of society. And if they led exciting, romantic lives, they still had about them the aspect of the clown or sideshow freak— something most women, with at least some inbred sense of social propriety, hardly cared to emulate.

In fact, it may be this sense of social propriety that accounts, at least in part, for cowgirls' invisibility. The desperadas needed notoriety, but the cowgirls wanted as little attention paid them as possible. They were not rebels or renegades. If they bucked a few conventions, they were not against society itself. In their journals and memoirs, and today in interviews, one finds a constant reference to social mores, as if each cowgirl carries with her the pervasive concept of feminine perfection—perhaps the Prairie Madonna, the Perfect Lady, or the Total Woman, depending on the era—and constantly measures herself against it. She acknowledges her departure from the model with a mixture of apology and pride.

I have seldom entered a countrywoman's home without being met by a perfunctory apology for the housekeeping. Then there is the apology for dress, for the roughness of hands, the untidiness of hair. I have to get through the apologies to find the honest pride in a life well lived.

The cowgirl is not so much a woman who, as Kittredge suggests, "seems never to have been bothered about who she was supposed to be," as a woman who has specifically chosen to be what she is—ever aware that she departs from the larger notion of what makes a "lady"; always attempting to

* William Kittredge, "Owyhee Buckaroo," *Rocky Mountain Magazine,* September/October 1980, p. 39.

Helen Bonham ("Miss Wyoming"), around 1920. The cowgirls were colorful and attractive, and they fascinated the public. This fact hardly eluded PR men from coast to coast.

compensate for that departure with apology. And the apology goes back for generations.

In her book *Frontier Women: The Trans-Mississippi West, 1840–1880,* Julie Roy Jeffrey notes that many pioneer women migrated West with a strong commitment to their place in the "woman's sphere." The women's magazines, journals, and novels of the day extolled the virtues of the "cult of domesticity." A woman's highest calling was to be the "guardian angel" of the nation's moral health. She should be soft and refined, able to provide a welcome retreat for her man from the rough-and-tumble world of business. While he handled the family finances, she took care of the family spirit, providing comfort, religion, and culture. She provided everything her man needed to be happy, healthy and productive; everything her children needed to grow into fine, upstanding citizens.

Jeffrey points out that most pioneer women came from middle-class backgrounds (it took money to migrate; few paupers hit the transcontinental trails) and were familiar with these ideas. They imagined the frontier as a wicked, wild place, a state of nature. Their duty was to soften it, to civilize it. Many women headed west imbued with an almost missionary zeal to do just that. And if the raw requirements of transcontinental travel and early settlement caused women to work outside the "woman's sphere"—to wear unfeminine clothes, do manly labor, and develop strong and calloused hands—many women never forgot they were *supposed* to be ladies:

> *Of course, assenting to ideas was not the same as living up to their prescriptions. Domesticity described the norms and not the actual conduct of American women. There was considerably more variety in the behavior of women than ideology would suggest. Still, norms were important because they established the behavioral context for those who tried to reject them as much as for those who attempted to realize them. They shaped personality and colored expectations. For many women the cult of domesticity provided a psychologically compelling meaning for their lives.†*

That frontier woman with which we are most familiar, the Prairie Madonna, fit within the context of frontier domesticity. In her long skirts, she was invariably beautiful, if a little lonesome and sad. She was strong and protective —as shown by the authoritative way she held that rifle—but also compassionate and nurturing. Her children clung to her with love and admiration. We sense that she provided a warm and welcoming home for her man. And if she had to help herd the oxen, milk the cows, or plow the field until the family became established, she turned her energies to the more refined tasks of culture, religion and education as soon as she was able.

But some women found that they *liked* to herd the oxen, milk the cows, and plow the field. They never missed their lace-edged cuffs and soft, pink hands. They, and their daughters and granddaughters, I have defined as cowgirls. And I suspect that they have still not fully outgrown their guilt that they turned their back on their duty, on the "woman's sphere."

Agnes Morley Cleaveland dearly loved her life and activities on a ranch during the late nineteenth and early twentieth centuries. There, she said, there was no "double standard." Yet she constantly felt torn between the rugged outdoor life she loved and the more gentle life of a lady she "should" like. Even the title of her autobiography—*No Life for a Lady*—bears the message of apology.

The vast majority of the couple hundred women's ranch reminiscences were written by ranchers' wives who worked outside when needed, but not everyday. In these the author tells about her day-to-day life on the ranch, of her help in calving or branding or fighting a grass fire. While she takes pride in her ranch

† Julie Roy Jeffrey, *Frontier Women: The Trans-Mississippi West, 1840–1880* (New York: Hill and Wang, 1979), p. 10.

skills, in her strength, and even in her sweat, there is often that underlying apology—If I were truly a lady, I wouldn't like this so much. "Somewhere I have read that 'horses sweat, men perspire—but ladies only glow,'" wrote Mary Kidder Rak in the thirties. "Well, I was working like a horse and shared his privileges."

These reminiscences often devote many of their pages to domestic accomplishments—the number of men the author cooked for, the primitive conditions under which she kept house, her involvement with church and school—as if to say, "I may have calloused hands. I may enjoy the great outdoors. But I do my duty as wife and mother too."

Few women ranchers—women who had a full-time commitment to out-of-doors work and hired their domestic work done or let it go—wrote memoirs. It is easy to say they didn't have time, but men ranchers found time to chronicle *their* lives. More likely the silence came from a desire to protect the invisibility which allowed them their quiet eddies of effectiveness, responsibility, and respect.

If cowgirls found they forever needed to justify their position in the woman's sphere, they felt more comfortable in the world of men. In woman's sphere they had to apologize for what they weren't; in man's sphere they earned an honest respect for what they were, what they could do, and the extent to which they made a hand. Most cowgirls learned their skills from men—a father, a brother, or a husband.

"I was my daddy's only boy," says Mildred Kanipe. "Amy and I were my father's boys," recalls Elsie Lloyd, "because my brother was away." "I got along with my mother," adds Marie Bell, "but it was Dad that was my pal. We did everything together."

In the rare case a cowgirl has a mother who was her outdoor mentor, the mother learned *her* skills from a man. "I think like a man," says Jerri Wattenberg, whose mother also "thought like a man." "If I have any trouble, it's relating to other women."

Cowgirls operate in two worlds, a fact they constantly confront. After her husband died and Margaret Duncan Brown decided to pay out their ranch herself, she wrote in her diary: "Please do not let me use physical disabilities as an excuse, nor the fact that I am a woman, but let me remember I am a woman in a man's place; that I must have the guts of a man and the patience of a woman." Mrs. Brown found that her venture into man's world suited her, for later she wrote, "I suppose living here alone is what other people call queer. No one can know the relief this quiet has been to me. I can stew my own little mess. I have spent the first half of my life explaining. I'm going to start the second half without explanation."

Man's world encompassed the things many cowgirls liked most about their lives and they looked on it with true affection. Quite possibly they saw their history not so much unwritten as included in the history of men.

The history of the West has traditionally been the history of men. From the first, the West was viewed as a particularly male domain. "Go West, young *man"* ran the popular wisdom, for it was men who would break the trails and quiet the natives. The women came later as an afterthought, a support crew, and no one paid them much mind. The nation was not predisposed to ask about the other half—at least not about unconventional members of the other half. When notice was made of a woman in an extraordinary role—such as the cattle business—no niche existed in which to catalog the information. It just floated in the nether lands of public consciousness, awaiting the time when scholars would grasp at the fragments and try to reconstruct the whole.

The desperadas were the exception. They carved out a niche for themselves. They wanted publicity and actively sought it, offering their life stories to eastern journalists, peddling their autobiographies in mining camps and cattle towns, holding court in rowdy saloons. Only a few, such as Calamity Jane, did this, but that was enough to alert the public to a phenomenon of note. Cowgirls, on the other hand, were thankful to remain in the shadows.

Many of the women introduced in these pages have found true fulfillment and happiness through their work on the range or in the rodeo. They respect themselves and are in turn respected by those who work around them. Some achieved this only after a struggle—not unlike that of urban career women who try to juggle a career with home and family. Still, cowgirls have little sympathy for "this Women's Lib stuff."

But ranchers have never been amenable to national movements of any kind. They didn't embrace "that populist stuff" or "that New Deal stuff" or "that American Agriculture Farm Strike stuff." Even though government programs, including pest control, lease of government land, and drought relief and other emergency programs are an integral part of modern ranch agriculture—as government programs are a part of every American industry—ranchers still see themselves as the last of the rugged individualists. Women subscribe to this as much as men. And individualists do not run off and get involved in movements.

Even so, I saw attitudes toward the Women's Movement change among both men and women during the course of this project. Gradually the glib concepts that attached themselves to the movement give way to a better understanding. As Westerners come to realize that Women's Liberation is not a matter of women dominating men, burning bras, or pushing their way into jobs they are ill-equipped for, sympathy for the movement grows. The real issues of self-respect and the opportunity to be respected, of just treatment before the law (including inheritance law), of recognition for work well done, are concepts Westerners embrace.

The West was never an easy place for a woman. Loneliness, isolation, and hard work took its toll in neuralgia, insanity, and long and lingering illnesses. But many women prospered in the West. Some of these were cowgirls, who found their answers to these problems by working outside. Through a combination of necessity, circumstance, and self-determination, they made a place for themselves in the larger world of horses, cows, and men. They operated in this world with dignity, strength, good humor—and sometimes joy.

This project has engaged me for the better part of four years, and I find it hard to put down. These women have changed me. They taught me to ask more of myself, to pay less mind to small encumbrances, to forge a life out of raw material and live it. Perhaps most important, as I watched many of them greet their elder years with humor, orneriness, and spunk, they taught me not to fear the process of aging but to greet it head-on as a worthy opponent, the ultimate challenge. No one says it better than Julia Kooken in *Country Women:*

> I want to live to be
> An outrageous old woman
> Who is never accused of being
> An old lady.
>
> I want to live to have ten thousand lovers
> In one love
> One 70-year-long-loving-love
>> There are at least
>> Two of me
>
> I want to get leaner and meaner
>> Sharp edged
>> Color of the ground
> Till I discorporate
> From sheer joy.

—Julia Kooken‡

‡ Julia Kooken, "Outrageous Old Woman," in *Country Women* by Jeanne Tetrault and Sherry Thomas (Garden City, N.Y.: Anchor Press/Doubleday, Inc., 1976), p. 241.

A Selected Bibliography

GENERAL, including bibliography, biography, and history

Clancy, Foghorn, *My Fifty Years in Rodeo: Living with Cowboys, Horses, and Danger*. San Antonio: The Naylor Co., 1952. This classic by an early rodeo announcer includes anecdotes and vignettes of all the early cowgirls, including Bertha Blancett, Lucille Mulhall, the Greenough sisters, Marie Gibson, Prairie Rose Henderson, and Tad Barnes Lucas.

Editors of Time-Life Books, with text by Joan Swallow Reiter, *The Old West: The Women*. Alexandria, VA: Time-Life Books, 1978. Has brief information on cowgirls in Wild West shows, rodeo, and on ranches; slightly more complete coverage of women outlaws. As in most Time-Life productions, the photos make the book.

Haney, Lynn, *Ride 'em Cowgirl!* New York: G. P. Putnam's Sons, 1975. This book gives a good behind-the-scenes look at all facets of women's rodeo from Little Britches and High School Rodeo competition to GRA barrel racing on the PRCA circuit. Included are sketches of many top cowgirls, including Sheila Bussey, Suzy Thomas, Jean and Becky Fuchs, Sammy Thurman, Bonnie Pleasant and Jeana Day Felts. She also looks into men's attitudes toward women's rodeo.

Jeffrey, Julie Roy, *Frontier Women: The Trans-Mississippi West, 1840–1880*. New York: Hill and Wang, 1979. Jeffrey bases this scholarly work on over 200 women's journals, memoirs, and collections of letters as well as other primary and secondary source material. She looks at the expectations women had for the frontier, their experiences on the overland trails, the tasks the frontier required of them, their civilizing influence, women in polygamous Mormon society, and women's political and social involvement. She attacks many accepted tenets, including the assumption that women realized more political and economic freedom and power on the frontier than in the East. Although Jeffrey does not deal extensively with women's experiences in agriculture, she provides a basis for understanding their attitudes and actions. A controversial and important book.

Lee, Katie, *Ten Thousand Goddam Cattle: A History of the American Cowboy in Song, Story and Verse*. Flagstaff: Northland Press, 1976. As the title suggests, this is a study of cow*boys,* but Lee does introduce the reader to some pretty substantial women and mentions the way they are treated in song. The book has extensive reference materials, including a discography, bibliography, song compendium, and index. Lee is a wild and vibrant storyteller and this book is pure poetry, gilded in cow dung and horse sweat.

Marriott, Alice, *Hell on Horses and Women*. Norman: University of Okla-

ROUGH RIDER

WEEKLY

THE BEST WILD WEST STORIES PUBLISHED

Issued Weekly. By subscription $2.50 per year. Entered according to Act of Congress in the year 1906, in the Office of the Librarian of Congress, Washington, D. C., by STREET & SMITH, 79-89 Seventh Avenue, N. Y. Application made at the N. Y. Post Office for entry as Second-class Matter.

No. 124   NEW YORK, SEPTEMBER 1, 1906.   **Price, Five Cents**

KING OF THE WILD WEST'S HELPING HAND

or Stella, the Girl Range Rider

By NED TAYLOR

She had snatched the blacksnake from Old Dennis as she passed the grub-wagon. Now she laid it into the stampeding herd with vicious strokes. Would she turn them in time?

Cover of a dime novel, 1906. The American love affair with the Wild West thrived on heroes made bigger than life in pulp fiction—dime novels published by such houses as Beadle and Adams, and Street and Smith. From the 1870s through the 1920s, heroes like Buffalo Bill, Deadwood Dick, and a host of tall, dark, forceful cowboys had a loyal audience. Although women usually served as the background against which these heroes could shine, a woman was occasionally given center stage. Then she coupled a buxom yet fragile beauty with excellence in range skills—riding, roping, shooting a gun or cracking a blacksnake, even gambling. Calamity Jane, Hurricane Nell, Bowie Knife Bessie—these were the Amazons.

homa Press, 1953. This is a series of sketches of ranchwomen drawn from eighteen months of interviewing in the western states. It includes both ranch wives and regular cowhands, but does not use their real names. Good reading.

Patterson-Black, Sheryll and Gene, *Western Women in History and Literature*. Crawford, NE: Cottonwood Press, 1978. If I could have only one book on women in the West, I just might choose this extensive bibliography. It includes nearly 3,000 annotated references to both published and unpublished works. Sections include bibliographies, regional and local history, women's history, oral history, biography, letters, diaries and journals, memoirs and autobiographies, literary bibliographies and criticism, novels and pulps, short stories, juvenile fiction, poetry, theater, and essays. Two excellent articles by the authors preface the work: "From Pack Trains to Publishing: Women's Work in the Frontier West"; and "Women Homesteaders on the Great Plains Frontier." The appendix outlines syllabi for courses on western women.

Roach, Joyce Gibson, *The Cowgirls*. Houston: Cordovan Corporation, 1977. This book is the closest thing available to a who's who of women in the West. Extensively footnoted, it treats women on ranches and in rodeo, bandittas and desperadas, and cowgirls in fiction, film, and music. The analysis of the media treatment of cowgirls could be more in-depth and the book suffers for want of an index and bibliography, but there is a wealth of information here.

Simpson, Charles. *El Rodeo*. London: The Bodley Head Limited, 1925. This account, along with over 100 paintings and sketches of the 1924 rodeo at Wembley Stadium in London is one of the rare rodeo accounts that pays as much attention to the women as to the men. This was the Englishman's first experience with rodeo, and the women fascinated him as they busted broncs and trick-rode. He bemoaned only the fact that they did not compete in bulldogging at Wembley.

Stratton, Joanna L., *Pioneer Women: Voices from the Kansas Frontier*. New York: Simon & Schuster, 1981. This book was conceived in the 1920s when the author's great grandmother, a lawyer, editor, and suffragist, collected reminiscences from eight hundred Kansas pioneer women for a book. The book was not written at that time, however, and eventually the collection was forgotten. Some fifty years later, Joanna Stratton discovered it in her grandmother's attic, and at last the book was born. Stratton organizes excerpts from the reminiscences around themes, including travel, settlement, daily life, Indians, the Civil War, temperance, and suffrage. She notes the limits of the reminiscences—they were all written several decades after the experiences described; personal subjects such as pregnancy and childbirth, sex and love, and personal problems and animosities were treated euphemistically if at all. Still, a picture of life for pioneer women in Kansas from 1854 to 1890 emerges that is extensive, sometimes humorous, and always touching. An important book. Includes index, bibliography, photos, and a guide to the Lilla Day Monroe Collection of Pioneer Stories (the original eight hundred reminiscences).

Tetrault, Jeanne and Sherry Thomas, *Country Women: A Handbook for the New Farmer.* Garden City, N.Y.: Anchor Press/Doubleday, 1976. This book grew out of the California-based *Country Women Magazine,* which itself is the product of a feminist collective of women who run or work on small "homestead-type" farms. The book has how-to articles on everything from butchering chickens to lambing, choosing your land to planting and harvesting grain. Whether or not you have use for the practical information, the book is a valuable testament to women's experiences on the land, by virtue of the personal experiences woven throughout (including excerpts from Sherry Thomas's journal), the poems by countrywomen, the pen-and-ink illustrations, and the photographs. A good read.

Van Steenwyk, Elizabeth, *Women in Sports: Rodeo.* New York: Harvey House, 1978. This book includes a short history of women in rodeo and a description of the seven Girls Rodeo Association events, neither of which is overly accurate. (Among other errors, she suggests that women regularly competed against men in early rodeo and that barrel race was the first regular all-women's event. She calls a bull rope a rigging.) Of more interest are her portraits of several top rodeo hands, including Sue Pirtle, Sammy Thurman, Sheila Bussey, and Becky Fuchs.

Westermeier, Clifford P., *Man, Beast, Dust: The Story of Rodeo.* Denver: World Press Inc., 1947. This rodeo history includes a short segment on women. Westermeier suggests that women were "never particularly welcome as participants in the work [but] carved a niche for themselves by sheer audacity, courage, and female persistence and . . . won the respect of all who . . . witnessed their daring and skill." Some good photos.

Western Writers of America, *The Women Who Made the West.* Garden City, N.Y.: Doubleday & Co., Inc., 1980. This anthology includes articles about eighteen women involved in all aspects of the frontier West—medicine, politics, reform, mining and mine ownership, ranching, horse trading, and even stagecoach driving. The women chosen were, for the most part, not known outside their own communities but led vital, varied lives and made substantial contributions. Authored by such writers as Peggie Simpson Curry, Nellie Snyder Yost, Joyce Gibson Roach, and Roberta Cheney, this is a lively, well-written and informative anthology.

AUTOBIOGRAPHIES, MEMOIRS, DIARIES, AND ORAL HISTORIES

Alderson, Nannie T., *A Bride Goes West.* New York: Farrar and Rinehart, Inc., 1942. Nannie Tiffany of Virginia married Walter Alderson in 1883 and went to live with him on his ranch along the Wolf Mountains of Wyoming. She had to learn to cook, keep house under primitive conditions, make her own clothes, and live for months without speaking to another woman. She writes much about the sheer physical demands of housekeeping and child-raising. When a teenage girl visits and prefers to ride and work cattle rather than help with the housework, Mrs. Alderson is not amused. A classic, reprinted by University of Nebraska Press in 1969.

Ashley, Daisy H., *A Cowgirl's Ups and Downs*. Philadelphia: Dorrance & Co., 1972. Daisy Hill, a city girl, married Tom Ashley while he was still in law school. He gave her two choices: they could live in Denver and he could begin a legal career; or they could "rough it" on a cattle ranch in the Colorado Rockies. Daisy chose the latter. She learned the ranch and could fill in when needed, but she did not work outside on a daily basis.

Baker, Pearl, *Robbers Roost Recollections*. Logan: Utah State University Press, 1976. Pearl grew up in the Robbers Roost area of Utah, and worked alongside her father, Joe Biddlecome, and her sister Hazel. After her father died in 1928, Pearl and her husband, Mel Marsing, bought the range rights. Two months later, Mel died of blood poisoning, leaving Pearl with two small boys. She ran the outfit for several years in the deepest part of the Depression, then remarried and moved to Oregon. The book focuses on Pearl's father but paints a good portrait of ranch life for a girl. She also talks about her mother, who was not "a hand" but gave the rest of the family the support they needed to make the ranch successful.

Bourne, Eulalia. *Woman in Levi's*. Tucson: University of Arizona Press, 1967. Eulalia took up country schoolteaching and a grazing homestead in the San Pedro Valley of southern Arizona in the 1930s. She bought fifty cows for $15 apiece from her $150-a-month salary and was in business. Except for a four-year disastrous marriage to a rancher she refers to as "The Cowboy," she managed her ranch alone. She talks candidly about the community's reactions to her, the difficulties a woman faces when she employs men, problems she had in business dealings. Her account is pithy and, unlike many ranch reminiscences, is not sugar-coated.

Bowman, Nora Linjer, *Only the Mountains Remain*. Caldwell, Idaho: The Caxton Printer, Ltd., 1958. Nora was the daughter of a Minneapolis doctor. She taught in Odgen, Utah. During the summer of 1919 she visited the expansive Utah Construction Company ranch in northeast Nevada where she met her husband-to-be, Archie Bowman. They lived and worked on the ranch until it broke up in 1945.

Brown, Margaret Duncan, *Shepherdess of Elk River Valley*. Denver: Golden Bell Press, 1967. Margaret and her bank-manager husband, Thornton (Dick) Brown, bought 160 acres on Elk River in northwest Colorado in 1915. When Dick died three years later, Margaret—then thirty-six years old—decided to stay on the ranch. She paid it out and expanded. She had kept diaries since she was fourteen years old, and this book is constructed posthumously by Paul E. Daugherty, the executor of her will. In her later years she waxes philosophic, but during the first few years on the ranch her writings are a moving testimony of a woman confronting loneliness, financial insecurity, and physical hardship. A wonderful book.

Call, Hughie, *Golden Fleece*. New York: Crown Publishers, 1942 and 1961. This is a classic among sheep-ranch wife stories. She helped out on the ranch, but raising three children kept her from working outside on a daily basis. Her daughter, Wezie, loved the ranch more than did the two boys, Andy and Leigh. Hughie does not talk much about Wezie, however, because Wezie had died of illness shortly before the book was written.

Cleaveland, Agnes Morley, *No Life for a Lady*. Boston: Houghton Mifflin, 1941. This is possibly the best woman's ranch reminiscence. Cleaveland describes her domestic mother's struggle to learn the cattle business after Agnes's stepfather deserted them; her and her brother Ray's natural love of the ranch; neighbors' reactions to women working on the range; and the conflict she felt between the natural, cowgirl side of herself and the side of the lady in whose guise she "masqueraded" when she was periodically sent off to finishing school. Reprinted by University of Nebraska Press, 1977.

Greenwood, Annie Pike. *We Sagebrush Folk*. New York and London: D. Appleton-Century Co., 1934. Annie Pike was born of a prominent family and grew up with contempt for farmers' coarseness, stupidity, and lack of style. She married Charles Greenwood, a well-educated and cultured man from Columbus, Ohio. He decided to leave a promising position with a sugar factory in Garden City, Kansas, to farm as part of the new Minidoka Irrigation Project in the sagebrush desert of southern Idaho. After fifteen lean, hard years in the twenties and thirties, they lost the farm. Annie never understood the agrarian way of life and was always an outsider, although she certainly did her fair share of work on the farm. The book is a valuable testimony to the hardship and agony a woman can experience on a farm, especially when she harbors an underlying contempt for that type of life.

Guerin, Mrs. E. J., *Mountain Charley; or the Adventures of Mrs. E. J. Guerin who was Thirteen Years in Male Attire*. Norman: University of Oklahoma Press, 1968. Mountain Charley passed as a man for thirteen years in order to support her child after the death of her husband. She prospected the Rocky Mountains for gold, ran an overland freight business, and drove her herd of cattle to California, where she made a handsome profit on them. Although several women claimed to be Mountain Charley (just as several women claimed to be Calamity Jane), the consensus of the introduction by Fred W. Mazzulla and William Kostka is that this is *probably* a true account. Her description of her wagon trek to California in 1855, for instance, is geographically true, and the places she mentions around Pikes Peak and Denver existed at the time she spoke of them. She remarried in 1860 and gave up her male identity.

Jeffers, Jo, *Ranch Wife*. Garden City, N.Y.: Doubleday & Co., Inc., 1964. Jo was born in Minnesota in 1931 and spent her childhood as an often bed-ridden asthmatic, in love with the Wild West where everyone was healthy and free.

She received her B.A. at Stanford and spent a year at the University of Nottingham in England before she met Coonie Jeffers—an Arizona rancher twice her age—and married him. Jo cooked for the men and took care of the house but also worked with Coonie on a regular basis. Like Eulalia Bourne (who suffered from colds before she started to wear men's clothes) and Margaret Brown (who had insomnia before she started to ranch), Jo realized an unexpected health through ranch work.

Jordan, Grace, *Home Below Hell's Canyon*. New York: Thomas Y. Crowell Co., 1954. Grace, her husband Len, and their three children moved to the Kirkwood Bar Ranch, just below Hell's Canyon on the Snake River in middle Idaho, in 1932. They raised sheep.

McGinnis, Vera, *Rodeo Road: My Life as a Pioneer Cowgirl*. New York: Hastings House, 1974. McGinnis, one of early rodeo's premier cowgirls, tells of her rodeo career from 1913 to 1934. She worked in Wild West shows; followed the gyp racetrack circuits and rode against men; competed in rodeo as a bronc rider, trick rider, and jockey. She traveled all over the United States, Europe, and the Far East, and had a brief stint in the movies. Vera stayed with her rodeo career even though it caused her first marriage to break up. She left rodeo only after a racehorse fell on her and broke all five lumbars in her back, her right hip, several ribs, her neck, and collapsed a lung. She was told she would die or at least never walk again; within six months she was back on a horse, although she could no longer compete. One of the best rodeo memoirs.

Powder River County Extension Homemakers' Council, *Echoing Footsteps: Powder River County*. Butte, Montana: Ashton Printing and Engraving Co., 1967. The Homemakers' Council contacted everyone they could find who lived or ever had lived in Powder River County, Montana, and asked them to write about their experiences there. The result is a fascinating collection of several hundred short pieces which, together, give a personal look into the homesteading years. An excellent—and very informative—approach to local history.

Rak, Mary Kidder, *A Cowman's Wife*. Boston and New York: Houghton Mifflin Co., 1934. *Mountain Cattle*. Boston and New York: Houghton Mifflin Co., 1936. These are two of the most cited city-woman-turned-ranchwife tomes. Mary ranched with her husband on the 20,000-acre Old Camp Rucker Ranch in the Chiricuahua Mountains of southwest Arizona, several hours from the nearest town. She recounts her struggle to learn the cattle business from those who always "knowd" it and aren't disposed to teach. She worked with her husband as much as a house with no amenities would allow. She draws interesting portraits of ranch life, Mexican and Indian neighbors, homesteaders, favorite critters, wolf hunts, and much more.

Rankin, Carol, *Spoken Words of Four Ranchwomen*. Sublette County, WY: Carol Rankin, 1979. This oral history of four Sublette County, Wyoming, ranchwomen is not commercially published. For further information, contact the author, Carol Rankin, Cora, Wyoming 82925.

Ross, Dorothy, *Stranger to the Desert*. London: Jarrolds Publishers, Ltd., 1958. Dorothy was born in Harborn, Staffordshire, in 1884 and met her husband on a visit to America in 1906. He secured a government homestead in the rugged country of southwest New Mexico and she brought her private-school education in language and music to these primitive surroundings. Dorothy did not work alongside her husband. Her accounts of hired men, visitors, domestic drudgery, and insanity among women in these isolated parts are insightful and well-written.

Stewart, Elinore Pruitt, *Letters of a Woman Homesteader*. Boston: Houghton Mifflin Co., 1914. Elinore came to Burnt Fork, Wyoming, in 1909 as a housekeeper for Clyde Stewart and homesteaded there with her baby daughter, Jerrine. She wrote these letters to a former employer in Denver between 1910 and 1913. In them she describes paying out her homestead, driving a mower for Mr. Stewart during haying, putting up huge amounts of vegetables from the garden she grew and harvested herself. She eventually married Stewart but would not allow him to help her in any way on her homestead. She was a great advocate of homesteading as a method for women to gain independence. The subject of the wonderful film, *Heartland,* 1981.

Smith, L. Walden, *Saddles Up*. San Antonio: The Naylor Co., 1937. Mrs. Smith and her husband Bryan started ranching in McCullen County, Texas, around 1906, in the height of the tick infestation. She generally worked right beside her husband. What distinguishes this reminiscence is Mrs. Smith's lack of emphasis on her sex. Nothing on the book jacket indicates she is a woman; she writes under an initial rather than her Christian name. She talks about ranching, but seldom about the experience of ranching from a woman's point of view.

Terry, Cleo Tom and Osie Wilson, *The Rawhide Tree: The Story of Florence Reynolds in Rodeo*. Clarendon, TX: The Clarendon Press, 1957. This really is an "As Told To" book, as the voice is that of Florence Reynolds. She and her husband John were part of the Miller Brothers 101 Ranch in Oklahoma during the twenties. Florence rode broncs, raced, and did whatever else needed doing. She had a long and successful career as a contract act at rodeos with one or more of her trained horses. This book is a guaranteed cure for insomnia despite the interesting subject matter.

Thomas, Sherry, *We Didn't Have Much, But We Sure Had Plenty: Stories of Rural Women*. Garden City, N.Y.: Anchor Press/Doubleday, 1981. This oral history by the co-author of *Country Women* looks at farm women in the Deep South, the Midwest, and New England. The thirteen women included form a diverse group. Some are black; some are white; some have been practically destitute all their lives; other have enjoyed a comfortable prosperity. This book is an extraordinary oral history for two reasons. First, Thomas asks intimate questions and has the rapport to get intimate answers. Secondly, she has struggled to preserve not only the women's words but the way they spoke them—their cadence, their emphasis, their particular vernacular. She succeeds so well you almost hear the women as you read. An admirable achievement.

Wallace, Charles, *The Cattle Queen of Montana: A Story of the Personal Experiences of Mrs. Nat Collins,* St. James, Minn.: Charles Foote, Publisher, 1894. (A 2nd edition, edited by Alvin Dyer, was published in Spokane, Wash., by Dyer Printing Co. and dated variously from 1898 to 1914.) Around 1860, Elizabeth Smith left Illinois with her family and moved to Iowa. She was ten, and this was the first of many westering experiences which eventually led her to Montana and her husband, Nat Collins. Mr. Collins was a miner and Elizabeth joined him in this. When they both broke their legs on the same day in separate accidents, had $1,500 worth of gold dust stolen, and lost their equipment to a flood, they decided to change occupations and go into the cattle business. Elizabeth gradually took more responsibility for the ranch as her husband's health failed. After he died, she ran it alone until her health also failed. She was always independent and gutsy—in the early 1890s, she went alone to Nome, Alaska, to prospect for gold. Although only the last thirty pages of this 260-page book deal with ranching, they include some fine anecdotes. Of especial interest because of the early time frame.

Ward, Elizabeth, *No Dudes, Few Women: Life with a Navajo Range Rider.* Albuquerque: University of New Mexico Press, 1951. When Dan Ward brought his wife, Elizabeth, to the huge Wagon Rod Ranch in southern Arizona he told her, "You'll get along. Just don't talk too much and keep plenty of coffee made." In the mid-thirties, Dan got a job as a range rider on the Navajo Indian Reservation and they moved to northwest New Mexico. Elizabeth rode with Dan when she could but often stayed home and took care of the ranch.

Wilson, Sonja, *Castle on the Prairie.* Boston: Branden Press, 1972. Sonja was a Missouri tenderfoot who married a Montana rancher and here she tells of her life on the ranch during the 1920s and '30s. Although the better part of the book focuses on her domestic chores, she helped her husband harvest grain, rope calves, and work cattle. Once she even roped a beaver. She did not stay on the ranch after her husband's accidental death.

Yates, Hadie, *70 Miles from a Lemon.* Boston: Houghton Mifflin Co., 1947. Hadie was a reporter for the *New Yorker* and her husband Ted worked in real estate when they decided to leave Manhattan for a small ranch in the heart of the Crow Indian Reservation in the Big Horn Mountains of Wyoming in 1927. They ranched for seven years before the Depression, drought, and legal entanglements with irrigation water on the Indian lands drove them out.

FICTION

Dime Novels: These pulp novels, popular from 1860 to 1930, often featured beautiful, dynamic, almost superhuman heroines—the Amazons. Neither wives nor mothers, these women were crack shots, exquisite horsewomen, unflinchingly brave, inestimably desirable. Before the turn of the century, the Amazons usually had a tragedy in their background that forced them to be on the range—murder of a family member, for instance, or the loss of their maidenhood. After 1900, two series heroines became popular—Arietta in the *Young Wild West* series from 1902 to 1927, and Stella in the *Rough Rider Weekly* from 1904 to 1907. They were healthy, normal ranch girls who needed no motivation besides their love for the outdoors and adventure. A few titles to look into:

Ingraham, Prentiss, *Buffalo Bill and the Renegade Queen; or, Deadly Hands Strange Duel*. Street & Smith No. 77, November 1, 1902.

An Old Scout, *Young Wild West's Curious Compact; or, Arietta as an Avenger*. Wild West Weekly No. 777, 1917.

Taylor, Ned, *King of the Wild West's Helping Hand; or, Stella the Girl Range Rider*. Rough Rider Weekly, No. 124, 1906.

Wheeler, Edward L., *Bob Woolf, The Border Ruffian; or, The Girl Dead-Shot*. Beadle's Half Dime Library, Vol. II, No. 32, 1878.

Wheeler, Edward L., *Deadwood Dick on Deck; or, Calamity Jane, the Heroine of Whoop-Up*. Beadle's Pocket Library, 1885.

Ranch Romances: This short-story magazine, directed primarily at a female audience, took up where the dime novels left off and ran through the 1950s. It frequently featured a range-worthy heroine. The formula ran something like this: young, beautiful woman has to run the ranch, the mine, or the freight line because of some wrong done to her and her family. Generally, her father has been killed or is wrongfully imprisoned. She makes a brave attempt but, being only a woman, can't handle it alone. Fortunately, a brave and handsome hero arrives just in the nick of time and the two of them rout the villain before riding off into the sunset together to live happily ever after. Although virtually every issue of *Ranch Romances* includes stories of this genre, here are three to ask for by name:

Denver, Robert Dale, "Trails to Disaster." *Ranch Romances*, August 2, 1935.

Lockhart, Sally (Carolyn King), "Lady Bandit Catcher." *Ranch Romances*, November 2, 1933.

Sinclair, Kenneth L., "Never Trust a Freighter." *Ranch Romances*, February 1, 1953.

Mainline Fiction:

Bower, B. M. (B. M. Sinclair), *Chip, of the Flying U*. New York: G. W. Dillingham Company, 1906. B. M. Bower was a woman, a fact she successfully hid from her readers for a good many years. The heroine, Della Whitcomb, is a doctor rather than a cowgirl but she can ride well and is a hand with a gun (in fact, she kills a coyote her first day at the ranch). She falls in love with the hero, Chip, a quiet, sensitive and artistic cowboy. Although the novel is replete with uncomplimentary "just like a woman" references, Della is portrayed as competent and professional as well as likable, human, and very, very much a woman. At one point of the book, critics acclaim an unsigned painting. Although Chip painted it, rumors abound that it is Della's work. However, the critics doubt this because it is such a "masculine" painting . . . interesting, since Bower was trying to pass her work as that of a man.

Cather, Willa, *My Antonia!* Boston: Houghton Mifflin Co., 1918. *O Pioneers!* Boston: Houghton Mifflin Co., 1913. Although both novels deal with midwestern farm women rather than "cowgirls," they are among the best and most sensitive portraits of women who love the land and understand how to work it. Antonia's father feels closer to her than to his sons because he realizes that she loves the farm more than they do and will carry it on. This she does after her father commits suicide. She has a child out of wedlock and keeps it; eventually marries a farmer and has many more children. In *O Pioneers!*, Alexandra Bergson takes over the family farm after her father's death and becomes the most respected farmer in the area. Through these novels the reader comes to understand why a woman—or anyone—grows to love the land and feel irrevocably tied to it.

Curry, Peggy Simson, *So Far from Spring.* New York: Viking, 1956. This novel of North Park, Colorado, ranch life around the turn of the century was written by a woman who herself grew up on a North Park ranch. Unlike most Westerns, it includes several women characters, drawn in depth with sensitivity. Six women deal with the demands of ranch life in a different—and realistic—way. They include Monte Maguire, a tough and competent woman rancher with a gaming house past; Prim (Mrs. Kelsey) Cameron, the protagonist's Scotch wife who lets the ruggedness and privations of her new life turn her into a shrew; Heather Cameron, Prim and Kelsey's cowgirl daughter who would rather work outside with her father than aid her mother with domestic chores; Amie Plunkett, a happy, easygoing ranch wife who loses herself in books at the expense of personal grooming and good housekeeping; Ellie Lundgren, a ranch wife who goes insane from loneliness and depression; and Dolly Gentry, the local gossip. Unfortunately, the novel is currently out of print.

Grey, Zane, *Riders of the Purple Sage.* New York: Harper & Brothers, 1912. Grey's women characters are usually one-dimensional props used to show off the hero's brave antics. *Riders* has one of his strongest women, Jane Withersteen. Jane inherited a vast cattle ranch in southern Utah from her Mormon father. Mormon Elder Tull wants to marry Jane for her ranch and cheats, lies, and murders in his attempt to force Jane into submission. Lassiter, the good-hearted gunman made vicious by previous Mormon wrongs, saves Jane from this fate worse than death. Jane is constantly referred to as a strong woman, but her strength is passive—as a woman's "should" be. She does not give in to the villain's wishes, but neither is she active in her defense. She hardly ever leaves the safety of her house at the Cottonwoods. She is an excellent horsewoman—as are many Grey women—but that is her only outdoor skill. And when she wants Lassiter to use her favorite Thoroughbred racer, she tells him, "He's too spirited for a woman." That makes Lassiter feel better about the gift.

Hough, Emerson, *North of 36*. New York: Grosset & Dunlap, 1923. Taisie Lockhart's father is killed and the ranch is in economic straits. Since cattle aren't worth anything in Texas, Taisie decides to herd the cattle north. Her men don't want her to go along for the trail is no place for a woman, but she insists. Of course, she takes along Black Milly (her cook), Anita (her Spanish woman), and two easy carts for them to ride in. She exhibits most of her business acumen by sobbing, weeping, or bursting into tears at opportune moments. Of more interest to the crew than the health or safety of the cattle is when and to whom Miss Taisie will get married. She is the Jonah of the journey by merit of her beauty, helplessness, and charm. Once she sells the cattle, she quickly discards the "men's attire" in which she appeared so alluring on the trail. She does have spunk, but it is a curiously masculine view of spunk. She doesn't *do* anything except go along.

L'Amour, Louis, *Ride the Dark Trail*. New York: Bantam Books, 1972. L'Amour often has two or more women in his books. Often one is pretty but "don't mean much," and the other is a daughter of the soil who can ride, rope, shoot, and handle herself in dangerous situations. In this novel, tall, gaunt, sixty-seven-year-old Emily Talon tries to defend her ranch of 100,000 acres of prime cattle land with her Colt Dragoons. She busts the knees of Jake Flanner, the man who killed her husband and is trying to take away her land. Logan Sackett and Em's two long-lost sons come to her aid and rout the ruffians, but Em carries her own weight all the way. A truly gutsy heroine.

Porter, William Sydney (O. Henry), "The Princess and the Puma." *Heart of the West*, Garden City, N.Y.: Doubleday, Doran & Co., Inc., 1904. Whenever O. Henry spins a yarn around a competent western woman, he usually plays her against a tender male ego. Such is the case in this story. Ranch foreman Ripley Givens falls in love with his boss's daughter, Josefa O'Donnell, a beautiful and intrepid crack shot and horsewoman. One day Givens comes upon Josefa at a water hole. He sees a mountain lion about to pounce on the young lady. Since his pistol is out of reach, he yells and runs between the lion and Josefa. The lion attacks him; Josefa shoots the lion and saves his life. Instead of being the savior, Givens is now the saved—a humiliating experience. To turn the situation back to his advantage, he pretends that the mountain lion was a camp pet he was trying to save from Josefa's gun. Her eyes immediately mist over with admiration for this man who would risk his life to save a gentle animal. They ride back to the ranch hand in hand. When Givens moves on to the next camp, Josefa casually tells her father that she shot a lion which, by the notch in its ear, she recognized as the Gotch-Eared Devil who killed a sheepherder and fifty calves. "Bully for you!" says her Pa. See also "Hearts and Crosses" in this same collection.

Robbins, Tom, *Even Cowgirls Get the Blues.* Boston: Houghton Mifflin Co., 1976. Most real cowgirls find this whimsical, mystical, counterculture novel downright offensive. No real cowgirl would let her land go to pot (either literally or figuratively), her goats starve, and her cows get mange. Nor are drugs or gay sex popular topics in the real cowgirl camp. But this is not a novel about real cowgirls. It was not meant to be. And as long as you accept that, it is delightful and thoroughly creative.

Index

Page numbers in italics indicate an illustration of the listed subject

TERESA JORDAN

Teresa Jordan was born and raised on a ranch in southeastern Wyoming and, while growing up, attended a one-room country school. She studied at Northwestern University and Colorado State University and graduated summa cum laude from Yale University, where she specialized in the history of the American West. For this book, Ms. Jordan traveled over 60,000 miles in the course of two years to find and interview over one hundred authentic cowgirls.

Ms. Jordan is a frequent lecturer on the topic of rural women and is also a photographer, whose most recent exhibition was *Photographs of the West*. She currently lives in Portland, Oregon, where she is at work on a novel.

What Readers Are Saying About
Accounting for Non-Accountants

"I have worked in accounting for over twenty-five years, and this is the best book that I have seen to help people with the basics of accounting. I highly recommend this book to anyone who does not have an accounting background. If accounting scares you, then this book will help relieve your anxieties."

—Cheryl K., Henderson, Tennessee

"Dr. Label's explanations are simple and straightforward. The step-by-step examples are easy to digest and make sense as they build on each other."

—J. Rose, Missouri

"Usually 'accounting' is intimidating for ordinary people, but I like this book very much because it explains the concepts in a simple manner. It helps you feel comfortable looking at financial statements and making basic analysis. This will help me a lot as I set up my own business."

—M. Singson, California

"For an engineer trying to do volunteer bookkeeping and accounting, this book is a good overview. It presents bookkeeping and accounting in a step-by-step, understandable manner."

—Ramon E. Hall, Colorado

"It's both an excellent cover-to-cover read as well as a great reference."

—Daniel Balfour, New York

"I bought this book because, as a non-accountant, I wanted to learn about it for work, and I found it very helpful. The author made ideas very easy to understand. I liked the examples and especially liked the glossaries at the end of each chapter."

—Chun J. Shin, Pennsylvania

"This book is an excellent refresher. It has certainly enhanced my accounting knowledge and practice after using it. Thank you Dr. Label very much for your good work!"

—Dorothy Do, California

"Excellent book. It was a real boon in helping me to review accounting practices."

—Wayne A., Stewart, Florida

Accounting *for*
Non-Accountants

Accounting *for* Non-Accountants

The *Fast* and *Easy* Way to Learn the Basics

WAYNE A. LABEL, CPA, MBA, PhD

2ND EDITION

Published by Sourcebooks, Inc.
P.O. Box 4410, Naperville, Illinois 60567-4410
(630) 961-3900
Fax: (630) 961-2168
www.sourcebooks.com

Library of Congress Cataloging-in-Publication Data
Label, Wayne A. (Wayne Allan)
   Accounting for non-accountants : the fast and easy way to learn the basics / Wayne Label.
      p. cm.
   Includes bibliographical references and index.
   1. Accounting. 2. Financial statements. I. Title. II. Title: Accounting for nonaccountants.

HF5636.L33 2006
657—dc22
                              2006012421

Printed and bound in the United States of America.
VP 10 9 8 7 6 5 4 3 2 1

Contents

- Other Types of Audit Reports
- Why Audits Are Useful to You
- Other Services Provided by Auditors

- Fraud Defined
- What Causes Fraud
- How Fraud is Committed
- Ethics

Acknowledgments

I would like to thank Sara Appino at Sourcebooks for her tireless efforts to make this book readable and understandable to the non-accountants of the world.

I would also like to thank Valarie Higgins for her time and effort in reading the manuscript, adding valuable insights, and using her English background to make the book a better read.

Another big thanks to Florencia Cordero for her patience with me as I worked on this second edition. Her support and encouragement made this possible.

Finally, I would like to thank the thousands of students and users of the first edition whose comments and suggestions have helped to improve this book.

Introduction

What is accounting? Who needs it? How does it benefit businesses? This book answers those questions for the non-accountant.

Accounting provides information that helps people in business increase their chances of making decisions that will benefit their companies. Accounting is the language of business, and like other languages, it has its own terms and rules. Understanding this language and learning to interpret it is your first step to becoming successful in your own business and in your personal financial life as well.

In your personal life you can use accounting information to make decisions about investing in the stock market, applying for a loan, and evaluating potential jobs. Banks use accounting information to make decisions about granting loans. Government agencies base their regulations on accounting information. Accounting information can even be useful to non-business entities with an interest in how businesses affect local, national, or foreign communities and community members. Businesses use accounting information for planning and budgeting and for making decisions about borrowing and investing. Overall, accounting aids businesses in the process of making better decisions.

The basics of accounting are the same regardless of the size or type of business. In *Accounting for Non-Accountants*, you will learn the basics of accounting through the examination of an imaginary small business, Solana Beach Bicycle Company. For more complex businesses, the economic transactions become more varied and complex, as does the process of reporting them to various users. The foundation of it all, however, remains the same. This book will give you a solid foundation you will be able to use in any accounting situation you encounter.

Whether you own a business or do not, even if you've never had any experience with accounting and financial statements, this is the book for you.

Several changes have been made to create this second edition. Chapter 2, Generally Accepted Accounting Principles, has been expanded to include a comparison of U.S. Standards to those of the International Accounting Standards Board and a discussion of these differences. In chapter 5, the entire approach to the Statement of

Cash Flows has been changed to make it more understandable to non-accountants. Many changes have been made to chapter 11, Audits and Auditors, to include more information on the Sarbanes-Oxley Act, which puts more responsibility on the management of companies as well as the auditors to better report areas of potential fraud and weaknesses in internal control. A new chapter has been added (chapter 12) to discuss fraud and ethics and how ignoring these issues can be the downfall of a small business. The appendix on websites to help accountants and non-accountants has been expanded, and a new appendix has been added with useful questions and answers for you to use as a reference after reading the book.

One of the biggest and most exciting changes in this second edition is reader access to two new websites that offer a wealth of accounting resources for the non-accountant. Free online tests and practice problems not found in the book are available exclusively to *Accounting for Non-Accountants* readers at www.sourcebooks.com/accountingquizzes. At www.LearnAcctgOnline.com, you can chat about questions you have concerning accounting and small business, and you can participate in a blog on important accounting topics. You will also be able to learn more about the study guide that accompanies this book, which includes practical questions and answers on topics covered throughout the second edition. I hope that you find this book useful in helping you to understand these accounting issues as they apply to your small business and to your personal life. Please feel free to contact me at AskDrL@ LearnAcctgOnline.com with your thoughts on the book, the other materials, or questions about accounting in general.

Chapter

Introducing Accounting and Financial Statements

- ▶ **What Is Accounting?**
- ▶ **Who Uses Accounting Information?**
- ▶ **Financial Statements**
- ▶ **How Different Business Entities Present Accounting Information**

What Is Accounting?

The purpose of accounting is to provide information that will help you make correct financial decisions. The accountant's job is to provide the information needed to run a business as efficiently as possible while maximizing profits and keeping costs low.

QUICK Tip

Finding an Accountant: Hiring a professional and ethical accountant to aid in your business operations can be critical to the success of your company. Meet with a few accountants before making a final choice so that you know your options and can select one whose experience and work style will be best suited to your needs and the needs of your business. Local chapters of your state societies of CPAs offer referral services that can help with this.

Accounting plays a role in businesses of all sizes. Your kids' lemonade stand, a one-person business, and a multinational corporation all use the same basic accounting principles. Accounting is legislated; it affects your taxes; even the president plays a role in how accounting affects you.

Accounting is the language of business. It is the process of recording, classifying, and summarizing economic events through certain documents or financial statements. Like any other language, accounting has its own terms and rules. To understand how to interpret and use the information accounting provides, you must first understand this language. Understanding the basic concepts of accounting is essential to success in business.

Different types of information furnished by accountants are shown in figure 1.1 on the next page.

**Figure 1.1: TYPES OF INFORMATION
PROVIDED BY ACCOUNTANTS**

- Information prepared exclusively by people within a company (managers, employees, or owners) for their own use.

- Financial information required by various government agencies such as the Internal Revenue Service (IRS), Securities and Exchange Commission (SEC), and the Federal Trade Commission (FTC).

- General information about companies provided to people outside the firm such as investors, creditors, and labor unions.

Accounting and Bookkeeping

Bookkeeping procedures and bookkeepers record and keep track of the business transactions that are later used to generate financial statements. Most bookkeeping procedures have been systematized, and, in many cases, can be handled by computer programs. Bookkeeping is a very important part of the accounting process, but it is just the beginning. There is currently no certification required to become a bookkeeper in the United States.

Accounting is the process of preparing and analyzing financial statements based on the transactions recorded through the bookkeeping process. Accountants are usually professionals who have completed at least a bachelor's degree in accounting, and often have passed a professional examination, like the Certified Public Accountant Examination, the Certified Management Accountant Examination, or the Certified Fraud Auditor Examination.

Accounting goes beyond bookkeeping and the recording of economic information to include the summarizing and reporting of this information in a way that is meant to drive decision making within a business.

Who Uses Accounting Information?

In the world of business, accounting plays an important role to aid in making critical decisions. The more complex the decision, the more detailed the information must be. Individuals and companies need different kinds of information to make their business decisions.

Let's start with you as an individual. Why would you be interested in accounting? Accounting knowledge can help you with investing in the stock market, applying for a home loan, evaluating a potential job, balancing a checkbook, and starting a personal savings plan, among other things.

Managers within a business also use accounting information daily to make decisions, although most of these managers are not accountants. Some of the decisions they might make for which they will use accounting information are illustrated in figure 1.2

Figure 1.2: AREAS IN WHICH MANAGERS USE ACCOUNTING INFORMATION

- Marketing (Which line of goods should the company emphasize?)
- Production (Should the company produce its goods in the United States or open a new plant in Mexico?)
- Research and Development (How much money should be set aside for new product development?)
- Sales (Should the company expand the advertising budget and take money away from some other part of the marketing budget?)

Without the proper accounting information these types of decisions would be very difficult, if not impossible, to make.

Bankers continually use accounting information. They are in the business of taking care of your money and making money with your money, so they absolutely must make good decisions. Accounting is fundamental to their decision-making process. Figure 1.3 looks at some of the decisions bankers make using accounting information.

Figure 1.3: AREAS IN WHICH BANKERS USE ACCOUNTING INFORMATION

- Granting loans to individuals and companies
- Investing clients' money
- Setting interest rates
- Meeting federal regulations for protecting your money

Government agencies such as the Internal Revenue Service (IRS), the Securities and Exchange Commission (SEC), the Federal Trade Commission (FTC), and the Bureau of Alcohol, Tobacco, and Firearms (ATF) base their regulation enforcement and compliance on the accounting information they receive.

Accountability in Accounting

A business's financial statements can also be of great interest to other members of the local or national community. Labor groups might be interested in what impact management's financial decisions have on their unions and other employees. Local communities have an interest in how a business's financial decisions (for example, layoffs or plant closings) will impact their citizens.

As the economy becomes more complex, so do the transactions within a business, and the process of reporting them to various users and making them understandable becomes more complex as well. A solid knowledge of accounting is helpful to individuals, managers, and business owners who are making their decisions based on the information accounting documents provide.

Financial Statements

Accountants supply information to people both inside and outside the firm by issuing formal reports that are called financial statements.

The financial statements are usually issued at least once a year. In many cases they are issued quarterly or more often where necessary. A set of rules, called Generally Accepted Accounting Principles (GAAP), govern the preparation of the financial statements. Generally Accepted Accounting Principles has been defined as a set of objectives, conventions, and principles to govern the preparation and presentation of financial statements. These rules can be found in volumes of documents issued by the American Institute of Certified Public Accountants (AICPA), the Financial Accounting Standards Board (FASB), the Internal Revenue Service (IRS), the Securities and Exchange Commission (SEC), and other regulatory bodies. In chapter 2 we look at some of the overriding principles of accounting as they apply to all businesses and individuals.

The Basic Financial Statements

The basic financial statements include the Balance Sheet, the Income Statement, the Statement of Cash Flows, and the Statement of Retained Earnings. We will look at these in depth in the following chapters and see how they all interact with each other. As we discuss these financial statements, you will see they are not as scary as you might think they are. Many of the concepts will already be familiar to you.

In the appendix you can see examples of these financial statements from the Coca-Cola Company.

The Balance Sheet is the statement that presents the Assets of the company (those items owned by the company) and the Liabilities (those items owed to others by the company).

The Income Statement shows all of the Revenues of the company less the Expenses, to arrive at the "bottom line," the Net Income.

The Statement of Cash Flows shows how much cash we started the period with, what additions and subtractions were made during the period, and how much cash we have left over at the end of the period.

The Statement of Retained Earnings shows how the balance in Retained Earnings has changed during the period of time (year, quarter, month) for which the financial statements are being prepared. Normally there are only two types of events that will cause the beginning balance to change: 1) the company makes a profit, which causes an increase in Retained Earnings (or the company suffers a loss, which would cause a decrease) and 2) the owners of the company withdraw money, which causes the beginning balance to decrease (or invest more money, which will cause it to increase).

Seeing the Bigger Picture: None of these financial statements alone can tell the whole story about a company. We need to know how to read, understand, and analyze these statements as a package in order to make any kind of decisions about the company. In addition to the financial statements, you must understand the industry you are operating in and the general economy.

Financial statements vary in form depending upon the type of business in which they are used. In general there are three forms of business operating in the United States: proprietorships, partnerships, and corporations.

How Different Business Entities Present Accounting Information

Proprietorships are businesses with a single owner like you and me. These types of businesses tend to be small retail businesses started by entrepreneurs. The accounting for these proprietorships includes only the records of the business—not the personal financial records of the proprietor of the business.

Alert!

Don't Mix and Match: The financial records of an individual owner of a business should never be combined with those of the business. They are two separate entities and need to be accounted for separately. Taking money from one of these entities (the business) for the other (the owner), must be accounted for by both entities.

Partnerships are very similar to proprietorships, except that instead of one owner, there are two or more owners. In general most of these businesses are small to medium-sized. However, there are some exceptions, such as large national or even international accounting or law firms that may have thousands of partners. As with the proprietorships, accounting treats these organizations' records as separate and distinct from those of the individual partners.

Finally there are corporations. These are businesses that are owned by one or more stockholders. These owners may or may not have a managerial interest in the company. Many of these stockholders are simply private citizens who have money invested in the company by way of stocks that they have purchased.

In a corporation a person becomes an owner by buying shares in the company and thus becomes a stockholder. The stockholders may or may not have a vote in the company's long-term planning, depending on the type of stock they have purchased. However, simply by being stockholders (owners), they do not have decision-making authority in the day-to-day operations. These investors (or stockholders) are not much different than the bankers that loan money to a proprietorship or a partnership. These bankers have a financial interest in the business, but no daily managerial decision-making power. As is the case with the stockholders who have invested money into the corporation, in general they have a nonmanagerial interest in the business. As with the other two types of business organizations discussed here, the accounting records of the corporation are maintained separately from those of the individual stockholders or owners.

The accounting records of a proprietorship are less complex than those of a corporation in that there is a simple capital structure and only one owner. In the case of a corporation, there are stockholders who buy a piece of the ownership of a company by buying stock. As we will discuss later, because of this stock ownership, the financial statements become more complex. Some of the basic differences between these three types of businesses are shown in figure 1.4.

Figure 1.4: DIFFERENCES IN THE THREE TYPES OF BUSINESSES

Business Type	Proprietorship	Partnership	Corporation
Number of Owners	One	Two or more	One or more
Accounting Records	Maintained separately from owner's records	Maintained separately from owner's records	Maintained separately from owner's records
Owner Has Managerial Responsibilities	Yes	Usually not	Usually not

In this chapter you have learned what accounting is, why you and other people in business need to understand accounting, what businesses use accounting for, and what the basic financial statements used in these businesses are. In chapter 2 you will learn about principles accountants use in the United States and worldwide on a regular basis.

GLOSSARY

Accounting: The process of recording, classifying, and summarizing economic events through the preparation of financial statements such as the Balance Sheet, the Income Statement, and the Statement of Cash Flows.

American Institute of Certified Public Accountants (AICPA): The professional organization of CPAs in the United States. The AICPA is charged with preparation of the CPA Examination, the establishment and enforcement of the code of professional ethics, and working with the Financial Accounting Standards Board in the proclamation of accounting standards.

Corporations: Businesses that are given the right to exist by an individual state in the United States. With this right to exist, the corporation is then allowed to sell stock. Those buying this stock become owners of the corporation. Corporations can be set up as for profit or not for profit, and make that decision when applying for their charter with the state.

Financial Accounting Standards Board (FASB): Sets the accounting standards to be followed for the preparation of financial statements. All rulings from the FASB are considered to be GAAP.

Financial Statements: Reports prepared by companies on the financial status of their business; examples are Balance Sheets, Income Statements, Statement of Cash Flow, and Statement of Retained Earnings.

Generally Accepted Accounting Principles (GAAP): The rules that govern the preparation of financial statements. These rules are developed by the American Institute of Certified Public Accountants, the Financial Accounting Standards Board, the Security and Exchange Commission, and other government agencies.

Internal Revenue Service (IRS): The government agency charged with the collection of federal taxes in the United States. There are different accounting rules for the preparation of taxes in the United States than for the presentation of financial statements.

Partnerships: A business entity with two or more owners. The accounting for partnerships is similar to that of proprietorships.

Proprietorships, Sole Proprietorships: Businesses with one single owner. Even though there is only one owner, the records of the owner's personal financial affairs are kept separate from those of the accounting records of the business. Separate tax returns are prepared for the business and for the individual.

Chapter 2

Generally Accepted Accounting Principles

- ▶ Who Are the SEC, AICPA, FASB, and IASB?
- ▶ Generally Accepted Accounting Principles (GAAP)

It is important that you understand the concepts of Generally Accepted Accounting Principles (GAAP), which form the basis of accounting and are part of the language of accounting and business. Third parties who invest in or provide loans to any company must know that they can rely on the financial information provided.

This chapter will introduce the agencies responsible for standardizing the accounting principles that are used in the United States and it will describe those principles in full detail. Once you understand these guiding principles, you will have a solid foundation on which to build a complete set of accounting skills. It is useful and necessary that whether an international company is reporting to its stockholders or a proprietor is presenting information to a bank for a loan, these reports follow a consistent set of rules that everyone understands and agrees to.

Who Are the SEC, AICPA, FASB, and IASB? (or What Is This, Alphabet Soup?)

Congress created the Securities and Exchange Commission (SEC) in 1934. At that time, the Commission was given the legal power to prescribe the accounting principles and practices that must be followed by the companies that come within its jurisdiction. Generally speaking, companies come under SEC regulations when they sell securities to the public, list their securities on any one of the securities exchanges (New York Stock Exchange or American Exchange, for example), or when they become greater than a specified size as measured by the firm's Assets and number of shareholders. Thus, since 1934, the SEC has had the power to determine the official rules of accounting practice that must be followed by almost all companies of any significant size.

Instead, for the most part, the SEC assigned the responsibility of identifying or specifying GAAP to the American Institute of Certified Public Accountants (AICPA). That role has now been transferred to the Financial Accounting Standards Board (FASB). All rulings from the FASB are considered to be GAAP.

A firm must adopt the accounting practices recommended by the FASB or the SEC unless they can identify an alternative practice that has "substantial authoritative support." Even when a company can find "substantial authoritative support" for a practice it uses that differs from the one recommended, the company must include in the financial statement footnotes (or in the auditor's report) a statement indicating that the practices used are not the ones recommended by GAAP. Where practicable, the company must explain how its financial statements would have been different if the company had used Generally Accepted Accounting Principles.

Generally Accepted Accounting Principles (GAAP)

Generally Accepted Accounting Principles begin with the three basic assumptions made about each business. First, it is assumed that the business is separate from its owners or other businesses. Revenue and expenses should be kept separate from personal expenses. Second, it is assumed that the business will be in operation indefinitely. This validates the methods of putting Assets on the Balance Sheet, depreciation and amortization. Only when liquidation of a business is certain does this assumption no longer apply. Third, it is assumed a business's accounting records include only quantifiable transactions. Certain economic events that affect a company, such as hiring a new employee or introducing a new product, cannot be quantified in monetary units and, therefore, do not appear in a company's accounting records.

Alert!

Accounting records must always be recorded using a stable currency. In the United States this is the dollar, in Europe it is the Euro, etc.

Financial statements must present relevant, reliable, understandable, sufficient, and practicably obtainable information in order to be useful.

Relevant Information

Relevant information is that information which helps financial statement users estimate the value of a firm and/or evaluate how well the firm is being managed. The financial statements must be stated in terms of a monetary unit, since money is our standard means of determining the value of a company.

In the United States, accountants use the stable monetary unit concept, which means that even though the value of the dollar changes over time (due to inflation), the values that appear on the financial statements normally are presented at historical cost. Historical cost presents the information on the financial statements at amounts the individual or company paid for them or agreed to pay back for them at the time of purchase. This method of accounting ignores the effect of inflation. In many other countries throughout the world, the accounting profession does account for inflation.

Alert!

Changes in the Works: In August 2008 the Security and Exchange Commission announced that within the next decade the United States will abandon GAAP, used by accountants for almost 75 years, and join the more than 100 countries worldwide in using IFRS (discussed in detail on page 20). A timetable was set for all United States companies to drop GAAP by 2016, with some larger companies in the United States possibly switching in 2009. Yet things can still change, and many questions are still unanswered.

Not all information about a firm is relevant for estimating its value or evaluating its management. For example, you don't need the information of how many individuals over forty years of age work for the company, or what color the machinery is painted in order to make financial decisions about a company. Even some financial information is not relevant, like how much money the owner of a corporation has in the bank, because as we reviewed in chapter 1, the business's accounting records are kept separate from its owner's, and the owner's financial information is irrelevant to the business.

Reliable Information

Reliable information is key in accounting. Sufficient and objective evidence should be available to indicate that the information presented is valid. In addition, the information must not be biased in favor of one statement user or one group of users to the detriment of other statement users. The need for reliable information has caused the federal government to pass laws requiring public companies to have their records and financial statements examined (audited) by independent auditors who will make sure that what companies report is accurate. This will be the topic of chapter 11.

Verifiable Information

The need for verifiable information does not preclude the use of estimates and approximation. If you were to eliminate all estimates from accounting, the resulting statements would not be useful primarily because the statements would not provide sufficient information. The approximations that are used, however, cannot be "wild guesses." They must be based on sufficient evidence to make the resulting statements a reliable basis for evaluating the firm and its management.

One example of a place in the financial statements where we estimate the value is with depreciation. Once we purchase a Long-Term Asset (anything that the company owns that will last longer than one year; for example, a building), we then need to spread the cost of this building over the life of the Asset. This is called depreciation. In order to do this we must estimate the life of that particular Asset. We can't know exactly how long that will be, but since we do have experience with these types of Assets, we can estimate the Asset's life. We assume that the building will be useable for, say, twenty years and depreciate (or spread) the cost of the building (the Asset) over twenty years (the estimated life).

For example, if we buy this building for $100,000 and assume that it is going to last twenty years, the annual depreciation would be $5,000 per year ($100,000/20). This $5,000 becomes one of the Expenses for the company and is shown on the Income Statement along with the other Expenses. We will look at this topic in depth in chapter 4.

Understandable Information

To be understandable the financial information must be comparable. Any item on the Balance Sheet that an accountant labels as an Asset or Liability, users of the financial statements should also call Assets and Liabilities. Statement users must compare financial statements of various firms with one another, and they must compare statements of an individual firm with prior years' statements of that same firm in order to make valid decisions. Thus the accounting practices that a firm uses for a particular transaction should be the same as other firms use for the identical transaction. This practice should also be the same practice the firm used in previous periods. This concept is called Consistency. Information that is both comparable and consistent becomes understandable to the users of the financial information.

Quantifiable Information

Information is easier to understand and use if it is quantified. Most information that accountants and users of financial information use is represented by numbers. The information that is presented in the financial statements is presented in a numerical form; however, where that is impossible, the information (if it is relevant, reliable, understandable, and practicably obtainable) will be presented in narrative form, usually in a footnote to the statements. Accountants include narrative information along with quantifiable information because of the need for adequate or full disclosure; statement users must have sufficient information about a firm.

An example of non-quantifiable information that might be included in the footnotes to the financial statements would be details of an outstanding patent infringement lawsuit against the company, which would be considered a contingent Liability.

Obtainable Information

Furthermore, to be useful, information must be reasonably easy to obtain. This fits into the concept of cost vs. benefit. The information must be worth more than what it will cost to obtain it and must be secured on a timely basis. Financial statements must be prepared at least once a year (in many cases, quarterly or monthly) and attempting to incorporate unobtainable information could seriously delay these schedules.

An example of obtainable information is the number of shares sold by the corporation during the year. Another example would be the amount of sales by the business during the year. An example of information that might not be considered obtainable would be the nitty-gritty details of the pension plan systems used in each of the subsidiaries of a multinational corporation. A more reasonable and easily obtainable piece of data might be the total amount of money that is being spent on the company's pensions around the world.

The Entity Concept

Financial statements must also present information representing each separate entity. This idea is called the Entity Concept. In other words, the transactions of each business or person are kept separate from those of other organizations or individuals. Therefore, the transactions of the subsidiaries of a multinational corporation must all be kept separate from each other. Even though at the end of the year the records of all of the subsidiaries might be consolidated into one set of financial statements, the records and transactions of each subsidiary are kept separate during the year.

The Going Concern

It is normally assumed that a company will continue in business into the future. This concept is called the Going Concern Principle. We make several estimates in order to complete the financial statement presentations (for example, depreciation of an Asset over its life), and if we did not assume that the company was going to remain in business in the indefinite future, we could not use this sort of information.

The alternative to the Going Concern Principle is to assume that management plans to liquidate the business. When this is known for sure about a business, a different set of accounting principles and rules are used. In general, when a company liquidates, the Assets of the company will be listed at the price at which they can be sold rapidly. This amount will usually be below the values stated on the Balance Sheet, since they will be sold at "fire sale" prices.

Realizable Value

Assets normally are not shown on the Balance Sheet at more than either their historical cost or an amount for which they can be sold below historical cost. For example, if a company has Inventory that is listed at a historical cost of $100,000, but due to the economy, the competition, or new technology, is today only worth $8,000, this Asset should be written down and shown on the Balance Sheet at $8,000. The section on conservatism (page 19) sheds more light on this topic. An example of an exception to this rule is with marketable securities (stocks). These Assets are shown on the Balance Sheet at their current market price.

Accounting Outside the United States: In the United States, for the purpose of preparing financial statements, accountants are not allowed to write up Assets to value higher than the historical cost (defined on page 29). This is not true in all countries of the world, where accountants may argue that if you can write down an Asset to reflect "reality," why not do the same when an Asset increases in value? Thus in many countries outside of the United States, the accountants are allowed to write up Assets when they increase in value to reflect "market value," as well as write them down when the market value is lower than historical cost. This is an important point to keep in mind when reviewing financial statements prepared in companies domiciled outside of the United States.

Materiality

Financial statements' data must be as simple and concise as possible. An item is considered material when its inclusion or exclusion in the financial statements would change the decision of a statement user. A rule of thumb in accounting might be that any item worth 10 percent of the business's Net Income is considered material and should be reported in financial statements; there is no firm dollar amount to be followed here. The important factor to remember is whether the amount in question will change the user's decision. This concept is called the Materiality Principle.

Items that are not material should not be included on the statements separately. If these items were included in the financial statements, they would obscure the important items of interest to the reader. Thus, in some cases, many immaterial items should be grouped together and called "miscellaneous" or the items could be added to other items, so that the total becomes material. That is, the items can be lumped in together with other items that are material and the entire bundle can be considered material.

QUIZ

The owners of a business decide to write up the value of their land, which ten years ago cost $10,000 to purchase and today sits in a prime location of the city and has been appraised at $40,000. Should they value their land on the Balance Sheet at $10,000 or $40,000?

See page 21 for the answer.

Conservatism

Another traditional practice that accountants use to guide them in preparing financial statements is called Conservatism. Whenever two or more accounting practices appear to be equally suitable to record the transaction under consideration, the accountant should choose the one that results in the lower or lowest Asset figure on the Balance Sheet and the higher or highest Expense on the Income Statement, so as not to be overly optimistic about financial events. This principle of accounting is highly controversial since while we are conservative, we may be violating other generally accepted accounting principles like consistency. In addition it is often asked, "Why is the lower value better, if the higher value better represents the true value of the Asset?"

An example of the Conservatism Principle in action might be in the presentation of Inventory on the Balance Sheet. There are several different generally accepted accounting methods that are allowed to assign a value to Inventory. The accountant should choose the one that presents Inventory at the lowest value so as not to overstate this particular Asset.

The conservatism idea is misused, however, when the accountant chooses a practice that is not as suitable to the situation as an alternative practice merely to report lower Assets and higher Expenses.

GAAP and Small Business

Small business owners have been asking for alternatives to GAAP for a long time. The feeling is that the GAAP used for public companies are irrelevant to small businesses and are very difficult and expensive to implement. To some people the solution is a separate set of standards for private companies—one that takes their needs specifically into account.

The FASB listened and appointed a committee in September 2006 to investigate the differences in reporting and accounting between private and public companies. It was determined that the final goal was to give small businesses a greater voice in standard setting and not to establish two sets of standards.

The Committee decided that it was not in the best interest of the public to have two classes of GAAP. They determined that two sets of standards would not only be confusing to the public, but also create the possibility of one set being considered more authoritative than the other.

International Financial Reporting Standards (IFRS)

International Financial Reporting Standards are issued by the International Accounting Standards Board (IASB), a committee of fourteen members from different countries headquartered in London. The Board has the goal of creating global accounting standards that are transparent, enforceable, understandable and of high quality. More than 100 countries currently use or coordinate with IFRS.

This Board and the standards that they issue are very important for the future of accounting. As globalization continues to connect businesses across the world, it is increasingly important for investors to be able to compare companies under similar standards. It is also much more cost efficient for a company doing business in several different countries to issue one set of financial statements that is understood in all of those countries, rather than having to use the accounting standards of each country.

IFRS puts all companies in all countries on a level playing field since they all have to present their financial information in a consistent, reliable manner. This certainly makes their financial results more comparable.

Differences between U.S. GAAP and IFRS

The biggest difference between U.S. GAAP and the International Accounting Standards is that the U.S. standards are based on rules and the International Standards are based upon principles. So what does this mean? It means that the U.S. standards have created a complex system of rules attempting to cover every situation that does or might occur, often masking economic reality. The U.S. rules fill a nine-inch, three-volume set of guidelines, while the International Standards are inside a single 2-inch book.

The principles-based system of accounting encourages company boards and accountants to do the right thing in allowing them to report what is correct for the user, rather than reporting based upon a set of rules. U.S. GAAP rules allowed trillions of dollars in securitized financial assets and liabilities to stay off the books of U.S. financial firms, while the international standards, more focused on the true underlying economics, kept these items on the books of firms based outside the United States.

The upcoming change to IFRS is going to be enormous for U.S. companies in dollars and methodology. While there will be some ambiguity in the reporting, the accountant will need to explain why certain reporting standards have been used for more accuracy.

In this chapter you have learned about Generally Accepted Accounting Principles in the United States as well as some of the differences between these and international reporting standards. In chapter 3 you will learn about the balance sheet and how it is used.

ANSWER

In the United States a company cannot write the value of their Assets above the historical cost of that Asset. The argument is that if they do write the value, it leaves too much room for manipulating the financial statements, which could mislead the users of the financial statements.

The practice of writing up Assets, though accepted in other foreign countries, would violate such generally accepted accounting principles as: 1) conservatism, 2) reliability, and 3) verifiability.

GLOSSARY

American Institute of Certified Public Accountants (AICPA): The professional organization of the Accounting profession. This group has the responsibility to set the ethics regulations for the profession as well as writing and grading the Certification Public Accountants' Examination (CPA Examination).

Conservatism Principle: Whenever two or more accounting practices appear to be equally suitable to the transaction under consideration, the accountant should always choose the one that results in the lower or lowest Asset figure on the Balance Sheet and the higher or highest Expense on the Income Statement.

Consistency: Practices and methods used for presentation on the financial statements should be the same year to year and process to process. If for any reason the company and their accountants decide to change the method of presentation for any item on the financial statements, they must present a footnote to the financial statements explaining why the methods were changed.

Entity Concept: The principle that requires separation of the transactions of each business or person from those of other organizations or individuals. For example, when a company is owned by one person, the personal finances of the individual who owns the company are not included on the company's financial statements. The opposite is also true: the financial information of the company is not included in the financial statements of the individual owner.

Financial Accounting Standards Board (FASB): The board that sets the accounting standards to be followed for the preparation of financial statements. All rulings from the FASB are considered to be GAAP.

Generally Accepted Accounting Principles (GAAP): A standardized set of accounting rules used in the United States and prescribed by various organizations, like the FASB and the SEC. These rules guide the uniform preparation of financial statements.

Going Concern Principle: This principle assumes that a company will continue in business into the future. Without this assumption most of the accounting information could not be presented in the financial statements since we are always making assumptions (e.g., what the life of a Long-Term Asset is). The only way to make this assumption is to further assume that the business will be in existence in the indefinite future.

Historical Cost Principle: According to this rule, most Assets and Liabilities should be represented on the Balance Sheet at the amount that was paid to acquire the Asset, or for the Liabilities, at the amount that was contracted to be paid in the future. No account is taken for either inflation or changing value of Assets over time.

International Accounting Standards Board (IASB): The board responsible for setting the International Accounting Standards used by more than 100 countries throughout the world. It is made up of 14 international members and is based in London.

International Financial Reporting Standards (IFRS): The standards issued by IASB, meant to level the playing field for better comparisons of financial data as companies become more global in their scope.

Materiality Principle: This principle states that an item should only be included on the Balance Sheet if it would change any decisions of a statement user. If, for example, a multimillion-dollar corporation were to donate $100 to a charity, this information would not change any decision that management or an owner would make. However, since corporate money was spent, this distribution of the $100 must be combined with other small expenditures and reported as a "miscellaneous Expense."

Monetary Unit: U.S. Dollars, Euros, Yen, etc. Since a business's accounting records can only include quantifiable transactions, these transactions need to be reported in one of these stable currencies.

Obtainable Information: Information reported in financial statements must be accessible in a timely manner without an unreasonable expenditure of resources—for example, time, effort, and money—to be included in the financial statements.

Quantifiable Information: Information is easier to understand and use if it is quantified. However, when the information cannot be quantified but is still relevant to the users of the financial statements, it must be shown in the financial statements in narrative form in the footnotes.

Realizable Value Principle: This indicates that Assets should normally not be shown on the Balance Sheet at a value greater than they can bring to the company if sold. If the original historical cost for example is $5,000, and the maximum that the company can sell that Asset for today is $4,000, this Asset should be shown on the Balance Sheet at the lower amount because of this principle.

Recognition Principle: This is the process of recording Revenue into the financial statements. Revenue is recorded at the point of the transfer of the merchandise or service, and not at the point of receiving the cash. That means, for example, that once a service is provided for which a charge has been incurred, that service should be shown on the financial statements regardless of whether money has actually changed hands. Similarly Expenses are recognized when incurred, not when the money is exchanged for that particular Expense.

Relevant Information: Information reported on financial statements must be relevant in that it helps statement users to estimate the value of a firm and/or evaluate the firm's management. Not all information about a company is relevant to this decision-making process. For example, the number of women versus men currently employed at the company would not be considered relevant, even though it might be important data in other contexts. Thus, this type of information is not included in the financial statements.

Reliable Information: There should be sufficient and objective evidence available to indicate that the information presented is valid.

Securities and Exchange Commission (SEC): The body created by Congress in 1934. One of its duties is to prescribe the accounting principles and practices that must be followed by the companies that come within its jurisdiction.

Separate Entities: See Entity Concept

Stable-Monetary-Unit Concept: Even though the value of the dollar changes over time (due to inflation), the values that appear on the financial statements in the United States are normally presented at historical cost and do not take inflation into account.

Understandable Information: Financial information must be comparable and consistent. If one accountant calls a particular item an Asset, the accountant must follow the set of rules known as generally accepted accounting principles to arrive at the definition of that Asset. Thus, when any user of the financial statements reads these statements, he understands the meaning and classification of the Asset.

Verifiable Information: Information on the financial statements must be based on sufficient evidence that can be substantiated and provides a reliable basis for evaluating the firm and its management.

Chapter 3

The Balance Sheet and Its Components

▶ **Understanding the Balance Sheet**

▶ **The Accounting Equation**

▶ **The Components of the Balance Sheet**

▶ **The Transactions Behind the Balance Sheet**

Understanding the Balance Sheet

Imagine that you make a list of everything that is important to you. Along with this list you attach values to all of these items. Then you make a list of everything that you owe to others, and again you attach values to these items. Then you subtract the total value of the second list from the total value of the first. Voilà! You have just created the basic components of a Balance Sheet.

In a business the first list of items is called Assets. Assets are valuable resources owned by the business and can be either short- or long-term in nature.

Your second list of items is called Liabilities. Liabilities are what you owe to others for resources that were furnished to the business. The parties to whom the company owes money are normally called creditors. The creditors are said to "have a claim against the Assets." Figure 3.1 illustrates the origin of some Liabilities a company or individual might incur.

Figure 3.1: WHERE DO LIABILITIES COME FROM?

What They Are Called	Where They Originate
Accounts payable	Purchase of items
Wages payable	Services from employees, not yet paid
Utilities payable	Utilities used, not yet paid for
Notes payable	IOUs
Rent payable	Unpaid rent

Your third list can be labeled Owner's Equity. Owner's Equity reflects the amount the owner has invested in the firm. There are two sources of Owner's Equity:

- The amount of money provided directly by the owner or other investors, called Owner's Investment; and,
- The amount retained from profits, called Retained Earnings.

QUICK Tip

Profit takes many forms: Profits are not always cash; profit can be made up of promises to pay money as well. For example, when there is a sale for a receivable, there will be Revenue, but no cash coming into the company. The money will come in during a later time period but can be considered profit for the company.

Let's look at an example. The Solana Beach Bicycle Company is a small business that makes, repairs, and sells bicycles. The company was started by Samantha Fernandez in January 2010. Sam (as all of her friends call her) has been an avid bike rider for many years and always felt she could build a "better mouse trap" or bicycle, that is. Sam invested some money she had saved and some that she had inherited into her business.

Take a look at the bicycle company's Balance Sheet in figure 3.2. This is a proprietorship, because Samantha is the sole owner of the company. The Balance Sheet would look a little different for a corporation. These differences are discussed in chapter 6. (See Appendix B for a real-life example of a Balance Sheet from Station Casinos, Inc.)

Figure 3.2: **SOLANA BEACH BICYCLE COMPANY**
Balance Sheet
December 31, 2010

Assets

Note: Parentheses indicate decreases in cash

Cash.	$17,385
Accounts Receivable.	9,175
Allowance for Bad Debts	(175)
Inventory.	23,000
Prepaid Insurance	1,000
Truck	8,000
Building	25,000

Land. 10,000
Total Assets $93,385

Liabilities And Owner's Equity

Liabilities:

Accounts Payable. $3,000
Mortgage Payable 20,000
Total Liabilities $23,000

Owner's Equity:

Owner's Investment $60,000
Retained Earnings 10,385
Total Owner's Equity $70,385
Total Liabilities & Owner's Equity. $93,385

By looking at the bicycle company's Balance Sheet, you can see that there are several Assets belonging to the company that together are valued at $93,385. You can also see that the company has several Liabilities, valued at $23,000. Finally, when you subtract the Liabilities from the Assets, you can see that the company has equity (also referred to as net worth) of $70,385. This represents a combination of the amount of money that the owner has invested into her business ($60,000), and the profit that was earned and retained in the business since its inception ($10,385). Since this is the first year of business, all of the profit must have been earned this year.

What Does the Date on the Balance Sheet Mean?

There is a great deal of disagreement as to how accountants arrive at the values that are shown on the Balance Sheet. Of most concern are the values attached to the Assets, and consequently to the Owner's Equity or net worth of the business. The Balance Sheet represents a "snapshot" of the financial position of the business on that specific date. In the case of Solana Beach Bicycle Company, this point in time is December 31, 2010.

The Balance Sheet Is a Snapshot: The numbers that are represented in a Balance Sheet *only* represent the financial position of the business at the exact point in time for which the Balance Sheet was prepared and no other. In figure 3.2, this means December 31, 2010, only, not December 30 or January 1. On any other date there might be more or less Assets and Liabilities, and thus the Balance Sheet would look different.

What Is Historical Cost?

As you saw, all of the items on the Balance Sheet have values attached to them, but where did these numbers come from? In the United States, accountants and other users of financial statements have agreed that financial statements (including Balance Sheets) must be based on historical cost.

This means that the values on the Balance Sheet for Solana Beach Bicycle Company do not represent what the Assets or the Liabilities would be worth today if they were to be sold. Instead, the values represent what was paid for the Assets and what the business agreed to pay to the creditors on the date of the obligation.

Does this confuse the reader of the financial statements? No. Because everyone has agreed to follow this convention, everyone preparing and using these financial statements understands the language that is being spoken.

The Accounting Equation

Often the relationships between Assets (A), Liabilities (L), and Owner's Equity (OE) are shown in terms of a formula.

QUICK Tip

A = L + OE
Assets = Liabilities + Owner's Equity

The total Assets of the company equal the sum of the Liabilities and the Owner's Equity.

The formula depicts the relationships of the various elements of the Balance Sheet. Balance Sheets are often set up with the Assets on one side (the left side) and the Liabilities and equity on the other (the right side).

The same formula can be stated this way:

QUICK Tip

A – L = OE
Assets – Liabilities = Owner's Equity

If you subtract the Liabilities from the Assets, you are left with the Owner's Equity of the business.

The Components of the Balance Sheet

Assets

As was previously discussed, Assets are items that are of value and are owned by the entity for which you are accounting. Let's make this idea more specific. For an Asset to be listed on a Balance Sheet of a company, the item must pass three tests.

**Figure 3.3: HOW DO WE KNOW WHEN
AN ASSET GOES ON THE BALANCE SHEET?**

The following items give us some hints.

• The company must control the item. (This usually means ownership.)

• The item must have some value to the company.

• The item must have value that can be measured.

Let's look at some examples. Because of the first test, a traditional Balance Sheet does not list the employees of a company, even though we may refer to them as "Assets" in a non-accounting sense, because the company does control, to a certain extent, but does not own these individuals. But what about basketball players or other professional athletes? Doesn't the team own them? The answer is no. What the team owns is not the players themselves, but the player's contracts. Therefore, in this situation, the basketball team ownership would list the contracts of the players as an Asset.

With the second test almost anything that is used in the business to earn income and to generate cash does have some value. Certain items that do meet the first requirement might be eliminated from being listed as Assets by this test. Examples might include an old truck that does not work or Inventory that cannot be sold any longer because it is now outdated; for example, old versions of computer software.

An example of the third test would be when the company purchases a used machine. The company purchased it for a fixed amount of money and has a record of this transaction that clearly indicates the value of the machine. (Note: Neither the company nor the Balance Sheet deals with an over- or under-paid amount for the machine. The Balance Sheet reflects only historical cost, which is what is recorded as the amount paid for the machine, whether the company paid too much or got a bargain!)

Let's assume that a company has built up a thriving business, and some of the reasons for this growth are the reputation of the owner and the location of the company. Neither the reputation of the owner nor the location of the company has been paid for. We also do not have any way of measuring a value to put onto these items. Therefore, they fail the third test, and cannot be listed as Assets of the business.

Another example of an Asset that would fail the test is any Asset that was given to the company. In this situation, there is no historical cost to the company and thus the Asset would not be reflected on the Balance Sheet, since it does not meet this third test. Now, you might say that we can determine a monetary value for this Asset. And you are right! In many countries, this Asset would then be reflected on the Balance Sheet at that value. However under generally accepted accounting principles in the United States, since there was no historical cost to this Asset, it would not be listed as one of the company's Assets.

QUIZ

The following is a list of items that might be considered Assets by a company. Indicate whether they should be listed on the Balance Sheet as an Asset and why or why not.

1. A bicycle that belongs to the owner of the company

2. A building used to build and sell the bicycles of the company

3. A broken tool that is not used in the business any longer

4. Employees

5. Money owed to the company from sales of bicycles

6. Money owed by the company to the gas company

7. The land that the company's building is on

8. A truck used to deliver the bicycles to customers

9. Money in the personal bank account of the owner

10. Money paid in advance for a three-year insurance policy on the business

See page 41 for answers.

Short-Term Assets

Assets are normally subdivided on the Balance Sheet into two categories. The first is called Short-Term Assets (or Current Assets). These items will be used or converted into cash within a period of one year or less.

Long-Term Assets

Long-Term Assets (also called Non-Current Assets) are not expected to be converted to cash or totally "used up" in a year or less. Rather, they are expected to be of value to the company for more than a year. Long-Term Assets would include equipment, land, and buildings.

Intangible Assets

Intangible Assets are Assets that cannot be physically touched. They must still meet the three tests mentioned earlier in order to be listed on the Balance Sheet as an Asset; however, they do not have any tangible characteristics. Some examples of intangible Assets include trademarks, copyrights, and patents, as long as they have been purchased from the prior owner of the business. You might be inclined to call goodwill an intangible Asset; goodwill is based on location of the business, reputation of the owners, and name recognition by the public, and is of great value to a business. Keep in mind, though, that because of the Generally Accepted Accounting Principles discussed in chapter 2, this and any valuable item which was not paid for and thus does not have a historical cost, cannot be listed on the Balance Sheet as an Asset.

Liabilities

Refer to the Balance Sheet of Solana Beach Bicycle Company (figure 3.2). The Total Liabilities of the business are equal to $23,000. As with the Assets, the Liabilities list represents both short-term and long-term items. Again, similar to the list of Assets, the Short-Term Liabilities will be paid off in a period not to exceed one year. The Long-Term Liabilities will remain as debt to the company for longer than one year.

With this or any long-term debt, a portion of it becomes due and payable each year. Thus, most companies' Balance Sheets show the current portion of all long-term debt separately in the Short-Term Liabilities section.

Owner's Equity

As we have previously discussed, the equity of Solana Beach Bicycle Company comes from two sources. The Owner's Investment of $60,000 represents the amount invested in the business by the owner through the purchase of various Assets or as money in the bank that is meant for the business. The Retained Earnings of $10,385 represent the amount of profit earned by the business since its inception minus any money that the owner may have taken out for his or her personal use.

Understanding Cash and Retained Earnings: Let's take a moment to clarify a very important point about Retained Earnings that often causes confusion among owners of small and large businesses alike. The Retained Earnings in a business are not equal to cash, that is, "money in the bank." Just because a company has kept profits in the business over the years does not mean that all of these profits have been retained in the form of cash. For example, after the company earns a profit, it may take that cash and purchase Assets or pay off some of its Liabilities. Business owners often assume that they are doing well because they are making profits without taking into account the amount of cash they have at their disposal. If they do not have sufficient cash, however, they will find themselves in dire straits since they may not be able to make the payroll, pay their taxes, or pay for other Liabilities. It is absolutely essential that businesses have a good cash management plan.

A revised Balance Sheet for Solana Beach Bicycle Company using the most common subheadings would look like the one shown in figure 3.4.

Figure 3.4: **THE EXPANDED BALANCE SHEET**
SOLANA BEACH BICYCLE COMPANY
Balance Sheet
December 31, 2010

Assets

Note: Parentheses indicate decreases in cash

Short-Term Assets:

Cash.	$17,385
Accounts Receivable.	9,175
Allowance for Doubtful Accounts	(175)
Inventory	23,000
Prepaid Insurance	1,000
Total Short-Term Assets	$50,385

Long-Term Assets:

Truck $8,000

Building 25,000

Land 10,000

Total Long-Term Assets $43,000

Total Assets $93,385

Liabilities and Owner's Equity

Short-Term Liabilities:

Accounts Payable $3,000

Current Portion of Mortgage Payable 1,000

Total Short-Term Liabilities $4,000

Long-Term Liabilities:

Mortgage Payable $19,000

Total Liabilities $23,000

Owner's Equity:

Owner's Investment $60,000

Retained Earnings 10,385

Total Owner's Equity $70,385

Total Liabilities & Owner's Equity $93,385

See Appendix C for an example of the Balance Sheet from a major corporation.

The Transactions Behind the Balance Sheet

Referring to the Balance Sheet in figure 3.4, let's examine the transactions that created it.

Sam Invests Money in the Company (Owner's Investment)

First, let's assume that on January 1, 2010, Sam invests $60,000 in her bicycle company. In other words, she takes $60,000 out of her personal bank account and sets up a new account with the bank for the new business. After this transaction, the company's Balance Sheet looks like the one presented in figure 3.5:

Figure 3.5: **SOLANA BEACH BICYCLE COMPANY**
Balance Sheet
January 1, 2010

Assets	Liabilities & Owner's Equity
Short-Term Assets:	**Liabilities:** $0
Cash. $60,000	**Owner's Equity:**
	Owner's Investment...$60,000
Total Assets $60,000	Total Liabilities and Owner's Equity. . . $60,000

On the Balance Sheet the cash and Owner's Investment are increased by $60,000. Note that the Balance Sheet continues to balance, i.e., Assets = Liabilities + Owner's Equity.

Sam Purchases Land, a Building, and a Truck (Long-Term Assets)

Next, on January 1, the bicycle company buys a piece of land with a building and a truck in order to operate her business. The land has a value of $10,000, the building's value is $25,000, and the truck that will be used for pick-ups and deliveries is $8,000. All of these values are the actual amounts that the company pays. Because the company does not have sufficient cash to pay for all of these Assets at the current time, it decides to borrow some money. It pays $23,000 in cash and takes out a mortgage on the land and building for $20,000 to purchase these Assets. This is a twenty-year loan. One thousand dollars of this loan is due and payable within one year. After these transactions, the company's Balance Sheet looks like the one presented in figure 3.6:

Figure 3.6: **SOLANA BEACH BICYCLE COMPANY**
Balance Sheet
January 1, 2010

Assets	Liabilities & Owner's Equity
Short-Term Assets:	**Liabilities:**
Cash. $37,000	Current Portion of Mortgage Payable. . $1,000
	Long-Term: Mortgage Payable. . . 19,000
Total Short-Term Assets $37,000	Total Liabilities . . . $20,000
Long-Term Assets:	**Owner's Equity:**
Truck $8,000	Owner's Investment . $60,000
Building 25,000	
Land 10,000	
Total Long-Term Assets $43,000	
Total Assets $80,000	Total Liabilities and Owner's Equity . . $80,000

As you can see in figure 3.6 the cash balance has decreased by $23,000 (the amount of cash contributed to the purchase of the land, building, and truck), the other Assets have increased to $43,000 (the truck, building, and land), and two new Liabilities have appeared (the current and long-term portions of the mortgage loan). The loan of $20,000 has been divided up between the short-term portion of $1,000 and the long-term portion (due in a period of greater than one year) of $19,000. Also, notice that the Owner's Equity is not affected.

What are the factors that change Owner's Equity? The items that follow give us a summary of the *only* items that have an impact on the beginning balance of Owner's Equity.

- The owner invests more money in the business
- The business makes a profit or loss
- The owner takes Assets out of the business.

Thus, when Sam invested the $60,000 into the bicycle company, this increased her Owner's Equity in the company by this same amount. When the company makes a profit, this is also an increase to her Owner's Equity. Finally, if Sam decides to take any money or other Assets out of the bicycle company for her own use, this will reduce the Owner's Equity as it shows up on the bicycle company's Balance Sheet.

Sam Purchases Insurance (Short-Term Asset)

On January 3, the company purchases a three-year insurance policy on the building. The cost of this insurance is $1,500. Because this purchase covers three years and at the time of purchase has not been used up at all, the expenditure represents an Asset. We call this Asset, "Prepaid Insurance." The company pays for this insurance with cash. After this transaction, the Balance Sheet looks like it does in figure 3.7:

Figure 3.7: SOLANA BEACH BICYCLE COMPANY
Balance Sheet
January 3, 2010

Assets	Liabilities & Owner's Equity
Short-Term Assets:	**Liabilities:**
Cash. $35,500	Current Portion of
Prepaid Insurance . . . 1,500	Mortgage Payable $1,000
	Long-Term:
	Mortgage Payable $19,000
Total Short-Term	
Assets $37,000	Total Liabilities $20,000

Long-Term Assets:		Owner's Equity:	
Truck	$8,000	Owner's Investment	$60,000
Building	25,000		
Land	10,000		
Total Long-Term Assets	$43,000	Total Liabilities and	
Total Assets	$80,000	Owner's Equity	$80,000

In figure 3.7 the only change in the Balance Sheet after the purchase of the insurance is that one Asset (cash) has been exchanged for another Asset (Prepaid Insurance, between Short- and Long-Term Assets) for the exact amount of $1,500.

Sam Orders and Buys Bicycles (Short-Term Assets)

On January 5, Sam orders and buys two different brands of bicycles from two different companies. She buys eighty of one kind that cost $100 apiece, and twenty-five of the other kind that cost her $200 apiece. The total cost of the 105 bicycles to the company is $13,000. This purchase represents a Short-Term Asset known as Inventory.

Inventory is a Short-Term Asset because the company anticipates selling these 105 bicycles in one year or less. As with the purchase of the Long-Term Assets, the company does not want to pay for all of these bicycles with cash. It pays $10,000 in cash and agrees to pay the additional $3,000 to the seller at a later date from the sale. This $3,000 becomes an Accounts Payable of the business, and is shown in the Short-Term Liabilities section.

As we saw in figure 3.1, there are several different types of payables. The term Accounts Payable is reserved for the purchase of Inventory items that are going to be resold by the company.

QUICK Tip

Keeping an Eye on Inventory: Having too little or too much Inventory in a small business will create problems for the company. Drawing up a budget is a critical part of the accounting process that will aid in the planning and control of the company's expenditures and help the business owner to maintain control of all aspects of the business. Budgets will be discussed further in chapter 10.

After this transaction, the Balance Sheet looks like the one in figure 3.8:

Figure 3.8: **SOLANA BEACH BICYCLE COMPANY**
Balance Sheet
January 5, 2010

Assets	Liabilities & Owner's Equity
Short-Term Assets:	**Liabilities:**
Cash. $25,500	Accounts Payable. . . $3,000
Inventory 13,000	Current Portion of
Prepaid Insurance . . . 1,500	Mortgage Payable . . . 1,000
	Long-term:
	Mortgage Payable . . 19,000
Total Short-Term Assets $40,000	Total Liabilities $23,000
Long-Term Assets:	**Owner's Equity:**
Truck $8,000	Owner's Investment $60,000
Building 25,000	
Land 10,000	
Total Long-Term Assets $43,000	Total Liabilities and
Total Assets $83,000	Owner's Equity . . . $83,000

Once again, the Balance Sheet stays in balance. Assets ($83,000) = Liabilities ($23,000) + Owner's Equity ($60,000).

You'll note that the Balance Sheet in figure 3.8 dated January 5, 2010, is quite different from the one dated December 31, 2010, in figure 3.4. This demonstrates how the Balance Sheet can change, representing the company's Assets, Liabilities, and Owner's Equity at any given point in time.

In this chapter, you have learned about the Balance Sheet and the definitions of all of its components. You have learned how these components relate to each other. You have also learned a very important point: Retained Earnings are not necessarily comprised of only cash, and therefore, cash management is a high priority to a business making a profit. Finally, you learned how various transactions affect the Balance Sheet of a small business.

In chapter 4 you will learn about the income statement and how you can use it in your business and personal life.

ANSWERS

1. No. This would not appear on the company's Balance Sheet, since this is an Asset that belongs to the owner and not the business.

2. Yes, because this Asset is used by the business.

3. No. This was once an Asset, but is no longer one since it is not used in the operations of the business.

4. No. Although a company's employees are often referred to as "Assets," they are not listed as Assets on a company's Balance Sheet since the company does not own them.

5. Yes. This is called Accounts Receivable.

6. No. This is a Liability, not an Asset (something owed rather than something owned).

7. This depends on whether the company owns the land. If it does, the land is considered an Asset because it has value.

8. Yes.

9. No. This is an Asset of the owner, not of the company, and these Assets are kept separate.

10. Yes, this has future benefit to the company since the insurance company owes them insurance for three years into the future.

GLOSSARY

Accounting Equation: The formula that depicts the relationships of the various elements of the Balance Sheet to each other: A(ssets) = L(iabilities) + OE (Owner's Equity).

Accounts Payable: A Short-Term Liability (debt) incurred from the purchase of Inventory.

Assets: Items of value that are owned by the company and are represented on the Balance Sheet. In order for an item to be shown on the Balance Sheet, it must meet three tests: 1) the company must control it or own it, 2) the item must have some value to the company, and 3) this value must be measurable. Assets are categorized as short-term or long-term items.

Balance Sheet: This financial statement is a listing of the Assets (items owned), Liabilities (items owed), and Owner's Equity (what belongs to the owner(s)). The relationships between all these items are represented by the accounting equation.

Creditors: Those individuals or companies to which money or other Assets are owed; for example, the supplier from whom Sam purchased the bicycles and to whom she owes an additional $3,000 is a creditor of the company.

Equity: See Owner's Equity.

Historical Cost: The amount paid for an item owned by the business (Assets), or the amount incurred in a debt on the date of the agreement to enter into the obligation (Liabilities). Even though over time the values of these Assets and/or Liabilities may change, they will always be shown on the Balance Sheet at their historical cost.

Intangible Assets: Those Assets that are of value to a business and meet all tests of being an Asset, but do not have tangible qualities; for example, trademarks and patents.

Inventory: An Asset held by a business for the purpose of resale. In the case of Solana Beach Bicycle Company, Inventory is the bicycles that the company intends to sell.

Liabilities: Debts owed by a business. They can either be short-term or long-term depending upon when they become due. Short-Term Liabilities are to be paid within a year. Examples in the bicycle company are the Accounts Payable, and the current portion of the Mortgage Payable. Long-Term Liabilities extend beyond one year.

An example in the bicycle company is the portion of the mortgage which is due to be paid beyond the current year.

Long-Term Assets: Those items that will be consumed or converted to cash after a period of one year. Examples of these Assets in the bicycle company are the truck, the building, and the land.

Owner's Equity: The difference between what is owned and what is owed; in a company, this amount belongs to the owners. The Owner's Equity is made up of the original and additional investments by the owner, plus any profit that is retained in the business, minus any cash or other Assets that are withdrawn or distributed to the owner(s).

Retained Earnings: The amount of profit earned by the business since its inception, minus any money that is taken out or distributed to the owner(s). At Solana Beach, this is whatever the company earns in selling bikes, minus whatever Expenses are incurred; for example, electricity, gas for the truck, mortgage payments, salaries, etc.

Short-Term Assets: Those Assets that are cash or will be converted to cash or consumed within a period of one year or less. Examples of these Assets in the bicycle company are Cash, Accounts Receivable, bicycle Inventory, and Prepaid Insurance.

Chapter 4

The Income Statement

At this point, we are familiar with the Balance Sheet and how it is helpful in showing what Assets Solana Beach Bicycle owns and what Liabilities the company owes. We also learned that the difference between these two items is called Owner's Equity and represents what the bicycle company is "worth" at the end of the year. The final thing that we learned was that the Balance Sheet represents these values for one particular point in time and for that point in time only. It can be considered a snapshot of the business.

Now that her business is up and running, Samantha is very interested in knowing, "What is the bottom line? How much money did I make?" For this information Sam should become familiar with the Income Statement.

Understanding the Income Statement

The Income Statement presents a summary of an entity's Revenues (what the company earned from sales of products and services) and Expenses (what was expended to earn this revenue) for a specific period of time, such as a month, a quarter, or a year. This period of time is known as the accounting period. One key difference between the Income Statement and the Balance Sheet is that the Income Statement reflects a period of time rather than a single moment in time as with the Balance Sheet. The Income Statement is also called a Statement of Earnings or a Statement of Operations.

The preparation of the Income Statement serves several purposes. Often the only reason one uses the Income Statement is to concentrate on the "bottom line" or Net Income (Revenue minus Expenses). The Income Statement can also be useful for analyzing changes in the Revenue data over a period of time, or determining ratios of particular Expenses to Revenue and how these ratios have been changing over certain periods of time. These two topics will be discussed in chapters 8 and 9. (See Appendix B for a real-life example of an Income Statement from the Coca-Cola Company.)

The Income Statement Illustrated

In figure 4.1 we can see all of the bicycle company's Revenue and Expenses for its first year in business. By reviewing these numbers Sam can also see her "bottom line," that is, her company's Net Income for the year.

In general Income Statements are organized into three sections. The first section shows the Revenues earned from the sale of goods and/or services for the period being reported. In the case of the Solana Beach Bicycle Company (figure 4.1), this period is one year. The second section lists the Expenses the business has incurred to earn these Revenues during the period represented by the Income Statement. The third section is the difference between these Revenues and Expenses in which we hope the Revenues outweigh the Expenses, indicating a profit. If the Expenses are greater than the Revenues, this would indicate a loss—not a great thing in a business.

In the following example, the numbers listed inside of parentheses represent subtractions.

Figure 4.1: **SOLANA BEACH BICYCLE COMPANY**
Income Statement
For the Year Ended December 31, 2010

Note: Parentheses indicate decreases in cash

Sales	$35,500	
Cost of Goods Sold	14,200	
Gross Profit		$21,300
Operating Expenses:		
Salaries and Wages	$5,200	
Bicycle Parts	1,625	
Insurance Expense	500	
Bad Debt Expense	175	
Tools Expense	50	
Bank Service Fee	15	
Total Operating Expenses		$7,565
Net Income from Operations		$13,735
Other Revenue and Expenses:		
Repair Revenue		$3,850
Repair Expenses		(1,100)
Interest Expense		(1600)
Net Income Before Taxes		$15,585
Less: Income Taxes		(4,500)
Net Income		$10,385

See Appendix C for an example of the Income Statement from a major corporation.

The Accrual Concept

The Accrual Concept addresses the issue of when Revenue is recognized on the Income Statement. Revenue is recognized when it is earned and Expenses are recognized as they are incurred regardless of when the cash changes hands; this is referred to as accrual basis of accounting. This type of accounting is used by businesses throughout the United States for the presentation of their financial statements. Some small firms and most individuals still use the cash basis of accounting to determine their income and Income Taxes. Under the cash basis of accounting, Revenue is not reported until cash is received, and Expenses are not reported until cash is disbursed.

QUICK Tip

Cash Basis of Accounting: The reason a small business might use the cash basis of accounting is that it is easier than the accrual system to keep track of the Revenues and Expenses. No assumptions have to be made (for instance, for depreciation), and no accruals have to be made for items such as Accounts Receivable and Accounts Payable. Accounting entries are only made when cash is actually exchanged.

Generally Accepted Accounting Principles require the accrual system of accounting, and thus most financial statements that you will encounter and that are used by investors and bankers will be prepared under the accrual system of accounting. It is for this reason that throughout the remainder of this book, we will use only the accrual basis of accounting for all of our examples.

Revenue

Revenue (or sales) is what the company earned during a particular period of time from the sale of merchandise or from the rendering of services to its customers. Revenue can come from several sources; a firm can generate Revenue from sales, interest, dividends, royalties, or any combination of these. The sum of all of these sources is the total Revenues of a business.

As shown in figure 4.1, Revenue of $35,500 is from the sale of bicycles. If you look towards the bottom of the Income Statement, you'll see that the bicycle company also earned Revenue from doing repairs ($3,850). This repair Revenue has been separated from the sales Revenue because the main business is sales and not repairs.

At this point there has been no discussion of Net Income. Revenue is one component of Net Income, but it is not the whole story. Expenses and other items need to be added to or subtracted from Revenue to arrive at the Net Income figure.

Revenue Versus Cash Flow: It is important to note that Revenue is not equal to cash flow. Revenue can be generated prior to a business receiving cash. In other words, a sale can be made in which only a promise to pay is generated, but cash does not change hands. Even though the cash will not be collected until some point in the future, the Revenue is recognized at the time that the merchandise has been transferred to the buyer, or the services have been performed by the seller. Therefore it is possible for a company to have a large amount of sales (or Revenue) and still have a cash flow problem, since they have not collected the money yet.

In figure 4.1 we can see that the $35,500 of sales was generated by collecting cash and promises to pay cash in the future. You cannot tell simply by reading this one number called Sales how much was generated from each of these two sources individually. But you can tell that at the end of the year, there is still $9,175 owed from the sales, meaning that $9,175 is expected but has not been received in cash yet. You know this from the Balance Sheet in figure 3.2 (Accounts Receivable at December 31, 2010). The reason that you cannot tell in total how much was sold on account during the year is because some of the Accounts Receivable could have been paid off during the year before this Balance Sheet was generated. The $9,175 only reflects how much is still owed to the business on December 31, 2010.

Expenses

Expenses represent the cost of doing business. Examples of Expenses are rent, utilities, bank service fees, tool and equipment Expenses, bad debt Expense, and salaries. In our current example, the Expenses of Solana Beach Bicycle Company fall under the title of Operating Expenses. These are all of the Expenses for the year 2006 that were incurred by the shop in order to generate Revenue in the operation of the business. The total is $7,565. Another Expense that does not appear in the listing of operating Expenses—but is necessary to generate Revenue—is Cost of Goods Sold ($14,200). This Expense is the cost of either the bicycles purchased by the company or the components used to build the bicycles that were sold during 2010.

There is an important distinction to be made between an expenditure and an Expense. An expenditure is the spending of cash. All Expenses are expenditures; however, not all expenditures are Expenses. It sounds confusing, but it's really quite simple. An Expense is an expenditure that generates Revenue. If the expenditure does not immediately generate Revenue, it is not an Expense. Consider the purchase of a building. When the purchase of a building is made, it does not immediately produce Revenue. At that point in time the purchase is considered an expenditure. However, over time this building will be used in the production of Revenue, and the building (and other such Long-Term Assets) depreciate or are used up. The depreciation of the building thus becomes an Expense and is matched with those Revenues it helped to generate.

Net Income

Net income represents the difference between Revenues generated during the period and the related Expenses, which generated that Revenue. Prior to calculating Net Income, a company first calculates gross income. The gross income is sales (or total Revenues) minus the cost of those goods that were sold. Gross income does not take operating Expenses into account; Net Income, on the other hand, is the gross income minus all of the operating Expenses, plus or minus other Revenues and Expenses.

Once again note that the term cash is not used. As with Revenue, part of the "bottom line" or Net Income could be made up of cash, but other parts could be made up of promises to receive cash or promises to pay cash in the future.

QUICK Tip

Expand Your Focus: When evaluating your business, you should not solely concentrate on Net Income in the financial statements. This is certainly a useful number (especially if it is compared to previous years' figures), but there are several other important numbers and ratios that ultimately might be important to your decisions. Some of these numbers might include gross income, the trend of salary Expenses (are they going up too fast?), how much cash is on hand at the end of the year, how sales have been increasing, if at all. Outside of the company it is important to pay attention to the competition as well as the economy as a whole. These are just a few examples of why, if you only focus on the Net Income figure, you will lose sight of the whole picture.

In figure 4.1 the term "Net Income" appears three times. The first time is "Net Income from Operations." This number, $13,735 represents the income earned from selling bicycles, the main product of Solana Beach Bicycle Company. In addition to selling bicycles, the company also did some repairs. These repairs generated Revenue of $3,850 during the year. This Revenue is shown separately because it is not the main business of this shop. Thus, after the other Revenues and Expenses are added to "Net Income from Operations," a new total is derived labeled "Net Income Before Taxes." This number is $15,585. After the taxes are paid on this total we arrive at the "bottom line" or "Net Income after taxes" of $10,385.

Confusing? Maybe a little, but accounting convention requires that we separate out Net Income from the main operations of the business and from other income earned from other types of sales and services. After these two numbers are shown separately on the Income Statement, we have to show what the government is going to take in taxes before we can finally arrive at the "bottom line."

Interest and Income Taxes

Other items subtracted from Revenues and Expenses before determining the total Net Income are Interest and Income Taxes. Most accountants classify interest and taxes as an "Other Expense" of the period, not as an operating expense. The reason for this is that interest and taxes do not produce mainstream Revenue but are necessary to pay in order to stay in business.

Bad Debt Expense

One operating Expense shown in figure 4.1 is Bad Debt Expense for $175. This Expense represents the amount of the Accounts Receivable that the company anticipates that it will be not be able to collect. Most businesses try to keep this number to a minimum, in order to keep their Expenses low. The amount of $175, in the case of the Solana Beach Bicycle Company, is an estimation made by management; in most businesses this estimate is made based upon prior year's experience of their collections of Accounts Receivable.

QUICK Tip

Keep Bad Debts in Check: In order to keep your Bad Debt Expense to a minimum, it is important that you do extensive credit checks on those customers to whom you are going to extend credit. This can be done with the help of professional services such as Dunn and Bradstreet and by reviewing and understanding their financial statements prior to extending this credit.

QUIZ

Based upon your knowledge of accounting so far, looking at the Income Statement in figure 4.1, would you say that the Solana Beach Bicycle Company had a good first year of business? What would you like to see them do differently next year? What additional information do you need to make these decisions?

See page 60 for the answer.

Transactions That Affect the Income Statement

Let's examine the transactions that created the Income Statement in figure 4.1.

Sales

In the Revenue section we looked at the total Revenue (or sales) for the year. Now let's look at an individual sale during the year, and see what effect it has on the Income Statement. What we have been looking at in figure 4.1 is the Income Statement at the end of the year. Now let's go back to the beginning of the year and see how these final figures in figure 4.1 were arrived at.

Assume that on January 6, the company makes its first sales—two bicycles—for a total of $500. The company originally bought the bikes for $100 each (a total of $200). After this transaction the Income Statement would look like the one in figure 4.2. (Note that this Income Statement in figure 4.2 is as of January 6, whereas the one in figure 4.1, is as of December 31.)

Figure 4.2: SOLANA BEACH BICYCLE COMPANY
Income Statement
For the Week Ended January 6, 2010

Sales	$500
Cost of Goods Sold	200
Gross Profit	$300
Expenses	—
Net Income	$300

This transaction has caused two changes to the Income Statement. First, it has increased the Revenue account called "Sales" by $500, and second, it has increased an Expense account called "Cost of Goods Sold" by the cost of the two bicycles or $200.

At the same time this transaction has changed the Balance Sheet in several ways. Assuming that these bicycles were sold for cash, the

Asset account (cash) on the Balance Sheet would increase by $500. A second Asset account called Inventory, where these bicycles were listed when they were bought, would be decreased by the cost of the two bicycles, $200.

The other change on the Balance Sheet is that the Retained Earnings figure goes up by the difference between the sales price of these two bicycles and the cost. Thus, Retained Earnings increases by $300 ($500–$200), the profit made through the sale of the bicycles.

(Note: Remember that Revenue minus Expenses equals Net Income, and Net Income increases Retained Earnings on the Balance Sheet. Once again, a very important part of this concept is that there is no mention of cash. Whether these bikes were sold for cash or the promise to pay cash in the future is of no importance to the "bottom line" although it is a very important concern from a cash flow management standpoint.)

Now let's look at the Accounting Equation, A = L + OE that we learned about in chapter 1. One Asset, cash, has increased by the sale price of $500. Another Asset, Inventory, has decreased by the cost of the bicycles that were sold, $200. Retained Earnings, part of Owner's Equity, has increased by the difference between the sale price and the cost, or $300. Thus the left side of this equation has increased by $300 (one Asset up $500 and the other down by $200), and the right side of the equation, Owner's Equity, has increased by the same amount, the Net Income of $300.

Using the equation, the transaction would look like this:

Assets = Liabilities + Owner's Equity
Cash + $500
Inventory – $200 = Net Income + $300

This concept is further demonstrated in chapter 7, "Double-Entry Accounting System."

Cost of Goods Sold and Gross Profit

During the complete year of 2010, the cost of the all of the bicycles sold was equal to $14,200. The difference between the sales price of the bicycles ($35,500) and the cost of these bicycles ($14,200) is called the Gross Profit. The word "gross" is used since it represents the profit of the bicycle company *before* the operating Expenses are subtracted. In the case of the bicycle company, the Gross Profit is equal to $21,300.

Operating Expenses

Operating Expenses are those costs that are necessary to operate the business on a day-to-day basis. On January 7, Solana Beach Bicycle Company pays the owner her first week's pay of $100.

Alert!

Paying the Owner: Remember that the owner of this company and the Solana Beach Bicycle Company are two separate entities and when the business pays the owner her salary, this constitutes one entity paying another.

After this second transaction, the Income Statement looks like the one in figure 4.3:

Figure 4.3: **SOLANA BEACH BICYCLE COMPANY**
Income Statement
For the Week Ended January 7, 2010

Sales	$500
Cost of Goods Sold	200
Gross Profit	$300
Expenses	100
Net Income	$200

The $100 paid to the owner is an Expense (Salary Expense) and as such it is shown in the Income Statement under Expenses. The Net Income is decreased by the entire $100, as is the Retained Earnings and the cash in the Balance Sheet. Assuming that the salary is paid in cash, the impact on the accounting equation would look like this:

Assets = Liabilities + Owner's Equity
Cash – $100 = Net Income – $100

Business Transactions

Selling Bicycles but Receiving Only Partial Payment

On January 21, the bicycle company sold ten more bicycles for a total of $5,000. The cost of these ten bicycles was $2,000. The buyers of these bicycles paid a total of $3,500 in cash and promised to pay the other $1,500 within sixty days.

After this transaction the Income Statement would look like the one in figure 4.4:

Figure 4.4: **SOLANA BEACH BICYCLE COMPANY**
Income Statement
For the Week Ended January 21, 2010

Sales	$5,500
Cost of Goods Sold	2,200
Gross Profit	$3,300
Expenses	100
Net Income	$3,200

Notice that on the Income Statement under the accrual system of accounting, income—like Revenue—is determined when it is earned and has nothing to do with when the cash is received. The entire $5,000 was added to the existing $500 in sales even though only $3,500 cash was received for the ten bicycles. This step is taken because a transaction has occurred in which the buyers have obligated themselves to pay the full $5,000.

The cost of the goods sold (which is an Expense) increased $2,000 because the ten bicycles that were sold had cost the business this amount of money (ten bicycles at $200 each). If we were looking at the Balance Sheet, the Inventory Asset would be decreased by this $2,000, the cost of the Inventory that was sold.

Also, on the Balance Sheet, the Retained Earnings increased $3,000. (Revenue of $5,000 minus Expenses of $2,000.) Now you can see that because of the relationship between Net Income on the Income Statement and Retained Earnings on the Balance Sheet, any time Net Income is changed, Retained Earnings is also changed by the same amount.

So the impact on the accounting equation of A = L + OE would look like this:

Assets	= Liabilities + Owner's Equity
Cash + $3,500	
Inventory – $2,000	= Net Income +,$3,000
Accounts Receivable + $1,500	

Repairing Bicycles and Receiving Cash

On February 14 five customers pick up bicycles they had brought into the shop for repair. The customers paid a total of $375 for the repair of these five bicycles. The cost of the parts to repair these bicycles was $105.

After this transaction the Income Statement would look like the one in figure 4.5:

Figure 4.5: SOLANA BEACH BICYCLE COMPANY
Income Statement
For the Two Weeks Ended February 14, 2010

Note: Parentheses indicate decreases in cash

Sales	$5,500
Cost of Goods Sold	2,200
Gross Profit	$3,300
Expenses.	100
Net Income from Operations	$3,200

Other Revenue:

Repair Revenue	$375
Repair Expenses.	(105)
Net Income	$3,470

This transaction of repairing the bicycles increased Net Income, cash, and Retained Earnings by $270. Also, the total Assets owned by the company increased by $270.

At this point you should assume that the bicycle parts were bought for cash immediately prior to being used to repair the bicycles. Therefore, there is no Inventory of bicycle parts.

Once again, let's look at the impact on the Accounting Equation:

Assets = Liabilities + Owner's Equity
Cash +$375 (from customers) = Net Income +$270
Cash –$105 (to buy parts)

Other Operating Expenses

During the year, Solana Beach Bicycle Company incurred other Expenses that were necessary to operate the business. The business had to pay interest on the mortgage that it held. Since the mortgage is for $20,000, and the interest rate on this loan is 10 percent, the total interest paid during the year is $2,000. In addition to the interest, the company bought some small tools to use on the repairs, which cost a total of $1,625. The company was also charged a service fee of $15 by the bank where it has its account. The total of these operating Expenses increased the Expenses on the Income Statement and reduced cash and Retained Earnings on the Balance Sheet.

At the end of the year, the owner concluded from prior experiences with business receivables that she was not going to be able to collect $175 from one of the customers that had promised to pay. In order to recognize this on the financial statements, she created an Expense category called Bad Debts Expense. This Expense is increased by the amount of the receivable that will not be collected, and a new account is set up, called Allowance for Doubtful Accounts for the other side of the transaction. This allowance account is called a "contra-Asset" account, and is used to reduce Accounts Receivable on the Balance Sheet.

The last Expense that is listed on the Income Statement, Insurance Expense is another Expense that reduces Net Income without using cash at the time the Expense is recognized. Remember from chapter 3, Prepaid Insurance is listed on the Balance Sheet as an Asset of $1,500. (Refer to page 40 in chapter 3, if you don't remember!) This came about because the bicycle company bought the insurance in advance of using it. Since this was a three-year policy, by the end of year one, one-third of it had been used by the business. To recognize the "using up" of this Asset (Prepaid Insurance), the Insurance Expense is increased by $500 which corresponds to the Expense of using the insurance for one year. Even though the insurance was paid for last year, it is being used one-third at a time during each of the three years. Each time we use the insurance, it represents an Expense to the company even though the cash was expended (an expenditure) in a prior year. Once again, we see the difference between an expenditure and an Expense. We also see that expenditures eventually become Expenses. In year one when the insurance was purchased, it was an expenditure of cash to the company. It does not become an Expense until the insurance policy is actually used for one year.

The Asset itself is no longer worth the full amount paid, since it now only represents the remaining two years. Therefore, the Asset is reduced by the same one-third (one year of the three years), or by $500.

Looking at the impact this would have on the accounting equation, we note the following:

Assets = Liabilities + Owner's Equity
Prepaid Insurance – $500 = Net Income (Insurance Expense) – $500

In this chapter you learned the components of an Income Statement and how they relate to each other. You also learned that Revenue and Net Income are not the same as cash because accountants usually use the accrual basis of accounting and not the cash basis. Finally you learned how individual transactions affect and change the Income Statement.

In chapter 5 you will find out how to prepare and use a Statement of Cash Flows.

ANSWER

It is not possible to make a complete analysis of a company just by looking at one financial statement. Sam, the owner, and we as outsiders would also need to look at the Balance Sheet as well as the Statement of Cash Flows (to be discussed in the next chapter).

It is important to note that the Solana Beach Bicycle Company did make a profit of $10,385. Many new small businesses do not make a profit for the first three or four years, so that is impressive.

In planning for the year ahead, Sam might decide to put more money into advertising and expand the repair business. Only 10 percent of the company's Revenue came from repairs, so there could be room for growth in that area of the business.

Other information that would be helpful to look at includes the other financial statements as well as the budgets for the next two years, 2011 and 2012.

GLOSSARY

Accounts Receivable: This is a term used to describe money that is to be received in the future for current sales of goods or services. Normally, Accounts Receivable appears on the Balance Sheet as a Short-Term Asset, since companies generally give credit to customers for thirty to sixty days.

Accrual Basis of Accounting: This accounting method recognizes transactions when Revenue is earned, Expenses are incurred, and purchases take place—whether or not cash changes hands at that moment. This is the method of accounting used by virtue of Generally Accepted Accounting Principle, and most businesses use this rather than the alternative, the cash basis of accounting.

Bad Debt Expense: This Expense appears on the Income Statement and is increased by the amount of the receivables that will not be collected (that is, debts owed to the company that will not be paid). When this Expense is created, a contra-Asset to Accounts receivable is also created called Allowance for Bad Debts. This contra-Asset reduces the Accounts Receivable account on the Balance Sheet and keeps the two sides of the Balance Sheet in balance.

Bottom Line: Another term used for Net Income, it represents all Expenses subtracted from all Revenues. This figure gets its name from the fact that it appears at the bottom of the Income Statement.

Cash Basis of Accounting: This accounting method only recognizes Revenue and Expenses when cash is exchanged. If the sale or Expense takes place in one period without cash changing hands, because of receivables and payables, the Revenue and the Expenses are not recognized until a future period. For this reason, the cash basis of accounting is typically not used for business according to GAAP, but is the method generally used in personal accounting.

Cost of Goods Sold: The cost of the entire Inventory that was sold during the period stated in the Income Statement. Cost of goods sold is an Expense and is subtracted from Revenue to arrive at Gross Profit.

Expenditures: The spending of cash. All Expenses are expenditures; however, all expenditures are not Expenses. Only expenditures that immediately generate Revenue are considered Expenses. When expenditures are made for items that have future benefits, they are classified as Assets and converted to Expenses as they are used up.

Expenses: These are expenditures made to generate Revenue. Whether or not cash changes hands, a company incurs an Expense as soon as it makes a commitment to pay for a product or service.

Gross Profit: The difference between Revenue and Cost of Goods Sold before operating Expenses, interest, and taxes are subtracted. A good analysis for the owner of a company is to compare Gross Profit from one year to another and determine whether it is increasing or decreasing and why.

Income Statement: This financial statement is a listing of all Revenues and Expenses of the business earned or incurred during a particular period of time. The Income Statement is usually produced by a company monthly, quarterly, or annually. It is one of the three major statements produced by businesses in the United States, the other two being the Balance Sheet and the Statement of Cash Flows.

Net Income: The difference between Revenue and Expenses for a designated period of time. In the case of Solana Beach Bicycle Company, we saw three uses of the term Net Income. The first, Net Income from operations, shows all normal Revenue and Expenses that deal with the main operations of this business—selling bicycles. The second usage was Net Income before taxes, where Net Income from operations is increased and reduced by other Revenue and Expenses that are outside the normal operations of this business—like repairing bicycles. The third usage was Net Income. This is what is referred to as the "bottom line" since it appears at the bottom of the Income Statement. It is derived by reducing Net Income before taxes, by the amount of Income Taxes for the year.

Other Revenues and Expenses: Those items that are derived from transactions that are not the main business of the company and that are listed on the Income Statement under "Other Revenues and Expenses." In the case of Solana Beach, sales of bicycles is the main business; repairs are not the shop's main business and are listed under "Other Revenues and Expenses."

Recognize: This term refers to the recording of the Revenues and Expenses in the records of the company. This occurs at the point in time when Revenue and Expenses are shown on the Income Statement. Revenues are recognized when services are performed or when title is transferred on goods sold. Expenses are recognized when they are incurred and become an obligation of the company.

Revenue: The amount earned by a business by selling goods or performing services is termed "Revenue." In the case of the Solana Beach Bicycle Company, Revenue represents the earnings in from the selling of bicycles as well as the repair of bicycles. Since the main business of the company is to sell bicycles, the Revenue that is earned from the repairs is shown as other income.

Chapter 5

Preparing and Using a Statement of Cash Flows

- ▶ What Is a Statement of Cash Flows?
- ▶ Cash and Cash Equivalents
- ▶ The Statement of Cash Flows Illustrated

After analyzing the Balance Sheet and the Income Statement for Solana Beach Bicycle Company, Samantha has a clear understanding of what her business owns and what she owes, as well as what its "bottom line" is for the year. Although things are looking good so far, Sam has a nagging concern, which she raises at a meeting with her business advisor: "I have read that many small businesses go bankrupt, not because they don't have a great product or a great service, but because they run out of cash. Is that right?"

Well, Sam is right. As we discussed in chapter 4, making a profit, or having a large amount in Retained Earnings, does not equal having cash. And if there is no cash, there is no way to pay the salaries, pay the IRS, or pay any other bills for that matter. In this chapter we will discuss the Statement of Cash Flows and the financial statement, which will help Sam in her quest to stay on top of the cash flow in her business.

What Is a Statement of Cash Flows?

For a company's financial statement to be in accordance with Generally Accepted Accounting Principles (GAAP), the Statement of Cash Flows must be included as one of the four required financial statements. Do you remember the other three? They are the Balance Sheet, the Income Statement, and Statement of Retained Earnings.

The Statement of Cash Flows shows the flow of cash within the business—where the cash came from and how it was spent during the period of reporting (which is generally a month, a quarter, or a year). It also shows the cash flows of the company, divided into categories according to three major activities: operating, investing, and financing. This is helpful to statement users, business owners, investors, and creditors because it indicates the type of transaction that gave rise to each one of the cash flows.

Additionally, the Statement of Cash Flows differs from the Balance Sheet and Income Statement in two key ways. The Balance Sheet shows the financial status of a company at the end of the reporting period (a snapshot), but both the Income Statement and the Statement of Cash Flows show the flow of activity during the reporting period (a short movie compared to the snapshot that is the Balance Sheet). The second difference is that the Income Statement reports this activity on the accrual basis, and the Statement of Cash Flows reports it on the cash basis. Remember from chapter 4, that under the cash basis of accounting, Revenue is not reported until cash is received, and Expenses are not reported until cash is disbursed.

What Is the Purpose of the Statement?

Like the other required financial statements you have learned about—the Balance Sheet and the Income Statement—the Statement of Cash Flows enables users to make decisions about the company. The Statement of Cash Flows is more like the Income Statement than the Balance Sheet in that it is a change statement. It shows the transactions that caused cash levels to change from the beginning of the period to the end. As was mentioned earlier, a company can make a profit or earn a large amount of Revenue but not have enough cash to pay its bills. The Revenue, thus the Net Income, may have been generated (wholly or in part) by promises to pay in the future (Accounts Receivable), so it is critically important to review both the "bottom line" as well as the company's position in cash to really forecast its future.

There are several ways in which you might use a Statement of Cash Flows in your own life. Will you have sufficient cash at the end of the month to purchase additional Inventory? Will you have the cash flow in the future to buy the new equipment you'll need to handle all the growth you're experiencing? Will you have the cash necessary to purchase a new building for the planned expansion? (See Appendix B for a real-life example of a Financial Statement from Station Casinos, Inc.)

Cash and Cash Equivalents

In business the term "cash" has a broader meaning than the amount of cash in the bank at the end of the year. It is also defined as liquid short-term investments; liquid investments are those that can quickly be converted into cash within a very short period of time, usually by cashing them in (in the case of certificates of deposit, for example) or by selling them. For this reason, they are also referred to as cash equivalents. (See figure 5.1 for examples.) Therefore, whenever the term "cash" is used in this chapter it refers to cash and all cash equivalents.

Figure 5.1: EXAMPLES OF CASH EQUIVALENTS

- Cash in the bank
- Commercial paper (a form of short-term loan)
- Any investment that has a maturity date of less than three months
- Certificates of deposit
- Money market accounts
- U.S. government treasury bills

The Statement of Cash Flows Illustrated

By looking at the Balance Sheet in chapter 3, figure 3.2, you can see how much cash the Solana Beach Bicycle Company has at the end of 2010—$17,385. By reviewing the Statement of Cash Flows in figure 5.2, we can see where the cash came from and where it went during 2010.

Figure 5.2: SOLANA BEACH BICYCLE COMPANY
Statement of Cash Flows
Year Ended December 31, 2010

Note: Parentheses indicate decreases in cash

Cash Flow from Operating Activities:

Cash Inflows:

From Customers	$35,500
Less: Accounts Receivable	(9,175)
Repair Revenue	3,850
Cash Outflows:	
Cost of Goods Sold	14,200
Inventory	23,000
Less: Accounts Payable	(3,000)
Salaries and Wages	5,200
Bicycle Parts	1,625

Insurance	1,500
Tools	50
Bank Service Fees	15
Repair Expenses	1,100
Interest	1,600
Income Taxes	4,500

Net Cash Flow from Operating Activities . . . . (19,615)

Cash Flow from Investing Activities:

Purchase of Truck. . . . .($8,000)
Purchase of Building. . . . .(25,000)
Purchase of Land . . . .(10,000)

Total Cash Flow from Investing Activities. . . . .($43,000)

Cash Flow from Financing Activities:

Borrowing for the Mortgage $20,000
Owner's Investment 60,000

Total Cash Flow from Financing Activities $80,000

Net Increase in Cash and Cash Equivalents $17,385

(Notice that this is the same number for ending cash on the Balance Sheet in figure 3.2, since there was no beginning balance in cash, $0 + this change = $17,385)

See Appendix C for an example of the Cash Flows Statement for a major corporation.

Now let's examine each of the statement's sections closely.

Operating Activities

As was mentioned earlier, the Statement of Cash Flows reports cash flow related to three areas: operating activities, financial activities, and investment activities. This is because a list of cash flows means more to business owners, investors, and creditors as they analyze the business if they can determine the type of transaction that gave rise to each one of the cash flows.

The operations section of the cash flow statement shows how much cash was generated from operations; that is, the day-to-day running of the business. In the case of Solana Beach Bicycle Company, the cash generated from operations would include the money brought in due to bicycle sales and repairs. In the case of Solana Beach's cash inflows, they are coming from two sources. The first is sales revenue of $35,500. (See Income Statement in figure 4.1) However, not all of the sales (revenue) were cash customers. Some of the sales were made on credit. We know this because accounts receivable has increased from a beginning balance of $0 to an ending balance of $9,175. This means that of all the sales for the year ($35,500), cash has not been received for $9,175 of that total. When the sales revenue minus the revenue is added to the Repair Revenue of $3,850, you arrive at total cash inflows from Operations.

Next it is necessary to calculate the cash outflows from Operations. This is comprised of Cost of Goods Sold (the amount of cash spent on the goods that were sold minus the portion that was loaned to the company, also called Accounts Payable) and all of the operating expenses on the Income Statement (figure 4.1), plus the other expenses on this same Income Statement. Thus, we will total Salaries and Wages, Bicycle Parts, Insurance expense, Tools Expense Bank Service Fees, plus Repair Expenses, Interest Expenses and Income Taxes. Notice that Bad Debt Expense does appear on the Income Statement, but not on the Cash Flows Statement. Why is that? It's because it is not a cash expense, it is just a guesstimate of what the company believes it will not be able to collect from the outstanding accounts receivable based upon past experiences and history. But the company does not expend any money for this expense.

One other point that might be a little confusing is that the insurance expense on the Income Statement is only $500, but the cash outflow on the Cash Flows Statement is more: $1,500. Why is this? Well, the company bought a 3-year Insurance Policy. So in year one of operations, the company expensed 1/3 of the total cost of the policy, or $500. However, the company did spend cash for the whole policy and thus the cash outflow is not just the $500, but is rather this plus the $1,000 that was also expended. The $1,000 shows up as an asset on the Balance Sheet because it does not become an expense until year two and three.

Now turning to the Balance Sheet, figure 3.4, we can find some other cash outflows from operations. What do you think these would be? If you said Inventory and Insurance, you would be correct. Cash was spent to purchase the goods that are still in Inventory, and thus becomes a cash outflow.

This gives us all of the cash inflows and outflows for the year, which is equal to a negative number, –$19,615. This means that the company had more cash outflows than cash inflows from operations for the year 2010.

Investing Activities

Any time a company makes a purchase of property, plant, or equipment, this addition is treated as an investment in the organization. This investment represents a cash flow from the company. Even though the entire purchase may not have been with cash, but with some borrowed money, the entire purchase is shown as a cash flow in the investing section of the Cash Flow Statement, and any borrowing of money is shown separately in the financing section.

In figure 5.2 we can see that the Solana Beach Bicycle Company purchased three Long-Term Assets during the year 2010. The land for $10,000, the building for $25,000, and the truck for $8,000 are all shown as negative cash flows in the investing activities section of the cash flow statement. The total of these three purchases represents a negative cash flow from investing activities of $43,000.

Financing Activities

The section called financing activities represents the cash that has come into or out of the company for the purpose of financing all of the other activities of the business. This could include Retained Earnings and money brought in by stock issued by the company, or as we can see in figure 5.2 the $60,000 that Samantha invested into the business on the first day. (Remember that Sam's personal money is accounted for separately from the company's money. If she invests personal funds in the business, while this is a decrease in her personal cash funds, it is an increase in funds for the business.) Because this investment was in cash, it is shown as an increase in the cash flow from financing activities. In addition to this investment by Sam, a fifteen-year loan was negotiated in order to purchase the land and the building. This loan for $20,000 is also shown as an inflow of cash to the business and thus an increase in cash flow from financing activities.

The total of these two items, $80,000, represents the total cash flow into the company from financing activities during the year 2010.

The total of the three cash flows—from operations, from investing, and from financing—represents the total increase or decrease in cash and cash equivalents for the business during the year being reported (in this example, an increase of $17,385). Notice that this total represents the change in cash from the beginning of the year to the end of the year. In our example, cash at the beginning of the year was $0, and at the end was $17,385, a net increase.

In this chapter you have learned how to prepare the Statement of Cash Flows. In chapter 6 you will learn how accounting for corporations differs from accounting for an individual proprietorship.

GLOSSARY

Cash: Includes currency and coins, balances in checking accounts, as well as any item that is acceptable into these checking accounts, such as checks and money orders.

Cash Equivalents: The cash held by a business as well as the liquid short-term investments that can quickly be converted into cash within a very short period of time.

Financing Activities: One of the three categories of business activity represented on the Cash Flow Statement. This section of the statement represents the cash that has come into or out of the company for the purpose of financing all of the other activities. In the case of Solana Beach Bicycle Company, this includes the money borrowed on the mortgage and the money Sam invested in the business.

Investing Activities: One of the three categories of business activity represented on the Cash Flow Statement. This section of the statement shows those purchases of property, plant, or equipment. These items are treated as an investment in the organization and represent a cash flow out of the company.

Operating Activities: One of the three categories of business activity represented on the Cash Flow Statement. This section of the statement shows how much cash was generated from operations; that is, the day-to-day running of the business. In the case of Solana Beach Bicycle, this would include cash generated from bicycle sales and repairs.

Statement of Cash Flows: One of the four required financial statements. This statement shows where the cash came from and how it was spent during the period of reporting.

Chapter 6

The Corporation

Up to this point we have been studying the Solana Beach Bicycle Company, which is an individual proprietorship. In other words, the business has one owner: Samantha. She has invested some of her own money into the company as well as borrowing some additional money.

Now Sam is thinking of growing her business. She has heard that by using other people's money, she will have more working capital and have the ability to expand the business. She has decided to investigate the possibility of incorporating her business and selling stock in her business.

But what is a corporation, really?

The Corporation Defined

A corporation has been defined as "an artificial being" independent from its owners, legally a separate entity. Corporations can be set up as for-profit or not-for-profit. For-profit corporations depend on making money in order to continue into the future. Not-for-profit corporations do not depend upon this profit to continue. These types of business, rather than depending on their profit, depend on gifts and grants from the public and private sectors for their continuation. Examples of not-for-profit corporations include charitable, governmental, educational, and recreational organizations.

QUICK Tip

The Other Side of Incorporation: Although incorporation has many benefits, it should also be noted that the proprietor loses partial or majority control to the other stockholders. The amount of paperwork and oversight also increases. Before making the decision to incorporate you should seek professional advice from your accountant, lawyer, and financial advisor regarding the pros and cons.

A corporation is given the right to operate (a charter) from the state in which it incorporates. However, the fact that a business is incorporated in one state does not mean that it cannot operate in the others. Due to differing tax laws and the incorporation fees, some states have become more advantageous to incorporate in than others.

Characteristics of a Corporation

There are several characteristics that differentiate a corporation from other forms of business. One of the characteristics of a corporation that distinguishes it from a partnership or a proprietorship is that it has limited liability. This means that the creditors of a corporation can lay claim only to the Assets of the corporation. Creditors of partnerships or proprietorships, on the other hand, can turn to the personal Assets of each owner whenever the Assets of the unincorporated firm are not sufficient to meet the creditors' claims. Because of this corporate characteristic, the states have laws that restrict the stockholders' right to withdraw Assets from the corporation. Each state has a law that prevents a corporation from paying dividends (that is, owners withdrawing Assets) whenever the net Assets (Assets minus Liabilities) are at or below a certain level. This minimum net Asset figure is often called the legal capital of a corporation.

Figure 6.1: **CHARACTERISTICS OF A CORPORATION**

- Is chartered as a legal and separate entity by an individual state
- Protects the personal Assets of the owners (stockholders) against creditors' claims (limited liability)
- Can issue capital stock to raise money
- Can issue dividends to stockholders
- May not issue dividends that would reduce the legal capital below a designated level

---

There are a number of reasons why a company would consider incorporation. Some of these reasons might include: 1) gaining the use of additional cash without the owner putting in his/her own personal funds; 2) removing legal liability from the individual and protecting his/her personal Assets; 3) securing various tax advantages. Incorporation may even provide the company with more credibility in the eyes of the business community and the general public.

What Is Capital Stock?

When a corporation receives its charter from the state, it also receives the right to sell a particular number of shares of stock to the public. Each share represents part ownership in the company. This number of shares the charter allows the corporation to sell is called the authorized shares. The corporation can sell as many shares as it chooses up to this authorized amount, but no more. When the stock is initially sold to the public, the corporation will receive the money. After the initial sale, when the stock is sold from one individual to another (on a stock market such as the New York Stock Exchange or the NASDAQ), this money does not affect the Assets of the corporation.

The shareholders are jointly the owners of a corporation and can legally receive a distribution of the Assets of the corporation in two ways. First, the corporation can play dividends. Second, the corporation can be liquidated—that is, all the Liabilities are paid off and the remaining Assets distributed to the shareholders, which means that the corporation ceases to operate.

Types of Capital Stock

Usually, two types of capital stock can be authorized by the state: common stock and preferred stock.

Figure 6.2: SOME CHARACTERISTICS OF COMMON STOCK AND PREFERRED STOCK

- Common stockholders have the right to vote for the directors of the corporation; preferred shareholders usually do not.

- Preferred shareholders have first claim to dividends; that is, in any year when dividends are declared by the board of directors, preferred shareholders must be allocated their share of the dividends before the common stockholders are entitled to any.

- The preferred shareholders have a fixed claim to dividends during any one year, whereas, the common shareholders' claims are not fixed.

- In the event the corporation is liquidated (that is, its Assets sold, Liabilities paid off, and the remaining cash distributed to the shareholders), the preferred shareholders' claim to the corporate Assets takes precedence over those of the common shareholders.

- Most preferred stock is cumulative. This means that if the preferred shareholders are not paid their full dividend in any year, in subsequent years dividend payments to the preferred shareholders must be sufficient to cover the previously inadequate dividend payments before any dividends can be paid to the common stockholders.

The common and preferred stock may or may not have a par value; par value is the value assigned to each share by a corporation in its corporate charter. If a stock has a par value, that value appears on the stock certificate (for example, $1 par or $5 par or $100 par, and so on). Stock rarely, if ever, is initially sold by a corporation for less than par value, either because state laws prevent such a sale or because the laws allow the creditors of the corporation to hold stockholders personally liable to the extent of any such discount.

In many states the total par value of all stock sold will be the corporation's legal capital. In some states, however, a corporation's legal capital is equal to the total amount received when the stock is initially sold. This can vary since par value stock is often sold for more than the par value figure. This legal capital amount is an important figure because a corporation may not issue dividends that would cause the net Assets (Assets-Liabilities) to go below the amount of this legal capital.

Alert!

Understanding Dividend Calculations: A 10 percent Common Stock with a par value of $100, should receive a $10 dividend each year. A 10 percent Preferred Stock with a par value of $100, should also receive a $10 dividend each year. But if only $6 is paid in dividends in year one, then the next year, the remaining $4 plus the $10 for year two must be paid to cumulative preferred stockholders before the common stockholders receive any further dividend.

When dividends on cumulative preferred stock are not paid, those dividends are said to be in arrears, and a footnote must be added to the financial statements indicating the amount of the dividends in arrears. The Balance Sheet will not show dividends in arrears as a Liability. Some preferred stock is non-cumulative, which means that if a year passes and the preferred stockholders do not receive a dividend, those shareholders never receive that dividend payment. The Common Stockholders will never receive the dividends that were missed in the past years.

Some preferred stock is participating preferred, which mean that the preferred shareholders' claim to dividends in any one year is not rigidly fixed. Those shareholders, in certain "good" years, will share with the common shareholders in the "excess" dividend payments. The amount or percentage of dividends that the preferred shareholders can receive in excess of the amount to which they have a prior claim varies considerably from company to company and is determined by the board of directors.

QUIZ

Assume that the Blanca Corporation has 10,000 shares of cumulative, participating, preferred stock outstanding. There are 20,000 shares of 10 percent Common Stock, and they will each receive $10 per share in dividends. This preferred stock is also 10 percent, with a $100 par value. The Preferred Stock participates at the 30 percent level, meaning that these stockholders will receive 30 percent of whatever excess dividends are left over after the initial dividends have been paid. The dividend declared by the board of directors this year is $500,000. How much in total do the preferred and common stockholders receive in dividends this year?

See page 94 for the answer.

The Stockholders' Equity Section of the Balance Sheet

As you recall from chapter 3, the Owner's Equity Section of the Balance Sheet contains two items, Owner's Investment and Retained Earnings. The only difference in the books of a corporation is that the Owner's Investment is replaced with Common Stock and Preferred

Stock and this section is called the Stockholders' Equity section in a privately-owned company. The reason for this is that the stockholders are the owners of the corporation.

Dividends and Splits

In general, a corporation cannot pay a dividend when such action would reduce the corporation's capital below its legal capital figure. Usually dividends can be paid, but only to the extent of the total Retained Earnings, i.e., the profit that has been retained in the business.

In addition, a corporation obviously cannot pay a cash dividend unless it has the cash to do so, and the cash is not needed for other purposes. Often, a corporation has sizable Retained Earnings as a result of successful operations in the past, but very little cash, which reduces its ability to pay dividends.

QUICK TIP

There are two goals of a corporation: 1) to maximize Net Income and 2) to satisfy the stockholders with the increase in their stock price or with the future expectation of a stock price increase. The act of issuing a cash dividend is a double-edged sword. On the one hand it will satisfy the immediate needs of the stockholders to receive cash, but on the other hand it will deplete cash in the company for future investment and growth. Therefore management needs to carefully adjust this balance to satisfy both the short- and long-term goals of the stockholders.

Dividends without Cash

Stock Dividends

Dividends can be divided into two categories, cash and stock. Companies often declare and issue stock dividends instead of cash dividends. Only when the board of directors declares dividends of any kind do they become legal liabilities of the corporation. Once the dividends are declared, the corporation is legally required to pay these dividends or issue the additional shares within a specified period of time. When stock dividends are issued, the corporation thus issues additional shares of stock in the corporation to each shareholder instead of cash.

There are several reasons why a corporation may issue stock dividends instead of cash. There may not be sufficient cash to pay a cash dividend, so rather than not issuing any dividends that year at all, the board may decide to issue the stock dividend instead. Another reason for issuing the stock dividend might be that the company needs the cash for other purposes. If, for instance, they are planning an expansion of operations to Brazil and need to accumulate cash in order to begin the new operation, they can issue stock dividends in order to keep sufficient levels of cash necessary for the expansion.

Alert!

Restrictions on Issuing Stock Dividends: In order for a corporation to issue stock dividends, it must have enough authorized stock that has not been issued. If it does not, the corporation will have to apply for the issuing of more stock from the Secretary of State in the state in which the corporation is incorporated.

Stock Splits

A company can also declare a stock split instead of issuing cash dividends. The stock split increases the number of shares outstanding and decreases the stock's par value. Stock may be split in a variety of ways—for example, two for one, three for one, three for two, and so on. (In a two for one stock split, each share becomes two shares. In a three for two stock split, every two shares becomes three shares. So, for example, a stockholder who held ten shares would have fifteen shares after the split.) Whether the company issues a stock dividend or a stock split, it must have the additional shares authorized by the state prior to the issue. If the company already has an amount of authorized shares that have not yet been issued, then this is unnecessary.

A company may split its stock for several reasons. One reason is that a stock split increases the number of shares on the market, which may mean that, in time, more people will own a part of the company. It is desirable to have more investors because it creates more interest in the company's stock, as well as in the company, which has the potential of driving up the stock price and getting more capital invested into the company as well. Another reason for a stock split is that increasing the number of shares reduces the price per share; thus, again, more people are able to buy the shares. Yet another reason is that many people would rather buy one hundred shares of $50 stock than fifty shares of $100 stock, even though the amount they would spend and the proportion of the company they would own would be the same. One reason for this decision is that the brokerage fee on round lots (one hundred shares or multiples thereof) is less than on odd lots (less than one hundred shares).

Incorporating Solana Beach Bicycle Company

Sale of Stock

Now Samantha has heard all of these definitions, and the prospect of getting more capital into her business is very interesting to her. By incorporating, she is able to expand her business without putting any more of her own money into it. She incorporates her business using close to the same name as before, so as not to confuse her current customers, and calls the business—The Solana Beach Bicycle Corporation.

When the new corporation sells stock, cash is increased (if the stock was sold for cash), and the common stock account is increased by the same amount. For example, when 120,000 shares of Common Stock with Par Value of $50 is sold for $60 per share cash, cash is increased $7,200,000, the common stock account increases $6,000,000 (120,000 shares x $50 par value), and another account called Paid-in Capital-Common (or Capital in Excess of Par) is increased by $1,200,000. This Capital in Excess of Par amount represents any amount paid into the corporation over and above the par value of the stock. This account is also part of Stockholders' Equity.

You may be wondering why the amount paid for the stock in the previous example is higher than the par value. Remember that the par value was simply a value assigned to each share of stock when the business was incorporated. By law in most states, the stock cannot be sold for below par, but can be sold for more than par value. The stock, when it is finally issued on the market, will almost always sell at above par, causing the account Paid-in Capital in Excess of Par to be created.

The impact on the Balance Sheet is shown in figure 6.3:

Figure 6.3: ASSETS AND STOCKHOLDERS' EQUITY CHANGES

Current Assets:	**Stockholders' Equity:**
Cash. . . . . . . +$7,200,000	Common Stock, $50 Par . . . . . .+$6,000,000
	Paid-in Capital in Excess of Par, Common. .+$1,200,000
	$7,200,000

When stock does not have a par value, but the Board of Directors has assigned a stated value to the no-par stock, the stock sale transaction is accounted for in a manner similar to that shown in the figure 6.3. The amount added to the common stock account equals the total stated value of the stock sold and any excess is added to the paid-in-capital account, now called Paid-in Capital in Excess of Stated Value, Common. The sale of preferred stock would cause the same changes as shown in the example, with the exception that the title of the accounts would be Preferred Stock and Paid-in Capital in Excess of Par, Preferred instead.

QUICK TIP

See Appendix B for more examples of the calculations discussed in this chapter.

When stock has neither a par value nor a stated value, the common stock account is increased by whatever amount is realized upon the sale of the stock. For example, if ten shares of no-par common stock sell for $100, the common stock and cash accounts are both increased by $100; if ten more shares are sold for $115 a few days later, the common stock account increases another $115, and so on.

Payment of Cash Dividends

When the board of directors declares cash dividends, the Retained Earnings figure is decreased and dividends payable, a Current Liability, is increased. For example if a corporation has 150,000 shares of common stock outstanding and the board of directors declares a $.20 dividend, the Retained Earnings would decrease by $30,000 and the dividends payable would increase by $30,000 (150,000 shares x $.20). The Balance Sheet changes are shown in figure 6.4. The Income Statement is not affected at all by this declaration.

Figure 6.4: **LIABILITIES AND STOCKHOLDERS' EQUITY CHANGES**

Current Liabilities:

Dividends Payable . . . . +$30,000

Stockholders' Equity:

Common Stock. XXX

Retained Earnings . . . .−$30,000

Total Liabilities and Stockholders' Equity . . . . No Change

---

When the dividend is actually paid, cash is decreased and dividends payable is decreased. Continuing the preceding example, when the dividend is paid, cash would decrease $30,000 and the Liability called "dividends payable" would be eliminated from the Balance Sheet.

Financial statements are affected in the same manner when cash dividends are declared and paid to preferred shareholders.

Stock Dividends Declared and Issued

Assume the Solana Beach Bicycle Corporation's Stockholders' Equity section looked like the one in figure 6.5 after the corporation has been in operation for a while:

Figure 6.5: STOCKHOLDERS' EQUITY BEFORE SMALL STOCK DIVIDEND DECLARED

Stockholders' Equity:

Common Stock, $50 Par	$10,000,000
Paid-in Capital in Excess of Par, Common	3,500,000
	$13,500,000
Retained Earnings	10,000,000
Total Stockholders' Equity.	$23,500,000

The corporation declared and issued a 10 percent stock dividend when its stock was selling on the market for $200 per share. We can tell from the Stockholders' Equity section that the corporation had two hundred thousand shares of common stock outstanding prior to the stock dividend ($10,000,000 common stock/$50 par = 200,000 shares). A 10 percent stock dividend will increase the number of shares by 20,000 (10 percent of 200,000 = 20,000). Since the market price of each share is $200, the Retained Earnings account is decreased by $4,000,000 (20,000 shares x $200 = $4,000,000), the common stock account is increased by $1,000,000 (20,000 shares x $50 Par = $1,000,000), and the paid-in capital account is increased by the difference, which is $3,000,000.

Figure 6.6: IMPACT OF STOCK DIVIDEND ON STOCKHOLDERS' EQUITY

Balance Sheet Changes

Stockholders' Equity:

Common Stock.	+$1,000,000
Paid-in Capital in Excess of Par, Common.	+$3,000,000
Retained Earnings	−$4,000,000
Total Liabilities and Stockholder's Equity	No Change

Alert!

Stock Dividends and Retained Earnings: Issuing stock dividends affects the corporation's Retained Earnings in exactly the same way as if it were a cash dividend. The only difference is that additional stock is being distributed to the stockholders instead of cash. Since it has the same impact on Retained Earnings, however, the corporation must still have sufficient Retained Earnings to make this declaration.

The equity section of the Balance Sheet appears as shown in figure 6.7, after the stock dividend:

Figure 6.7: STOCKHOLDERS' EQUITY AFTER SMALL STOCK DIVIDEND DECLARED

Stockholders' Equity:

Common Stock, $50 Par $11,000,000

Paid-in Capital in Excess of Par, Common 6,500,000

$17,500,000

Retained Earnings 6,000,000

Total Stockholders' Equity. $23,500,000

Notice that the total Stockholders' Equity ($23,500,000) does not change. Furthermore, neither the Assets nor the Liabilities of the corporation are affected by a stock dividend nor are the income or Expense items.

The accounting for a stock dividend is somewhat different whenever the dividend is greater than 20 percent to 25 percent of the shares previously outstanding.

Whenever such large stock dividends are issued, the market value of the stock is not relevant in determining the change in the Balance Sheet figures. Instead, the Retained Earnings are reduced by the par value of the new shares.

Had Solana Beach Bicycle Corporation in the example shown in figure 6.7 declared and issued a 50 percent instead of a 10 percent stock dividend, for example, the Balance Sheet would have been changed to look like the example in figure 6.8. Since there are 200,000 shares outstanding in figure 6.5, a 50 percent stock dividend would entail the issuing of an additional 100,000 shares. (There would be no change to the Paid-in Capital in Excess of Par, Common amount from figure 6.5.)

Figure 6.8: IMPACT OF LARGE STOCK DIVIDEND DECLARATION ON STOCKHOLDERS' EQUITY

Stockholders' Equity:

Common Stock, $50 Par	$15,000,000
Paid-in Capital in Excess of Par, Common	3,500,000
	$18,500,000
Retained Earnings	5,000,000
Total Stockholders' Equity.	$23,500,000

Notice that Total Stockholders' Equity does not change from figure 6.5 because all we have done is shift dollars out of Retained Earnings into Common Stock.

Now assume that the board of directors of the Solana Beach Bicycle Corporation declared a two-for-one stock split instead of a 50 percent stock dividend. Four hundred thousand shares (remember, there were two hundred thousand shares outstanding) of new $25 par stock would have been sent to the shareholders and the old $50 par stock would have been called in so that only the $25 stocks are held by shareholders. The Stockholders' Equity section of the Balance Sheet would now look like figure 6.9:

Figure 6.9: IMPACT OF STOCK SPLIT ON STOCKHOLDERS' EQUITY

Stockholders' Equity:

Common Stock, $25 Par	$10,000,000
Paid-in Capital in Excess of Par, Common	3,500,000
	$13,500,000
Retained Earnings	10,000,000
Total Stockholders' Equity	$23,500,000

Notice that there are no differences in this partial Balance Sheet and the one shown in figure 7.5 (before the stock split) except that the par value has changed from $50 to $25 and the number of shares outstanding has changed from 200,000 to 400,000.

What Is Treasury Stock?

When a corporation buys back its own stock and does not cancel it or resell it, it is known as treasury stock. A corporation may buy its own stock for a variety of reasons. For example, it may need the stock to distribute for stock dividends or to satisfy a stock option contract with its employees.

Purchase of Treasury Stock

To begin operation Solana Beach Bicycle Corporation sold one hundred thousand shares of $50 par stock for $60 each on July 1, 2010, the day Solana Beach Bicycle began doing business as a corporation. Two years later, it bought back ten thousand shares of its own stock for $700,000 (notice that the price of the stock has increased from the original sale price of $60 to $70). Until this stock is legally canceled or resold, it is known as treasury stock.

Before the Solana Beach Bicycle Corporation acquired its own stock, its Stockholders' Equity section of the Balance Sheet looked like figure 6.10:

Figure 6.10: STOCKHOLDERS' EQUITY BEFORE TREASURY STOCK PURCHASE

Stockholders' Equity:

Common Stock, $50 Par (120,000 shares) $6,000,000

Paid-in Capital in Excess of Par, Common 1,200,000

$7,200,000

Retained Earnings 10,000,000

Total Stockholders' Equity $17,200,000

After the Solana Beach Bicycle Corporation acquired ten thousand shares of its own stock, its Stockholders' Equity section of the Balance Sheet looked like figure 6.11:

Figure 6.11: STOCKHOLDERS' EQUITY AFTER TREASURY STOCK PURCHASE

Note: Parentheses indicate decreases in cash

Stockholders' Equity:

Common Stock, $50 Par

(10,000 Shares of which are Treasury Stock) $6,000,000

Paid-in Capital, Common 1,200,000

$7,200,000

Retained Earnings (See Footnote 1) 10,000,000

$17,200,000

Less: Cost of Treasury Stock . . . . (700,000)

Total Stockholders' Equity $16,500,000

The following footnote would be included below the Balance Sheet of the current year:

Footnote 1: Although the Retained Earnings totals $10,000,000, the acquisition of treasury stock has reduced the Retained Earnings available for dividends by $700,000, the cost of the treasury stock; thus, the Solana Beach Bicycle Corporation may legally declare and pay dividends of not more than $9,300,000 ($10,000,000 Retained Earnings – $700,000 Treasury Stock).

You should be aware of several changes caused by the purchase of the treasury stock:

- The total Stockholders' Equity has decreased from $17,200,000 to $16,500,000. The Balance Sheet is still in balance because cash has decreased by the same amount $700,000 (the amount of cash paid for the purchase of the treasury stock).
- A treasury stock purchase reduces the Retained Earnings of a company and as a result reduces the amount of dividends the corporation can pay. A corporation usually cannot buy treasury stock unless its Retained Earnings is equal to or exceeds the cost of the treasury stock. This restriction is necessary to prevent a corporation from reducing its capital below its required legal capital figure.
- The Balance Sheet would not be complete without some notation in the Stockholders' Equity section of the statement regarding the reduction of Retained Earnings due to treasury stock, as is accomplished by the footnote in figure 6.11 on the previous page.
- The number of shares of common stock now outstanding is 110,000 shares (the number of shares *issued* has not changed from the original 120,000).

Alert!

Treasury Stock Is NOT an Asset: The purchase of the stock by the corporation merely reduces the amount that the owners have invested in the business.

If cash dividends were declared today, they would be paid only to the owners of the 110,000 shares; the corporation would not pay dividends to itself on the ten thousand shares of treasury stock. Dividends are paid only on outstanding stock, and treasury stock is not considered to be outstanding. Each corporation is authorized to issue a maximum number of shares as specified in the corporate charter. The number of shares authorized can be greater than or equal to the number of shares issued, but a corporation can issue no more shares than authorized. Most firms show the number of shares authorized, issued, and outstanding, in the Stockholders' Equity section of the Balance Sheet.

Notice in Figure 6.11 that the number of shares issued and authorized has not changed since the purchase of the treasury stock. The only change is to the number of shares outstanding. Even though the treasury stock is no longer outstanding, those shares are considered to still be part of the issued shares of the corporation.

Selling the Treasury Stock

The company can hold, sell, or cancel its treasury stock. If the Solana Beach Bicycle Corporation sold four thousand shares of its treasury stock for $80 per share, its cash would increase by $320,000. Further, its Treasury Stock account would decrease by $280,000, which is equal to the four thousand shares being sold times its original cost of $70 per share. The difference between the $320,000 and $280,000 (or $40,000) represents an increase in Paid-in Capital In Excess of Par, Treasury. This is also a Stockholders' Equity account, thus we increase Stockholders' Equity by the same amount as cash increases.

After the sale of the four thousand shares of treasury stock, the Stockholders' Equity section would look like figure 6.12:

Figure 6.12

Note: Parentheses indicate decreases in cash

Stockholders' Equity:

Common Stock, $50 Par (6,000 shares of which are Treasury Stock)

Authorized 500,000 Shares

Issued 120,000 Shares

Outstanding 114,000 Shares. $6,000,000

Paid-in Capital in Excess of Par, Common 1,200,000

Paid-in Capital in Excess of Cost, Treasury. 40,000

$7,240,000

Retained Earnings (See Footnote 1). 10,000,000

$17,240,000

Less: Cost of Treasury Stock . . . . (420,000)

Total Stockholders' Equity. $16,820,000

You should be aware of several changes caused by the sale of the treasury stock:

- The total Stockholders' Equity increased (from figure 6.12) by $320,000—the amount of cash received for the sale of the treasury stock.
- The Treasury Stock account decreased by only $280,000, the amount the four thousand shares had cost the company when they were purchased: 4,000 shares x $70 per share. (Remember, the company bought these shares at the market rate of $70 per share.)
- The sale of Treasury Stock for more than it cost (bought at $70 per share and sold for $80 per share, so the original cost to the corporation was $280,000 while the sales price was $320,000) did not result in a profit of $40,000. The rules of accounting do not allow a corporation to make a profit on the sale of its own stock. The Income Statement is not affected by the transaction; the Retained

Earnings do not change; and the $40,000 simply creates a new Balance Sheet account that is called Paid-In Capital in excess of Cost, Treasury. This account is somewhat like the Paid-in Capital, Common account that results when stock is initially sold for more than its par value.

Alert!

When treasury stock is sold for less than it cost, the Paid-In Capital, Treasury account is reduced. If this account does not exist or if the account is not large enough to absorb the difference between the sales prices and the cost of the treasury stock, the Paid-In Capital in Excess of Par, Common is reduced. If this account is not sufficient, Retained Earnings is reduced.

In this chapter you have learned about how the financial statements in a corporation differ from those of a proprietorship. You have also learned about the corporate structure and how individual transactions affect the financial statements of a corporation. In chapter 7 you will learn about the double-entry system of accounting and how transactions are recorded in the accounting records.

ANSWER

Preferred Stock	**Common Stock**
10,000 Shares x $10 = $100,000	20,000 Shares x $10 = $200,000

Remainder to be divided =
$500,000 – $100,000 – $200,000 = $200,000

30 percent of Remainder = $60,000	70 percent of Remainder = $140,000
Total for P.S. = $160,000	Total for C.S. = $340,000

GLOSSARY

Arrears: The amount of money that has not been paid on cumulative preferred stock. Since the stock is cumulative, in most cases, the dividends for common stock and other non-cumulative preferred stock may not be paid until the dividends in arrears have been paid.

Authorized Shares: The number of shares a state allows a corporation to issue to the public when the company is incorporated. If a corporation needs or wants to issue more stock than authorized in order to raise more capital, it must request the authorization of additional shares.

Capital Stock: A term used to refer to both the Common and Preferred Stock of a corporation, which the company is initially authorized to issue when it receives its incorporation charter.

Cash Dividends: Dividends declared by the board of directors and paid in cash to stockholders. These become a Liability on the corporation's Balance Sheet when they are declared by the Board of Directors. The corporation must have sufficient Retained Earnings and cash to make this declaration. After the declaration, once dividends are paid, cash and Retained Earnings are reduced.

Common Stock: One of the two types of stock that a corporation can issue to the public when it is chartered by the state. Common stock usually does not have a defined dividend amount per year, but only receives dividends when they are declared by the board of directors. Common stockholders usually have voting rights to elect the board of directors.

Corporation: An incorporated business is "an artificial being" independent from its owners. It is a legal separate entity. A company will request permission to exist from the secretary of state of any state. Once it has been granted the charter to operate, it may sell stock in order to raise capital.

Cumulative Preferred Stock: When holders of this type of stock are not paid a full dividend in any year (usually this dividend amount will be stated on the share of stock), then subsequent years' dividend payments to them must be sufficient to cover the current year as well as the amount that was not paid in any previous years, before any dividends can be paid to the common stockholders. (See also Preferred Stock.)

Legal Capital: In many states, this is the total par value of all stock sold. In some states, however, a corporation's legal capital is equal to the total amount of money received when the stock is initially sold.

Thus, in this second case, the legal capital would be equal to the par value and the paid in capital in excess of par.

Paid-in Capital in Excess of Par: The amount of money received by a corporation from the sale of stock above the par value. In some states, it is both the par value and the paid in capital in excess of par that represents the legal capital of the corporation.

Participating Preferred Stock: Preferred stockholders, in certain "good" years, will share with the common shareholders in the "excess" dividend payments. For example, after the preferred stockholders receive their 10 percent dividend, and the common stockholders receive their declared amount of dividend, if there is money left in total declaration for the year, the common and the preferred will share in that amount. If preferred stock is not participating, the total remaining amount will go to the common stockholders. (See also Preferred Stock.)

Par Value: The value assigned by a corporation to each share of stock, common or preferred, when it is incorporated. In most states, the common stock cannot be sold at below par. Generally, stock sells for more than the par value rather than at the par value itself.

Preferred Stock: One of the two types of stock that a corporation can issue upon receiving its charter from the state. This type of stock has preference over the Common Stockholders for when dividends are issued and also will receive its money back from the corporation first if there is a liquidation. (See also Cumulative Preferred Stock and Participating Preferred Stock.)

Stock Dividends: Dividends declared by the board of directors and issued to the stockholders in the form of additional shares of stock rather than cash. The corporation must have sufficient Retained Earnings and authorized stock to make this declaration.

Stock Split: A stock split is declared by the board of directors to split the number of shares that a stockholder currently holds. These splits can be for two for one, three for one, etc. The corporation must have a sufficient number of authorized shares to make the split. Often, stock splits are declared by the board of directors when the price of the stock is very high and the corporation wants to encourage more stockholders in the corporation by lowering the price of each share.

Treasury Stock: The corporation's own stock that it holds when it buys shares back from existing stockholders. This stock remains on the books of the issuing corporation until it cancels the stock or resells the shares back to the public. Treasury stock appears on the Balance Sheet as a reduction of Retained Earnings.

Chapter 7

Double-Entry Accounting

- ▶ The General Journal
- ▶ The General Ledger
- ▶ Adjusting Journal Entries
- ▶ Closing Journal Entries

The terms "debit" and "credit" are enough to induce fear in even the most intrepid non-accountant. But even though you may never become an accountant, you will need to understand these concepts in order to have a solid grasp of accounting and business. In this chapter you'll learn what these terms mean and how they are used in the world of accounting.

What Is a Debit?: The word debit simply refers to the left side of the amount columns and the word credit identifies the right side of the amount columns. Nothing more, nothing less. Debit does not mean something unfavorable and credit does not mean something favorable, as some non-accountants often believe.

The General Journal

Some time after a business transaction occurs it is recorded in a book called the general journal. While there are many different kinds of journals, it is most important to focus on the general journal. A general journal is often referred to as the book of original entry because this journal is the book in which a transaction is first recorded.

If a company were to buy land for cash, the pages of a general journal will look like the one shown in figure 7.1 (the entries in this figure do not come from Solana Beach Bicycle Company but are simply examples):

Figure 7.1:
JOURNAL

Date	Entries	Reference	Amounts Debits	Credits
01/05/10	Land		$10,000	
	Cash			$10,000
(Bought Land for cash for new warehouse)				
01/31/10	Salary Expense		$400	
	Cash			$400
(Paid Salary for the month of January with cash)				

Journal Entries

To illustrate how transactions are recorded in the general journal, you can use the transactions described in chapters 3 and 4. But first let's go back to the Accounting Equation we talked about in chapter 1.

$$A = L + OE$$

The standard accounting rule is that Assets, or the left side of the equation, are increased with debits, and decreased with credits, while the right side of the equation, the Liabilities and the Owner's Equity items are just the opposite; that is, they are increased with credits, and decreased with debits. When you increase or decrease the debits by the same amount as you increase or decrease the credits on each transaction, you make sure that the debits always equal the credits, a key goal of bookkeeping. If the debits do not equal the credits at the end of the period (month, quarter, or year), it indicates that a mistake was made somewhere along the line and one of the transactions was entered improperly. By using this system, the Accounting Equation always stays in balance after each transaction is recorded, since you are increasing or decreasing both sides of the equation by equal amounts. There is a standard way of dealing with debits and credits assigned to Assets, Liabilities, Owner's Equity, Revenues, and Expenses. Figure 7.2 summarizes this concept:

Figure 7.2:
INCREASES/DECREASES IN ACCOUNTS

Transaction	Journal Entry
Assets Increase	Debit
Assets Decrease	Credit
Liabilities Increase	Credit
Liabilities Decrease	Debit
Revenue (OE Increases)	Credit
Expense (OE Decreases)	Debit

Now let's record in the general journal some of the transactions of the previous chapters. It is important to remember that every single transaction in the journal must be recorded as both a debit and a credit. First, Sam invested $60,000 in her bicycle company. This transaction would be recorded as shown in figure 7.3:

Figure 7.3:
JOURNAL

Date	Entries	Reference	Debits	Credits
			Amounts	
2010				
Jan 1	Cash		$60,000	
	Owner's Investment			$60,000
	(Owner Invests $60,000 in Cash)			

You already know that whenever the owner of a business invests cash into his or her business, cash is increased and so is the Owner's Investment (part of Owner's Equity). If cash (an Asset) increases, this is shown as a debit in the journal; the increase in Owner's Equity is listed as a credit. (See figure 7.2.)

In the next transaction, the company buys a building, land, and a truck for $43,000. Since the bicycle shop does not have sufficient cash to pay for all of these Assets, the owner needs to borrow $20,000 and pays the remainder in cash ($23,000). This transaction would be recorded in the general journal as shown in figure 7.4:

Figure 7.4:
JOURNAL

Date	Entries	Reference	Amounts Debits	Credits
2010				
Jan 3	Truck		$8,000	
	Building		$25,000	
	Land		$10,000	
	Cash			$23,000
	Mortgage Payable			$20,000
			(Purchase of Assets for Cash and Mortgage)	

Notice in the journal entry that **debits** were used to increase the Assets (land, building, and truck), while **credits** were used to decrease Assets (cash), but to increase the Liability Mortgage Payable. Thus, depending upon which side of the accounting equation the account appears, this will determine if it is recorded as a debit or a credit (see figure 7.2).

Now we'll move on to the transactions from chapter 4, which were recorded on the Income Statement.

On January 5 the bicycle company sold two bicycles for a total of $500. As you remember, this one transaction caused two changes to the Income Statement. First it increased the Revenue account called "Sales" by $500, and second it increased an Expense account called "Cost of Goods Sold" by the cost of these two bicycles or $200. Remember also that at the same time that this transaction causes a change to the Income Statement, it also causes the Balance Sheet to change in several ways. These bicycles were sold for cash; thus, the Asset cash would increase by $500. The Asset Inventory would decrease by their cost, $200 (since the bicycles (Inventory) do not belong to the company any longer). The $300 difference between the sale price and the cost ($500 – $200) would be an increase to Retained Earnings, which is part of Owner's Equity.

Notice in the transaction in figure 7.5 that there is no entry for Retained Earnings or Owner's Equity. The "profit" from this transaction of $300 simply appears in the Balance Sheet (as Retained Earnings) when the Revenue ($500) and the Expense ($200) are recorded.

These two transactions would be recorded in the general journal as seen in figure 7.5:

Figure 7.5:
JOURNAL

			Amounts	
Date	Entries	Reference	Debits	Credits
2010				
5 Jan	Cash		$500	
	Sales			$500

Also:

5 Jan	Cost of Goods Sold		$200	
	Inventory			$200
	(Sold Bicycles)			

Referring back to the Accounting Equation, A = L + OE, the sales transaction has increased the left side (the Asset Cash) by $500, and increased the right side (Owner's Equity) by the same amount. The second part of this transaction that reduces the Inventory also keeps the accounting equation in balance, the Expense of the bikes (the debit), and the decrease in Inventory (the credit). In both of these transactions, the debits to record these transactions are equal to the credits.

Looking at another transaction in chapter 4, Operating Expenses, you can see the impact on the General Journal. On January 7 Solana Beach Bicycle Company pays Sam her first week's pay of $100. This transaction would be recorded in the General Journal as shown in figure 7.6:

Figure 7.6:

JOURNAL

			Amounts	
Date	Entries	Reference	Debits	Credits
2010				
7 Jan	Salary Expense		$100	
	Cash			$100
	(Paid Salaries)			

This transaction has decreased the left side of the accounting equation, Assets or Cash, by $100, and has also decreased the right side, Owner's Equity, with an Expense by the same amount. Once again, the debits equal the credits.

Finally look at one more transaction from chapter 4, where Solana Beach Bicycle Company repairs some bicycles for $375. The parts for these repairs cost the company $105, paid for in cash. This transaction is recorded in the General Journal as follows in figure 7.7:

Figure 7.7:

JOURNAL

Date	Entries	Reference	Debits	Credits
2010				
14 Feb	Cash		$375	
	Repairs Revenue			$375

Also:

14 Feb	Repairs Expense		$105	
	Cash			$105
	(Performed Repairs)			

Once again, notice that in the first part of this transaction, the left side of the accounting equation is increased by $375, and the right side, Owner's Equity (via a Revenue item), is increased by the same amount.

In the second part of the transaction, the right side is decreased with a credit to an Asset (cash) by $105, and the left side is decreased with a debit to an Owner's Equity account (Repairs Expense). Thus the equation (A = L + OE) stays in balance, and the debits equal the credits.

The General Ledger

During the month, the journal entries made to record the January transactions would be posted from the general journal to the general ledger. The general ledger is a book containing a record of each account. (See boxed section below figure 7.8.) Posting is simply the process of transferring the information from the general journal to the individual account pages in the general ledger. The cash account, which probably is the first page (or pages) in the general ledger, would look like the example in figure 7.8:

Figure 7.8

| | | | **CASH** | | | | **Account #101** |

Date	Comments	Ref.	Debit Amount	Date	Comments	Ref.	Credit Amount

Notice that the account has two sides. As before, the left side is used to record the debits and the right side is used to record the credits.

Notice that the sample ledger account in figure 7.8 lists an account number, 101, in the upper right hand corner. Every Asset, Liability, Owner's Equity, Revenue, and Expense item has a number assigned to it. Usually, the Assets are the 100s; the Liabilities, the 200s; the Owner's Equity, the 300s; the Revenues, the 400s; and the Expenses, the 500s. In the ledger each item (or account) has a separate page with a separate number. In this case, cash has been assigned the number 101, and all cash transactions are recorded on this page.

The accounts are usually numbered for a variety of reasons; for example, to facilitate referencing or for use instead of the account name. This listing of accounts is normally called the chart of accounts.

After posting the first journal entry (January 1), the cash account would look like figure 7.9:

Figure 7.9

| | | | **CASH** | | | | **Account #101** |

Date	Comments	Ref.	Debit Amount	Date	Comments	Ref.	Credit Amount
Jan 1		J-1	$60,000				

The date of the transaction is entered in the date column on the left-hand side since the entry was a debit. J-1 is entered in the reference column and that tells you that the journal entry that recorded the transaction can be found on page one of the general journal. Sixty thousand dollars is entered in the left-hand amount column.

The other half to this first journal entry (the credit) would be posted to the Owner's Investment account and would be recorded as shown in figure 7.10:

	Figure 7.10						
OWNER'S INVESTMENT						**Account #301**	
			Debit				Credit
Date	Comments	Ref.	Amount	Date	Comments	Ref.	Amount
Jan 1		J-1					$60,000

Of course, in this instance the data is posted to the right-hand column since the entry is a credit to the account.

Now after posting the first entry, the general journal would appear as shown in figure 7.11:

Figure 7.11: TO RECORD $60,000 INVESTMENT BY OWNER

	JOURNAL			Page 1
Date	Entries	Ref.	Amounts	
			Debits	Credits
2010				
Jan 1	Cash	101	$60,000	
	Owner's Equity	301		$60,000

You see that the account numbers for the cash and Owner's Investment accounts have now been entered in the reference column of the journal. This step completes the posting process for the first journal entry. The same procedure is repeated until all the journal entries have been posted to the general ledger.

After posting all the journal entries recorded in January, the cash account would look like figure 7.12:

Figure 7.12

		Cash				**Account #101**	
Date	Comments	Ref.	Debit Amount	Date	Comments	Ref.	Credit Amount
Jan 1	Investment	J-1	$60,000	Jan 1	Assets	J-1	$23,000
				Jan 3	Insurance	J-1	$1,500
				Jan 5	Inventory	J-1	$10,000
Jan 6	Sales	J-1	$500	Jan 7	Salary	J-1	$100
Jan 21	Sales	J-1	$3,500				
	Total		$54,000		Total		$34,600

If you add the debit and credit sides of the cash account, you will find that the debits total $54,000 and the credits total $34,600. The difference between these two figures is $19,400. You could say that the cash account has a debit balance at the end of January. Remember, in order to increase an Asset, we record a debit. If at the end of the period there is a debit balance in an Asset account, that means that there is a positive balance, or in this case with cash, "money in the bank." Debits and credits will generally not be equal for each individual account, but once all the accounts are considered together, the debits and credits should be equal. This is reflected on the trial balance for the cash account before adjustments. A discussion of the trial balance follows.

Trial Balance

Typically, accountants and bookkeepers will prepare a trial balance from the general ledger after all transactions have been recorded and posted. A trial balance is merely a list of all accounts in the general ledger that have a balance other than zero, with the balance in each account shown and the debits and credits totaled. A trial balance of Solana Beach Bicycle Company at January 31, 2010, would look like the one in figure 7.13:

Figure 7.13: SOLANA BEACH BICYCLE COMPANY

Trial Balance
(Before Adjusting & Closing Entries)
January 31, 2010

	Debits	Credits
Cash	$19,400	
Accounts receivable	1,500	
Inventory	20,800	
Prepaid Insurance	1,500	
Truck	8,000	
Building	25,000	
Land	10,000	
Accounts Payable		$3,000
Mortgage Payable (Long-Term)		20,000
Owner's Investment		60,000
Retained Earnings		-0-
Sales		5,500
Repair Revenue		-0-
Cost of Goods Sold	2,200	
Expenses (Salary)	100	
	$88,500	$88,500

A trial balance is prepared by first turning through the pages of the general ledger and locating each account with a balance other than zero, as in figure 7.12 where the cash account had a debit balance of $19,400. Once it is determined what the balance in each account is, this is noted on the trial Balance Sheet. Generally speaking the trial balance is prepared for two reasons. The first reason is to determine whether the total debits equal the total credits. If they are not equal, some kind of error has been made either in the recording of the journal entries or in the posting of the general ledger. In either case the error must be located and corrected. The second reason is to facilitate the preparation of adjusting entries (discussed in the next section), which are necessary before the financial statements can be prepared.

You should note that if Solana Beach Bicycle Company had been in operation prior to this year, a Retained Earnings figure would appear on the present trial balance. The Retained Earnings account will show the beginning Retained Earnings until the accountant closes the accounts that affect the Retained Earnings by the amount of the profit or loss for the period (month, quarter, or year). For more information on closing accounts, see Closing Journal Entries, page 115.

Adjusting Journal Entries

Accounting records are not kept up to date at all times. To do so would be a waste of time, effort, and money because much of the information is not needed for day-to-day decisions. Adjusting entries is a step taken to recognize financial events that have occurred prior to the financial statements' issuance date which have not been recorded in the journal. These are not transactions with a particular date attached, but they are financial realities that require documentation in order to maintain accurate records. In the case of the Solana Beach Bicycle Company, there are five items that need to be adjusted at the end of each month: Accumulated Depreciation on the building and on the truck, Prepaid Insurance, Interest on the mortgage, and the portion of Account Receivable that the company does not believe it will ever be able to collect (bad debts). After the adjusted journal entries are recorded in the journal, they must be posted to the accounts in the general ledger, just like the earlier journal entries.

Prepaid Insurance

Remember, in chapter 3, Prepaid Insurance is listed on the Balance Sheet as an Asset. This came about because Solana Beach Bicycle Company bought insurance in advance of using it. By the end of January, one thirty-sixth of the three-year policy had been used up and became an Expense. To recognize the "using up" of this Asset (called Prepaid Insurance), an Expense called Insurance Expense is increased by $41.67 ($1,500/36 months). The Asset itself is no longer worth the full amount paid, since it now only represents the remaining thirty-five months. If you think back to the accounting equation again (A = L + OE), the left-hand side of the equation is reduced by $41.67 (because the Asset called Prepaid Insurance has decreased), and the right side is also reduced by the same amount because of insurance Expense (which causes a reduction in Owner's Equity). An adjustment for this amount will be made in the journal.

Depreciation Expense

Long-Term Assets like the building and truck have a finite life. Their original (historical) cost is therefore spread over their useful lives. This process is called depreciation. In order to depreciate these two Assets, you need to know what the life expectancy of each is; that is, how long these Assets will produce income for the business. In our example, you can assume that the building has a life expectancy of twenty-five years, and the truck of five years. To depreciate these two Assets, you can divide the historical cost by the life expectancy.

Truck:
$8,000 (historical cost)/5 years (life expectancy) = $1,600 Depreciation per year

Building:
$25,000 (historical cost)/25 years (life expectancy) = $1,000 Depreciation per year

Since you are only looking for the depreciation adjustment for these two Assets for the month of January, each number would be divided by twelve (months) to arrive at depreciation adjustment for the month of January.

Truck = $1,600 (depreciation per year)/12 (months per year) = $133.33
per month

Building = $1,000 (depreciation per year)/12 (months per year) $33.33
per month

QUICK Tip

The Life Expectancy of an Asset: One of the assumptions you as the owner of a business need to make is what the life expectancies of Long-Term Assets are. How should you do this? The easiest way is to estimate based on your experience of similar Assets used in the business in the past. You can also get information from the library on what averages are used for similar Assets in your industry. Finally, the IRS has a schedule of Long-Term Assets, with life expectancy figures that they will accept. The final decision is yours, and if it is reasonable, it is acceptable.

Interest Expense

As you remember, Solana Beach Bicycle Company has to pay interest on the mortgage that it took out on the land and building. The mortgage was for $20,000 for ten years at 8 percent per year. The total interest per year is $1,600 ($20,000 x 8 percent). Therefore each month the business owes the mortgage company one-twelfth of the year's total interest or $133.33 ($1,600/12 months). Since the cash is not owed until the end of the year, Solana Beach Bicycle Company has created another Liability called Interest Payable that is due at the end of the year. The amount of this Liability is the same as the Interest Expense of $133.33 for the month of January.

Accounts Receivable Write-Offs

At the end of January, the company assumed that it was not going to be able to collect $50 from some of the customers that had promised to pay. (This was a guesstimate or assumption, since the company will not know until next month who is going to pay and who is not.) In order to recognize this assumption on the financial statements, Sam created an Expense category called Bad Debts Expense. The other half of this entry is to increase an account called "Allowance for Doubtful Accounts." This account is called a "contra-Asset"; it is a reduction to Accounts Receivable that factors in the expectation that certain Accounts Receivable will not be paid and keeps the Balance Sheet in balance. You should note that even though the Bad Debt Expense does not use cash, it reduces the Net Income in the same way as other Expenses that do use cash. In the case of Bad Debt Expense, the Asset reduced is Accounts Receivable (rather than cash).

QUICK Tip

Estimating Bad Debts: Like depreciation, the management of the company must estimate bad debts for the period. This estimation can be done based on past experience that a certain percent of receivables cannot be collected. It is also possible that management has specific information on particular accounts that will not be collected and can incorporate this data into the adjustments.

QUIZ

How would you "journalize" the following transactions?

1. January 1: Brad invests $100,000 into his new book publishing business.

2. January 3: Brad buys a delivery truck for $20,000. He gives the car dealership $15,000 and takes out a 2-year loan at 6 percent interest per year for the balance.

3. January 3: Brad rents space in a warehouse to do his printing. Beginning in January, the rent is $1200 per month and is due at the beginning of the month. Brad pays for this in cash.

4. January 10: Brad buys a printing press for $6,000. He makes a cash payment of $4,000, and takes out a long-term 8 percent loan for $2,000. He also buys supplies for $3,000 (with a cash payment of $1,000 and a short-term loan of $2,000). Hint: these are two separate entries.

5. January 15: Finally, Brad pays his two employees their first half of the month's salary. He pays $3,000 total for the two of them, half of the amount will be paid in cash today, and the other half will be paid in two days.

See page 120 for answers.

Trial Balance After Adjustments

After the adjusting entries are posted to the journal, the accountant may prepare another trial balance to help in the preparation of the actual financial statements, or the accountant may be able to prepare the statements by using the general ledger only. A trial balance prepared at the end of January 2010 would look like figure 7.14:

Figure 7.14: SOLANA BEACH BICYCLE COMPANY

Trial Balance
(After Adjustments, Before Closing)
January 31, 2010

	Debits	Credits
Cash	$29,400.00	
Accounts Receivable	1,500.00	
Allowance for Doubtful Accounts	(50.00)	
Inventory	10,800.00	
Prepaid Insurance	1,458.33	
Land	10,000.00	
Building	25,000.00	
Accumulated Depreciation-Building	(33.33)	
Truck	8,000.00	
Accumulated Depreciation-Truck	(133.33)	
Accounts Payable		$3,000.00
Interest Payable		133.33
Mortgage Payable (Long-Term)		20,000.00

Owner's Investment		60,000.00
Retained Earnings		-0-
Sales	5,500.00	
Repair Revenue	-0-	
Cost of Goods Sold	2,200.00	
Salaries Expenses	100.00	
Insurance Expense	41.67	
Depreciation Expense	166.66	
Interest Expense	133.33	
Bad Debt Expense	50.00	
	$88,633.33	$88,633.33

There are some differences between this trial balance and the one on page 108, which shows the trial balance before the adjusting journal entries. First, four new accounts have been created: Insurance Expense, Depreciation Expense, Accumulated Depreciation, and Interest Expense.

The account called Insurance Expense represents the amount of the used up Prepaid Insurance for one month. It was increased by $41.67 at the same time that Prepaid Insurance (the Asset) was decreased by the same amount.

The Depreciation Expense account was created to represent the depreciation on the two Long-Term Assets, truck, and building. Instead of reducing the Long-Term Assets directly as they get older, accountants set up another separate contra-Asset account. This, like the one previously discussed for Allowance for Doubtful Accounts, was a reduction to Accounts Receivable. For Long-Term Assets the contra account is called Accumulated Depreciation. Each Long-Term Asset has a separate contra-Asset account. (Accumulated Depreciation-Truck and Accumulated Depreciation-Building.) On the Balance Sheet, the contra-Assets would appear like those shown in figure 7.15:

Figure 7.15: **PARTIAL BALANCE SHEET**	
Current Assets:	
Accounts Receivable	$1,500
Less: Allowance for Doubtful Accounts	(50)
Net Accounts Receivable	$1,450
Long-Term Assets:	
Truck	$8,000
Less: Accumulated Depreciation—Truck	(133)
Net Truck	$7,866.67

Land, even though it is a Long-Term Asset, does not depreciate and does not have an accumulated depreciation contra-Asset account.

The last new account is Interest Expense. This account represents the amount of interest that has been paid. In our example, this is $133.33 per month on the Mortgage.

Closing Journal Entries

In general, accounting records are closed at the end of the year. After the closing journal entries have been made and posted, all the Income Statement accounts (also called temporary accounts) begin the new year with a zero balance. For example, next year we want to accumulate and show in the sales account the total sales made during that year and that year only; to do this, the sales account must have a zero balance at the beginning of the year so the figures from the previous year don't carry over.

When Solana Beach Bicycle Company decides to make the financial statements for the end of the month, the accountant would make the following entries in the general journal, as shown in figure 7.16, to close the records for January, 2010:

Figure 7.16: **JOURNAL**

Page 5

Date	Entries	Ref.	Amounts	
			Debits	Credits
2010				
Jan 31	Sales		$5,500.00	
	Cost of Goods Sold			$2,200.00
	Salaries Expense			100.00
	Insurance Expense			41.67
	Depreciation Expense			166.66
	Interest Expense			133.33
	Bad Debt Expense			50.00
	Retained Earnings			2,808.34

Each Revenue and Expense account is closed (brought to a zero balance) by 1) determining the balance of the account and 2) placing this amount (the account balance) on the opposite side of the account; that is, a debit balance for an account is balanced out on the credit side of the journal, and a credit balance is balanced out on the debit side. For example, prior to closing, the sales account had a credit balance of $5,500. To close the sales account, it was debited for $5,500 to achieve the desired zero balance. The Cost of Goods Sold account had a debit balance of $2,200; thus, to close this account it was credited for $2,200.

After all of the Revenues and Expenses have been closed (made to have a zero balance), and the debits and credits are added in the journal, there will be a dollar difference. In the example, this difference is the difference between the sales debit and the credits for the various Expenses: $2,808.34. This represents Net Income for the month of January. In order to make the closing entry balance an additional credit is needed; this credit is to Retained Earnings. As you learned in previous lessons, Retained Earnings is the account where profits are accumulated from year to year.

QUICK Tip

Handling Revenue and Expense Accounts: Revenue and Expense accounts are temporary accounts. You can close them any time you want summarized information about their financial position. At the end of the accounting period all Revenue and Expense accounts are closed into the Retained Earnings account. This leaves all of the Revenue and Expense accounts with a zero balance after the closing process and lets the statement reader know how much profit or loss has been created by the business.

Before posting the closing entries, the sales and Cost of Goods Sold accounts (for example) looked like figure 7.17:

Figure 7.17: LEDGER

Sales #401					Account		
Date	Comments	Ref.	Debit Amount	Date	Comments	Ref.	Credit Amount
				2010			
				Jan 6		J-1	
			500.00				
				Jan 21		J-1	
			5,000.00				

Cost of Goods Sold #501					Account		
Date	Comments	Ref.	Debit Amount	Date	Comments	Ref.	Credit Amount
2010							
Jan 6		J-1	200.00				
Jan 21		J-3	2,000.00				

After posting the closing entries, the sales and Cost of Goods Sold accounts would look like figure 7.18:

Figure 7.18: **LEDGER**

	Sales						**Account #401**
Date	Comments	Ref.	Debit Amount	Date	Comments	Ref.	Credit Amount
				2010			
				Jan 6		J-1	500.00
Jan 31	Closing	J-5	5,500.00	Jan 21		J-1	5,000.00

	Cost of Goods Sold						**Account #501**
Date	Comments	Ref.	Debit Amount	Date	Comments	Ref.	Credit Amount
2010							
Jan 6		J-1	200.00				
Jan 21		J-3	2,000.00	Jan 31	Closing	J-5	2,200.00

Notice that in the trial balance in figure 7.19, there are no Revenue or Expense accounts listed. However, the difference between the Revenue and Expenses prior to their closing has now been closed and appears in the Retained Earnings account.

The double lines drawn across the accounts in figure 7.18 are meant to indicate that the accounts are closed. Entries for the following period (in this example, February 2010) would be posted to these accounts in the spaces under the double lines. All of the accounts that were closed would look like the sales and Cost of Goods Sold accounts illustrated in the figure, in that the debits and credits would balance, except, of course, the dates and dollars figures would be different.

Often accountants will prepare an after-closing trial balance to see that the debits and credits are still in balance and to see that all the temporary accounts have been closed. Solana Beach Bicycle Company's after-closing trial balance would look like figure 7.19. Notice that accumulated depreciation is listed as a subtraction on the debit side.

Figure 7.19: **TRIAL BALANCE AFTER CLOSING ENTRIES**

Solana Beach Bicycle Company

Trial Balance
(After Closing)
January 31, 2010

	Debits	Credits
Note: Parentheses indicate decreases in cash		
Cash	$29,400.00	
Accounts Receivable	1,500.00	
Allowance for Doubtful Accounts	(50).00	
Inventory	10,800.00	
Prepaid Insurance	1,458.33	
Land	10,000.00	
Building	25,000.00	
Accumulated Depreciation—Building	(33.33)	
Truck	8,000.00	
Accumulated Depreciation—Truck	(133.33)	
Accounts Payable		$3,000.00
Interest Payable		133.33
Mortgage Payable (Long-Term)		20,000.00
Owner's Investment		60,000.00
Retained Earnings		2,808.34
	$85,941.67	$85,941.67

The closing process is a fairly routine one. It merely reverses the balances in the Income Statement accounts, bringing the ending balances to zero. Thus, since sales has a credit balance at the end of the accounting period, to close this account you must debit it to bring its balance to zero. Just the opposite happens with Cost of Goods Sold and all of the other Expenses; that is, they normally have a debit balance and to close them, they are credited for the same amount. Once all these debits and credits from the closed accounts are totaled on the trial balance, the difference should be a credit that is applied to Retained Earnings. This credit balance represents Net Income. If for some reason the debits are greater than the credits from the closed accounts this amount will represent a Net Loss.

In this chapter you have learned how to record business transactions into the original book of entry—the General Journal. You have also learned how to post to the accounting ledgers and how to make adjusting entries. Finally you have learned how to close the accounting records of a company. In chapter 8 you will be introduced to how to use financial statements for short-term decision making.

ANSWERS

<u>January 1</u>

Dr: Cash $100,000

    Cr: Investment $100,000

(Brad invests $100,000 in cash)

<u>January 3</u>

Dr: Truck (Long-Term Asset) $20,000

    Cr: Cash $15,000

    Cr: Notes Payable (Long-Term Liability) $5,000

(To purchase a Truck with cash and credit)

<u>January 3</u>

Dr: Rental Expense $1,200

    Cr: Cash $1,200

(To pay January Rent)

<u>January 10</u>

Dr: Printing Press (Long-term Asset) $6,000

    Cr: Cash $4,000

    Cr: Notes Payable $2,000

(To purchase Printing Press with Cash and Long-Term Debt)

January 10

Dr: Supplies Expense $3,000

       Cr: Cash $1,000

       Cr: Accountants Payable (Short-Term Debt) $2,000

(To buy supplies for the month with cash and on credit)

January 15

Dr: Salaries Expense $3,000

   Cr: Cash $1,500

   Cr: Salaries Payable $1,500

(To pay salaries for the first half of January)

GLOSSARY

Accounts Receivable Write-Offs: The process of identifying an account receivable that is never going to be paid and taking it off the books. These accounts are written off to an Expense account with the amount being estimated by management based on past experiences of collection rates. When the entry is made, two accounts are created, an Expense account called Bad Debts Expense and a contra-Asset account (contra to Accounts Receivable).

Adjusting Journal Entries: Journal entries made at the end of the accounting period (month, quarter, and/or year) to recognize transactions that have occurred prior to the statements' issue date, but which have not yet been recorded in the journal. Examples of these entries include: depreciation; salaries earned, but not yet paid; adjustments to prepaid items, like insurance and interest on the mortgage that has not yet been paid.

Chart of Accounts: A listing of account numbers for each of the accounts. These numbers are usually divided into five groups; 100s for Assets, 200s for Liabilities, 300s for Owner's Equity, 400s for Revenues, and 500s for Expenses. Every time an accounting entry is made, the accountant will use the same account number for that particular Asset, Liability, Owner's Equity, Revenue, or Expense.

Closing Journal Entries: The process required to bring all accounts to a zero balance. This process is done at the end of the period (month, quarter, or year) prior to the preparation of the financial statements. Only Revenues and Expenses (also called temporary accounts) are closed and the difference between Revenues and Expenses is recorded as Net Income or net loss.

Credit: The right side of the amount column in a journal or ledger. Credits are recorded when Assets and Expenses are reduced and when Liabilities, Owner's Equity, and Revenue accounts are increased.

Debit: The left side of the amount column in a journal or ledger. Debits are recorded when Assets and Expenses are increased and when Liabilities, Owner's Equity, and Revenue accounts are decreased.

Depreciation: The process of spreading the historical cost of a Long-Term Asset over its useful life. In order to determine this amount, management must make an assumption as to the life of all of the Long-Term Assets. The historical cost is then spread evenly over this life expectancy. When this method of depreciation is used (evenly spread over the life) it is called the straight-line method of depreciation.

General Journal: The book in which transactions are first recorded, often referred to as "the book of original entry." As soon as a business transaction takes place, it is recorded in the general journal. The accounts impacted by the transaction: the date, the debits, credits, and an explanation of the transaction are also recorded.

General Ledger: A book containing a page (or pages) for every account in the business. After a transaction is recorded in the general journal, the components are then transferred (or posted) to the individual accounts in the general ledger. Thus at any one time one can review the individual accounts in the general ledger to determine their current balances.

Journal Entries: As soon as a business transaction occurs, an entry is made in the general journal to recognize this transaction. A debit (or debits) and a credit (or credits) will be made to the accounts that are impacted by this transaction. The debits and credits for each transaction will always be equal.

Posting: The process of transferring the information in the general journal to the individual accounts in the general ledger. At any time, one can review the individual accounts in the general ledger to determine their balances.

Trial Balance: A list of all accounts in the general ledger that have a balance other than zero. This is prepared right before the financial statements to make sure that the accounts are in balance and that all journal entries have been prepared correctly and accurately. If the trial balance does not balance (that is, debits do not equal credits), it indicates that there has been an error made in either the recording of the transactions, in the general journal, or in the posting of those transactions to the general ledger. (This does not include a trial balance, which has been completed after the closing of accounts.)

Chapter 8

Using Financial Statements for Short-Term Analysis

Using Short-Term Ratios

Financial statements can be extremely useful for evaluating a company's future in the near-term (usually defined as one to twelve months) as well as beyond the near-term. This chapter will focus on near-term evaluation; evaluation beyond the near-term will be the focus of chapter 9.

The most important question to be answered when evaluating a company's near-term future is whether or not the company will be able to pay its debts when they come due. If the firm cannot, it may be forced into bankruptcy or perhaps even forced to cease operations. As you learned earlier, even a profitable company can become short on cash and place its future in jeopardy.

Certain financial statement users will be particularly interested in the short-term prospects of a company. For example, bankers who have made or are contemplating making short-term loans (thirty-day, sixty-day, or even six-month loans) are mainly concerned with determining whether the borrowing company will be able to repay their loans when they come due. These statement users will attempt to forecast the company's cash flow for the period of time during which their loans are expected to be outstanding. For this reason the Statement of Cash Flows discussed in chapter 5 becomes very important.

Even those users who are mostly interested in the short-term will also have an interest in the long-term. Again taking banks as an example, bankers must be aware of what is happening now and what the future looks like for all of their customers in order to decide to whom they can loan money and in order to estimate their own future cash flows.

Figure 8.1 gives some examples of how certain financial statement users might use short-term ratios.

Figure 8.1: HOW SHORT-TERM RATIOS ARE USED		
Users	**Ratios**	**Used For**
Bankers loans	Current Ratio	To make short-term
	Working Capital	
Vendors	Quick Ratio	To extend credit for purchases
	Inventory Turnover	

Users	Ratios	Used For
Credit Card Company	Current Ratio Working Capital	To issue credit cards
Business Owners	All	Ongoing short-term analysis of their businesses

There are a number of key figures that are useful in these assessments. They are highlighted in figure 8.1 and listed in figure 8.2.

Figure 8.2: KEY SHORT-TERM RATIOS

Ratio	Calculation
Current Ratio	Current Assets/Current Liabilities
Quick Ratio	Quick Asset/Current Liabilities
[Quick Assets = Current Assets − Inventory − Prepaid Items]	
Working Capital	Current Assets − Current Liabilities
Inventory Turnover Ratio	Cost of Goods Sold/Average Inventory
[Average Inventory = (Beginning Inventory + Ending Inventory)/2]	
Average Collection Period	Accounts Receivable/Average Sales per day
(Average Sales/Day = Annual Sales/365)	

Current and Quick Ratios

To figure out whether a company is going to survive in the short-term, you should look first at the Balance Sheet. Compare the company's Current Assets with their Current Liabilities (debts that must be paid within twelve months) using the current ratio.

Current Ratio = Current or Short-Term Assets/Current or Short-Term Liabilities

Also widely used is the comparison of the firm's quick Assets—those Current Assets that can be quickly turned into cash—to the Current Liabilities. Usually quick Assets include cash, current receivables, and marketable securities, or in other words, Current Assets minus Inventory and prepaid items. This ratio of quick Assets to Current Liabilities is referred to as the quick (or acid test) ratio.

Quick Asset Ratio = Quick Assets/Current or Short-Term Liabilities

Referring to Figure 3.4 in chapter 3, the current ratio for the Solana Beach Bicycle Company would be 12.6. This is calculated by dividing the Short-Term Assets on December 31, 2010, of $50,385 by the Short-Term Liabilities on the same day of $4,000. Again using the values from figure 3.4, the quick ratio for the bicycle company would be 6.6. This is calculated by taking the quick Assets on December 31, 2006, of $26,385 and dividing them by the Current Liabilities of $4,000. But what do these numbers mean?

Before you can decide whether a firm has sufficient Current Assets or quick Assets to cover their Current Liabilities, you need to know what the current and quick ratios were in the preceding periods. The rule of thumb is that the current ratio should be greater than 2.0. What this means is that the Current Assets available to the company to pay their debts are at least double their Current Liabilities. The quick Asset ratio rule of thumb is that this ratio should be 1.5 or larger. These ratios vary from industry to industry, and therefore your company's current ratio should not only be compared to prior years and to the rule of thumb figure, but should also be compared to similar companies in the same industry.

In general the larger the current and quick ratios are, the greater the probability that a company will be able to pay its debts in the near term. In the case of the Solana Beach Bicycle Company, the current and quick ratios are well above the rule of thumb, which means the business is in a very good position to be able to pay its Current Liabilities.

Alert!

Bigger Isn't Always Better: These ratios can also be too large. A company's profitability is reduced whenever it has too large a proportion of any particular type of Asset including cash. A current or quick ratio that is way over the industry average may be an indication that this is the case.

Knowing the environmental conditions that existed in prior periods as compared to now and having data about similar companies in the same industry are also useful. You can get the average ratios for various industries from publications such as *Moody's, Standard & Poor, Dun & Bradstreet,* or *Robert Morris Associates.*

QUICK Tip

Stay Informed: Unfortunately, there is no easy or shortcut method for obtaining the information on present and past environmental conditions. You must read widely and be sensitive to changes in the marketplace.

Working Capital

Another important factor to consider in the short-term in addition to these two ratios is the firms' working capital. This is calculated by subtracting the Current Liabilities from the Current Assets.

Working Capital = Current or Short-Term Assets – Current or
Short-Term
Liabilities

Working capital is a cushion. It allows management to make errors in its estimate of future cash receipts and disbursements and still be able to pay its debts when they come due. For example, if management estimates both cash receipts and disbursements for the next thirty days to be $30,000, and for some reason receipts only total $25,000 and disbursements total $35,000, the firm must have either sufficient working capital at the beginning of the month to cover the shortfall or good credit with its bankers. If this is not the case it will find itself unable to settle its debts and possibly be out of business or have the creditors taking control.

Alert!

It's All Relative: How do we know what is a good enough cushion? The calculation of working capital will not help a great deal unless it is related to the firm's cash flow and to prior year's figures. For example calculating a working capital of $20,000 does not mean anything by itself. However, to know that working capital three years ago was $10,000, two years ago was $14,000, and last year was $17,000 indicates a positive trend that gives more meaning to this year's figure of $20,000. Also important is the economy, the budget for future Current Liabilities, and the need to have excess cash in the business.

In addition it is necessary to compare the working capital to the cash flow of the firm, as you calculated in chapter 5. How much working capital a firm should have depends upon its cash flow. It makes sense that a business that receives and/or disburses an average of $7,000,000 per week should have a larger working capital balance than a firm that receives and/or disburses $7,000 per week, because the first business's needs for cash are higher.

In the case of our bicycle company, the working capital cushion is very good. It is $46,385 (Current Assets of $50,385 minus the Current Liabilities of $4,000).

QUICK Tip

Working Capital Cushion: Is your working capital cushion large enough? What is your cash flow per month? Is it ever negative? What is your cash flow budget for the future? If you had a normal negative flow of cash in the past, and you have projected a negative flow of cash for the next twelve months, you will need a larger working capital cushion than if your projections are the opposite. Also what are your predictions for the economy over the next twelve months? If you expect a slow down that might affect your industry and company, you will want to have a larger cushion for working capital since you will likely have less Revenue coming in to help you cover your debts.

Composition of Assets

In deciding whether a company is going to survive the near-term, you also want to look at the composition of their Current Assets; that is, you want to see that each of the various Current Asset items is a desirable size. Your main interest here centers on receivables and Inventory items.

Inventories and receivables may sometimes become too large. Receivables may become too large because customers delay their payments or because the company changed its credit policy so that sales are made to people or firms who are greater credit risks or who are slower in paying off their debts. Inventories get too large when, for example, management overestimates the demand for the company's products and either buys or makes too many items. These situations have negative implications for the near-term business prospects. To determine whether inventories are a reasonable size, you can calculate the Inventory turnover ratio.

Inventory Turnover Ratio

Inventory turnover ratio is calculated by dividing Cost of Goods Sold by the average Inventory.

Inventory Turnover Ratio = Cost of Goods Sold/Average Inventory

Average Inventory is defined as (beginning Inventory balance + ending Inventory balance)/2. This represents the number of times that the Inventory "turned over" (was sold during a particular period of time). If a business sells and replaces its stock of Inventory at a rapid rate, turnover is high; if items sit without being sold for long periods, Inventory turnover is low. There is no widely used rule of thumb available. To decide whether the Inventory turnover figure for a firm is desirable, you must look at previous turnover figures of the firm, turnover figures of other similar firms, and industry-wide averages. A relatively high turnover figure would suggest that sales are being lost due to shortage of Inventory; a low turnover figure may suggest that demand for the goods is falling, that some of the Inventory cannot be sold, or that prices must be reduced. A low turnover figure may also indicate that as of the Balance Sheet date too much cash has been invested in Inventory items.

In a grocery store you would expect to see an Inventory turnover of one to two days because the Inventory is perishable. In a fur coat boutique, on the other hand, you would expect this ratio to be one or two months since fur coats are bought much less frequently and in much smaller quantities than foodstuffs. It is critical to know and understand the industry you are analyzing in order to be able to evaluate the ratios.

What would you want the Inventory turnover ratio be for the Solana Beach Bicycle Company? Their Inventory certainly will not move as fast as the perishable commodities in a grocery store; however, if they are going to stay in business and not end up with a lot of Inventory that they can't sell, it should move faster than the fur coats discussed earlier. So what do you think? One week? One month? Two Months? Let's see.

To find the Cost of Goods Sold, we need to move to figure 4.1 in chapter 4. On December 31, 2010, the Cost of Goods Sold was $14,200.

Then to calculate the average Inventory, we go back to figure 3.4 in chapter 3, and see that Inventory on December 31, 2010, is $23,000. What was Inventory on December 31, 2009? Well, the bicycle company was not in business then, so it was zero. Now to calculate the average Inventory of beginning ($0) and ending ($23,000), we add these two numbers together and divide by two. Thus, average Inventory is $11,500.

To arrive at Inventory turnover, we divide Cost of Goods Sold ($14,200) by average Inventory ($11,500) and arrive at 1.24. What does this mean? Well, it means that Inventory is turning over on the average of 1.24 times per year. That is about every twelve months. Not good! The bicycles are being built and/or bought, and then not sold for twelve months. If this ratio is not improved, the company is going to have a lot of money tied up in Inventory, since it's not getting it back for a long time—nearly one year. Sam may need a better marketing plan. Or it may be that there is just too much Inventory in the shop for what can be sold at this location. What other possibilities do you see?

Average Collection Period

To determine whether the balance in Accounts Receivable is too large (or too small), you can calculate the average collection period.

Average collection period = Accounts Receivable/average sales per day

(Average sales per day is equal to Annual Sales/365 days.)

You must rely more on the firm's previous average collection period figures in evaluating the result and less on the figures of other firms and industry-wide figures in this case, because firms' credit policies and their mix of cash sales and sales on account differ widely. If the average collection period has been increasing, it may indicate the firm's increasing difficulty in collecting its receivables as they come due.

Once again let's look at the Solana Beach Bicycle Company and see how they are doing in collecting their receivables. To find Accounts Receivable we go to figure 3.4 and see that at the end of 2010, Accounts Receivable is $9,000. (This is net receivables: Accounts

Receivable minus allowance for doubtful accounts.) Then we look at figure 4.1 and see that sales for the year 2010 are $35,500. To arrive at average sales per day, we divide $35,500 by 365 days and get $97.26. To arrive at the average collection period we divide the Accounts Receivable $9,000 by the average sales per day of $97.26 and get 92.5. This means that it is taking the company ninety-two and one-half days to collect their receivables. Solana Beach Bicycle Company has a policy that generally gives customers thirty to sixty days to pay. The fact that the average collection period for Solana Beach Bicycle is longer than this means that it is taking the company too long to collect their money and be able to use it again in the activities of the business. This is not a good sign. The company must figure out how to get the customers to pay them sooner or stop giving them credit at all.

Once you decide that the company is going to survive in the near future, you can turn to estimating its long-term future prospects. As you begin to look beyond the short-term success of a company, the main focus of your attention shifts from information presented on the Balance Sheet to information presented on the Income Statement in order to look at past performance and project any trends into the future.

The long-term future of a company depends, to a very large extent, upon the capability of the company's employees. One of your main goals is to determine how well the employees have done in the past and how well they are doing now. The information that you have already gathered at the beginning of this chapter with regard to the short-term future prospect gives you valuable clues as to current performance. However, this is not sufficient to draw a reliable conclusion about the long-term prospects of the company. Chapter 9 will detail how to approach making this sort of evaluation.

GLOSSARY

Average Collection Period: A short-term financial analytical tool calculated by dividing Accounts Receivable by average sales per day. This figure is used by management to determine how long it is taking them to collect their Accounts Receivable. If a company offers payment terms of thirty days to its customers, and the average collection period is longer than thirty days, management needs to determine how to start collecting these receivables faster.

Current Ratio: A short-term financial analytical tool calculated by dividing Current Assets by Current Liabilities. The rule of thumb is that this ratio should be greater than 2.0; however, this will vary somewhat from company to company and industry to industry. Thus it is necessary to know prior year figures as a basis of comparison.

Inventory Turnover Ratio: A short-term financial analytical tool that is calculated by dividing Cost of Goods Sold by Average Inventory. (Average Inventory = Beginning Inventory + Ending Inventory/2.) What is good or bad for this ratio depends on the industry. If the company is in a business where there are perishable goods, then this number needs to be very low. In a business selling nonperishable goods such as clothes, it would be higher. In a business where producing the goods takes a long time—building airplanes, for instance—the ratio would be even higher.

Quick Ratio (or Acid Test Ratio): A short-term financial analytical tool calculated by dividing Quick Assets by Current Liabilities. The rule of thumb for this ratio is that it should be above 1.5. However, as with the current ratio, the history of the company's ratio and the averages in the industry should be considered.

Working Capital: A short-term financial analytical tool calculated by subtracting Current Liabilities from Current Assets. To determine what is a safe and comfortable cushion (sufficient to cover whatever debts may come due), this figure needs to be compared to the cash flow of the company as well as to prior years' data.

Chapter 9

Using Financial Statements for Long-Term Analysis

- ▶ Quality of Earnings
- ▶ Rate of Return on Investment
- ▶ Sales-Based Ratios or Percentages
- ▶ Earnings Data
- ▶ Long-Term Debt Position
- ▶ Dividend Data
- ▶ Footnotes

Quality of Earnings

In analyzing financial statements, it is important to keep in mind the "quality of earnings" of the company being analyzed. But what is quality of earnings? In general, companies with a high quality of earnings have a strong history of earnings and strong ratios for both the short- and long-terms, and thus are considered to be in a good position to maintain higher earnings in the future. The "quality of earnings" concept is used by both creditors and investors who understand that the bottom line of all organizations is not equal. Companies with higher quality of earnings receive higher credit limits, lower interest costs, and higher stock prices. You can see in figure 9.1 what produces a higher quality of earnings for a business.

Figure 9.1: WHAT PRODUCES A HIGHER QUALITY OF EARNINGS?

- A majority of Net Income coming from continuing operations as opposed to one-time transactions.
- The quick conversion of sales into cash, i.e., relatively low average collection period
- An appropriate debt-equity ratio
- A fully funded pension Liability
- Stable earning trends
- Highly developed brand loyalty among consumers
- Stable or increasing market share
- An unqualified audit opinion
- Good labor relations

In chapter 8 we reviewed several ratios that are beneficial in analyzing the short-term viability of a company. In figure 9.2, we see that there are also several ratios that need to be reviewed and evaluated to understand the long-term strength of a company. Each of these ratios will be discussed in this chapter.

Figure 9.2: LONG-TERM INFORMATION USED TO EVALUATE A COMPANY

1. Rate of return on investment

2. Net profit as a percentage of sales

3. Percentage of various Expenses to sales

4. Rate of growth of sales

5. Earnings per share

6. Extraordinary gains and losses

7. Price/earnings ratio

8. Number of times interest and preferred stock dividends were earned

9. Total Liabilities to total Assets

10. Dividend payout ratio

Rate of Return on Investment

The rate of return on investment is probably the single most important financial statistic. It comes as close as any figure can to reflecting how well a company has done.

Return on Investment (ROI) is usually calculated as follows:

Rate of return (as a ratio) = Net Income/Average Stockholders' or Owner's Equity

Rate of return (as a percentage) = Net Income/Average Stockholders' or Owner's Equity (x 100)

Note: Stockholders' Equity is the term used in a corporation, whereas Owner's Equity is the term used in a proprietorship and partnership. They are similar in that they both show how much the owner(s) invested in the business plus their accumulated earnings (Retained Earnings).

This ratio depicts how much money was earned as compared to the amount the owners invested in the business. In the example in chapter 3, Sam had invested $60,000 into the business on January 1. Since the beginning Owner's Equity was $0 on January 1, and the ending Owner's Equity was $70,385 on December 31, the average for the year was $35,193. Since Net Income for 2010 was $10,385, the owner earned 29.5 percent on her investment ($10,385/$35,193).

Is 29.5 percent a good return on the Owner's Investment? The only way to answer this question is to know what alternative investments an investor might consider. Can the owner invest his or her money elsewhere and make more money? If the answer is no, then the return is a good one. This analysis should be made on an ongoing basis in order to continually determine where to invest one's money.

Having said this, there are exceptions. In the early years of a new company, the owner may not make a great return or any return. But he or she may be "betting" on the future, in the belief that the returns will outpace other alternatives. In addition, a company should consider how well it does in the current year as compared to the previous year by comparing the rate of return figure for each of the two years. Comparing one company's results to those of another company in the same industry is also a useful indicator of how the company is doing compared to the competition.

Alert!

Know Your Estimates: In making these comparisons between two years within the same company or between one company and another, you must be alert as to what estimates were made and which generally accepted accounting principles were used. Since Net Income is comprised of several estimates, if these estimates and accounting standards are not the same between years, or between companies, this ratio cannot be compared.

Sales-Based Ratios or Percentages

In order to be able to predict future profitability, you need to examine your company's and other companies' past sales and Expenses.

Net Profit as a Percentage of Sales

One such ratio that aids in the analysis of future profitability is the Net Profit as a percentage of Sales.

Net Profit as a Percentage of Sales = (Net Income/Sales) x 100

An increase in this percentage as compared to previous years may indicate that the company is operating more efficiently. More sales were made with fewer Expenses. Also, when the net profit as a percentage of sales is higher for one company than another, it may indicate that one company has been operating more efficiently than the other.

In the case of the Solana Beach Bicycle Company, Net Income for 2010 was $10,385. Sales for the year were $35,500. Thus the net profit as a percentage of sales would be 29.25 percent. Is this good? Bad? Helpful? Since this is the first year of operations for the company, we do not have any prior years to compare this number to. However, it does tell us that the company is making over 29 percent on their sales. Not bad. Why? Where else can you invest your money and earn 29 percent? Not very many places, and not on a regular basis. If we had the data, we could compare this to other similar small businesses and in the future we will be able to compare it to prior years for the bicycle company. (Once again, keep in mind that the different companies being compared must have used the same GAAP to arrive at their Net Income calculations in order for comparisons to be meaningful.)

Sales Ratios

To help verify these hunches and to gain better insight into operational changes, it is also helpful to compare a variety of different Expenses to the total sales figure. By understanding these ratios of various Expenses to sales, one can determine if a larger or a smaller percentage during the year is being spent on these Expenses. If a company is going to be competitive and successful, it must control its Expenses. These ratios show the areas of the business where the company has been able to control these Expenses. See figure 9.3 for several examples.

Figure 9.3: IMPORTANT SALES RATIOS

1. Cost of goods sold/Sales
2. Selling and delivery Expenses/Sales
3. General and administrative Expenses/Sales
4. Depreciation Expenses/Sales
5. Lease and rental Expenses/Sales
6. Repairs and maintenance Expense/Sales
7. Advertising/Sales
8. Research and development/Sales

Another sales based ratio that is helpful is the rate of growth of sales from one period to the next, calculated by comparing the increase (or decease) in sales between two periods to the sales in the first period. You would find it very informative to learn that Solana Beach Bicycle Company sales increased 10 percent from one year to the next, and 20 percent from year two to three, and 30 percent from year three to four, etc. The pattern of sales over the most recent years of a company's life can help you form an estimate of expected future sales.

Earnings Data

The earnings per share figure (EPS) and the price/earnings ratio (P/E) are, along with the rate of return on investment ratio, the most widely used information about corporations. The price/earnings ratio is calculated by dividing the market price per share of that company's stock by the earnings per share of the company.

Price/Earnings Ratio = Market Price Per Share/Earnings Per Share

Corporations Only: Both the P/E ratio and Earning Per Share can only be calculated for businesses that have been incorporated. Why? Because if the businesses have not been incorporated, they do not sell capital stock, and therefore cannot perform any calculations involving common or pre-ferred shares. An additional note: if you own a small business that has been incorporated, there may not be a market price for shares. Thus the P/E ratio cannot be calculated, but EPS can be determined.

The price/earnings ratio can give you some very useful ideas about what other people expect for the future of a company. For example, when a company's stock is selling for fifty times earnings (P/E ratio of fifty to one) and the average P/E ratio for most stocks in that industry is fifteen to one, you may conclude that 1) the company's earnings are going to increase considerably in the future or that 2) the price of the stock is going down between now and the time the present buyers will want to sell the stock.

In general, when the P/E ratio of a company's stock is significantly higher than average, the buyers of the stock expect that the company will prosper; when the ratio is lower than average, buyers are not opti-mistic about the company's future.

After calculating EPS, you will want to compare the earnings per share figures of a company for a period of five to ten years and should compare the EPS figures with those of other companies.

When looking at Net Income for a company, you must also consider the makeup of that number. Often there are extraordinary gains or losses included. These are gains/losses from the sale of items that are not considered to be recurring. Since you want to project the past into the future, you want to eliminate from the past data those gains and losses that are not expected to occur again in the future. Therefore the figure that you will find most useful is the EPS before extraordinary gains and losses when the earnings figure used in the calculation does not include gains or losses that are considered an anomaly or highly unusual in some way. However, you should be sure to look carefully at the extraordinary items and determine the likelihood that they may occur again in the future.

Long-Term Debt Position

Some people believe that a company that borrows money is not as good or as well managed as a company that operates without borrowing. This is not necessarily true. Often, by borrowing money, a company can increase the Net Income for the stockholders without increasing the stockholders' investment.

For example, say that Company A, whose Assets total $100,000, Liabilities total $10,000, and Stockholders' Equity totals $90,000, expects a Net Income next year of $9,000. This represents a return on investment of 10 percent.

Now assume that management is considering the purchase of $40,000 worth of Assets. These Assets will produce additional annual Net Income (before Interest Expense) of $4,000. The company has two choices: it can borrow the $40,000 at 6 percent interest or it can have the investors put the additional $40,000 into the business.

In scenario one, Company A borrows the needed $40,000. Company A's Net Income next year would be $10,600 ($9,000 + $4,000 − $2,400) before Income Taxes. The $2,400 reduction to Net Income is the interest on the loan ($40,000 x 6 percent). Thus, the return on investment would be 11.7 percent ($10,600/$90,000 = 11.7 percent).

In scenario two, instead of borrowing the $40,000, the owners invest their own money. Net income would still increase by $4,000 to $13,000 ($9,000 + $4,000). There would be no Interest Expense, and the Return on Stockholders' Equity would be $13,000/$130,000 (the original $90,000 + the additional $40,000). Thus, its Return on investment remains at 10 percent.

As you can see, scenario one, where Company A borrowed the additional $40,000 and ended up with a return on investment of 11.7 percent, was a more favorable outcome.

Alert!

Dangerous Debt: Too much debt can make a company too "risky." During economic downturns, these companies may not be able to repay their debts. On the other hand, little or no debt may not be a good thing either. If a company can borrow money at 7 percent interest and earn 10 percent on its investment, borrowing will increase its overall rate of return.

One way to help you determine if a company has put itself into a risky position is to calculate two ratios: the number of times interest was earned and the ratio of total Liabilities to total Assets.

To calculate the number of times that interest was earned, divide the Interest Expense into the Net Income before Interest Expense and before Income Taxes. You use the income figure before Income Taxes because Interest Expense is deductible for Income Tax purposes.

Number of Times Interest Was Earned = Net Income before Interest and Taxes/ Interest Expense

The larger this ratio, the easier it is for the company to meet its interest payments, and the less likely it is that the company will default on its loans.

To calculate the ratio of Liabilities to Assets, you divide total Liabilities by total Assets.

Ratio of Liabilities to Assets = Total Liabilities/Total Assets

The idea here is that the larger the ratio, the more risky the company. Of course a company with a large Liability to Asset ratio may prosper while a company without any debt at all may fail. The Liability to Asset ratio, as well as any ratio, only gives you a part of the total picture and must be analyzed along with other ratios and outside information about the company, the industry, and the economy.

Dividend Data

Additional information about a company can be obtained by looking at the cash dividends that it has paid over the past several years and calculating the dividend payout ratio, the total cash dividends declared during the year divided by the Net Income for the year.

Dividend Payout Ratio = Dividends Declared/Net Income

If the ratio is large, the company is paying out to the stockholders a large portion of the funds earned and not reinvesting them in the company. If this ratio is small or if the company pays no dividends whatsoever, the company may be growing rapidly and using the funds to finance this growth. Which is better? This is completely determined by your personal investment needs if you are a stockholder, or by the goals of the business if you are part of management.

Figure 9.4 illustrates examples of which long-term ratios are useful for various users.

Figure 9.4: HOW LONG-TERM RATIOS ARE USED

Users	Ratios	Used For
Lenders	Number of Times Interest Was Earned	Evaluating the Safety of Your Loan
	Total Liabilities/ Total Assets	Making Long-Term Loans
Stockholders Holding	EPS, P/E Ratio	Purchasing Stock
	Dividend Payout Ratio	Analyzing Earnings Payouts to Stockholders
Owners/Managers	Sales-Based Ratios	Ongoing Long-Term Analysis

Footnotes

Almost all financial statements of companies larger than average small businesses have footnotes attached to them. The footnotes are as important as the fine print in a contract. When you examine a company's annual report, consider reading the footnotes first. Examine the financial statements next and read the president's message and the rest of the "advertising" last.

Information contained in the footnotes is quite varied. It can include terms of pension plans, terms of stock options outstanding, the nature and expected outcome of any pending lawsuits, terms of a long-term lease agreement, and probable effects of forced sale of properties in a foreign country. You may find an abundance of clues about a company's future from the footnotes.

Analyzing financial statements can be extremely helpful, but without the use of historical data, no predictions could be made about the future of a company. The more you read financial statements, use them, and work with them, the better your decisions about the future of your company and those you wish to invest in will become.

In this chapter you have learned how financial statements and various ratios can be used to evaluate the long-term success of a business. In chapter 10 you will learn how to prepare and use a budget.

GLOSSARY

Dividend Payout Ratio: A long-term financial analytical tool calculated by dividing Dividends Declared by Net Income. This ratio is useful when analyzing how much of the earnings for the year have been distributed to the stockholders. As with all other ratios, it must be compared to prior years and to other companies.

Earnings Per Share: A long-term financial analytical tool calculated by dividing Net income by the average number of common shares outstanding for the year. This ratio can only be calculated for corporations. Sometimes this ratio gets too much attention when potential investors are making their decisions. This number is only as accurate and useful as is Net Income itself and must be used in conjunction with many of the other ratios in this chapter.

Extraordinary Gains and Losses: Gains and losses from the sale of items that are neither considered to be recurring nor a normal part of the business operations. For this reason, it is required by GAAP that these gains and losses be separated on the Income Statement from income from operations.

Net Profit as a Percentage of Sales: A long-term financial analytical tool calculated by dividing Net Income by sales and multiplying the results by one hundred. This ratio should be compared with prior years' figures as well as with industry averages to determine its value to management.

Number of Times Interest Was Earned: A long-term financial analytical tool calculated by dividing Net Income before Taxes by Interest Expense. The larger this number, the more satisfied the lenders will be since they will have a higher coverage of the interest due to them by the Net Income of the company.

Price/Earnings Ratio: A long-term financial analytical tool calculated by dividing market price per share by earnings per share. This ratio can only be calculated for corporations since partnerships and proprietorships do not have stock and thus have no market price or earnings per share. In general for corporations, the higher this ratio the better, and a positive upward trend in this ratio from year to year is looked on favorably by investors.

Rate of Return on Investment: A long-term financial analytical tool calculated by dividing Net Income by the average Stockholders' Equity. The average Stockholders' Equity is determined by adding the beginning of the year equity with the end of the year and dividing by two. A good rate of return is one that would be greater than what could be earned investing that money in other places, like with the bank or in bonds or securities.

Rate of Sales Growth: A long-term financial analytical tool; the percentage change in sales between two or more years. Generally businesses look for this figure to grow from year to year.

Chapter 10

Budgeting for Your Business

What Is a Budget?

The budget is a detailed plan that outlines future expectations in quantitative terms. Budgets in accounting can be used for a variety of reasons. You can use a budget to plan and control your future Income and Expenses, which would look like the Income Statements we have been reviewing throughout the book. Or you can use budgets to plan for future capital expenditures, which would show when the company may plan to buy Long-Term Assets and where this money is to come from. Governmental agencies can use budgets of Revenues and Expenses in order to determine their future tax needs.

Planning and Control

So why would Sam want to do a budget for her business? The answer to this question is that Sam is going to produce a budget each year for the purpose of **planning** for her company into the future and to **control** the amount she is spending.

The terms "planning" and "control" are often used interchangeably in an accounting sense, but they are actually two distinct concepts. Planning is the development of future objectives and the preparation of budgets to meet these objectives. Control, on the other hand, involves ensuring that the objectives established during the planning phase are attained. A good budgeting system takes into consideration both the plan and the control.

Advantages of Budgeting

Whether the budget is for personal use or for your business, the major advantage of using a budget is that it gives formality to the planning process. If the budget involves other people, it also serves as a way of communicating the plan to these other people. One of the major processes within an organization is to coordinate and integrate the plans and goals of the various departments. Once the budget has been established it serves as a benchmark for evaluating the actual results.

Without preparing a budget, Sam would not know how much money the bicycle company is going to have at the end of the month, how much it must borrow to buy the capital Assets needed for the business, or if the Revenues are going to exceed the Expenses or vice versa. The process of preparing the budget will be critical to Sam as she plans for the future.

Most small businesses that go out of business do so, not because they don't have a good product or service, but because they have not planned well and have run out of cash. Preparing a budget can help avoid this undesirable end.

QUICK Tip

Using Budgets in Your Business: With the use of personal computers and spreadsheet programs, the budgeting process has been simplified. Budgets can be implemented and maintained at little cost. In addition it is easy to make changes on a regular basis to view potential situations that may come up. This allows the individual or the manager to more easily make decisions based on these anticipated results, thus implementing the control feature of a budget.

The Master Budget

The master budget is a compilation of many separate budgets that are interdependent. An example of this network is exhibited in figure 10.1. The major budgets that together comprise the Master Budget will be the focus of this chapter.

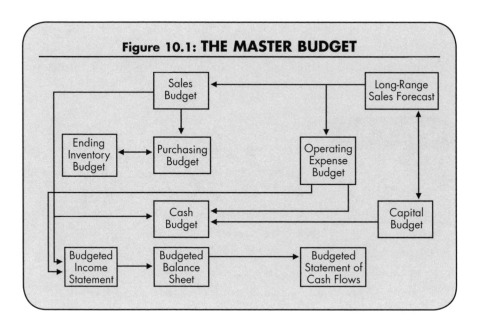

Figure 10.1: THE MASTER BUDGET

Sales Budget

Let's assume that Sam wants to prepare a master budget for the bicycle company for the year 2011. In order to prepare this budget, Sam is going to have to guesstimate how much sales the business will generate for the year. As indicated in figure 10.1, without this first step of creating a sales budget, none of the other budgets can be prepared.

To calculate the total sales figure, it is necessary to multiply the expected unit sales for each product by its anticipated unit selling price. Sam calculates that total will be $85,000 for anticipated sales of new bicycles. (She expects to sell 170 bicycles at an average price of $500 per bicycle; 170 bicycles x $500 per bicycle = $85,000.)

In addition to the normal sales of bicycles, the bicycle company has been increasing its Revenue from repairs. During 2011, the Revenue from repairs will be budgeted at $9,500. The Expenses associated with these repairs are budgeted to be $3,600.

Cost of Goods Sold and Ending Inventory

Ending Inventory at the end of December 2010 is $13,000. (See figure 3.2.)

Assume that on average, the company has had a 60 percent profit margin. Since sales are budgeted to be $85,000, the Gross Profit would be $51,000 ($85,000 x 60 percent). Further assume that since the company is growing, the bicycle company determines that it wants ending Inventory to grow from the previous year in anticipation of growing sales in the future, so Sam has budgeted ending Inventory for 2011 to be $32,000.

QUICK Tip

Inventory and Budgeting: Determining Inventory needs is not an easy process but is an extremely important one for a small business. Excess Inventory that cannot be sold may become spoiled or out of date. A shortage of Inventory will cause a loss of sales because the product is not available and customers will take their business elsewhere. As a small business owner, careful planning and control is critical to maintaining proper levels of Inventory. This number should be based upon past experiences as well as careful budgeting of sales.

In order for the company to achieve the ending Inventory of $32,000 for 2011, additional Inventory must be purchased. The amount that the company needs to purchase is calculated by the following formula:

Beginning Inventory
+ Purchases
– Ending Inventory
= Cost of Goods Sold

In the case of the bicycle company, we know three out of the four numbers:

Beginning Inventory
(2010 Ending Inventory:
See figure 3.3, chapter 3) $13,000
+ Purchases   ???
– Ending Inventory $32,000
= Cost of Good Sold $34,000

But wait, how do we know Cost of Goods Sold? Well, we know budgeted sales is $85,000, right? We also know that Gross Profit = $51,000. And lastly, we know that sales – cost of good sold = Gross profit. So voilà, $85,000 – X = $51,000. X = $34,000. Whew!

By working backwards, we can calculate that purchases for 2011 must be $53,000.

Operating Expenses

By looking back at the Master Budget in figure 10.1, we can see that the sales budget flows directly into the budget for operating Expenses. As indicated in figure 4.1, these Expenses were $7,565 or 21 percent of sales for 2010. Again assuming that this percentage remains fairly constant and that during the year 2011 sales are budgeted to be $85,000, operating Expenses would be budgeted at $17,850 (21 percent of $85,000).

Capital Budget

The capital budget is concerned with those items that will last longer than one year: the company's Long-Term Assets. To determine if any additional space would need to be rented or built, the business must do a long-range sales forecast. Assuming that the business is growing at a fairly constant rate, Sam has predicted that within two years another building must be purchased in order to meet the business's production and sales demands. Sam's research of local real estate indicates that the cost of a building with sufficient space for the next five years would be $48,000. Therefore the capital budget per month for the next two years (when the purchase will actually have to be made, since Sam does not want to incur any additional debt by taking out a mortgage on this building) would be $2,000 ($48,000/24 months). In order to purchase the building two years from now, $2,000 must be set aside every month for the next two years. (This assumes no inflation during the next two years.)

With the information that has been gathered to this point, it is now possible to create a cash budget and a budgeted Income Statement, Balance Sheet, and cash flow. Let's examine this information.

Budgeted Income Statement

Using the figures calculated earlier, Sam can create a budgeted Income Statement like the one shown in figure 10.2:

Figure 10.2: SOLANA BEACH BICYCLE COMPANY
Budgeted Income Statement
For the Year Ended December 31, 2011

Sales	$85,000
Cost of Goods Sold	34,000
Gross Profit	$51,000
Operating Expenses	17,850
Net Income from Operations	$33,150

Other Revenue:

Repair Revenue	$9,500

Other Expenses:

Repair Expenses. 3,600

Net Income $39,050

Why does the bicycle company need this Income Statement? They might use it to show to the bank to get a loan. They might want to show it to potential partners looking for information about the future of the business. And of course, they will also need it for planning how they are going to expand in the future!

The Cash Budget

Next, the company needs to calculate how much cash they are going to have at the end of the year. Sam needs to know this figure in order to prepare the budgeted Balance Sheet, but more importantly, to make sure the company has enough cash to pay its bills in the following periods, and keep the cash balance at a "safe level."

In order to calculate the budgeted ending cash balance for 2011, we need to know the beginning cash balance. This figure is the same as the ending cash balance on December 31, 2010, because the business starts the new year with the amount of cash it ended the last year with. This figure is $17,385 (see figure 3.2). A number of assumptions need to be made as well. Sales for 2011 were predicted to be $85,000 plus $9,500 for repairs (for a total of $94,500), but it must also be determined how much of these sales will be in cash and how much will be on Accounts Receivable. In the past, 75 percent of both the bicycle sales and repair work have been paid for with cash, so it is safe to assume that this will be the case for 2011 as well. Thus, the cash receipts for 2011 from sales and repairs will be $70,875 ($94,500 x 75 percent).

Assuming the same ratio applies to the preceding year (that is, 75 percent of the sales were for cash, and the other 25 percent were on account) then the 25 percent that was still owed to the bicycle company on December 31, 2010, will be collected in 2011. This is making the assumption that there were no bad debts. (If there were bad debts, then the amount estimated for bad debts would be deducted from the amount to be collected.) Again, since the sales and the repair work for 2010 totaled $39,350, the cash to be collected in 2011 on these 2010 sales would be $9,837 ($39,350 x 25 percent).

Now we need to calculate the cash expenditures for 2011. The first expenditure is that of purchasing Inventory. The general rule at Solana Beach Bicycle Company is that 80 percent of the purchase is paid in cash in the year of purchase, and 20 percent is paid the following year. In 2010 the bicycle company purchased $23,000 of bicycles (Inventory) and in 2011, they purchased bicycles costing $53,000. Thus, the cash expenditure for 2011 is $47,000 (20 percent of $23,000 for 2010 and 80 percent of $53,000 for 2007).

So continuing with this assumption, 80 percent of the other expenditures at Solana Beach Bicycle Company are paid with cash in the year of use, and 20 percent are charged on account. (Every company will have its own past data to guide their assumptions for the purposes of preparing budgets and will calculate this ratio (80/20, 65/35, etc.) based upon its own experiences.) Operating Expenses for 2011 have been budgeted at $17,850, and operating Expenses in 2010 totaled $7,565 (see figure 4.1). Based on the 80/20 breakdown of cash versus account payment at Solana Beach Bicycle Company, we know that the total cash outlay for operating Expenses in 2011 would be $15,793: the sum of the cash outlay for 2011 expenditures ($17,850 x 80 percent = $14,280) plus the cash spent to settle Accounts Payable for 2010 operating Expenses ($7,565 x 20 percent = $1,513).

Each year another cash expenditure is made for repair Expenses. All of these expenditures are made in the year in which they occur. Thus the $3,600 for repairs in 2011 are all paid in the year 2011.

The last cash "expenditure" that the bicycle company made during 2011 is the $2,000 per month that the business "put aside" for the future purchase of a building. This cash transaction is neither an expenditure nor a reduction in cash. It is simply going from one bank account to another. The only reason for the transaction at all is to make sure that the cash left in the operating cash account is not accidentally spent prior to the purchase of the building.

Let's take a look at figure 10.3 to see how we can actually calculate the ending cash balance.

Figure 10.3: SOLANA BEACH BICYCLE COMPANY
Budgeted Ending Cash Balance
For the Year Ended December 31, 2011

Beginning Cash $17,385

Add:

Cash Receipts from 2011 Sales. 70,875

Cash Receipts from 2010 Sales. 9,837

Subtract:

Cash Payments for Inventory Purchases 2011 42,400

Cash Payments for Inventory Purchases 2010 4,600

Cash Payments for Operating Expenses in 2011 14,280

Cash Payments for Operating Expenses in 2010 1,513

Cash Payments for Repairs Expenses in 2011 3,600

Ending Cash Balance $31,704

(Note to the Cash Budget: Of the $31,704 ending cash balance, $24,000 has been set aside in a separate bank account for the future purchase of a new building.)

The example presented here is for a small business such as Solana Beach Bicycle Company. However, the same concepts can be applied to preparing a personal budget and the same benefits will be derived.

QUICK Tip

Participation Is Key: The success or failure of budgets within an organization is usually enhanced by the participation of the managers, who are generally more apt to fulfill the goals that they have had a direct role in developing. This isn't to say that these budgets should not be subject to review by higher management; however, any changes that are made should be done with the involvement of the individuals who played a part in creating the budget.

In this chapter you learned the meaning of a budget, the value of preparing one, and the ways in which the components interrelate. In chapter 11 you will find out who auditors are, what type of reports they issue, and why those reports are useful to you.

GLOSSARY

Budget: A detailed plan that outlines future expectations in quantitative terms. The major purposes of a budget are to plan for the future and to control the operations of the company. The budget is prepared on an ongoing basis and adjusted continually with the acquisition of additional information.

Capital Budget: The budget for Long-Term Assets. Not only does this budget help determine what future capital (long-term) Assets are needed for the business, but also how much money needs to be set aside each month or quarter to acquire these Assets in the future.

Control: Involves ensuring that the objectives established during the planning phase of the budget preparation are attained. For example, once it is determined that the amount of cash needed at the end of the year is $40,000, all during the year the cash account needs to be monitored by careful review of the budget and decisions made to ensure the desired ending balance is attained.

Master Budget: A network of many separate budgets that are interdependent. The master budget starts with the Sales Budget. Once it is estimated how much in sales is going to occur during the year, all of the other budgets for Inventory, purchases, cash, and Expenses, et al, can be determined.

Planning: The development of future objectives and the preparation of budgets to meet those objectives. Without a budget, there is no planning, and companies that attempt to operate their businesses without this type of planning base their success on luck.

Chapter 11

Audits and Auditors

What Is an Audit?

One of the rules that the Securities Exchange Commission (SEC) has issued is that the financial statements of public companies (those companies selling stock to the public) must be examined by an independent public accountant through the process of an audit. This rule means that an accountant, who is not an employee of the company and who is licensed to practice as a public accountant by the state where the financial statements are being prepared, must audit (or examine) the records of the company and must determine whether or not the financial statements are in accordance with the rules of Generally Accepted Accounting Principles (GAAP). In addition, the auditor has the responsibility to give reasonable assurance that the financial statements are free of any material misstatement.

The American Accounting Association defines auditing as "a systematic process of objectively obtaining and evaluating evidence regarding assertions about economic actions and events to ascertain the degree of correspondence between those assertions and established criteria and communicating the results to interested users." (From American Accounting Association Committee on Basic Auditing Concepts, *A Statement of Basic Auditing Concepts*; Sarasota, FL, American Accounting Association, 1973.)

When auditors issue their reports they must follow a set of rules known as Generally Accepted Auditing Standards (GAAS). These standards are made up of 1) the ten Generally Accepted Auditing Standards, 2) the Statements on Auditing Standards (SASs), and 3) the Interpretations of these Standards.

These standards have been the jurisdiction of the American Institute of Certified Public Accountants and their Auditing Standards Board. With the passage of the Sarbanes-Oxley Act of 2002, Congress has now taken the responsibility for creating standards for public companies and created the Public Company Accounting Oversight Board (PCAOB) for this purpose. The board has the additional responsibility to make sure that audit quality is not compromised and that auditor performance meets public expectations.

In addition to the auditing standards, CPAs are expected to follow the Code of Ethics established by the American Institute of Certified Public Accountants. Adhering to such a code ensures the auditor's independence—the major attribute the auditor has to sell to the public. (The topic of ethics will be discussed in depth in chapter 12.)

A typical auditor's report (known as the unqualified report) is issued when the financial statements are in accordance with GAAP. This report is written and issued by the auditors and is submitted to the public with the financial statements.

QUICK TIP

Remember that the financial statements are prepared by and are the responsibility of the management of the company and not the auditors. Since the major corporate failures of the 1990s and early 2000s, the Sarbanes-Oxley Act of 2002 requires company management to sign a letter stating that the financial statements are presented fairly in accordance with Generally Accepted Accounting Principles, just as the auditors must.

Accounting Versus Auditing

As discussed in previous chapters, accounting is the process of recording, classifying, and summarizing economic events in a process that leads to the preparation of financial statements.

Auditing, on the other hand, is not concerned with the preparation of the accounting data, but with the evaluation of this data to determine if it is properly presented in accordance with the rules of accounting (GAAP) and whether it properly reflects the events that have occurred during the period in question.

Types of Auditors

An auditor is an individual or company who checks the accuracy and fairness of the accounting records of a company and determines whether the financial statements are in accordance with the Generally Accepted Accounting Principles. There are many different types of auditors. The three most common types are described in the following section.

The Certified Public Accountant (CPA)

Certified Public Accountants (CPAs) are auditors who serve the needs of the general public by providing auditing, tax planning and preparation, and management consulting services. CPAs can work as individuals or as employees of a firm; these firms range in size from one individual to international organizations with thousands of employees.

The largest of these firms have offices worldwide and are referred to as the "Big Four." Even though they only employ about 12 percent of all of the CPAs in the United States, they actually perform the audits of about 85 percent of the largest corporations in the world. These four companies are: Deloitte & Touche, Ernst & Young, KPMG, and PricewaterhouseCoopers.

Those individuals who act as independent auditors must be licensed to perform audits by the state in which they practice. The laws vary from state to state as to the requirements that must be met in order to obtain such licenses. However to be issued a license to practice as a CPA, all states require the individual to pass a uniform examination, which is prepared and graded by the American Institute of CPAs (AICPA). Prior to taking this examination, an individual must have a minimum of four years of college education, with many states now requiring five years. Depending upon the State, this will either result in the earning of a master's degree, or the fifth year becoming part of the undergraduate degree.

In addition to passing this examination, most states require an individual to have some experience working with another CPA prior to being licensed. Most states also require that after being licensed to practice as a public accountant, CPAs must take at least a certain minimum amount of continuing education coursework each year in order to have their license renewed.

Internal Auditors

Internal auditors are employed by companies to audit the companies' own records and to establish a system of internal control. The functions of these auditors vary greatly depending upon the needs and expectations of management. In general the work includes compliance audits (to make sure the accounting is in compliance with the rules of the company and the laws under which they operate) and operational audits (a review of an organization's operating procedures for efficiency and effectiveness). Operational Audits review the business for efficient use of resources; they are meant to help management make decisions that will aid the company in becoming more profitable.

As with CPAs, many internal auditors are also certified by passing a nationally prepared examination. This examination is for the Certificate of Internal Auditing and is prepared by the Institute of Internal Auditors.

Internal auditors generally must report to the highest level of responsibility within the company; this may include the Board of Directors or the Audit Committee of the Board of Directors. This is important because it gives the internal auditors more independence from the management team that they are reporting on.

During a company's audit, internal auditors work closely with external auditors (CPAs) in order to reduce the amount of time that the outside auditors need to spend with the company. Given the size of the internal audit staff and their independence within the company, they may be asked to perform several of the tasks that would have been prepared by the external auditors. The external auditors still have the ultimate responsibility to determine if the financial statements are presented in accordance with Generally Accepted Accounting Principles, and they are the ones who sign the report that is presented to the public. Using internal auditors is simply meant to reduce the number of detailed procedures that would otherwise have to be performed by the external auditors. This in turn reduces the cost of the external audit to the corporation.

Governmental Auditors

As you would expect, governmental auditors are individuals who perform the audit function within or on behalf of a governmental organization. As with the other two types of auditors described earlier, these individuals also must be independent from the individuals or groups that they are auditing.

Examples of governmental organizations that hire and use auditors include: 1) The United States General Accounting Office (GAO), whose major function is to perform the audit function for Congress; 2) The Internal Revenue Service, which hires auditors to enforce the federal tax laws as defined by the Congress and interpreted by the courts; 3) The Bureau of Alcohol, Tobacco and Firearms (ATF); 4)

The Drug Enforcement Agency (DEA); and 5) The Federal Bureau of Investigation (FBI). Rather than following Generally Accepted Accounting Principles, government audits are done in accordance with a set of accounting rules established by the Governmental Accounting Standards Board (GASB).

The Standard Audit Opinion Illustrated

The most common document issued by auditors as part of their reports is the standard unqualified audit opinion. It is issued in the following situations:

1. All financial statements have been examined by the auditor.
2. It is determined that these financial statements were prepared in accordance with GAAP.
3. The auditor has gathered sufficient evidence to give an opinion on these statements.
4. The auditor is independent of the company being audited.
5. The auditor has followed the generally accepted rules of auditing called Generally Accepted Auditing Standards (GAAS).

The Generally Accepted Auditing Standards that auditors must follow are spelled out in the rules of the auditing profession in a set of standards that is always changing. The rules come from two sources, the AICPA and the SEC. With the standards always changing, this provides an example of how the SEC and the AICPA complement and support each other to help ensure that the financial statements issued to the public present useful information that is relevant, reliable, understandable, and sufficient for use in making decisions about firms and their management.

When all of these conditions are met, a report like the one in figure 11.1 will be issued. Notice that the report is issued on a comparative basis, and therefore the management of the company must attach two years of financial statements.

The report has three basic segments: 1) the introductory paragraph, 2) the scope paragraph, and 3) the opinion paragraph.

Figure 11.1: THE UNQUALIFIED AUDIT OPINION (STANDARD)

Sydney and Maude
Certified Public Accountants
7 Circle Drive
Cape Cod, MA 02117

Report of Independent Registered Public Accounting Firm

To: the Board of Directors and Shareholders, The Las Brisas Company

We have audited the accompanying Balance Sheets of The Las Brisas Company as of December 31, 2011, and 2010, and the related statements of income, shareholders' equity, and cash flows for the years then ended. These financial statements are the responsibility of the Company's management. Our responsibility is to express an opinion on these financial statements based on our audits.

We conducted our audits in accordance with auditing standards of the Public Company Accounting Oversight Board. Those standards require that we plan and perform the audit to obtain reasonable assurance about whether the financial statements are free of material misstatement. An audit includes examining, on a test basis, evidence supporting the amounts and disclosures in the financial statements. An audit also includes assessing the accounting principles used and significant estimates made by management, as well as evaluating the overall financial statement presentation. We believe that our audits provide a reasonable basis for our opinion.

In our opinion, the financial statements referred to above present fairly, in all material respects, the financial position of the Las Brisas Company as of December 31, 2011, and 2010 and the results of its operations and its cash flows for the years then ended in conformity with accounting principles generally accepted in the United States.

Sydney and Maude, CPAs

Cape Cod, Massachusetts

March 17, 2012

See Appendix C for an example of the Auditor's Report for a major corporation.

See Appendix B for the audit opinion for the Coca-Cola Company's Annual Report.

The Parts of the Report

There are seven parts to every standard audit report. They include:

Figure 11.2: **STANDARD AUDIT REPORT**

1. The report title—"Independent Auditor's Report"

2. The audit report address—"To the Stockholder's..."

3. Introductory paragraph—"We have audited..."

4. Scope paragraph—"We conducted our audits..."

5. Opinion paragraph—"In our opinion..."

6. Signature of CPA firm—"Sydney and Maude, CPAs"

7. Audit report date—"March 17, 2012." This date represents when the work on the audit was completed, not the date the report was issued. Depending on the size of the company being audited, the review of the evidence may take two to three months.

The wording on this report may vary slightly from auditor to auditor; however, the overall structure and meaning remain the same.

Other Types of Audit Reports

The following is a brief overview of three other types of audit reports that you might encounter when reviewing financial statements and with which you should be familiar.

A qualified audit report is issued by the auditor when they conclude that the financial statements are presented in accordance with GAAP, except for some specified items being different. An example of such a difference would be if the company did not use historical cost to report their assets (one of the Generally Accepted Accounting Principles) and used replacement cost accounting instead. With this method, the assets are valued at what it costs to replace them rather than what it cost the company to buy them. Although this method is currently not allowed in the United States under the Generally Accepted Accounting

Principles, it is allowed by international accounting standards and used in several other countries.

An adverse audit report is issued by auditors when they conclude that the financial statements are not presented fairly in accordance with the rules of accounting (GAAP).

A disclaimer audit report is issued by auditors when they do not have enough information to determine whether the financial statements are in accordance with the accounting rules. Auditors would also issue this type of report if they were not independent of the company being audited.

Why Audits Are Useful to You

As the business world becomes more global and complex, so do the financial reports that companies issue. The information provided and the rules that govern their presentation have exploded in number and complexity during the past twenty years. Today it is becoming more and more difficult for the layperson (non-accountants) to fully understand these presentations. The auditor's report of a company's financial statements gives the reader and user of these financial statements an assurance that this information is in accordance with an established set of rules (GAAP) and reviewed by the auditor who is independent of management.

The use of an independent audit can generally assure the user that the information contained in a company's financial statements is free of material errors and fraud. This assurance supports the user in making investment and analytical decisions about the company being reviewed.

Audits Have Their Limits: These audits do not guarantee the dollar accuracy or predictive ability of these financial statements. It only guarantees that they are presented in accordance with a set of accounting rules (GAAP). Many people believe that the auditor will either stop or detect all fraud within an organization, but this is not necessarily the case. Even though auditors do follow procedures that help detect fraud, they cannot detect or disclose all such instances.

Other Services Provided by Auditors

In addition to audits, CPAs perform many other types of assurance and accounting services, including historical financial information reporting and non-historical information reporting.

Examples of historical information reporting are:

Special reports

Special reports by a CPA might be on cash-basis financial statements or reports to outside parties showing that a company complied with certain agreements, like leases.

Financial statements prepared for use in other countries

If a CPA is to prepare financial statements for use in other countries, they must be familiar with both the accounting and auditing standards used in that country.

Personal financial statements

Politicians and private individuals who use their personal assets to buy companies often have a need for a CPA to audit their financial statements for presentations to third parties.

Reviews of interim financial information

Public companies are required to file quarterly financial information with the SEC on what is called a 10-Q form. Unlike annual financial statements (which on submitted on a 10-K form), the interim information is reviewed rather than audited. The objective of the review is to provide a basis for communicating whether the CPA is aware of any material modifications or errors with the interim statements. This review must include:

- A statement as to whether the financial statements are in accordance with GAAP
- Any complex situations affecting the interim financial statements
- Any significant events that have happened near the end or after the end of the period of time being reviewed
- Whether management or employees are aware of any fraudulent events that would affect the financial statements.

An example of a review report by a CPA is shown in figure 11.3.

Figure 11.3

We have reviewed the balance sheet and related statements of income, retained earnings and cash flows of the Solana Dreams Publishing Company as of September 30, 2011, and for the three-month and nine-month periods then ended. These financial statements are the responsibility of the company's management.

We conducted our review in accordance with standards established by the American Institute of Certified Public Accountants. A review of interim financial information consists principally of applying analytical procedures to financial data and making inquiries of persons responsible for financial and accounting matters. It is substantially less in scope than an audit conducted in accordance with generally accepted auditing standards, the objective of which is the expression of an opinion regarding the financial statements taken as a whole. Accordingly, we do not express such an opinion.

Based on our review, we are not aware of any material modifications that should be made to the accompanying financial statements for them to be in conformity with generally accepted accounting principles.

Compilations of financial statements

Compilations involve the preparation of financial statements from accounting records and other information from management. In order to perform a compilation, a CPA must have knowledge of the client's business and industry. At a minimum the CPA must read the statements for any material errors or major discrepancies from generally accepted accounting principles. If the CPA knows or suspects that the financial statements are going to be relied upon by a third party, they should attach a report, similar to the one in figure 11.4, to the financial statements.

Figure 11.4

We have compiled the accompanying balance sheet of the Solana Dreams Publishing Company as of December 31, 2011 and the related statements of income, retained earnings, and cash flows for the year then ended, in accordance with the Statements on Standards for Accounting and Review Services issued by the American Institute of Certified Public Accountants.

A compilation is limited to presenting in the form of financial statements information that is the representation of management. We have not audited or reviewed the accompanying financial statements and, accordingly, do not express an opinion or any other form of assurance on them.

It is also possible for CPAs to issue reports on information that is non-historical. Examples of non-historical reporting include:

- Reports on internal control over financial reporting
- Reports on financial forecasts and projections
- Reports on compliance with laws, regulations, and contracts

In this chapter you learned about the importance of audits and other kinds of reports issued by CPAs, besides audits. In chapter 12 you will learn about how fraud and ethics have affected not only the accounting profession specifically, but the business world in general including small businesses.

GLOSSARY

Adverse Audit Report: A type of report issued by a CPA firm at the completion of an audit. This report is issued when the CPA concludes that the financial statements being audited are not in accordance with Generally Accepted Accounting Principles.

Audit: The accumulation and evaluation of evidence about a company's financial statements to determine if they are in accordance with GAAP.

Auditor: The individual who checks the accuracy and fairness of the accounting records of a company and issues a report as to whether the company's financial records are in accordance with Generally Accepted Accounting Principles.

"Big Four" Accounting Firms: The four largest CPA firms in the world with offices worldwide. PricewaterhouseCoopers, KPMG, Deloitt & Touche, and Ernst & Young perform the audits of the majority of the world's large companies.

Certified Public Accountant (CPA): Auditors who serve the needs of the general public. These individuals have passed an examination, in most cases have 150 hours of college credits, have worked with another CPA for a minimum of two years, and complete a required twenty to forty hours of continuing education each year. Their work includes auditing, tax planning and preparation, and management consulting.

Code of Ethics: A set of rules established by the American Institute of Certified Public Accountants to be followed by all CPAs in their work.

Compilation: The preparation of financial statements from accounting records and other information from management. A report may be issued on these statements if the CPA believes that a third party will rely on the statements.

Compliance Audits: An audit that makes sure the accounting is in compliance with the rules being reviewed. Most often these types of audits are governmental audits, in that they determine whether the financial statements are in compliance with government regulations. They can, however, also be used to check compliance in other instances, such as when a bank requires certain stipulations be met in order for a company to receive or to continue with a loan.

Compliance Report: A report that makes sure the accounting is in compliance with the rules being reviewed. Most often these types of reports are governmental, in that they determine whether the financial statements are in compliance with government regulations. They can, however, also be used to review compliance in other instances.

Disclaimer Audit Report: A type of report issued by a CPA firm at the completion of an audit. This report is issued when the CPA concludes that he or she does not have enough information to determine whether the financial statements are or are not in accordance with the accounting rules.

Generally Accepted Auditing Standards: A set of standards established by the AICPA and the SEC.

Governmental Accounting Standards Board: Issues a set of rules other than the Generally Accepted Accounting Principles to be followed by governmental accountants.

Governmental Auditors: The individuals who perform the audit function for a governmental organization such as the U.S. General Accounting Office (GAO), the Internal Revenue Service (IRS), the Securities and Exchange Commission (SEC), Bureau of Alcohol, Tobacco, and Firearms (ATF), Drug Enforcement Agency (DEA), and the Federal Bureau of Investigation (FBI), as well as state and local governments. Rather than following Generally Accepted Accounting Principles, government audits are done in accordance with a set of accounting rules established by the Governmental Accounting Standards Board (GASB).

Internal Auditors: These auditors are employed by companies to audit the company's own records. These individuals are not necessarily certified public accountants (CPAs), but many are certified internal auditors (CIA). To ensure autonomy these individuals report directly to the audit committee or board of directors of the company rather than to company management.

Operational Audit: A review of an organization's operating procedures for the purpose of making recommendations about the efficiency and effectiveness of business objectives and compliance with company policy. The goal of this type of an audit is to help managers discharge their responsibilities and maximize profitability.

Public Company Accounting Oversight Board (PCAOB): Established by Congress as part of the Sarbanes-Oxley Law of 2002, the PCAOB is charged with the responsibility of creating accounting standards for public companies. The Board has the additional responsibility to make sure that audit quality is not compromised and that auditor performance meets public expectations.

Qualified Audit Report: A type of report issued by a CPA firm at the completion of an audit. This report is issued when the CPA concludes that the financial statements being audited are presented in accordance with GAAP, except for some specified items being different; for example, the use of a nonstandard type of Inventory evaluation is used.

Review: The objective of a review is to provide a basis for communicating whether the CPA is aware of any material modifications or errors with the interim statements.

Sarbanes-Oxley Act (2002): Passed by Congress to include a set of reforms toughening penalties for corporate fraud, restricting types of consulting services for audit clients, and creating the Public Company Accounting Oversight Board (PCAOB).

10-K Form: A form used to submit annual financial statement information to the SEC.

10-Q Form: A form used to submit quarterly financial statement information to the SEC.

Unqualified Audit Report: Issued by a CPA when the financial statements are in accordance with GAAP, the auditor is independent and has gather sufficient evidence in order to give an opinion.

Unqualified Audit Report: A type of report issued by a CPA firm at the completion of an audit. This report is issued when the CPA concludes that the financial statements being audited are completely in accordance with Generally Accepted Accounting Principles.

Chapter 12

Fraud and Ethics

Fraud Defined

Let's first understand the definitions of fraud and embezzlement. Fraud is defined as an intentional deception or manipulation of financial data to the advantage of an individual, who is often an entrusted employee. Embezzlement, on the other hand, is defined as the crime of stealing the funds or property of an employer, company or government or misappropriating money or assets held in trust. Some other terms that have been used for fraud and embezzlement include: white-collar crime, defalcation, and irregularities.

Fraud is big business.

According to the Association of Certified Fraud Examiners, the fraud losses incurred in the smallest companies are 100 times greater than those incurred by the largest companies. It was further reported that the median fraud loss suffered by organizations with fewer than 100 employees averaged $190,000. This is higher than the median loss in even the largest organizations. Small businesses continue to suffer disproportionate fraud losses.

What Causes Fraud

It is tough to know exactly why the frequency of fraud has increased. It may be due to tougher economic times or to specific personal circumstances causing more people to steal.

Two forms of fraud that impact businesses are management fraud and employee fraud. Employee fraud usually involves the stealing of assets belonging to the company. Management fraud usually doesn't directly benefit the person committing the fraud, but is committed to make the company look better for the stockholders or for bankers when the company is attempting to borrow money. The individual or group involved in the management fraud may benefit indirectly through receiving larger bonuses or stock options.

In the accounting literature, the basic elements of fraud have been described by what has been called the "fraud triangle." This triangle looks something like this:

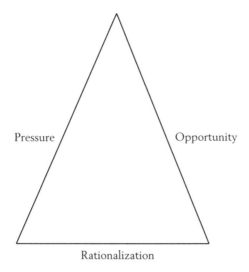

The reasoning for the decision by an individual to commit fraud can be explained by the three sides of this triangle.

To begin with there is the **pressure** to commit fraud. We see this lot of this in a struggling economy. The reasoning here goes something like this: "If I don't take this money, I am going to lose my house" or "if I don't take this money I can't pay for my kids to go to college" or "if I don't alter the financial statements I will not make the goal of a 10% increase in net income or earnings per share and I may lose my job." The list goes on and on!

Secondly there has to be the **opportunity** for an individual to have access to either the physical assets or the accounting records to be able to steal. Having untrustworthy employees is one of the key reasons fraud occurs and why it is more frequent and severe in the small business environment. In a smaller business office, employees are often entrusted with more responsibility and greater authority because the financial resources do not exist to spread the responsibility and authority by hiring more people. This situation leads to the lack of segregation of duties, which is a critical internal control concept.

Thirdly, there is **rationalization**. This is a state of mind that allows the individual to commit the fraud. Reasoning goes something like this: "I am just going to borrow the money and will pay it back when my horse wins at the track" or "the company does not pay me enough money and I deserve this little extra" or "it is really a small amount compared to the total assets of this company and no one will notice" and on and on.

How Fraud Is Committed

Many business owners are simply unaware of the risks that fraud can pose to their businesses. As a result, they fail to adequately monitor these risks, causing a significant amount of fraud to go undetected and unreported.

There are several different types of frauds that business owners need to be aware of. These include embezzling of cash (probably the most common method), or taking other company assets (whether it be inventory or supplies or even something larger). Often times employees engage in kickback schemes or straight forgeries of unauthorized checks. Other common methods include false invoicing, misuse of company credit cards, stealing from the petty cash fund, manipulation of financial information, and fraudulent access to bank accounts.

Alert!

Minimizing Your Company's Risk: It is interesting to note that nearly half (46%) of all frauds within small businesses are detected by tips from other employees, according to the Annual Report to the Nation on Occupational Fraud and Abuse, 2008 (ACFE). Here is the rest of the breakdown:

20% of frauds are detected by accident

20% of frauds are also detected by the companies' internal auditors (a difficult thing to have if you are a small business)

23% of frauds are discovered by a good system of internal control (which you should work with your auditors to help implement)

9% of frauds are discovered by external auditors.

Note: these numbers do not add up to 100% because some of the respondents indicated more than one method was useful in discovering the frauds.

The following are key steps you can take to make sure you are not victimized by your own employees or outsiders. Consider using them as a checklist for keeping your small business safe from fraud.

- Obtain a bond on certain key employees
- Perform criminal and credit background checks on employees
- Require employees to take vacation time every year so that others can perform their duties
- Look for changes in employees' lifestyles
- Monitor your financial statements and management reports (See chapter 1 for a discussion of financial statements and how they can be used, and in this case misused.)
- Prosecute those who commit fraud, and communicate this internally and externally
- Always have an invoice or other support attached to the back of any check you sign
- Run a vendor history showing invoices and amounts (if the invoices were sequential, this would mean that you are the only customer of that vendor—highly unlikely, and thus a false vendor was established by one of your employees)
- Conduct seminars about workplace fraud
- Instruct your bank to never allow a check to be written to an individual from an operating bank account. This account should only be used to pay vendors.
- Hand out employee paychecks at least once per year (this ensures that there are not employees who have been set up to receive pay checks who do not exist)
- Participate in a fraud program by your CPA or CFE
- Encourage staff feedback: develop an anonymous process for staff to report breaches in internal controls and suspicious behavior. Most fraud is detected by staff tipping off the auditors, owners, or accountants.
- Hire a CPA to examine the books
- Have a written code of ethics
- Set a good example (the tone of ethical behavior has to begin at the top)
- Have reasonable expectations (don't set goals so high that the employees are forced to lie or cheat in order to meet these goals)

- Treat employees with respect and understanding
- Restrict bank account access
- Perform regular bank reconciliations
- Adequately secure inventory and supplies

Ethics

Most people involved in business—whether functioning as a small business owner, employee or chief executive officer of a multi-national company—eventually face ethical or moral dilemmas in the workplace.

The number of companies that engage in ethics training and initiate socially responsive programs has increased dramatically over the course of the past two decades. Even with this increased attention being paid to ethical behavior in companies, we have also seen large corporate frauds and the emphasis on the bottom line rather than on developing a business strategy that is long-term.

Very often an employee's ethical choices have an impact on a relatively small number of people, usually co-workers or their employers. However, the ethical choices of business owners—whether to use inferior materials in preparing goods for customers, or to lay off a dozen workers because of careless personal financial expenditures—often have far more impact on the community and possibly the world.

Ethical behavior in your business must start with top management. As part of more comprehensive compliance and ethics programs, many companies have put ethics codes in place.

To be successful, these codes should include at least the following:

- Be given the unequivocal support of top management
- Be monitored by top management
- Be explained in writing and orally
- Be doable
- Be backed up by clearly stated consequences in the case of disobedience
- Remain neutral and non-sexist

Some companies even require their employees to sign agreements stating that they will abide by the company's rules of conduct.

Some degree of fraud likely occurs in every organization, and you may not be able to totally eliminate it. However, you can certainly do something to minimize the risk. Don't be a victim—putting simple processes in place will help improve business operations and minimize the risk of fraud and related its financial loses.

GLOSSARY

Code of Ethics: A set of standards established by a company to guide their employees in making ethical decisions.

Embezzlement: The crime of stealing the funds or property of an employer, company, or government, or misappropriating money or assets held in trust.

Employee Fraud: Usually involves the stealing of assets belonging to the company.

Ethics: The ability to make the "right" decision when there is pressure to do otherwise.

Fraud: An intentional deception, misappropriation of a company's assets, or manipulation of its financial data to the advantage of an individual, often an entrusted employee. Some other terms that have been used include: white-collar crime, defalcation, embezzlement and irregularities.

Fraud Detection: Ways in which fraud are discovered within an organization. These include tips from other employees, detection by accident, the use of internal auditors and good systems of internal control. External auditors are also useful in this detection process.

Fraud Triangle: Describes the basic reasons for fraud as opportunity, rationalization and pressure.

Management Fraud: A fraud that usually doesn't benefit the person committing the fraud, but is committed to make the company look better for the stockholders or for bankers when the company is attempting to borrow money.

Appendix

Internet for Accountants

What Resources Are Available for Accountants?

The amount of information available to accountants and other professionals in business continues to grow each day. In the past accessing this information was extremely burdensome and time-consuming, but the advent of computers and the Internet have placed an abundance of information at your fingertips.

The Internet has also changed the way in which accountants and auditors do their work. Financial reporting, financial information systems, practices in auditing, management and control, tax accounting, and forensic accounting have all been changed for the better by the

Internet. Without understanding the power of the Internet, an accountant is at a loss to access the wealth of information that is available.

The listing that follows is only partial and does not cover all topics of interest to accountants. However, part of the fun of being on the Internet is surfing the Web to find the links that are most interesting to you and to your particular interests. Here are some sites to get you started:

Accounting Organizations

The American Institute of Certified Public Accountants
www.aicpa.org

The American Accounting Association
www.aaahq.org

The Institute of Internal Auditors
www.theiia.org

The Association of Certified Fraud Examiners
www.acfe.com

State Accounting Societies and Boards
www.aicpa.org/states/index.htm

A listing of CPA Firms
www.cpafirms.com

Financial Accounting and Auditing

Learn the Accounting Basics Online
www.learnacctgonline.com

The Financial Accounting Standards Board
www.fasb.org

The Sarbanes-Oxley Act
http://sarbanes-oxley.com

Free Annual Reports
http://ftcom.ar.wilink.com

Access to Free Audit Programs
www.auditnet.org

Top 10 Accounting Software Programs
www.2020software.com

Glossary of Accounting Terms
www.accountz.com/glossary.html

Corporate SEC Filings
http://edgar-online.com

Public Company Accounting Oversight Board
www.pcaob.com

Managerial Accounting

The Institute of Management Accountants
www.imanet.org

International Information Management Association
www.iima.org

Management Accounting Guidelines
http://fmcenter.aicpa.org/Resources/Management+Accounting+
Guidelines

IMA Ethical Standards
www.imanet.org/about_ethics_statement.asp

Governmental Accounting

The Governmental Accounting Standards Board
www.gasb.org

The Government Accountability Office
www.gao.gov

American Accounting Association—Governmental and Not-for-Profit
Section
http://aaahq.org/GNP/index.htm

Tax Information and Organizations

The IRS Homepage
www.irs.ustreaqs.gov

The National Association of Enrolled Agents
www.naea.org

Top 50 Overlooked Tax Deductions
www.jacksonhewitt.com/resources_library_top50.asp

International Accounting

The International Accounting Standards Board
www.iasb.org

International Federation of Accountants
www.ifac.org

American Accounting Association—International Accounting Section
http://www.aaaiasection.org/

Financial Calculators

www.bcspa.com/calcs/index.htm

www.fool.com/calcs/calculators.htm?source=LN

Stock Quotes

Nasdaq
http://quotes.nasdaq.com/asp/MasterDataEntry.asp?page=flashQuotes

New York Stock Exchange
www.nyse.com

Business Newspapers and Magazines

New York Times
www.nytimes.com

Wall Street Journal
http://wsj.com

Financial Times
www.ft.com

Business Week
www.businessweek.com

Forbes Magazine
www.forbes.com

Once, again, this is just a starter list. Have fun surfing the Net!

Appendix B

Frequently Asked Questions

So what is accounting?
Accounting is the act of preparing financial statements and other reports that will help you make correct financial decisions.

How is accounting different from bookkeeping?
Bookkeeping is the act of recording the daily business decisions that will be used by the accountant to prepare the financial statements. Many companies use the various computer programs to do their bookkeeping.

Is GAAP different from "the Gap"?

Well, this is just a joke in some ways! The Gap is a clothing chain of stores in the United States, and GAAP is Generally Accepted Accounting Principles—those rules that guide accountants in their role of preparing and analyzing financial statements.

Why is it important to understand international accounting standards?

It is increasingly important to understand International Accounting Standards because the world is getting smaller and business is international—even small business! Do you in your small business buy parts from outside of the United States? Do you sell products or services outside of the United States? The answers to these questions are probably yes, if you are growing and are staying competitive in today's marketplace.

More and more countries are now following International Accounting Standards rather than their home countries' standards. At the time of this printing, the United States is considering a project to converge International Accounting Standards into their current GAAP.

How are the international standards different from the U.S. standards?

There are many areas where there are significant differences between the two set of accounting rules. While it is the goal of the Financial Accounting Standards Board (FASB) to work together with the International Accounting Standards Board (IASB) to eliminate many of these differences, the success will also depend on both local governments and industry groups not to issue their own rules that will make for exceptions from the IASB's rules.

How many financial statements are normally found in a company's annual report?

There are usually four financial statements that are included in a company's annual report. These statements include:

- The Income Statement
- The Balance Sheet
- The Statement of Cash Flows
- The Statement of Owner's Equity

What is the relationship between the balance sheet and the income statement?

Net Income (the Bottom Line) is added to Owner's Equity on the Balance Sheet each time the financial statements are prepared.

How important is the Cash Flows Statement and why?

In my opinion it is the most important of all of the financial statements. A very high percentage of small businesses go bankrupt each year, not because they don't have a good idea or good products or services or a good location or good employees, but because they did not do good cash forecasting (budgeting) or analysis (the Statement of Cash Flows).

Do debits always have to equal credits on the trial balance and Balance Sheet?

Yes, they do! The reason is because the accounting system used to record business transactions—the double entry accounting system is based upon recording a debit and an equal credit for each business transaction. Thus when it is time to prepare the trial balance and the Balance Sheet, each transaction that comprises the information for these reports has already been entered with one debit and one equal credit.

What are some of the benefits of incorporating your company?

These benefits include: limited liability for the owners, the ability to issue capital stock to raise funding, and the right to issue dividends to the stockholders (owners).

Is there a difference between common stock and preferred stock?

Yes, and in some ways it is a very large difference. Some of the differences include: Common Stockholders can vote for the directors of the company. Preferred Stockholders have first claim to the dividends that are declared by a company. Preferred Stockholders have a fixed claim to these dividends, and normally must be paid all of their dividends for every year before Common Stockholders can be paid any. In the case of a company declaring bankruptcy, Preferred Stockholders have claim to the remaining assets before the Common Stockholders.

If you want to have a feeling for the short-term sustainability of your company, which ratios would you consider?

- The Current Ratio
- Working Capital
- The Quick Ratio
- Inventory Turnover
- Average Collection Period of the Accounts Receivables

The short-term is normally defined as twelve months or less. These ratios help evaluate the most important question of whether a company can pay its debts in the near term and not be forced into bankruptcy.

If you want to have a feeling for the long-term sustainability of your company, which ratios would you consider?

This is a little more complex question than the prior one. In addition to evaluating some ratios, it is important to evaluate a company's quality of earnings. Some hints on doing this can be found in figure 9.1 on page 138. In figure 9.2 on page 139, you can find a list of Long-Term ratios that can be used to evaluate a company's Long-Term viability. Once we evaluate if a company will survive the Short-Term, it is important to determine how competitive they will be in the Long-Term. These ratios will aid in this decision. In addition to these ratios, don't forget to evaluate the company's footnotes to the financial statements. A great deal of information might be found there to further evaluate their Long-Term viability.

What is a budget?

A budget is a detailed plan that outlines future expectations in quantitative terms.

Why is a budget important?

Budgets are important because they give formality to the planning process. If the budget involves other people, it also serves as a way of communicating the plan to these other people. The process of preparing a budget is critical for planning the future.

Do small businesses need audits?

Yes, just as much as large businesses need them. Since these audits are performed by outside independent accountants, they give reasonable assurance to the users of the financial statements that they are free of any material misstatement.

What is the difference between accounting and auditing?

Accounting is the process of recording, classifying and summarizing economic events. Auditing is not concerned with the preparation of the accounting data, but with the evaluation of this data to determine if is properly presented in accordance with the rules of GAAP, and whether it properly reflects the events that have occurred during the period.

Is fraud an issue in a small business?

You bet it is! The average loss that a small business takes due to fraud of one of their employees or owners is much larger as a percentage of total assets than those losses of a large business.

How can the owner limit or control fraud?

1. Establish a system of internal control, no matter how basic, and oversee it on a regular basis
2. Set the "tone from the top" by showing by example how important good ethical behavior is
3. Have a company code of ethics, which is reviewed by all employees on a regular basis through classes and seminars on fraud and ethics
4. Have a system where employees can report fraud to upper management anonymously

5. Incorporate ethics and fraud prevention goals in employee evaluations

The list goes on, but whichever of these techniques are used (or all of them), it is important to apply them on a regular basis to show all employees that the company is serious about fraud and ethics within the company.

Do you have more questions after reading this book? Learn more about accounting basics by visiting Dr. Label's blog at www. learnacctgonline.com. Get a chance to personally discuss accounting and business issues with other individuals and small business owners like yourself. See you there, and in the meantime have fun (yes that is possible with accounting) and good luck!

Appendix

C

Financial Statements— The Coca-Cola Company

The financial statements contained here are from the actual 2008 annual report of the Coca-Cola Company. They will give you an excellent idea of what these statements look like for major corporations.

The Coca-Cola Company and Subsidiaries
Condensed Consolidated Statements of Income (UNAUDITED)
(In millions except per share data)

	Three Months Ended March 28, 2008	Three Months Ended June 27, 2008	Three Months Ended September 26, 2008	Three Months Ended December 31, 2008
NET OPERATING REVENUES	$7,379	$9,046	$8,393	$7,126
Cost of goods sold	2,624	3,162	3,020	2,568
GROSS PROFIT	4,755	5,884	5,373	4,558
Selling, general and administrative expenses	2,803	3,108	3,139	2,744
Other operating charges	78	97	47	108
OPERATING INCOME	1,874	2,679	2,187	1,706
Interest income	65	69	105	94
Interest expense	117	89	111	121
Equity income (loss)—net	137	(843)	272	(440)
Other income (loss)—net	(11)	80	(8)	(89)
INCOME BEFORE INCOME TAXES	1,948	1,896	2,445	1,150
Income taxes	448	474	555	155
NET INCOME	$1,500	$1,422	$1,890	$995
BASIC NET INCOME PER SHARE	$0.65	$0.61	$0.82	$0.43
DILUTED NET INCOME PER SHARE	$0.64	$0.61	$0.81	$0.43
DIVIDENDS PER SHARE	$0.38	$0.38	$0.38	$0.38
AVERAGE SHARES OUTSTANDING	2,322	2,316	2,311	2,312

	Three Months Ended March 28, 2008	Three Months Ended June 27, 2008	Three Months Ended September 26, 2008	Three Months Ended December 31, 2008
Effect of dilutive securities	29	27	18	9
AVERAGE SHARES OUTSTANDING ASSUMING DILUTION	2,351	2,343	2,329	2,321

[1] Full year amounts do not add due to the reclassification of prior quarter amounts to conform with the full year presentation.

Note:
The financial information included in this section should be read in conjunction with Management's Discussion and Analysis of Financial Condition and Results of Operations and Notes to Consolidated Financial Statements contained in our Company's 2008 Quarterly Reports on Form 10-Q and 2008 Annual Report on Form 10-K.

The Coca-Cola Company and Subsidiaries
Condensed Consolidated Balance Sheets
(UNAUDITED)
(In millions except par value)

	March 28, 2008	June 27, 2008	September 26, 2008	December 31, 2008
ASSETS				
CURRENT ASSETS				
Cash and cash equivalents	$6,199	$6,571	$7,797	$4,701
Marketable securities	221	286	287	278
Trade accounts receivable, less allowances	3,500	4,073	3,674	3,090
Inventories	2,447	2,531	2,321	2,187
Prepaid expenses and other assets	2,521	2,628	2,741	1,920
TOTAL CURRENT ASSETS	14,888	16,089	16,820	12,176
INVESTMENTS				
Equity method investments:				
Coca-Cola Hellenic Bottling Company S.A.	1,571	1,699	1,667	1,487
Coca-Cola FEMSA, S.A.B. de C.V.	1,065	1,095	1,176	877
Coca-Cola Amatil Limited	836	887	786	638
Coca-Cola Enterprises Inc.	1,661	623	695	0
Other, principally bottling companies and joint ventures	2,440	2,511	2,567	2,314
Other investments, principally bottling companies	549	552	530	463
TOTAL INVESTMENTS	8,122	7,367	7,421	5,779
OTHER ASSETS	2,702	2,634	2,625	1,733

	March 28, 2008	June 27, 2008	September 26, 2008	December 31, 2008
PROPERTY, PLANT AND EQUIPMENT—net	8,675	8,712	8,527	8,326
TRADEMARKS WITH INDEFINITE LIVES	5,323	6,025	6,138	6,059
GOODWILL	4,334	4,062	4,011	4,029
OTHER INTANGIBLE ASSETS	2,960	2,842	2,638	2,417
TOTAL ASSETS	$47,004	$47,731	$48,180	$40,519
LIABILITIES AND SHAREOWNERS' EQUITY				
CURRENT LIABILITIES				
Accounts payable and accrued expenses	$7,805	$7,978	$7,659	$6,205
Loans and notes payable	7,285	7,752	8,111	6,066
Current maturities of long-term debt	130	531	536	465
Accrued income taxes	368	359	281	252
TOTAL CURRENT LIABILITIES	15,588	16,620	16,587	12,988
LONG-TERM DEBT	3,259	2,874	2,877	2,781
OTHER LIABILITIES	3,287	3,267	2,803	3,401
DEFERRED INCOME TAXES	1,838	1,788	2,168	877
SHAREOWNERS' EQUITY				
Common stock, $0.25 par value; Authorized— 5,600 shares	880	880	880	880
Capital surplus	7,662	7,805	7,927	7,966
Reinvested earnings	36,843	37,386	38,397	38,513

	March 28, 2008	June 27, 2008	September 26, 2008	December 31, 2008
Accumulated other comprehensive income (loss)	1,199	1,352	759	(2,674)
Treasury stock, at cost	(23,552)	(24,241)	(24,218)	(24,213)
TOTAL SHAREOWNERS' EQUITY	23,032	23,182	23,745	20,472
TOTAL LIABILITIES AND SHAREOWNERS' EQUITY	$47,004	$47,731	$48,180	$40,519

Note:
The financial information included in this section should be read in conjunction with Management's Discussion and Analysis of Financial Condition and Results of Operations and Notes to Consolidated Financial Statements contained in our Company's 2008 Quarterly Reports on Form 10-Q and 2008 Annual Report on Form 10-K.

The Coca-Cola Company and Subsidiaries
Condensed Consolidated Statements of Cash Flows
(UNAUDITED)
(In millions)

	Three Months Ended March 28, 2008	Six Months Ended June 27, 2008	Nine Months Ended September 26, 2008	Year Ended December 31, 2008
OPERATING ACTIVITIES				
Net income	$1,500	$2,922	$4,812	$5,807
Depreciation and amortization	307	637	943	1,228
Stock-based compensation expense	75	152	223	266
Deferred income taxes	(8)	(222)	(221)	(360)
Equity income or loss, net of dividends	(122)	856	638	1,128
Foreign currency adjustments	(18)	(43)	(39)	(42)
Gains on sales of assets, including bottling interests	(8)	(111)	(128)	(130)
Other operating charges	78	159	141	209
Other items	11	34	57	153
Net change in operating assets and liabilities	(695)	(1,166)	(758)	(688)
Net cash provided by operating activities	1,120	3,218	5,668	7,571
INVESTING ACTIVITIES				
Acquisitions and investments, principally beverage and bottling companies and trademarks	(238)	(621)	(655)	(759)
Purchases of other investments	(42)	(140)	(212)	(240)
Proceeds from disposals of bottling companies and other investments	97	387	454	479

	Three Months Ended March 28, 2008	Six Months Ended June 27, 2008	Nine Months Ended September 26, 2008	Year Ended December 31, 2008
Purchases of property, plant and equipment	(386)	(896)	(1,370)	(1,968)
Proceeds from disposals of property, plant and equipment	14	46	46	129
Other investing activities	(2)	(10)	(57)	(4)
Net cash used in investing activities	(557)	(1,234)	(1,794)	(2,363)
FINANCING ACTIVITIES				
Issuances of debt	3,204	4,317	5,308	4,337
Payments of debt	(1,825)	(2,478)	(3,211)	(4,308)
Issuances of stock	316	459	570	586
Purchases of stock for treasury	(254)	(1,031)	(1,079)	(1,079)
Dividends	–	(884)	(1,764)	(3,521)
Net cash provided by (used in) financing activities	1,441	383	(176)	(3,985)
EFFECT OF EXCHANGE RATE CHANGES ON CASH AND CASH EQUIVALENTS	102	111	6	(615)
CASH AND CASH EQUIVALENTS				
Net increase during the period	2,106	2,478	3,704	608
Balance at beginning of period	4,093	4,093	4,093	4,093
Balance at end of period	$6,199	$6,571	$7,797	$4,701

Note:
The financial information included in this section should be read in conjunction with Management's Discussion and Analysis of Financial Condition and Results of Operations and Notes to Consolidated Financial Statements
contained in our Company's 2008 Quarterly Reports on Form 10-Q and 2008 Annual Report on Form 10-K.

Report of Independent Registered Public Accounting Firm
Board of Directors and Shareowners
The Coca-Cola Company

We have audited the accompanying consolidated balance sheets of the Coca-Cola Company and subsidiaries as of December 31, 2007 and 2006, and the related consolidated statements of income, shareowners' equity, and cash flows for each of the three years in the period ended December 31, 2007. These financial statements are the responsibility of the Company's management. Our responsibility is to express an opinion on these financial statements based on our audits.

We conducted our audits in accordance with the standards of the Public Company Accounting Oversight Board (United States). Those standards require that we plan and perform the audit to obtain reasonable assurance about whether the financial statements are free of material misstatement. An audit includes examining, on a test basis, evidence supporting the amounts and disclosures in the financial statements. An audit also includes assessing the accounting principles used and significant estimates made by management, as well as evaluating the overall financial statement presentation. We believe that our audits provide a reasonable basis for our opinion.

In our opinion, the financial statements referred to above present fairly, in all material respects, the consolidated financial position of the Coca-Cola Company and subsidiaries at December 31, 2007 and 2006, and the consolidated results of their operations and their cash flows for each of the three years in the period ended December 31, 2007, in conformity with U.S. generally accepted accounting principles.

As discussed in Notes 1 and 17 to the consolidated financial statements, in 2007 the Company adopted FASB Interpretation No. 48 related to accounting for uncertainty in income taxes. Also as discussed in Note 1 to the consolidated financial statements, in 2006 the Company adopted SFAS No. 158 related to defined benefit pension and other post-retirement plans.

We also have audited, in accordance with the standards of the Public Company Accounting Oversight Board (United States), the Coca-Cola Company's internal control over financial reporting as of December 31, 2007, based on criteria established in *Internal Control—Integrated Framework* issued by the Committee of Sponsoring Organizations of the Treadway Commission and our report dated February 27, 2008, expressed an unqualified opinion thereon.

Ernst + Young LLP

Atlanta, Georgia
February 27, 2008

Report of Independent Registered Public Accounting Firm on Internal Control Over Financial Reporting Board of Directors and Shareowners
The Coca-Cola Company

We have audited the Coca-Cola Company's internal control over financial reporting as of December 31, 2007, based on criteria established in *Internal Control—Integrated Framework* issued by the Committee of Sponsoring Organizations of the Treadway Commission (the COSO criteria). The Coca-Cola Company's management is responsible for maintaining effective internal control over financial reporting, and for its assessment of the effectiveness of internal control over financial reporting included in the accompanying Report of Management on Internal Control Over Financial Reporting. Our responsibility is to express an opinion on the Company's internal control over financial reporting based on our audit.

We conducted our audit in accordance with the standards of the Public Company Accounting Oversight Board (United States). Those standards require that we plan and perform the audit to obtain reasonable assurance about whether effective internal control over financial reporting was maintained in all material respects. Our audit included obtaining an understanding of internal control over financial reporting, assessing the risk that a material weakness exists, testing and evaluating the design and operating effectiveness of internal control based on the assessed risk, and performing such other procedures as we considered necessary in the circumstances. We believe that our audit provides a reasonable basis for our opinion.

A company's internal control over financial reporting is a process designed to provide reasonable assurance regarding the reliability of financial reporting and the preparation of financial statements for external purposes in accordance with generally accepted accounting principles. A company's internal control over financial reporting includes those policies and procedures that 1) pertain to the maintenance of records that, in reasonable detail, accurately and fairly reflect the transactions and dispositions of the assets of the company; 2) provide reasonable assurance that transactions are recorded as necessary to permit preparation of financial statements in accordance with generally accepted accounting principles, and that receipts and expenditures of the company are being made only in accordance with authorizations of management and directors of the company; and (3) provide reasonable assurance regarding prevention or timely detection of unauthorized acquisition, use, or disposition of the company's assets that could have a material effect on the financial statements.

Because of its inherent limitations, internal control over financial reporting may not prevent or detect misstatements. Also, projections of any evaluation of effectiveness to future periods are subject to the risk that controls may become inadequate because of changes in conditions, or that the degree of compliance with the policies or procedures may deteriorate.

As indicated in the accompanying Report of Management on Internal Control Over Financial Reporting, management's assessment of and conclusion on the effectiveness of internal control over financial reporting did not include the internal controls of Coca-Cola Bottlers Philippines, Inc. (CCBPI) and 18 bottling and distribution operations in Germany, which are included in the 2007 consolidated financial statements of the Coca-Cola Company and subsidiaries and constituted approximately 5.0 percent of the Company's consolidated total assets as of December 31, 2007 and approximately 3.5 percent of the Company's consolidated net operating revenues for the year then ended. Our audit of internal control over financial reporting of the Coca-Cola Company also did not include an evaluation of the internal control over financial reporting of CCBPI and the 18 bottling and distribution operations in Germany.

In our opinion, the Coca-Cola Company maintained, in all material respects, effective internal control over financial reporting as of December 31, 2007, based on the COSO criteria.

We also have audited, in accordance with the standards of the Public Company Accounting Oversight Board (United States), the consolidated balance sheets of the Coca-Cola Company and subsidiaries as of December 31, 2007 and 2006, and the related consolidated statements of income, shareowners' equity, and cash flows for each of the three years in the period ended December 31, 2007, and our report dated February 27, 2008, expressed an unqualified opinion thereon.

Ernst + Young LLP

Atlanta, Georgia
February 27, 2008

Report of Management on Internal Control Over Financial Reporting
The Coca-Cola Company and Subsidiaries

Management of the Company is responsible for the preparation and integrity of the consolidated financial statements appearing in our annual report on Form 10-K. The financial statements were prepared in conformity with generally accepted accounting principles appropriate in the circumstances and, accordingly, include certain amounts based on our best judgments and estimates. Financial information in this annual report on Form 10-K is consistent with that in the financial statements.

Management of the Company is responsible for establishing and maintaining adequate internal control over financial reporting as such term is defined in Rules 13a-15(f) under the Securities Exchange Act of 1934 ("Exchange Act"). The Company's internal control over financial reporting is designed to provide reasonable assurance regarding the reliability of financial reporting and the preparation of the consolidated financial statements. Our internal control over financial reporting is supported by a program of internal audits and appropriate reviews by management, written policies and guidelines, careful selection and training of qualified personnel and a written Code of Business Conduct adopted by our Company's Board of Directors, applicable to all Company Directors and all officers and employees of our Company and subsidiaries.

Because of its inherent limitations, internal control over financial reporting may not prevent or detect misstatements and even when determined to be effective, can only provide reasonable assurance with respect to financial statement preparation and presentation. Also, projections of any evaluation of effectiveness to future periods are subject to the risk that controls may become inadequate because of changes in conditions, or that the degree of compliance with the policies or procedures may deteriorate.

The Audit Committee of our Company's Board of Directors, composed solely of Directors who are independent in accordance with the requirements of the New York Stock Exchange listing standards, the Exchange Act and the Company's Corporate Governance Guidelines, meets with the independent auditors, management and internal auditors periodically to discuss internal control over financial reporting and auditing and financial reporting matters. The Audit Committee reviews with the independent auditors the scope and results of the audit effort. The Audit Committee also meets periodically with the independent auditors and the chief internal auditor without management present to ensure that the independent auditors and the chief internal auditor have free access to the Audit Committee. Our Audit Committee's Report can be found in the Company's 2008 Proxy Statement.

Management assessed the effectiveness of the Company's internal control over financial reporting as of December 31, 2007. In making this assessment, management used the criteria set forth by the Committee of Sponsoring Organizations of the Treadway Commission (COSO) in *Internal Control—Integrated Framework.* During 2007, the Company acquired the 65 percent interest in Coca-Cola Bottlers Philippines, Inc. which it did not already own and 18 bottling and distribution operations in Germany. Refer to Note 20 of Notes to Consolidated Financial Statements for additional information regarding these events. In accordance with SEC Staff guidance, management has excluded these businesses from its evaluation of the effectiveness of the Company's internal control over financial reporting as of December 31, 2007. The net operating revenues attributable to these businesses represented approximately 3.5 percent of the Company's consolidated net operating revenues for the year ended December 31, 2007, and their aggregate total assets represented approximately 5.0 percent of the Company's consolidated total assets as of December 31, 2007. Based on our assessment, management believes that the Company maintained effective internal control over financial reporting as of December 31, 2007.

The Company's independent auditors, Ernst & Young LLP, a registered public accounting firm, are appointed by the Audit Committee of the Company's Board of Directors, subject to ratification by our Company's shareowners. Ernst & Young LLP has audited and reported on the consolidated financial statements of the Coca-Cola Company and subsidiaries and the Company's internal control over financial reporting. The reports of the independent auditors are contained in this annual report.

E. Neville Isdell
Chairman, Board of Directors,
and Chief Executive Officer
February 27, 2008

Harry L. Anderson
Vice President and Controller
February 27, 2008

Gary P. Fayard
Executive Vice President
and Chief Financial Officer
February 27, 2008

Index

About the Author

Kevin Thomas Roberts

Wayne A. Label, CPA, MBA, PhD, was born and raised in San Francisco. He completed his undergraduate work in accounting at the University of California, Berkeley, and then went on to the University of California, Los Angeles, where he received his MBA and a PhD in accounting. He is a certified public accountant in the state of Texas.

Dr. Label has taught at several universities in the United States and abroad. He was the director of the School of Accountancy at the University of Hawaii and chairman of the accounting department at the University of Nevada, Las Vegas. Dr. Label also taught for the Harvard Institute of International Development, where he helped to start the master's degree program in auditing in La Paz, Bolivia. He received a Ford Foundation grant to aid the beginning of an MBA program at the Catholic University in Rio de Janeiro, Brazil. He has also taught accounting courses in Peru, Chile, Mexico, Germany, Korea, and Thailand.

Dr. Label has published three books on accounting and over thirty articles in professional journals. He is currently teaching online courses for the University of Maryland University College and UCLA. Dr. Label has also given seminars in accounting and international business in numerous locations throughout the United States, as well as in Latin America, Europe, and Asia. He has also served as an expert witness in many civil and criminal cases.

Dr. Label divides his time between Puerto Vallarta, Mexico, and San Diego, California.

You can learn more about Dr. Label at his website: www. LearnAcctgOnline.com. He can be contacted at AskDrL@ LearnAcctgOnline.com.